AN UNWANTED WAR

An Unwanted War

THE DIPLOMACY OF THE

. . . .

UNITED STATES AND SPAIN

. . . .

OVER CUBA, 1895 – 1898

. . . .

BY JOHN L. OFFNER

. . . .

The University of North Carolina Press Chapel Hill & London

© 1992 The University of

North Carolina Press

Manufactured in the

United States of America

The paper in this book meets the guidelines for

permanence and durability of the Committee on

Production Guidelines for Book Longevity of

the Council on Library Resources.

96 95 94 93 92   5 4 3 2 1

Library of Congress Cataloging-in-Publication

Data

Offner, John L.

An unwanted war: the diplomacy of the

United States and Spain over Cuba, 1895–1898/

by John L. Offner.

p. cm.

Includes bibliographical references and index.

ISBN 0-8078-2038-5 (alk. paper).—

ISBN 0-8078-4380-6 (pbk. : alk. paper)

1. Spanish-American War, 1898—Diplomatic

history. 2. United States—Foreign relations—

Spain. 3. Spain—Foreign relations—United

States. 4. Cuba—History—Revolution, 1895–

1898—Diplomatic history. I. Title.

E723.O44 1992

973.8'92—dc20 91-48198

CIP

To

VERA BLINN REBER,

teacher and scholar,

wife and mother

CONTENTS

• • • • • • • • • • • • • • • •

A map of Cuba will be found on page xiv,
and a section of illustrations will be found
beginning on page 101.

PREFACE

. . . .

The Spanish-American War was inevitable. Cuban nationalism and Spanish colonialism were irreconcilable forces allowing for no compromise. The United States and Spain tried to find a peaceful resolution to the stalemated Cuban-Spanish war, but Cuban nationalists were unyielding, and powerful domestic forces propelled Washington and Madrid into a conflict.

McKinley dominated American foreign affairs. His objectives were to free Cuba and to prevent a war with Spain. His minister to Spain erred in believing that, under pressure, the Spanish government would evacuate Cuba; as a result, the White House held unfounded hopes for peace. During the intense diplomatic negotiations preceding the war, McKinley, believing that Spain was about to withdraw from Cuba, worked hard for more time to prevent war. Congressional Republicans rejected his pleas, however, and the United States entered the Cuban-Spanish war.

Legislators willingly entered a war with Spain primarily because of national politics. The Republican Party feared an election defeat in 1898. Facing the start of a critical election campaign, Republicans wanted to get out in front of the Cuban issue rather than provide an opening for Bryanites and Populists. The American people took a deep interest in the Cuban revolution. They sympathized with Cuban independence, favored the underdog, looked with horror on the numerous deaths in Cuban reconcentration camps, wanted to avenge the *Maine*, and by March 1898 were willing to use military force to remove Spain from Cuba. Both Republican and Democratic politicians maneuvered to enlist these sentiments in the approaching election. In the final analysis, Republicans made war on Spain in order to keep control of Washington. Expansionism, markets and investments, the sensational press, and national security interests were much less important in carrying the United States into the war.

The war altered American foreign affairs. Military victories and heightened nationalism led to expansionism. U.S. interests were moderate; when Spain was prostrate, Washington took none of Spain's Atlantic, Mediterranean, or African colonies. America's goal was to remove Spain from the Caribbean. Dewey's victory aroused interest in the Pacific, but by the end of the war, the McKinley administration and the American people were undecided about the future of Spain's Pacific colonies.

I base these conclusions on a multi-archival study of American and foreign documents. My approach has been to seek a balanced and sympathetic understanding of Spanish, Cuban, and American perspectives. In addition to conducting research in U.S. archives, I have examined document collections in Spain, France, England, Austria, the Vatican, Cuba, Mexico, Brazil, and Argentina. The European archives have provided much information about Spain but little new on the United States. Latin American archives were disappointing. Brazil took no interest in Cuba; Mexico stood aloof; and although well represented in Madrid, Argentina never was at the center of diplomatic discussions. French diplomats, closest to Spain and involved in ending the Spanish-American War, were knowledgeable and energetic. The Austrian ambassador, having a close relationship with the queen regent, was well informed about the inner workings of the Spanish government. But the Spanish cabinet and its friends on the continent were suspicious of England and its colonial interests. Nevertheless, the British government set the tone for Europe's careful relations with the United States. The Vatican nuncio was a minor player, except during the month preceding the outbreak of war.

Taken as a whole, the European diplomatic archives nicely complement the historical records found in Madrid. Spain's diplomatic archives are well organized and completely open. But Cuban colonial papers at the national archives are scattered and often hard to locate. And I was unable to obtain access to Spain's military archives at Segovia. A valuable unpublished source of information on Spanish politics and the war is the doctoral dissertation of Thomas Hart Baker, Jr. Armed with a richer understanding of Spanish politics and diplomacy, one gains a better understanding of the diplomacy of the McKinley administration.

For the researcher, Cuba presents the problem of finding sufficient information. Although Havana has published ten volumes of correspondence for 1895–98, the material provides a sketchy story. And Havana's national archives hold little more than what is available in print. One looks in vain in Havana for a collection of new records that will illuminate

Cuban politics and diplomacy. But some nuggets of information exist, and a visit to Havana can provide a clearer understanding of Cuban policies. For me, the puzzle was trying to understand why the Americans and the Cubans did so little to prepare for the day when Spain would be gone. McKinley initially adopted contradictory policies toward the Cubans and then hardened his position against them when the war came; staunch Cuban nationalists looked on as the American eagle threw a larger and larger shadow over the island. Inflexible to the end, the Cubans stood by as America went to war with Spain and unleashed a military attack on the island that inevitably defined the coming era in Cuban-American relations. My suggested answers to this enigma are tentative; I hope, however, that I have thrown some light on the formative months of Cuban-American relations.

I am often asked how my investigation compares with Ernest R. May's classic contribution, *Imperial Democracy*, which is now three decades old. Our works differ in scope. May focused on the U.S. entry into world politics; European attitudes toward the United States and American acquisition of the Philippines were central to his account. I have emphasized Spanish-American relations and the struggle over Cuba. My monograph ends with the protocol that brought a cease-fire to Cuba rather than the Treaty of Paris, which settled the fate of the Philippines. The Cuban issue united the American people and provides insights into those things that they championed. In contrast, Philippine expansionism divided Americans and raised fundamental constitutional and democratic questions.

I have had one important advantage over May. During the last three decades there have been several excellent studies of McKinley, his presidency, and the Spanish-American War. Margaret Leech, H. Wayne Morgan, Lewis L. Gould, and David Trask have illuminated the way. Their revisionist works, solidly based on imaginative, fresh scholarship, have added a new dimension to understanding McKinley and his administration. May did not have the benefit of these changed perspectives. I hope that I have carried revisionism one step further by clarifying a portion of McKinley's foreign affairs.

As I read the sources, one thing that struck me was that none of the major participants wanted war. McKinley searched for an arrangement that would satisfy both Spain and Cuba; Sagasta gave as much ground as he could to prevent an unwinnable war; and Cuban nationalists did not want American troops in Cuba. In each case, internal politics limited the flexibility needed for diplomatic accommodation. Although McKinley made mistakes and suffered from errors of judgment, his efforts to prevent the war were commendable. The reader will have to judge whether the facts support my conclusion that the war was both inevitable and necessary.

The diplomacy of the Spanish-American War is a large subject, and I have relied on many people for assistance. I wish to give special recognition to my teacher, John A. DeNovo, who first suggested that I study the war. I am also indebted to David Trask, who pioneered in writing a balanced history of the war, showing that an even-handed monograph was possible. He read and commented on my manuscript in draft. My debt to Lewis L. Gould is deep and abiding; he encouraged my research and writing in many ways and provided me with bits and pieces of archival material that I would have overlooked. His depiction of McKinley's presidency is a tribute to the quality of his research and thoughtful analysis. I am thankful to Franklin W. Knight, who assisted me in entering Cuba, and to Julio Le Riverend, who graciously received me in Havana and provided me with unhindered access to the Cuban national library and archives. I am grateful to José Varela Ortega, who assisted my work at his institute in Madrid and who gave me the benefit of his expertise on Spanish history. I want to thank William Bassin, who read and commented on the manuscript, and Hans-Dietrich Meurer, who translated the handwritten Austrian diplomatic documents. I am also thankful for the financial support of the Professional Development Committees of Shippensburg University and the Pennsylvania State System of Higher Education. Many librarians and archivists across three continents have helped me, often struggling to comprehend my badly spoken foreign languages; and at Shippensburg, librarians have cheerfully aided me on many occasions. Finally, there are insufficient words to cover my debt to Vera Blinn Reber, to whom this book is dedicated. Without her support, advice, encouragement, and professional contributions as a Latin Americanist, this book would never have been written. She also read and commented on the draft manuscript. Together we visited Washington, Madrid, London, Paris, Rome, Vienna, Havana, Mexico City, Rio de Janeiro, and Buenos Aires. We share many fond memories of this project. S. F. Bemis was right: multi-archival research offers many rewards. Obviously, I take full responsibility for all the shortcomings that follow.

AN UNWANTED WAR

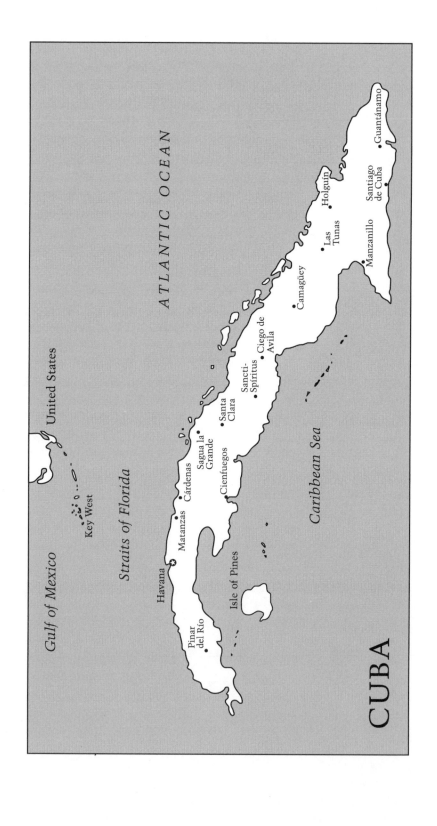

Gulf of Mexico

United States

Key West

Straits of Florida

ATLANTIC OCEAN

Pinar
del Río

Havana

Isle of Pines

Matanzas
Cárdenas

Sagua la
Grande

Cienfuegos

Santa
Clara

Sancti-
Spíritus

Ciego de
Avila

Camagüey

Las
Tunas

Holguín

Manzanillo

Santiago
de Cuba

Guantánamo

Caribbean Sea

CUBA

CHAPTER I

. . . .

THE CUBAN

. . . .

REVOLUTION

. . . .

THREE PERSPECTIVES

. . . .

The war for Cuban independence that began in February 1895 involved three participants—Cuba, Spain, and the United States. Each witnessed the events in Cuba from its own historical and national perspective, viewpoints that differed widely and that still color the histories of each nation. To understand the diplomacy of the Spanish-American War, one must appreciate these differing perspectives.

For the leaders of the Cuban revolution, the *Grito de Baire* that began the struggle in 1895 represented the renewal of a war for independence that had started in 1868. All the leaders had taken part in the earlier Ten Years War, and although they had ended armed struggle in 1878, many had never ceased to dream of Cuban independence. Nevertheless, from 1878 to 1895, changes had taken place in Cuba that affected the renewal of the war. During these years, rationalization of the Cuban sugar industry and the end of its forced labor system altered the fundamental economic and social conditions on the island. Abolition of Cuban slavery during the 1880s coincided with a severe depression in the cane sugar industry. European nations were expanding beet sugar production, which decreased the international market for cane sugar and caused a fall in the price. Toward the end of the 1880s, however, the Cuban sugar industry had begun a revival based largely on American markets and capital. Mechanization of mills and transport resulted in larger cane plantations and more efficient sugar-refining mills.[1]

As sugar exports shifted from Europe to North America, much of the innovation was paid for by American dollars. Part of the increase in U.S. investment in the Cuban sugar industry resulted from many Cuban, Spanish, French, and British plantation owners acting to protect their property by becoming naturalized American citizens. But native Americans made some of the largest investments in land, mills, and transportation. Edwin F. Atkins of Boston, for instance, acquired the twelve-thousand-acre Soledad Plantation, which he valued at about $1 million. In 1892 Atkins joined Henry O. Havemeyer of the American Sugar Refining Company in purchasing the Trinidad interests for $600,000, the largest single investment of that year. Atkins, one of Cuba's largest sugar producers, became an active lobbyist in Washington. After the Cuban revolution resumed in 1895, Atkins lobbied against the insurgents and for continued Spanish sovereignty.[2]

Prosperity came to the island's sugar plantations in the early 1890s. As Cuban sugar production and exports soared, large amounts of new American capital were attracted to the island, further accelerating the rationalization of the industry. The boom was cut short in 1895 by changes in U.S. and Spanish tariff legislation, the general economic decline of the 1890s, and the onset of the Cuban revolution. Cuban sugar production peaked in 1894/95 at just over a million tons, and the U.S. market absorbed more than 91 percent of it. By contrast Spain imported slightly more than 2 percent of Cuba's crop. In 1895 American imports fell to 769,000 tons, and the following year they skidded to 235,000 tons, by this time reflecting the devastating effects of the Cuban revolution. Alarmed by the accelerating economic collapse, some Cuban planters looked to Madrid for relief through tariff negotiations with Washington; many others defined their future in terms of autonomy in economic affairs or annexation to the United States.[3]

There were many causes of the Cuban revolution. Working-class Cubans existed in extreme poverty on the fringe of the sugar and tobacco industries. Recently freed slaves faced continued economic and social repression. Social and economic injustice fed the long-smoldering political sources of rebellion. The 1890s depression caused additional economic hardship. Many Cuban leaders who had started the 1860s rebellion and who now lived in exile in Spanish America or the United States still longed for independence. Spain's failure to provide autonomy as promised in 1878 weakened Cuba's political moderates. During the late 1880s, expatriate revolutionaries began a new campaign for independence. José Martí organized and directed the movement, and General Máximo Gómez became its military head; closely associated was Antonio Maceo, a charismatic Afro-Cuban general. Martí inspired Cuban-American emigré communities in the United States and kept in close contact with Gómez and Maceo, the former having returned to his native Santo Domingo and the latter in exile in Costa Rica. In 1892 Martí capped his organizational efforts with the formation of the Cuban Revolutionary Party, and in the following months Cubans contributed funds for the renewal of the revolution and encouraged rebellion on the island. Because of Spanish vigilance and several false starts, the timing of the outbreak of the Cuban war was delayed until February 1895. When the struggle finally began, the Cuban sugar industry was just starting to feel the effects of a slowdown. Several weeks later, when Gómez, Martí, and Maceo landed on a beach in eastern Cuba, the Cuban sugar plantations had completed the 1894/95 harvest and were laying off laborers, many of whom joined the independence fight. *Cuba Libre* was the cry that rallied the rebels. No longer seeking autonomy under the Spanish flag, they demanded independence and social justice.[4]

United against Spain, the revolutionary leaders were divided in how they saw their future relations with the United States. Insurgent opinion ranged from fear of U.S. annexation to willingness to consider a close association with the American neighbor. Martí was apprehensive over the signs of growing U.S. interest in Hawaii and the Caribbean. One of his goals was to secure Cuban independence before the United States projected an annexationist policy toward the island. Gómez and Maceo were also wary of U.S. interest and believed Cubans could win independence without American intervention.[5]

But Tomás Estrada Palma, who briefly had been president of the Cuban Republic during the Ten Years War, believed that a special relationship with the United States was inevitable and desirable. When Martí died in 1895 in a military clash in Cuba, the civilian leadership of the

Cuban Revolutionary Party fell largely to Estrada Palma. He reasoned that since the United States provided the only large market for Cuban sugar, the island's prosperity required commercial access to the United States. Moreover, the immense destruction of the Cuban war necessitated new capital investment, which after independence could come only from the United States.[6]

Another divisive issue for the Cuban insurgents was the design and direction of the revolutionary leadership and future government. The possibility existed that at the end of a successful war, governmental power would be in the hands of victorious military caudillos. Before the rebellion began, Martí argued for civilian control, but Gómez and Maceo were wary of outside interference, recalling the failures of the Ten Years War. Gómez, a stubborn and dictatorial general who liked to issue political proclamations, was suspected of political ambitions, despite his promises that after the war he would accept civilian authority. Maceo, a politically attractive leader, was more openly contemptuous of civilian government, although he pledged to follow Gómez's lead. Covering these conflicting views was a loose agreement worked out by Martí, Gómez, and Maceo over how the revolutionary movement was to be directed and what its outcome should be. When Martí died, the new Cuban civilian leader, Estrada Palma, exercised little influence over Cuba's military leaders. In addition, Estrada Palma questioned the ability of the Cuban masses to govern themselves in an orderly way and to protect property. Although an ardent champion of independence from Spain, he believed that at the end of the war some form of association with the United States would be essential to ensure Cuban political liberty. Thus, Gómez, a tough field commander, and Estrada Palma, a civilian diplomat in New York City, did not have an understanding on how Cuba should be ruled.[7]

Cuba's racial makeup was another factor affecting the diplomacy of the war. The island had a large population of Afro-Cubans. The census of 1887 recorded 1,631,687 people; nearly one-third were of African descent. Most had been freed from slavery during the 1880s, and many lived in squalor on the fringe of plantation society. The ranks of the Cuban revolutionary army contained large numbers of Afro-Cuban soldiers. Upper-class Spaniards and Cubans—planters, merchants, and professionals—often described the war against Spain as a racial and social struggle for control of the island, a struggle that pitted black against white, poor against rich, and rural against urban. There were predictions that if Spain left Cuba, the island would descend into anarchy, racial warfare, and ultimately division into two parts, much like Santo Domingo. As a result some propertied Cubans and Spanish, who feared a triumphant Afro-Cuban army, wanted annexation to the United States.[8]

As the Cuban rebellion engulfed the island, Gómez employed a strategy of destroying the Cuban economy in order to persuade the Spanish to leave, thereby increasing upper-class fears of property destruction, banditry, and anarchy. After losing the Ten Years War, Gómez had brooded over the failure, concluding that the next rebellion must be more savage if it was to succeed. So he set out to turn the island into an economic desert that would become such a burden on the Spanish that they would withdraw. During the Ten Years War the rebellion had been confined to the eastern and mountainous portion of the island and therefore had never crippled the island's economy. This time widespread popular participation contributed to Gómez's military successes which carried revolutionary troops from the eastern to the western tip of Cuba and allowed them to torch the island's wealth.[9]

Initial insurgent successes in Cuba were matched by the broad support the Cuban Revolutionary Party obtained in the United States and other nations. Martí had successfully organized thousands of Cubans residing abroad, many naturalized Americans. Involved in clubs and committees, workers, businessmen, and professionals contributed time and money to the patriotic cause. Political support was strongest in Florida and New York City, where most emigrant Cubans lived. Another important unit, under the leadership of Dr. Ramón Betances, a Puerto Rican physician, was located in Paris, France. Betances hoped the war would unify Cuba and Puerto Rico into a single republic. Exiles in France provided significant financial support for the revolution, and Betances sometimes held covert talks with Spanish agents.[10]

Cuba's major civilian leaders lived in New York City. Estrada Palma was the delegate of the Cuban Revolutionary Party and the chief diplomatic agent of the Republic of Cuba. Benjamín Guerra was the party treasurer; Gonzalo de Quesada Arôstequia, the party secretary, held the post of Washington lobbyist; and Horatio Rubens, a North American, functioned as legal counsel. All were American citizens. Of these Cuban leaders, Estrada Palma was much older. Since release from a Spanish prison, he had taken up residence in a small New York State community and taught school. He lived frugally and was respected for his personal honesty and integrity. Rubens, young, ebullient, and full of his self-importance, was passionately caught up in the drama of the revolutionary events. He was eager to provide spirited leadership to the Cuban cause. Quesada was also young and carried into prominence by the independence movement. He frequently represented the Cubans, meeting in Washington with American congressmen sympathetic to the island's independence. All together, the Cuban organization was popularly known as the Junta. It promoted the revolution through public appeals, meetings, financial campaigns, press releases, political lobbying, and outfitting filibustering expeditions for Cuba. During the fall of 1895 the Cubans adopted a constitution and formed a government, which never had as much authority as the military field commanders or the party officers living abroad.[11]

The success of the military efforts in Cuba and the political and financial support overseas were impressive but inadequate to win Cuban independence. Gómez and Maceo initially carried the war across the island, crippled the Cuban economy, and held the support of the Cuban people, achieving far more in one year than during the entire Ten Years War. Nevertheless, the Spanish killed Martí in 1895 and Maceo the next year, which were grievous losses to the revolution. More important, Gómez was unable to drive the Spanish from the island. With a small army, never totaling more than forty thousand men and divided into small, poorly armed units scattered across the island, Gómez could not confront the Spanish in a decisive battle or force them from their entrenched fortifications associated with towns and cities. The Cuban army had no artillery and relied on machete charges, which were ineffective against trenches and barbed-wire emplacements. Thus the war settled down to one of attrition and destruction, with the insurgents roaming over much of the countryside and harassing Spanish troops and outposts where possible. Avoiding large battles, Gómez decimated the Cuban economy; his military success lay in Spain's inability to defeat his army or strategy. Gómez believed that, in time, economic strangulation would free Cuba, but time became the issue; how long and at what human and economic cost would it take to free Cuba?[12]

Estrada Palma also had difficulty in bolstering the revolution. Although the Junta enjoyed American popular approval, it was impossible to transform the many meetings, marches, and press accounts into enough soldiers, guns, and medicines so that Gómez could win the war. Congress passed belligerency resolutions, but the executive branch failed to act; and financial campaigns never raised sufficient funds to satisfy the needs of Gómez. Of seventy-one filibustering expeditions outfitted in the

United States, only twenty-seven reached Cuba. Supplies arrived in Cuba from other Caribbean ports, but Estrada Palma and the emigrés were unable to deliver the guns, ammunition, and quinine needed to end the war. Gómez was largely dependent on the men and materiel he obtained within Cuba to keep his army in the field.[13]

Just as the Cubans were unable to bring the war to a quick conclusion, the Spanish also failed to do so. Spain had changed greatly since the independence struggle had begun in the 1860s. The first Cuban rebellion had coincided with many years of peninsular political upheaval that had shaped Spanish political and economic society during the last third of the nineteenth century. A coup in 1868 unseated Queen Isabel II, who had reigned since 1833, and unleashed years of political turbulence on the peninsula. Spanish political factions could agree neither on the choice of the next monarch nor on the definition of what powers the monarchy should have. Thus political cleavages divided monarchists, republicans, clericals, militarists, provincial nationalists, and urban and rural elements. The years of political upheaval ended in 1875 with the restoration of the Bourbon monarchy. Alfonso XII, the son of Isabel, gained the throne through the efforts of the army, led by General Arsenio Martínez de Campos, and the support of professional politicians, headed by Antonio Cánovas del Castillo. The new king agreed to accept constitutional restrictions, thus meeting one of the major demands of political liberals. Cánovas then worked to decrease the influence of the army in politics and thereby end the recurring military coups carried out by *pronunciamientos*, political proclamations of leading generals. He believed that Spain should have a two-party system, which would allow for peaceful changes of ministries and thereby end the revolutionary plots and coups. He encouraged all politicians to accept the restored monarch and the 1876 constitution and to participate in Spanish political life. Those who refused were largely excluded from office—Carlists (supporters of Don Carlos as monarch), republicans, and some provincial autonomists, particularly Catalonians and Basques of the north.[14]

Cánovas's solution to Spain's political disorders lasted into the twentieth century; it defined the governmental system and established the generation of politicians that the United States faced in 1895. The leadership of the Spanish government came from an oligarchy of wealthy, landed, and often titled politicians who controlled local and national offices both through appointments and elections. The monarch had the important powers of selecting the head of the cabinet, dissolving the

Cortes, and decreeing new elections. When Alfonso died of tuberculosis in 1885, this authority fell to María Cristina, his Austrian wife, a Hapsburg, who held it until her only son, Alfonso XIII, became sixteen in 1902. Although a foreigner, untrained in Spanish politics, and little loved by her Spanish subjects, the young queen regent took her position seriously. She was intelligent and diligent. Her primary goal was to conserve the Spanish throne for her son. By 1895 the queen regent was an important political presence in Spain's governing councils.[15]

The new Spanish political system contained managed national elections. When Spain's principal political figures—the monarch, cabinet ministers, generals, and loyal opposition leaders—decided that a particular cabinet had reached an impasse solvable only by dismissal, the monarch would select a new prime minister and give him the necessary decree to hold new elections. The incoming prime minister and his interior minister would appoint urban and rural officials throughout Spain who could be counted on to provide an election majority. These officeholders and election managers were called *caciques*. When candidates for office were determined, a few spaces were reserved for the opposition. Often only one person ran for each office, and the results of the election came as no surprise; sometimes they were published before the election occurred. Obviously the Spanish electoral system was not democratic; it was not designed to be so. Rather it allowed for peaceful changes of ministry, an opposition voice in the Cortes, and freedom from military coups, thereby bringing order and centralized control to Madrid after years of political upheaval.[16]

During the Restoration, two governing political parties emerged, the Conservatives and the Liberals. Cánovas led the Conservatives until his assassination in 1897. He tended to be closer to the military officers and ultra-clericals. The Liberals were headed by Práxedes Mateo Sagasta, who retained direction of the party until his death in 1903. Before 1868, Liberal politicians had been excluded from office, and they had generated much of the revolutionary instability of the 1870s. When the Liberal Party entered office, it pressed for a large number of reforms. Opposing ultra-clericals, Liberals sought greater freedom of religious conscience and expanded secular education. One progressive goal, the elimination of slavery, was provided by Cánovas just before he left office in 1881. Liberals also promoted a free press, union legality, and an expanded suffrage. Universal male suffrage, adopted in 1890, was corrupted by the electoral system, yet during the 1890s more people voted, and municipal elections in particular became more responsive to the ballot box. Sagasta also attempted to reform bloated military budgets, but his efforts chiefly alienated the officers. Despite political differences, Liberals and Conservatives shared a common determination to make the Restoration succeed, thereby ending military coups and securing centralized authority throughout Spain. Conservatives accepted limited liberal reform, and Liberals supported the restored monarchy. Thus Cánovas and Sagasta alternated in the office of prime minister from 1875 to 1899, the *turno pacífico*, which brought internal peace and over two decades of stability to Spain.[17]

Though Cánovas and Sagasta shared much, they had contrasting personalities and did not work easily or closely together. Born of lower-middle-class parents in southern Spain, Cánovas came to represent the large landholders of Andalusía. He was a brilliant intellectual, a prominent historian by age twenty-five, who moved easily in the highest social circles and was the center of attention at Madrid salons. A forceful public speaker, he commanded attention by his sparkling intellect. Hard-working, ambitious, and shrewd, he was Spain's most important nineteenth-century politician.[18]

Sagasta had no intellectual pretensions, and to Cánovas, he was barely literate. Born in 1825 in Torrecilla of middle-class parents, he was educated as an engineer. The young Sagasta entered politics as a progressive, championing ideas that were out of favor in Isabel's Spain. Faced by repression, Sagasta turned revolutionary, attempting coups, manning barricades, and leading civil guards. After being imprisoned and exiled, he turned to foreign plotting and edited a revolutionary journal. On his return to Spain, he took an important part in the agitated political events of the post-Isabel years. Sagasta held several cabinet posts, including foreign minister, and was prime minister in 1875 when Martínez de Campos and Cánovas overthrew the government and placed Alfonso XII on the throne. In the years that followed, Sagasta decided to accept the constitutional Bourbon monarchy; other progressive politicians approved his decision and rallied to the new order. From these supporters Sagasta formed the Liberal Party, which he held together until his death. More retiring that Cánovas, Sagasta shunned the social circles and avoided the Madrid salons. Instead he worked ceaselessly to unify the party factions.[19]

By the 1890s the Restoration was showing signs of old age. Cánovas and Sagasta had brought many beneficial changes to Spain but now seemed more involved in retaining office than adopting new programs. Each man was having greater difficulty holding together a group of politicians with which to form a ministry. Cánovas's major political supporter and election manipulator, Francisco Romero Robledo, left his political following. A blatantly corrupt municipal election in Madrid had caused such an outcry against Romero Robledo that the two men separated. Moreover, Francisco Silvela, who supported greater local rule and honesty in government, had left Cánovas's entourage. After Cánovas's death, Silvela bested Romero Robledo and others to become the leading Conservative. Sagasta also had difficulty harmonizing his coalition of politicians. Antonio Maura broke with him over the issue of autonomy for Cuba, and Germán Gamazo, Maura's father-in-law, coveted Sagasta's leadership role. Moreover, with the resumption in the 1890s of colonial wars in Cuba and the Philippine Islands, military leaders had become more important and assertive in Madrid politics. The aged Martínez de Campos and other generals who lead the colonial campaigns, such as Camilio García de Polavieja and Valeriano Weyler y Nicolau, assumed greater prominence.[20]

By 1895 there were many peninsular political and economic issues affecting the Cuban war and Spain's diplomacy with the United States. Spanish politicians, mindful of earlier revolutionary turbulence, were united in trying to maintain political authority at the center against all divisive threats. The fundamental point of the Restoration was the continuation of the Bourbon constitutional monarchy. Restoration politicians feared a return to *pronunciamientos* and saw a threat in generals who might turn to coups; but junior officers and common soldiers tended to listen to Republican politicians. On the fringe of Spanish politics were the Carlists, who longed to change the monarchy in their favor by wrapping themselves in the flag of ultra-nationalism and ultra-clericalism. Don Carlos lived in Venice, but he had many Spanish supporters in northern rural Catalonian and Basque villages. Carlists often made common cause with disaffected provincial autonomists and ultra-clericals. When the Cuban war began, Carlists divided: some supported military suppression by Weyler and believed Madrid was fighting to defend the faith in Cuba; others saw in Spanish military failures the opportunity to overthrow a discredited regime. The Spanish government carefully monitored Carlist activities and successfully held them in check. Another group of excluded politicians were the Republicans, who were strongest in urban areas. Inherently opposed to monarchy, they were largely excluded from office, yet they had leaders of national stature. In a crisis, urban workers, soldiers, and junior officers might form behind them to end the Restoration. Republicans, however, were even more divided by the Cuban war than the Carlists. Some took a fraternal interest in the aspiring insular republic, but others, needing the support of the army, took a strong stand against the Cuban Republic. Thus many Carlists and Republicans supported military repression of the insurrection.[21]

Part of the political scene in Spain was the unfettered press. Journalists enjoyed press freedom, and a few newspapers, such as *El Imparcial*, provided broad news coverage and political independence. The bulk of them, however, were allied to a particular politician or party and provided limited news slanted to what their owners wanted. As the war developed in Cuba and the threat of U.S. intervention grew, newspapers often glorified Spanish heroism, patriotism, and noble behavior and characterized Americans as greedy Yankees lacking military virtues. As a result, many Spaniards had unrealistic expectations, believing their navy had a superior fighting spirit and would be victorious.[22]

The Restoration also affected the colonial administration of Cuba and helped to define Madrid's response to the *Grito de Baire*. To obtain a settlement in 1878, the Spanish government promised autonomy to the insurgents but subsequently failed to provide it. Restoration politicians, suppressing the local aspirations of Catalonians and Basques, were unwilling to extend autonomy to Cubans. If Madrid granted home rule to Cuba, some peninsular provincial leaders might demand the same status, and local control would inevitably weaken the power of managed national elections. Instead, Spanish politicians chose to regard Cuba as an inherent part of Spain, much as Asturias or Andalusía. As late as 1893, Antonio Maura presented to the Cortes a Cuban autonomy plan, which Cánovas and Sagasta sharply rejected. The Restoration system allowed Cuba to send members to the Cortes, but insular elections were just as cynically controlled as peninsular ones. On the island a political organization of Spanish officials and community leaders, the Constitutional Union, dominated the administrative process through appointed offices and corrupt elections. Moreover, the bloated military regime found the colonies an opportunity for offices, promotions, and personal financial gain. This regime was unresponsive to Cuba's basic social and economic problems.[23]

In addition, Madrid regulated Cuban trade to benefit Spanish industrial and agricultural interests. During the last third of the nineteenth century, Spain experienced some industrial development. Barcelona's expanding and high-priced textile production, sheltered by high tariff walls, profited from the Cuban market, and Spanish wheat farmers enjoyed flour sales to Cuba. At the same time, Spain encouraged domestic beet production, with the result that Cuba's cane sugar exporters faced declining peninsular sales. Although Spain had an unfavorable balance of trade with the outside world, soaring Cuban sugar sales to the United States helped offset the nation's unfavorable import account. Madrid never solved the problem of rising Spanish exports to the island and decreasing imports from it; indeed during the 1890s, tariff changes worsened the imbalance.[24]

When the Cuban rebellion began, Cánovas, who became prime minister a few weeks after the outbreak, sent Martínez de Campos to Cuba. Arriving in April, the captain general, who had negotiated the end of the previous Cuban uprising, quickly realized that the scope of the new insurrection was much greater than the last and that a political solution modeled after that of 1878 was out of the question. Pressured by *peninsulares* (Spaniards residing in Cuba) for a military solution, he advised Cánovas in July that he was unwilling to wage all-out war, which would involve a massive loss of life; instead he suggested that General Valeriano Weyler, a vigorous and ruthless officer, assume the command.[25]

Weyler arrived in Cuba in February 1896, bringing with him authority to fight war with war. During the campaign, about two hundred thousand Spanish troops went to Cuba; in addition, Weyler could count on an additional fifty thousand spirited Spanish and Cuban *voluntarios*. Weyler initiated a plan of warfare designed to eliminate insurgency from the economically developed western and central portions of the island and to restrict it to the eastern mountainous region, where it could be gradually reduced. He divided the island into several war zones, separated by north-south military barriers of trenches, barbed wire, and watchtowers. His plan was to concentrate his forces in the west to defeat the insurgents there and to use the military barriers to prevent insurgent reinforcements from the east. After reestablishing control of the west, he intended to move his troops to the central portion of the island, where they would end that insurgency, thereby containing the remaining Cuban forces in the eastern portion of the island, sealed off by a military barrier. During 1896 Weyler realized some successes. He reduced insurgency in the western zone but did not completely eliminate it. The central region became more secure, but insurgent bands still roamed widely throughout much of the area and often crossed the military barriers. Weyler's troops killed Maceo in December 1896, which raised Spanish hopes. Despite his determined efforts and some successes, however, Weyler did not end the insurrection in the western two-thirds of Cuba, and he never reduced the eastern stronghold. Gómez remained in the field and continued to harass Spanish military units and destroy economic assets.[26]

Associated with Weyler's failed military campaign was his civilian reconcentration program designed to separate insurgents from civilians. To cut off manpower, food, supplies, and information from the insurgents, Weyler ordered the peasants to leave their homes and villages and to relocate in towns and cities where the Spanish military could control them. The order was first directed at only a portion of the island, but in a few months it was expanded to include most of the island's rural population. He also called for a cessation of sugar production and tobacco exports in an effort to prevent Cuban planters from bribing insurgents to allow their businesses to operate. Weyler's directives, added to those of Gómez, rapidly reduced the island's productive capacity. More important than the collapse of the economy was the plight of unemployed *reconcentrados* in the fortified towns. Within months about four hundred thousand rural refugees entered concentration sites that were unprepared to receive them. The *reconcentrados* lacked housing, food, sanitation, and medical care. The results were predictable; indeed, Martínez de Campos had foreseen the inevitable effects even as he placed the plan before Cánovas in 1895. Starvation and disease soon gripped the island, and by 1897 the concentration centers had become death camps, with tens of thousands dying and thousands more living under the threat. The fate of the *reconcentrados* grew more grim with each passing month. In 1896 the numbers affected were relatively small, but by 1897 the condition of the *reconcentrados* had reached disaster proportions.[27]

As Spain increased its military pressure on Cuba, Cánovas tried to negotiate a settlement with the insurgents. During 1896 he initiated secret talks with Betances in Paris and continued the meetings sporadically until April 1897. The Cubans rejected an offer of autonomy, one of suzerainty, and a request to pay $200 million for their independence.[28]

By the spring of 1897, Spain's military and diplomatic campaigns had produced limited results at an extremely high cost. The Cuban insurgents were entrenched in eastern Cuba and able to disrupt economic life throughout most of the island. About 250,000 Spanish soldiers and Cuban volunteers had failed to defeat Gómez; some had died in combat, and tens of thousands had succumbed to tropical diseases; makeshift hospitals were filled with sick and dying troops. Those able to fight were insufficient to mount large-scale operations to search out and destroy insurgents. To this military failure were added the thousands of Cuban civilians who had perished in reconcentration camps and the thousands more condemned to starvation, disease, and death. On the peninsula, Cánovas and Weyler were encountering political opposition as Liberals decried military methods and called for a political settlement based on home rule. Abroad, the U.S. government was increasing its demands for an early settlement.[29]

The United States also had changed since the Ten Years War, but some things remained constant. The geographic situation of Cuba was the same; the island, located about ninety miles from the Florida coast, commanded vital sea lanes to the Gulf of Mexico and had many fine natural harbors. It had a subtropical setting for its rich and well-watered soil, which offered a basis for a commercial exchange of sugar and other subtropical products for North American foodstuffs and manufactures. Another constant was the American belief that Spain was decadent and declining and that its remaining colonies would inevitably strike off their chains. Deeply imbued with nineteenth-century liberalism and a belief in progress, Americans identified with Cuba's struggle for political and economic freedom. But American views of Cuban independence were tempered by racism and bigotry, since many opposed annexing Cuba because of its African heritage, Creole population, and Catholic faith.[30]

A significant development since the Ten Years War was the enormous change in relative strength between Spain and the United States, a difference that was evident in nearly every phase of economic life. Spain lagged farther and farther behind in population growth, technological development, manufacturing and mining output, transportation improvements, agricultural production, and financial strength. These economic resources affected military power as well; by 1898 the new American navy outclassed the Spanish fleet.[31]

American economic development during the latter half of the nineteenth century encouraged businessmen and government officials to reappraise commercial and investment opportunities abroad. Periodic economic depressions had sharpened American awareness of the importance of foreign markets to secure national prosperity. Sugar dominated American interest in Cuba, but there were also substantial investments in mining, cattle ranches, and tobacco. The exact amount of investment is unknown, but Americans considered it important. Secretary of State Richard Olney, for instance, estimated U.S. investment at $50 million, and although this was exaggerated, his figure was accepted as a measure of the significance of American economic interest. Moreover, investment was rising rapidly in the 1890s; the largest single annual increase, $1.2 million, came in 1892. More accurate figures were available for commerce; customs data showed a rapid growth in American-Cuban trade, which peaked at just over $103 million in 1893. These figures, $50 million in investment and $100 million in trade, were often cited to illustrate America's economic involvement in Cuba.[32]

Cuba became part of the American political scene of the 1890s as both U.S. political parties faced instability and unprecedented challenges. During the late 1870s and 1880s, the parties had been closely matched. The balance of the 1880s, however, gave way to political turbulence during the next decade as voters shifted traditional party allegiances. New political movements and parties challenged both Republicans and Democrats, who suffered humiliating defeats at the polls. The first to feel the new currents were the Republicans in the 1890 election. Democrats had a field day as 238 gained seats in the House of Representatives, compared with a mere 88 Republicans. William McKinley was among those swept out of Washington. Traditional politicians found little comfort in the formation of the Populist Party in 1891, which, through fusion with discontented Democrats and Republicans, won stunning victories in the West and South. The 1894 election, which took place during the depression and amid bitter partisan divisions, resulted in a rout for the Democrats.[33]

These seesaw election returns set the stage for the presidential election of 1896, the most hotly contested one in twenty years. A coalition of Democrats and Populists formed behind the candidacy of William Jennings Bryan on a platform of silver coinage, which terrified eastern business interests. The contest divided both political parties as silver Republicans supported Bryan and as gold Democrats backed McKinley. Unprecedented campaign innovations, Bryan's extensive electioneering throughout the nation, and Mark Hanna's massive financing, changed the character of presidential campaigning. Although McKinley won, Republican politicians feared another election debacle and expected future desperate contests.[34]

Into this unstable and passionate political scene came the Cuban issue.

Politicians of all stripes tried to use the Cuban insurrection to promote their cause. Republicans, Democrats, and Populists weighed in on the side of Cuba's insurgency, demonstrating their enthusiasm in public meetings and congressional debates. It was left to the presidents, Cleveland and McKinley, to try to find a way to accommodate popular politics at home to diplomatic responsibilities abroad.

CHAPTER 2

. . . .

CUBA, CLEVELAND,

. . . .

AND CÁNOVAS

. . . .

S hortly after the Cuban war for independence began,
Congress and the Cleveland administration clashed
over it. Differing in their responsibilities and perspectives, these branches of government wrangled over foreign policy and
competed for leadership of domestic political forces. Their division
shaped America's response to the Cuban war. At the heart of the Cuban
issue was partisan politics and the approaching election. The American
people wanted to see the Cuban revolution succeed, and most politicians
were eager to take a stand favoring it; there was no better pulpit than the
floor of Congress. Only a small congressional minority attempted to restrain the majority. Within this political context, President Grover Cleveland and Secretary of State Richard Olney conducted their diplomacy
with Spain.

From the outset, congressional interest was partisan. A Democratic
and unpopular administration held the White House; Cleveland was concluding his second term in office, and crucial national elections were imminent. It was tempting for the Republican-controlled Congress to raise
the popular Cuban issue to show that the Cleveland administration was
failing to represent the true feelings of the American people. And many
Democrats willingly joined the critics rather than defend the president.

Much of the congressional debate turned on the issue of constitutional powers. Although executive prerogatives governed the conduct of diplomacy, some congressmen claimed jurisdiction. Congress had the constitutional authority to declare war, and some pro-Cuban members asserted that Congress could also recognize the belligerent rights of the Cuban Republic. Congressional debates, therefore, often centered on constitutional arguments over U.S. recognition of the Cuban insurgents, most legislators favoring either belligerent rights or immediate independence.

There was one area of legislative-executive agreement; both branches expected the State Department to make a maximum effort to protect the lives, property, and commerce of American citizens. Since many Cubans had become naturalized citizens and some of them were engaged in filibustering expeditions, vigorous protection of American citizens satisfied American patriotism and at the same time projected the U.S. government into Cuban events.

Congressional consideration of the Cuban war began with a series of resolutions submitted by Senate and House members, nearly all of them offered after Congress reconvened in December 1895. A few of the resolutions dealt with the protection of American citizens; the majority asked the executive branch for information about affairs in Cuba or called for the immediate recognition of Cuban belligerency or independence. These resolutions were routinely sent for consideration to the Senate Foreign Relations Committee or the House Foreign Affairs Committee. The Senate committee was the first to act; on 28 January 1896 it introduced two resolutions, one sponsored by the committee majority and the other the minority. Senator John T. Morgan, Democrat of Alabama, spoke for the majority, and Senator Don Cameron, Republican of Pennsylvania, presented the minority view. The majority resolution was concurrent; it had to be approved by both houses of Congress and did not require presidential action. It declared that since a state of war existed in Cuba between the government of Spain and the Cuban Republic, the U.S. government "should maintain a strict neutrality between the contending powers, according to each all the rights of belligerents in the ports and territory of the United States." Cameron's minority resolution added that the president should offer the friendly offices of the United States to the Spanish government "for the recognition of the independence of Cuba."[1]

Debate on the resolutions began on 20 February and lasted eight days. Those senators favoring U.S. intervention presented arguments that fell into three broad categories: American interests, Cuban interests, and Spanish misdeeds. The war directly involved America because of the strategic location of the island. It damaged American investment and trade and required the government to spend money to enforce U.S. neutrality laws. Moreover, the United States had sufficient power to bring peace, liberty, and independence to Cuba. Since the Cuban insurgents were engaged in war, belligerency was a fact that should be recognized; true neutrality would exist only when both Spain and Cuba had equal rights in the United States to borrow money, buy arms, and support their military efforts. The Cubans had created a government, they deserved to be governed by their own will, and they wanted recognition of belligerent rights. As a result of misrule, Spain had forfeited its right to the island, and its war atrocities must end. U.S. recognition of Cuban belligerency should not anger Spain, since Spain had recognized the Confederacy during the American Civil War and that had not touched off a war between the Union and Spain.[2]

The speech by Senator John Sherman, Republican of Ohio and chairman of the Senate Foreign Relations Committee, received a lot of attention. Sherman delivered an emotional account of conditions in Cuba, branding the Spanish as "barbarous robbers and imitators of the worst men who ever lived in the world," and he predicted that the American people would not tolerate conditions much longer before intervening "to put an end to crimes . . . almost beyond description." Sherman took his examples of butchery and rape from a book published by the *New York Journal*; these stories later proved to be false, embarrassing the proponents of intervention.[3]

Opposition senators replied that the debate was simply political posturing, since a concurrent resolution did not require executive action. Moreover, senators had insufficient information. There was no evidence that the Cubans had established a government worthy of recognition; it had no capital, no ports, no commerce, and no navy. If the U.S. government recognized Cuban belligerent rights, it would harm rather than help American and Cuban interests; Americans would lose the right to demand protection of property and compensation for losses from the Spanish, and the Spanish navy would gain the right to search ships in international waters, thereby improving its ability to intercept filibustering expeditions. Even with belligerent rights, the Cubans would not be able to raise additional money or outfit more ships.[4]

The Senate voted to join the Morgan and Cameron resolutions together and then passed them 64 to 6, with 10 abstentions. The vote was bipartisan, with 35 Republicans, 25 Democrats, 3 Populists, and 1 independent in favor. Of the 6 who opposed, half were Republicans and half Democrats. The abstentions were split between 3 Republicans and 7 Democrats. Half the opposition votes came from New England and the other half from Gulf Coast states.[5] During the debate two amendments were proposed; one recognized the Cuban government and the other only extended sympathy to the Cubans. Both were defeated; of the two, the independence amendment received 17 votes, an indication of support for immediate U.S. intervention in the Cuban war.[6]

After passage, the Morgan-Cameron resolutions went to the House for consideration. The Foreign Affairs Committee had already received many proposals from House members, and it produced its own set of resolutions. On 2 March, the chairman of the committee, Robert R. Hitt, Republican of Illinois, reported out of committee three resolutions: the United States should recognize Cuban belligerency and maintain neutrality between the two contestants; the United States should use its "good offices and friendly influence" to obtain a government in Cuba satisfactory to the island's people; and the United States should protect legitimate American interests in Cuba "by intervention" if necessary.[7]

Hitt and Robert Adams, Jr., Republican of Pennsylvania and chairman of the subcommittee on Cuba, managed the House debate. They explained to House members that the resolution was an effort to make Spain do its duty toward American property. They estimated U.S. investment in Cuba at $20 to $30 million. At first they had believed that the U.S. government could hold Spain responsible for any property losses resulting from the war, but the State Department held that Spain need not pay any compensation if it could prove that it had not been negligent. Hitt and Adams argued that the House resolutions would pressure Spain to act more vigorously. As for the Senate resolutions, Hitt objected to Cameron's addition; instead of independence, the United States should acknowledge Cuban belligerency and adopt strict neutrality between the contending forces.[8]

The House debate on the resolutions was completed in one day. Positions taken for and against mirrored those of the committee reports and Senate debates. House members stressed the popularity of Cuba's insurgency, Adams noting that the American people had sent thousands of petitions to the House asking the government to extend a helping hand to the Cubans. Those favoring the resolution likened the American Revolution to the Cuban revolution. The most important opposition spokesman was Charles A. Boutelle, Republican of Maine, who complained of the lack of information. At the close of debate, House members voted 262 to 17 in favor, with 76 not voting. As in the Senate, the support was bipartisan, with eight negative votes coming from New England and the rest scattered among the coastal states from Virginia to Texas.[9]

Since the Senate and House had passed different resolutions, a conference committee met and decided to send the House resolutions to the Senate for approval, which initiated a second Senate debate in mid-March. This debate became more rancorous. Senators George F. Hoar, Republican of Massachusetts, and Eugene Hale, Republican of Maine, sarcastically criticized the Foreign Relations Committee for lack of information. Hale ridiculed Sherman's use of patently false *Journal* stories. Since the concurrent resolution would have no effect, Hale charged senators with making political speeches; in particular he accused Sherman of having presidential ambitions. Hale also belabored the Cubans for destroying American property and questioned their "liberty loving" nature.[10] Morgan countered that the public wanted Congress to act. He introduced thirty-nine petitions that had come from all parts of the country, but especially the Midwest, and remarked that the House had many more.[11] As the debate dragged on, a filibuster threatened, and Senate leaders decided to return the House resolutions to the conference committee, with the intent that the original Senate resolutions be sent once again to the House for passage.

On 3 April, Hitt introduced the Morgan-Cameron resolutions to the House. This time, debate was extensive as two dozen members had a chance to speak. Hitt and Adams repeated many familiar arguments on behalf of the Cubans, stressing the large number of public petitions in favor of aiding them. Adams said that older House members could not recall an issue that had aroused so much public support. Hitt noted that only the business community opposed congressional action. About half of those who spoke wanted the Cuban patriots to be free of Spanish misrule and cruelty and to establish an independent government. They often favorably compared American and Cuban patriotism and love of liberty. Fewer urged only recognition of belligerency, and just two favored annexation to the United States. There were only a few references to protecting American economic interests and considerably greater condemnation of the business community for opposing congressional action. Those who objected to the resolutions complained of voting without facts and feared risking a war. Only one opponent argued that passage of the resolutions would harm American business.[12]

The tally taken on 6 April showed 247 for the resolutions, 27 against, and 80 abstentions. The favorable vote was heavily Republican, 186 joined by 56 Democrats, 4 Populists, and 1 silverite. The negative vote, however, was nearly 2-to-1 Republicans over Democrats. Fourteen negative votes were concentrated in New England and New York, with the other 13 opposition votes coming from Atlantic and Gulf Coast states. Only 1 vote, from Texas, came from west of the Mississippi River. The heartland of the nation and the Pacific Coast either voted for the resolutions or abstained.[13]

Certainly the Senate and House votes contained a political message. The Republicans had succeeded in an election year in demonstrating greater commitment than the White House to Cuba, and this was especially true in the agricultural regions, where Populism was challenging traditional parties. Only a few eastern and southern congressmen were willing to stand up against the popular mood, and hardly anyone had a good word for the business community. Although nearly everyone but Morgan admitted that Congress did not have the constitutional right to recognize Cuban belligerency and that the concurrent resolutions had no more weight than an expression of congressional opinion, the vote provided a lift to the Cuban insurgents and was seen as threatening to Spain. In addition, congressional action encouraged the Cleveland administration to make a diplomatic initiative.

Confronted by the growing war in Cuba, which involved many American interests, the Cleveland administration acted firmly to assert legal and treaty rights and more hesitantly took up the issue of independence. The first problems were legal: the enforcement of treaties and neutrality laws, largely in the interest of protecting American citizens and property and stemming the flow of arms and men to Cuba. Richard Olney, who became secretary of state in July 1895, handled these legal issues. Hannis Taylor was minister to Spain, and Ramon Williams was consul general in Havana. Olney, a lawyer, previously served as attorney general. Taylor, a southern lawyer, had received his diplomatic appointment because he had steadfastly supported the Democratic Party against Populism; he did not speak Spanish and had no training in diplomacy. At the time the Cuban insurrection began, he was in Madrid pressing Spain to settle claims that had originated during the Ten Years War.[14]

The claims against Spain were handled much like legal actions: evidence was collected and presented, counterarguments were introduced, and some cases ended up in arbitration. This was a familiar procedure for lawyers and bureaucrats. Despite the careful, legalistic procedures followed, many of the cases irritated government officials, and some made their way into the press, becoming sensational stories that inflamed public opinion. The intense controversy and publicity, however, neither produced a war scare nor threatened a break in diplomatic relations. In fact, the closer the two nations came to war, the harder Spain worked to prevent these incidents from causing a crisis.

A few examples of the more inflammatory cases provide some appreciation of the anger aroused. Of the American citizenship cases, one of the most tendentious was that of Julio Sanguily. A youthful insurgent general at the close of the Ten Years War, Sanguily became a naturalized American citizen. On 24 February 1895 he was arrested in his home in Havana and charged with rebellion, which under courts-martial was punishable by death. Although he had associations with insurgents, the evidence showing participation in the rebellion was flimsy and circumstantial. In a trial held nine months after his arrest, the judge found him guilty and sentenced him to life in prison. The State Department did everything in its power to protect and defend Sanguily; it insisted that his American citizenship be respected and that he have a trial in a civilian court, and it repeatedly pressured the Spanish government to pardon him.[15]

More sensational was the case of José M. Delgado, a sugar planter, who was also a naturalized citizen. One morning in March 1896, Maceo's troops came to Delgado's plantation and stopped to prepare breakfast. Maceo and his officers took over the plantation house for their meal. While they were eating, Spanish troops arrived, and there was a brief battle. Maceo retreated, leaving the cane fields burning. When the Spanish confronted the men and women who had taken refuge in the plantation house during the battle, Delgado explained to the general that he was an American citizen and displayed his U.S. documentation. The officer contemptuously dismissed it and ordered the men shot. Delgado received three bullet wounds and three machete cuts. Left for dead, he and a Cuban laborer, who served as a witness, survived. Frightened and desperate for medical help, Delgado's father, also an American citizen, managed to contact Consul General Williams, who obtained protection from the Spanish captain general. Delgado was moved to Havana and nursed back to health, but his leg was permanently damaged. Strongly supported by the American government, he sought $178,543 in financial compensation. The United States also insisted that Spain punish the general who had spurned U.S. documentation and ordered the shooting of innocent civilians. The Spanish government never admitted any fault and claimed the insurgents shot Delgado. After six months of intensive litigation, Delgado dropped the case.[16]

Another incident that troubled Spanish-American relations was the capture of the *Competitor*, a filibustering schooner with two American citizens aboard, and a few days later, the capture of two other Americans who had gone ashore from the ship. Since the ship was seized in the process of delivering arms and men to Cuba, the Spanish promptly tried the men as pirates under admiralty law, found them guilty, and condemned them to death. The State Department managed to prevent the executions from taking place. Despite a weak case, it brought the prisoners under civilian jurisdiction, improved their condition of imprisonment, and eventually obtained a pardon for them.[17]

These three cases were just the tip of the iceberg; by early 1897 there were seventy-three citizen-protection cases, seven expulsion cases of American newspaper reporters, and eighty-three personal and property compensation claims totaling just under $10 million. Much of the energy of the State Department and Spanish foreign ministry was devoted to pursuing these cases. Many of the incidents were carried in the newspapers and featured in congressional debates. They fed the public's perception that Spanish rule was cruel and unjust.[18]

During 1895 and the first half of 1896 the Cleveland administration took a few hesitant steps toward intervention in the Cuban war. Olney examined a number of possibilities and discussed them with Cleveland, but nothing came of these early talks. Olney first considered intervention during September 1895. He informed Cleveland that there were two sides to the Cuban question. The Spanish contended that the rebels were of the lowest class, without property, and were led by adventurers incapable of forming a government. Should they win, anarchy would result; therefore Spain believed the United States should support its efforts. On the other hand, Paul Brooks, a wealthy American planter in Cuba and consular agent, told Olney that every prominent Cuban family had at least one member associated with the insurrection. Brooks estimated that 90 percent of Cubans supported the insurgents. The Cuban propertied class was disgusted with Spanish misrule, which had brought high taxes and debt and at the same time was unable to protect life or property.

Brooks predicted that the insurgents would ultimately win and were capable of governing the island. Continuation of the barbarous war, however, meant destruction of the economy and heavy loss of life. In addition, Olney reminded Cleveland of the large domestic political interest. Given the favorable public attitude toward the Cuban cause, politicians of all persuasions were setting their sails "to catch the popular breeze." The war harmed many American economic interests, Olney noted, and Cuban sympathizers swarmed over Washington, demanding recognition of belligerency. Given these circumstances Olney recommended that the administration strictly enforce its neutrality laws but that it also obtain better information. He proposed sending an agent to Cuba, particularly one with military experience, to investigate the true nature of the war. If Brooks proved to be right, then the government should protest Spain's inhumane warfare and ultimately recognize Cuba's belligerency and independence. Olney sent Brooks to see Cleveland, who was favorably impressed by him. Nevertheless, nothing came of these initial exchanges.[19]

Olney had another source of information, Edwin Atkins, also a prominent Cuban sugar planter. Atkins disdained the Cuban insurgents, regarding them as little more than arsonists. At first he held that they could not govern Cuba, but he eventually came to believe that they could provide local government under Spanish autonomy.[20] As the months passed, Olney and Cleveland moved closer to Atkins's point of view.

The Cleveland administration reviewed the Cuban issue while Congress debated its resolutions. During a cabinet session that considered the Republican partisan views expressed in the Senate, particularly those of Sherman, Olney reiterated his idea of sending an investigative commission to Cuba to gather better information on the military situation, but he obtained no cabinet support.[21]

A month later, on 20 March 1896, Olney informally discussed Cuba with the Spanish minister, Enrique Dupuy de Lôme. In a candid exchange, Olney declared that the United States was preoccupied with the Cuban issue largely because the war was grinding on without an end in sight. Olney assured Dupuy that he opposed Cuban independence because he did not believe the insurgents could govern successfully. Yet continuation of the war harmed American interests and threatened the complete destruction of the island. Olney insisted that the U.S. government wanted to help Spain to end the war; thus Dupuy could be certain that the Cleveland administration would not recognize Cuban belligerency or send an investigative commission to the island. Olney suggested that Spain bring the war to an early conclusion by providing meaningful political reforms that would attract the mass of Cubans. If Spain did this, Olney promised that the United States would throw its weight behind the reforms, and the insurrection would lose its moral force. With public support for the insurrection diminishing, the rebellion would end.[22]

During the next two weeks, while Congress continued its debate, Olney prepared a diplomatic note, which was dated 4 April but which was not delivered until the eighth, two days after Congress approved its resolutions. In the note, Olney described the year-long military standoff in Cuba. Given the interest of the American people in struggles for freer political institutions, the geographic proximity of Cuba, the excesses committed by both combatants, the loss of trade, the destruction of property, and the impoverishment of American citizens, the United States could not be expected to refrain from intervention for ten years. The president was anxious to have a "prompt and permanent pacification of that island." Olney agreed with Spain that the insurgents could not govern the island; he admitted that Spanish withdrawal might lead to a bloody "war of races," the establishment of two republics—one white and one black—and recurring bloodshed until one finally defeated the other. He assured Spain that the Cleveland administration did not want to annex the island; rather, it desired an early end to the insurrection through the establishment of good government on the island. Olney suggested that Madrid propose a political solution that would leave "Spain her rights of sovereignty . . . yet secure to the [Cubans] all such rights and powers of local self-government as they [could] reasonably ask." It was up to Spain to define the measures that would achieve this end. Olney promised that the U.S. government would back such a solution and offered to provide presidential good offices and mediation if desired.[23]

Having alerted Spain of American impatience, Olney took an additional step: he chose a new consul general for Havana. For six months, Cleveland and Olney had mulled over sending a special agent to Cuba, a person familiar with military affairs and of high rank, who could use his experience to size up the war. Deciding against a special mission, they selected a new consul general, Fitzhugh Lee, a former Confederate cavalry general, nephew of Robert E. Lee, and recent governor of Virginia. Although Lee had no diplomatic experience and could not speak Spanish, they expected him to provide better military analysis. At the time of appointment, newspapers noted that Lee favored the Cuban cause. He quickly upset Cleveland and Olney with his proinsurgent reports and diplomatic methods. Self-assured, opinionated, talkative, and with an eye for investments, Lee quickly irritated the Spanish authorities and endeared himself to American reporters. Toward the end of his stay in Havana, Lee wore a holstered revolver on his hip.[24]

By the time Lee arrived in Cuba, Cleveland and Olney had largely turned away from the insurgents. They were therefore displeased by Lee's first reports, which advocated American intervention. Lee asserted that the war was a military stalemate and that the Spanish would never grant meaningful political reform. Even if Spain granted autonomy, the Cubans would not accept it. Lee advocated that to end the deadlock, the United States should intervene, perhaps even purchase the island. He proposed sending a naval ship to Havana to encourage the Spanish to protect American interests or risk having the marines do it. If the United States did nothing, Lee warned, conditions on the island would continue to deteriorate, and there might be war with Spain. Lee noted that Spanish military officers considered it dishonorable to lose the island to the Cubans and would prefer to surrender it honorably to superior U.S. armed forces.[25]

Annoyed by Lee's advice, Cleveland remarked to Olney that the consul general rolled "intervention like a sweet morsel under his tongue." Since the United States did not want the island, the president considered it foolish to buy it and then give it to the Cubans. As for a gunboat, the United States had to take "prudent measures" to safeguard American citizens and their interests, but a naval visit might provide a convenient excuse for trouble with Spain. Nevertheless, Cleveland mulled over eventual intervention. He confessed to Olney that he thought a "great deal about Cuba" but that he could not see "the place where we [could] get in."[26] Despite Lee's urging, Cleveland and Olney were not ready to give up the search for a Spanish solution.

American frustration with Spain was matched by that of Spain with the United States. To the Spanish government, the root cause of the Cuban problem was the Junta. Ignoring all internal Cuban grievances, the Spanish believed that the Junta was the engine that drove the revolution. It spread lies about Spain, raised money, purchased arms, sent shiploads of men and arms to Cuba, and coordinated efforts of hostile emigrant Cubans throughout Latin America and Europe. Spain believed that because the Junta operated freely in the United States and with public opinion behind it, the Cuban insurgents were encouraged to fight on, hoping for even greater aid and ultimately American intervention. From the start of the rebellion until the Spanish-American War began, the Spanish government complained about the Junta and held the United States responsible for encouraging the rebellion.[27]

When Dupuy received Olney's 4 April note, he advised Madrid that the Cleveland administration was friendly and sincere. Having no desire for the island, the United States hoped that Spain would pacify Cuba. Dupuy emphasized that the secretary of state had not questioned Spain's sovereignty over the island and that he had demonstrated a clear understanding of what would happen if the insurgents gained control of Cuba.[28]

The Spanish reply to Olney, written by Cánovas, relied on the advice given by Dupuy. Cánovas emphasized the positive parts of Olney's note. On the other hand, he criticized some of Washington's misunderstandings. Cánovas asserted that Cuba had "one of the most liberal political systems in the world." Moreover, during 1895 the Cortes had passed reforms providing local government to the Cubans. Cánovas promised that as soon as the insurrection ended, he would implement them. Cánovas rejected the offer of presidential good offices and mediation, since Spain could not negotiate as an equal with the insurgents. "In brief," he declared, "there is no effectual way to pacify Cuba apart from the actual submission of the armed rebels to the mother country." The United States should aid in pacification by prosecuting those who organized filibustering expeditions and exposing the American public to the lies of the Cuban emigrants. If Washington displayed its support for the Spanish cause, popular approval of the Junta would diminish, ending rebel hopes for outside aid.[29]

Cánovas had several reasons for rejecting Cleveland's offer of good offices and mediation. He believed that any involvement of the United States in Cuban affairs, no matter how trivial, diminished Spanish sovereignty and demonstrated the impotence of the nation to deal with the insurrection. U.S. involvement would inevitably increase the morale of the insurgents and encourage them to fight harder. Once started, American involvement would tend to increase over the years and would eventually result in a protectorate or annexation. The United States had a long history of interest in the island, and therefore Spain could not expect it to mediate impartially. Congress had just passed a resolution favoring recognition of Cuban belligerency, even though Cleveland disapproved, which was one more indication of U.S. interest. In addition, the Cleveland administration would be in office for only nine more months. Cáno- vas was unwilling to place Spanish interests in the hands of a nation facing elections, with the outcome unknown.[30]

Having turned down Cleveland's offer, Cánovas sought European sup- port against potential U.S. intervention in Cuba. Carlos Manuel O'Don- nell y Abreu, the duke of Tetuán and Spain's minister of state, prepared a twenty-three-page memorandum for circulation to Europe's Great Pow- ers. Dated 28 July 1896, the memorandum presented Spain's case against the United States and asked for assistance in Washington. Tetuán cov- ered the familiar points already made to Olney: Cuba was well governed before the revolution; the insurgents did not want autonomy but the end of Spanish sovereignty, which Spain would not concede; and the Spanish administration was not responsible for the rebellion. He pointed to the contented and prosperous Puerto Ricans, who lived under the same laws as the Cubans. Since the Cuban insurgents refused to fight openly, the struggle would be long; having already sent 127,000 soldiers to Cuba, Spain was readying more and would send as many as were needed. As for the United States, Cleveland had done his duty, but Congress had passed resolutions favoring the Cubans, and the coming presidential election, given the Republican platform in support of Cuban independence, in- creased the danger of conflict. The worst was that the U.S. government allowed the Cuban Junta to function openly despite Spain's complaints and contrary to treaties of friendship. Ever since the founding of the U.S. Republic, Tetuán asserted, Americans had coveted Cuba; now the Re- publican Party wanted to eradicate all European colonial interests from the New World. Therefore, those European nations with American colo- nies or maritime interests should support Spain. The Great Powers should explain to Washington the difficult situation facing Spain—the sacrifices it had made as a result of the support the American people had given the insurrection—and they should ask Washington to take effective steps to halt the aid. This would avoid the danger that the American people, stimulated by the election, would provide even greater aid to the insurrection and cause a conflict between Spain and the United States, a conflict that might involve all of Europe. As for Cuba, once peace re- turned, Spain would see that it enjoyed local self-government.[31]

With the draft memorandum in hand, Tetuán met separately with the ambassadors of the Great Powers, asking each of them to consider mak- ing a joint demarche on Spain's behalf in Washington. During these ini- tial talks, Tetuán believed that England, Austria, and Italy were favorable to his request and that Germany was willing to join in collective action if it was unanimous. The Russian ambassador was personally favorable, and the French diplomat put off replying until Paris received a response from its minister in Washington.[32]

While Tetuán was waiting for all the European powers to reply, Hannis Taylor learned of the memorandum. The British ambassador, Henry Drummond Wolff, leaked it to a British reporter, who in turn informed Taylor. Angered, Taylor confronted Tetuán, protesting that Spain's action would be offensive to Cleveland and Olney because it showed a lack of confidence in their sincerity toward Spain. Taylor insisted that no administration could be friendlier toward Spain; should Spain attempt to organize European action against the United States, it would end the Cleveland administration's efforts to cooperate. American public opinion would be greatly excited against Spain and result in a more favorable attitude toward the insurgents and increased filibustering. Placed on the defensive, Tetuán agreed to change his circular memorandum by deleting the part asking for European support in Washington. This turned the draft message into an informative report on the Cuban situation, which satisfied Taylor. After giving in to Taylor, Tetuán commented to Cánovas that although he agreed not to request joint action, circulation of his memorandum to Europe's capitals would prepare the way for action when it became appropriate.[33]

The final European response to Tetuán's initiative disappointed the Spanish government. London, Rome, Vienna, and Paris opposed concerted action in Washington. The French, for instance, explained that any European demarche would offend American national pride and antagonize public opinion against Spain. Should any president appear to give way to foreign pressure, he would immediately be suspect in the eyes of the public. The French minister suggested that Spain's best hope was to win some battles in Cuba, to provide significant governmental reforms, and to accept Cleveland's proposal of good offices.[34] Thus Spain's first attempt to secure European backing failed.

Cánovas also looked into the possibility of negotiating a settlement with the Cubans. In late March 1896 Ramón Betances, the Cuban representative in Paris, received several Spanish contacts. From these talks it appeared that Madrid was prepared to offer local self-government, including an insular constitution and cortes. The Spaniards hinted that they represented the highest levels of the Spanish government, and Betances took this to mean Cánovas and the queen regent. He turned away the advances, insisting that Cubans would settle only for independence. Six weeks later Tetuán attempted to bribe Betances and other Cuban leaders, offering fifty million Spanish pesetas to desert the insurrection. In September, a few weeks after Tetuán failed to secure European support, several Spanish financiers proposed to Betances that Cuba buy its independence from Spain for $200 million and Puerto Rico for $25 million. Certain that Spain would have to give up the islands, they proposed arranging a status for Cuba, such as South Africa had, under which the Cubans would receive complete sovereignty in exchange for a financial indemnity. Having met several times with the Spaniards, Betances urged Estrada Palma to empower him to negotiate, but the New York leader failed to respond, and the contacts broke off at the end of the month.[35]

Spain's diplomatic feelers coincided with the American presidential election. During the summer and fall of 1896, U.S. attention focused on the national campaign, and there was remarkably little consideration of the Cuban war and Spain. The presidential candidates concentrated on the money and tariff issues; in all the recorded campaign speeches of William McKinley, there was no mention of Cuba or any other international topics. The nominating conventions, however, did write platform planks on foreign affairs. The Republican platform was more ambitious and aggressive than the Democratic one. Republicans ran on a program of control of the Hawaiian Islands, construction of an American-owned Nicaraguan canal, and purchase of the Danish West Indies. As for Cuba, Republicans took a "deep and abiding interest [in] the heroic battle of the Cuban patriots against cruelty and oppression" and hoped for the success of liberty. Since Spain had lost control of Cuba and was unable to protect American lives and property, the U.S. government should "use its influence and good offices to restore peace and give independence to the island." By contrast, the Democrats only put in a good word for the Monroe Doctrine and extended "sympathy to the people of Cuba in their heroic struggle for liberty and independence."[36] In November the Republicans swept the elections, gaining the White House and control of both houses of Congress.

Between election day and the inauguration of the new president, however, there was an interim period of four months, during which several attempts were made to solve the Cuban problem. In his last annual address to Congress, Cleveland presented his Cuban policy to the nation. The president characterized the war in Cuba as a stalemate; both sides were willfully destroying American property, and many American citizens were being harmed. He reiterated his April offer of good offices and warned Spain that it could not count indefinitely on the current American policy; the United States might not continue to refrain from intervention. On the other hand, Cleveland asserted that recognition of Cuban belligerency would do more harm than good to American interests and contended that the United States could not extend recognition to a Cuban government that did not exist. He warned, however, that when Cuban developments showed that Spain's "sovereignty [was] extinct," and when the war meant "nothing more than the useless sacrifice of human life and the utter destruction" of the island, U.S. respect for Spanish sovereignty would "be superseded by higher obligations, which [the United States could] hardly hesitate to recognize and discharge."[37]

Despite the threat, Dupuy considered Cleveland's message favorable to Spain. The president had opposed Congress and declared that the insurgents had no government. His message rallied conservatives and was attacked by those supporting the revolution. As for intervention, Dupuy concluded that the Cleveland administration would do nothing during its remaining months in office.[38]

The Republican Congress, however, was anxious to take up the Cuban issue. Several congressional leaders returned to Washington in early December determined to pass a joint resolution that would recognize the independence of Cuba. Cameron led the campaign, and many congressmen believed that in a few weeks they would secure Cuban independence. As the Senate Foreign Relations Committee met to consider a flurry of resolutions, news arrived from Cuba of Maceo's death, which provided a shock and an emotional response favorable to Cuba. Initial newspaper reports erroneously alleged that the Spanish had treacherously murdered Maceo under a flag of truce, and this provoked widespread indignation. Some feared that the loss of Cuba's boldest general might end the insurgency and that therefore Congress had to act quickly to shore up the revolution.[39]

On 21 December Cameron reported out of the Foreign Relations Committee a joint resolution that the U.S. government "acknowledge" the independence of the Cuban Republic and "use its friendly offices with the Government of Spain to bring to a close the war." The resolution was bipartisan, since all the committee members approved it. They expected Congress to pass the resolution, Cleveland to veto it, and Congress to override, thereby forcing recognition of the Cuban government.[40] When the resolution came out of committee, there was a war scare, and stocks tumbled in New York and London. But Olney quickly met the challenge; in an extraordinary press meeting, he stated that the joint resolution, even if passed over a presidential veto, would have no constitutional force. The power to recognize a state rested "exclusively with the Executive."[41]

Pro-Cuban congressmen fumed over Olney's declaration but did nothing more. Congress adjourned for the holidays, and when members returned, the drive for Cuban recognition had lost its force. Olney had succeeded in changing the Cuban issue into one of defining the constitutional prerogatives of the branches of government, and many legislators agreed with him. Some congressmen also responded to the nation's businessmen who pressured them to stop roiling the economic recovery waters. The Cuban Junta lamented that the dying Cleveland administration governed without concern for public opinion or party interests. There was talk of impeaching the president if he refused to respect a congressional veto, but this was impossible in the two remaining months of the administration. Instead, after the holiday recess, the Senate never took up the Cameron resolution.[42]

Meanwhile Cánovas made an effort to blunt American criticism of Spanish rule, and a joint Spanish-American attempt was made to end the Cuban war. During March 1895 the Cortes had passed legislation that empowered the Spanish government to extend limited self-government to Cuba and Puerto Rico. With the Cuban revolution under way, Cánovas had not implemented the law, declaring that he would not extend it until after the insurrection ended. But there was no disturbance in Puerto Rico, and therefore Cánovas applied the law to that island as an example of what Cubans might expect if they laid down their arms. The timing of the reform took into account Weyler's victory over Maceo.[43] Just after New Year's Day, Tetuán asked Taylor what he thought of the Puerto Rican reforms. The American minister candidly responded that the self-government law lacked substance, since Madrid chose the majority of the new administrative council members and the council was only consultative. Tetuán retorted that this was only a first step, and Taylor, with Olney's consent, pressed the Spanish government to provide genuine autonomy on which to build peace.[44]

During the closing weeks of the Cleveland administration, Madrid and Washington concerted their efforts to end the war. Cánovas attempted to pull several threads together at once: he tried to bribe Gómez to leave Cuba, proposed autonomy for Cuba together with the recall of Weyler, and suggested a change in Cuban tariffs favorable to the United States. Moreover, Oscar B. Stillman, the director of the Trinidad sugar estate, informed Olney that, except for Gómez, insurgent leaders were willing to make peace based on autonomy guaranteed by the United States. Sensing the possibility of peace, Olney sent Stillman to Cuba to talk to the rebels and pressed Lee for facts. Early in February Cánovas published some administrative reforms that were to take effect when the insurrection ended. Dupuy optimistically reported that the Cleveland administration, and even McKinley, considered these reforms "as extensive as could be asked and more than expected." But Lee was skeptical the insurgents would end the war, and Gómez insisted on complete independence.[45]

These Spanish-American efforts to end the war failed for several reasons. Cánovas offered only minimal reforms; for instance, he kept the power over sugar tariffs in Madrid's hands, which was unlikely to attract Cuban moderates. And Cánovas would not consider the insurgents' demand for an American guarantee of Spanish autonomy; his government was unwilling to cede authority over Spanish reforms to Washington. Moreover, Stillman's information proved to be incorrect; he located only two rebel officers who were ready to lay down their arms.[46]

As the Cleveland administration came to a close, a new American prisoner outrage erupted in Cuba. Ricardo Ruiz, a dentist in Havana who had become a naturalized American while studying dentistry in Philadelphia, was arrested on 5 February at his home and charged with dynamiting a train. Placed in solitary confinement and refused communication with an American consul, he died twelve days later from congestion on the brain. Ruiz left his wife and children a pathetic note that could have been interpreted as a suicide note or as a farewell written by someone who believed he was about to be killed. Lee charged Spanish prison officials with placing Ruiz in a four-by-six-foot cell that was not cleaned and with either driving Ruiz insane to the point that he killed himself by hitting his head against prison bars or murdering him by beating him over the head. Lee wanted Spain to release all American prisoners, and he urged Washington to send a warship to Havana. The "murder" case made sensational reading in American newspapers.[47]

The Spanish denied Lee's charge of prison brutality. They claimed Ruiz's cell was large, contained furnishings, and was kept clean; noting that Ruiz had not been in the United States since 1880, they also questioned his American citizenship. They insisted that Ruiz committed suicide, allowed Lee to witness an autopsy performed by an American physician, and proposed a joint investigation of the death, which Olney accepted.[48] Olney and Cleveland were so angered by Lee's failure to force Spanish jailers to end Ruiz's solitary confinement and by the consul general's freewheeling talks with newspapermen that only hours before the administration ended, Cleveland considered firing Lee.[49]

Many congressmen rejected Spanish explanations. As February ended, there was talk of war; one legislator wanted to send the fleet to bombard Cuba. The Senate hastily passed a resolution requesting information about Ruiz, and the Foreign Relations Committee reported a resolution demanding the immediate release of Sanguily. In an attempt to ease the American prisoner issue, the queen regent pardoned Sanguily, but the sensational Ruiz case was still news on 4 March when McKinley took office.[50]

As the new administration began, many of the underlying themes of the Spanish-American conflict were apparent. Both Cleveland and Cánovas had given an initial cast to the diplomacy. Cleveland and Olney had decided that the Cuban insurgents were unworthy of recognition, yet Spain appeared unable to defeat them. Not wanting to annex Cuba, Cleveland and Olney offered cooperation with Spain if it made substantial political reforms and accepted presidential good offices. Worried that Spain would take too long to end the war, they warned there were limits to American patience. If the United States intervened, it would be for humanitarian reasons.

Behind the diplomacy was the American public's approval of Cuban independence, which Congress reflected. Although congressional resolutions has been largely bipartisan, Republicans had assumed a greater commitment to Cuban liberty, and it was expected that the new president and Congress would support Cuba's cause.

The Spanish government was angered by the open operation of the Junta in the United States. Placing responsibility for the rebellion on the Junta, Cánovas sought a military solution and courted European backing against potential U.S. intervention. He made only feeble efforts to provide political reforms and to open talks with the Cubans.

Ever since 1898, historians have compared the roles of Cleveland and McKinley, with the former often seen as strong and dominating Congress and the latter as weak and giving in to Congress. This simplistic comparison fails to account for many major variables. Cleveland was more responsive to Congress and public opinion than he let on, and the Cuban situation then was not as serious as the one McKinley later faced. During

Cleveland's administration, the results of Weyler's devastating campaign on the Cuban population were not fully revealed, and the stalemated war was just becoming apparent. Cleveland still had hope that Spain would adopt reforms that would end the rebellion.

The situation was quite different for McKinley. The military stalemate was ever more apparent; civilian deaths and misery climbed rapidly; political reforms failed; and a series of accidental events united the American people behind intervention. No one can say how Cleveland and Olney might have reacted to these changed circumstances, but Cleveland had raised the possibility of intervention under much less daunting conditions.

CHAPTER 3

. . . .

MCKINLEY AND

. . . .

CÁNOVAS

. . . .

Du- uring the first five months of the McKinley administration, the new president appointed his foreign affairs advisers, gathered information about Cuba,
and defined his policy toward Spain. Although many legislators wanted
the administration to recognize Cuban belligerency, Congress provided
time for McKinley to organize and attempt to negotiate a solution. In
Spain during these months, Cánovas faced growing domestic opposition
to the military suppression of Cuba; Sagasta and others called for political reforms to end the war. The situation changed dramatically in August,
when an assassin killed Cánovas.

The new American president was experienced in domestic issues yet a
novice in foreign affairs. Born to a lower-middle-class family, McKinley
obtained a modest education, which eventually led to the practice of law.
Caught up in the fiery events of the Civil War, he volunteered at the start,
and during four years he rose in the ranks from private to major, with
several citations for bravery. After the war McKinley practiced law in
Canton, Ohio, and began a successful political career. He served fourteen years in the House of Representatives, rising to chairman of the
Ways and Means Committee, and served two terms as governor of Ohio.
Before becoming president, McKinley had shown little experience or in-

terest in foreign affairs. By the 1890s he shared with many Republicans a belief that the United States should play a larger role in the world as defined by the issues of the day. He supported annexation of the Hawaiian Islands, construction of an American-owned Nicaraguan canal, expansion of the merchant marine, greater foreign trade, and reciprocal trade agreements. Aware of the need for gunboats, he showed only moderate interest in constructing a larger navy. McKinley never proposed a special global program or strategy.[1]

An able politician and an astute manager of men, McKinley controlled his administration. The new president had many attractive personal attributes. Unfailingly courteous and affable, he was kindly, considerate, tactful, and a good listener. A sincere, decent man, McKinley generated loyalty and respect. He carefully guarded his own views, sometimes gaining his point without others realizing it. He left few personal written records of his presidency; there is no diary, only a few scrawled notes and some official letters written for the record. McKinley preferred personal contact and face-to-face discussions. When dealing with legislators, cabinet members, and White House staff, the president sought harmony and consensus; nevertheless, he could take a stand and hold it stubbornly when he believed he was right, such as during the April 1898 battle with Congress over recognition of the Cuban Republic.

On the stump he tended to speak in generalities about patriotism, national unity, duty, and destiny, which corresponded to his view of the nation's history and his religious convictions. The president shared the deep moral concern of the American people aroused by massive civilian suffering in Cuba. He was genuinely moved by descriptions of starving and diseased women and children in reconcentration camps.

McKinley dominated the foreign relations of his administration; he established its policies and directed its diplomacy. McKinley's diplomatic strength was handling his own government, and his weakness was lacking knowledge of foreigners. The president managed well within the system of democratic society and constitutional government. In setting policy, he worked hard for consensus and support, listening carefully to many voices and especially key congressional Republicans. When weighty decisions had to be made, he conferred for hours with cabinet members and legislators in an attempt to keep the government together. Yet he made some important tactical moves without broad consultation, such as sending the *Maine* to Havana. Despite his control of policy, he gave subordinates considerable latitude for implementation. McKinley empowered his minister in Madrid to handle most of the negotiations with Spain; by contrast, Cleveland and Olney dealt with Spain through Dupuy de Lôme in Washington.

McKinley developed a close working relationship with the press. His administration kept newspapermen informed, and the general public could intelligently follow diplomatic events by reading the press. McKinley kept in touch with public opinion by reading many newspapers every day and establishing a clipping service within the White House. There is no evidence that the sensational press affected his policies directly. Much of the 1890s press was partisan, and the *Journal* and the *World*, sensational newspapers of New York City, were Democratic and had opposed his election. He did not need these papers to win reelection. The extent to which the sensational press whipped up public excitement and thereby affected government policies is unknowable; but its impact on changing public opinion may have been limited. Eager to expand circulation, the sensational press tended to slant its news and editorials toward the popular view and therefore often echoed rather than shaped public opinion.[2]

The first task McKinley had in foreign affairs was to select people to fill the cabinet posts, diplomatic missions, and State Department offices. The president-elect chose a politically balanced cabinet, which contained several poor choices in the area of foreign relations. For secretary of state, he picked John Sherman, who at seventy-three years old was infirm and increasingly senile. McKinley named Russell A. Alger as secretary of war, who proved to be an ineffective administrator and wartime leader. John D. Long, chosen to head the Navy Department, was loyal and able but conservative and unimaginative when challenges faced the administration. As a result, McKinley carried a greater burden in initiating and implementing foreign policy.[3]

Given these cabinet choices, McKinley had to reach deeper into the ranks for help. After it became apparent that Sherman was unable to perform his duties, McKinley asked William R. Day to be assistant secretary of state. Day was a close friend, political adviser, and neighbor from Canton, Ohio. Although Day had no Washington or foreign experience, McKinley trusted him. From the outset he turned the Cuban issue over to Day, and when Sherman resigned, McKinley named him secretary of state. Day was a lawyer and judge; he had never traveled abroad or had any association with diplomacy. Suddenly thrust into the center of foreign relations, Day was uncertain of his role. Loyal to the president, he made no move in Cuban affairs without consulting McKinley. Taciturn and guarded, reserved in manner and speech, he took no pleasure in dealing with diplomats and Washington society. He disliked the limelight of high office and left Washington as soon as the Cuban crisis was resolved. His ambition was to join the Supreme Court, to which he was appointed by Theodore Roosevelt.[4]

Aware of his inexperience and limitations, Day sought expert advice. Within the Department of State there was Alvey A. Adee, a career employee who knew the correct forms and protocol of diplomatic usage. Adee often coupled policy suggestions with advice on precedents. Day soon contacted John Bassett Moore of Columbia University, a prominent scholar of international law. Asked to assist with technical issues, such as the recognition of belligerency and independence, the means to declare war, and the management of a naval blockade, Moore proved so useful that when Day advanced to secretary of state, he named Moore as assistant secretary of state. Moore later served Day as secretary of the American delegation that negotiated the Treaty of Paris.[5]

For missions overseas, McKinley chose John M. Hay to be ambassador to Great Britain. Hay had been a private secretary to Abraham Lincoln, and after the Civil War he gained fame as a celebrated author who married well. He had represented the State Department in Madrid, and he often traveled abroad, where he was at ease with the British upper class. Of all McKinley's diplomatic appointments, Hay was the ablest, and he eventually became secretary of state.[6] The president had a hard time filling the key position of minister to Spain. Offering the post to many, he finally selected Stewart L. Woodford, a Civil War general and New York state politician and lawyer. Woodford was sixty-three years old, had no previous diplomatic service, and did not know the Spanish language. Yet he was intelligent, courteous, ambitious, and hard-working, and he endeavored to serve the president well. Although McKinley set policy, he relied heavily on Woodford for advice and implementation. The president never indicated dissatisfaction with Woodford's mission, yet after the war started, McKinley never consulted him or sought his knowledge of Spain in formulating the peace.[7] The president sent to Paris another former general, Horace Porter, who was equally lacking in diplomatic experience and language facility and who provided mediocre assistance. As for Havana, Cleveland strongly urged McKinley to replace Lee. The new president intended to do so, and there were many applicants, but when an opportune time came to remove Lee, McKinley retained the popular Virginian. The assertive southerner could be counted on to defend American interests and to provide a steady stream of political information. Lee held views that corresponded with those of the administration, and he gave bipartisan continuity to a sensitive post.[8] In sum, McKinley's top foreign policy advisers were largely inexperienced. But McKinley's level of appointments conformed to that of other presidents of his day; the White House was expected to use public offices to reward political factions and friends, a practice that paid dividends at home but showed scant regard for foreign affairs.

McKinley began to consider Cuban policy before entering office. After the election, his first concern was to avoid entering a war at the start of the administration. During the rush of events in December 1896, he worried that Cleveland and Congress would start a Spanish war that he would have to deal with when he entered the White House. And he was sensitive to business opinion, which wanted the Cuban situation solved without disturbing the revival of prosperity.[9] McKinley also shared the public's desire that the Cuban cause should prevail. Before taking office, he talked to many legislators, some of them backers of Cuba, who then informed Junta members that the president-elect was sympathetic to their cause and willing to side with them against Spain to secure independence.[10]

The night before inauguration, McKinley had a long discussion with Cleveland about Spain. Cleveland reviewed his policies and was impressed by McKinley's sincere desire to avoid war. As McKinley later recalled, Cleveland stated that war would come within the next two years. "Nothing [could] stop it."[11] At his inaugural the next day, McKinley carefully refrained from saying anything about Cuba. Speaking in generalities, he expressed his determination to protect the rights of American citizens, cautioned against wars of territorial conquest, and promised to seek peace. "Peace is preferable to war in almost every contingency."[12]

When McKinley entered the White House, he faced all the nagging problems of his predecessor: American prisoners, property protection, filibustering incidents, and conflicting information about the war. The State Department shouldered the task of assisting American prisoners and handling property claims, many recent ones involving confiscated tobacco. It pressed Spain to protect American investments, particularly iron company properties. Businessmen engaged in commerce with the island petitioned the State Department to end the war so that they could resume a profitable trade. McKinley met with one group of petitioners from New York City, who also spoke on the behalf of Philadelphia and Mobile merchants. Countering American demands on Spain were frequent Spanish requests to the State Department to prevent filibustering expeditions from leaving American ports. A sensational incident occurred when a Spanish gunboat, believing the *Valencia* was running arms, fired a shot to stop it. The ship was on legitimate business, and the incident was quickly settled. Much more troubling were the confusing reports on the Cuban war—some favorable to the Spanish, others to the insurgents, and many detailing the grim condition of *reconcentrados*.[13]

The first step McKinley took to fashion a Cuban policy was to send an agent to Havana to investigate conditions. After listening to Cleveland the night before the inauguration, the new president must have been uncertain about Lee's reliability. There was a way to check on his reports. The incoming administration inherited the Ruiz affair, which contained Olney's agreement to a joint U.S.-Spanish commission to investigate the death. McKinley used this opportunity to send an agent to Havana to examine Cuban affairs. He first chose Day, but after talking to him, McKinley decided Day would be more useful in Washington at the State Department. Instead the president picked another old friend, William J. Calhoun, a former congressman and a judge in Danville, Illinois. Calhoun had worked for McKinley's election in a key state, and the president had a high regard for him. That Calhoun knew nothing of Cuba and the Spanish language was less important. The president's commissioner arrived in Havana the second week of May and spent three weeks on the island.[14]

While the Calhoun mission was under way, McKinley had to take up another Cuban problem, that of restraining congressional action. During the election campaign the president had promised to revise the tariff; to do so, he called a special session of Congress, which began in late March 1897. Once in session, however, the legislators turned from the tariff to Cuba. In the House, McKinley could count on Speaker Thomas B. Reed, Republican of Maine, to prevent any action. The Republicans had a comfortable majority, 206 to 122 Democrats, with 29 Populists and independents. Reed and McKinley were not on good terms, since they were rivals for party leadership. The speaker was arrogant, sarcastic, and domineering, which earned him the title "Czar." Among his many intense dislikes, however, were the Cuban insurgents. Accordingly, despite personal differences, McKinley could count on Reed to use his authority to block pro-Cuban resolutions. When the special congressional session met, Reed named members to only two committees, Rules and Ways and

Means; these controlled the floor debate and handled the tariff bill. Since the Foreign Affairs Committee was unorganized, it could take no action; and Republicans were unlikely to challenge Reed because he controlled the remaining committee assignments.[15]

The leader of the House Democrats, Joe Bailey of Texas, was staunchly pro-Cuban and a good friend of the Junta. A southerner, Bailey likened the Cuban situation to that of reconstruction. He sympathized with those who lived under military occupation, without political rights and ruled by a distant despotic government. Politically shrewd, he saw the continuing Cuban problem as a means of rallying congressional Democrats and the country against the McKinley administration. Bailey did not want war with Spain, and he later opposed expansionism. But he was willing to accept war if it came, seeing in it an opportunity for the South to prove its patriotism and loyalty.[16]

Republicans organized the Senate but had difficulty in holding the line on Cuba. Nominally there were 48 Republicans, 35 Democrats, 6 Populists, and 1 independent. The Republicans, however, were divided; 6 were silver Republicans who had opposed McKinley's election. On some issues, such as currency, the Republicans could not count a majority. The Cuban question also divided the Republicans, since up to thirteen were inclined to support the Junta's cause. The Senate Republican leadership, often referred to as "The Four," was staunchly loyal to McKinley and would follow whatever policy he wanted on Cuba. The Republican caucus leader was Senator William B. Allison of Iowa, and his three closest associates were Nelson W. Aldrich of Rhode Island, Orville H. Platt of Connecticut, and John C. Spooner of Wisconsin.[17] The head of the Senate Foreign Relations Committee, Cushman K. Davis of Minnesota, however, was staunchly pro-Cuban, and all but one of his committee members shared that view. Only George Gray, Democrat of Delaware, was anti-Junta.[18] When Congress met in March, therefore, the Senate was expected to pass a resolution favorable to the Junta, but McKinley could count on Reed to prevent House action.

Shortly after Congress met, Senator Morgan introduced a joint resolution recognizing Cuban belligerency. The language was exactly the same as the Senate concurrent resolution passed a year earlier; since war existed between the governments of Spain and Cuba, the United States—in order to be neutral—should extend belligerency rights to both contenders. Morgan introduced the resolution on 6 April and spoke in favor of it for four days; there was little new in his extended remarks.

Morgan also introduced a resolution requesting the latest consular information from Cuba, a resolution the Senate passed.[19]

Senate debate on the Morgan resolution began on 4 May and lasted more than two weeks, allowing ample time for all who wanted to speak. Although all the Republicans on the Foreign Relations Committee supported the recognition of Cuban belligerency, two of them, Henry Cabot Lodge and Joseph B. Foraker, opposed forcing the president's hand, since he had been in office less than three months. Morgan countered by reading into the record the Republican platform and remarking tongue in cheek that he was not acting in a partisan manner but rather was trying to aid the president.[20] Senator Hale, the chief opponent of Morgan's resolution, asked for a delay until Calhoun could return from Cuba with the latest information. Several other senators agreed that nothing should be done until Calhoun had a chance to report.[21]

Much of the debate covered the old questions: Had the Cubans formed a government that could be recognized? Were the Spanish vicious and inhumane rulers? Must American citizens and property be subject to more outrages? Did newspaper reports constitute sufficient information on which to base a judgment? Would recognition of belligerency help or hinder the Cubans? And would passing a joint resolution violate the constitutional separation of powers?[22]

While the debate continued, the State Department responded to Morgan's second resolution by allowing the Senate subcommittee on Cuba—Davis, Morgan, and Foraker—to read the most recent consular dispatches from the island. Besides describing the terrible conditions in reconcentration camps and the devastated economy, the consuls reported that many starving people were American citizens. This news startled the senators and quickly drew in the president. McKinley met with Sherman, Day, Long, and the three senators, and Day cabled Lee for more particulars. Lee calculated the number of destitute Americans at six hundred to eight hundred. The result was an administration-backed bill to provide $50,000 for relief of destitute Americans and to pay repatriation costs for those who wanted to return to the United States. Without debate, the Senate passed the bill by voice vote.[23]

The senators then returned to the Morgan joint resolution and passed it 41 in favor, 14 opposed, 33 abstentions, and 2 absent. The vote showed that several Republicans did not want to embarrass the president by attempting to force his hand on Cuba. Of the 10 members of the Foreign Relations Committee, 4 abstained, including Lodge, William P. Frye,

Republican of Maine, and Democrats Gray and John W. Daniel of Virginia. In the yes column were 18 Republicans and 18 Democrats, with the others being Populists or independent. Of the 14 negative votes, 12 were Republican and 2 Democratic. There was no particular geographic pattern to the voting. In effect the Senate showed much less enthusiasm for Cuba than it had a year before, largely because Republicans were reluctant to challenge their new president.[24] Foreign policy considerations aside, McKinley was in the process of making appointments to federal offices, and this was no time to annoy him.

When the Senate joint resolution on Cuban belligerency reached the House, Reed held it up, since there was no Foreign Affairs Committee. The Senate $50,000 relief bill was a different matter. Reed wanted to pass it and first tried to get it through by unanimous consent. Bailey objected unless Reed joined the belligerency resolution to the aid bill. Therefore, Reed produced a rules committee resolution that, if approved by a simple majority, would allow a vote on the Senate relief bill. Bailey challenged the procedure, which forced a two-hour debate on Reed's ruling and which was devoted to speeches on Cuba. The brief House debate and vote disclosed a partisan division; House members, both Republican and Democratic, favored the Cubans, but the issue was one of Republicans sustaining their speaker and the president. Bailey condemned the Republicans for refusing to allow a vote on Cuban belligerency, which he asserted would pass easily. He accused the Republicans of currying favor with rich business interests rather than standing by their party platform, and he appealed to them to be patriotic and humanitarian. To keep the Republicans united, House leaders responded with categorical declarations that McKinley would take effective action favorable to the Cubans. Hitt attacked Bailey for making politics of the Cuban war and assured the House that McKinley was working for Cuban independence. Charles H. Grosvenor, Republican of Ohio and a close friend of the president's, declared that Cuba would be given its belligerent rights and independence. One Republican sided against Reed: Edward E. Robbins of Pennsylvania told of a recent trip to Cuba where he saw the Spanish exterminating the Cubans, and he accused them of "cold, cruel, [and] deliberate murder." A partisan House vote sustained Reed, and then the members passed the relief bill. The brief exchange, though, demonstrated the passions aroused by the Cuban issue; moreover, House leaders had pledged McKinley to bring about a settlement in Cuba favorable to the insurgents.[25]

While Calhoun was still in Cuba, the McKinley administration considered the possibility that Spain would sell the island. Edwin Atkins called on the president and described Weyler's failing military campaign, which was unable to restore peace. The following week McKinley met with John J. McCook, an influential New York City lawyer whom the president had considered for a cabinet position. McCook was the general manager of the Ward Line steamship company, which called at Cuban ports, and he was associated with R.A.C. Smith, a wealthy investor in Cuban electricity and the Ward Line. McCook also represented the Junta in its attempt to exchange Republic of Cuba bonds for independence from Spain. In late May, McCook and Smith told McKinley and Day about Cuba's efforts to buy its freedom, and McCook optimistically assured McKinley that Spain would sell. Estrada Palma also informed Day of the Junta's willingness to buy Cuba but not at the price Spain asked. Reports of these discussions appeared in the press, and the Spanish minister firmly denied that Spain would ever sell any part of its soil. A short time later Whitelaw Reid, the editor of the *New York Tribune*, political adviser to McKinley, and the U.S. representative at the diamond jubilee of Queen Victoria, asked Spanish officials in London about selling Cuba; the response was sharply negative.[26]

Calhoun returned to Washington the first week of June, and on the basis of his findings, the McKinley administration prepared its Cuban policy. Calhoun drafted two reports and had lengthy conversations with McKinley and Day. As for Ruiz, Calhoun concluded that it was impossible to determine how he had died. Whatever the cause, the Spanish had illegally detained him incommunicado, and if this had not been done, Calhoun surmised, Ruiz would probably still be alive. The blame for his death, therefore, rested on the Spanish authorities.[27]

In a long and thoughtful treatise, Calhoun took up the Cuban issues. Examining economic aspects, he remarked on the war's devastating effect on American trade and investment; since the island was dependent on selling sugar to the United States, any settlement would have to provide Cubans with access to the American market. As for American citizens on the island, nearly all were naturalized, some of them fraudulently, and they were more Cuban than American in their background and interests. Taking up the revolution, Calhoun condemned Spanish officials who had abused their offices. All classes of Cubans throughout the island backed the insurrection, and there was no end in sight to the war. The worst part was the terrible suffering of the unfortunate *reconcentrados*. If not for them, the United States might simply stand by and wait for the conflict to end through exhaustion of one side or the other. In traveling from Havana to Matanzas, Calhoun found the countryside depopulated: "Every house had been burned, banana trees cut down, cane fields swept with fire, and everything in the shape of food destroyed. . . . I did not see a house, a man, woman or child; a horse, mule or cow, not even a dog." The people had been forced into protected zones, where "destitution and suffering" made his "heart bleed for the poor creatures." Calhoun noted, "We saw children with swollen limbs and extended abdomens, that had a dropsical appearance; this, I was told, was caused by a want of sufficient food." He added, "There is no use to dwell on the sad and grewsome [*sic*] picture." If Spain continued to try to end the insurrection through force of arms, Calhoun predicted the complete destruction of property and the almost total elimination of the island's population.[28]

With respect to the future, Calhoun observed that Cubans with property wanted annexation to the United States; they feared complete independence because the masses were uneducated and ignorant of self-government, which would lead to disorder and revolution and not true peace. Spain might grant political autonomy, but the insurgents in the field were unlikely to accept a proposal that incorporated any degree of Spanish sovereignty. At the same time, they had only a paper government. Calhoun did not urge any particular solution; nevertheless, his report leaned toward an early end to the war by providing Cubans with economic liberty and local self-government under Spanish sovereignty.[29]

Calhoun's reports laid the basis for McKinley's policy. The early months of indecision ended; the president was now certain of the facts and in sympathy with the mood of Congress and the nation. He was committed to restoring peace to Cuba and ending the suffering of the Cuban people. The president directed the preparation of two documents, a diplomatic note sharply rebuking the Spanish for the inhumane conditions of the Cuban *reconcentrados* and a diplomatic instruction to guide Woodford in his mission to Madrid. Since Woodford was in Washington before leaving for Spain, Calhoun, Day, and Woodford drew up the new minister's instructions. Although Lee took no part in formulating these policies, his advice, through Calhoun to McKinley, was an essential ingredient. Calhoun probably put in a favorable word on behalf of the consul general, since two months later, when Lee visited Washington fully expecting to be relieved of his Havana assignment, the president asked him to continue in Havana.[30] Lee's pro-Cuban stance and skepticism about Spain's military prospects fit in with McKinley's view of Cuban affairs.

McKinley's first step toward intervention in Cuba was contained in an emotional protest against reconcentration. As early as January, the president-elect had indicated his concern for the suffering Cuban civilians and considered the possibility of basing intervention in Cuba on humanitarian grounds. With Calhoun's graphic testimony in hand, McKinley supervised the preparation of a diplomatic note that accused Weyler of deliberately inflicting suffering on innocent civilians and destroying property in order to win a war, which his military efforts had been unable to do. Spanish relief for starving and diseased Cubans was "illusory." Bound by the "higher obligations" of his office, McKinley protested "in the name of the American people and . . . common humanity" against the "uncivilized and inhumane" war, and he demanded that Spain at least follow the "military codes of civilization." The fact that American citizens and property were affected by Spain's "wanton destruction" added to the president's "right of . . . remonstrance."[31]

McKinley's sharp criticism of Weyler reached Madrid at a time of growing demands within Spain for Weyler's ouster. From March through June, Cánovas confronted an erosion of his political power as other Spanish leaders increasingly questioned Weyler's harsh methods. Criticism of the Cuban campaign came from leading generals, the Liberal Party, bankers and businessmen, and Conservative political factions.

From the early months of the war, Martínez de Campos had distrusted a policy of all-out war against the insurgents. Initially sent to Cuba to reach a political settlement, he had refused to undertake a reconcentration program. As a result, Martínez de Campos's return to Spain was tinged with failure. He soon had company. General Ramón Blanco y Erenas, marqués de Piña Plata, was captain general in the Philippine Islands when an insurrection started there. The rebels turned back Blanco's offensive, and under a cloud of criticism, he lost his command. When the unpopular Blanco came back to Madrid, only Martínez de Campos welcomed him at the railroad station. As an added indignity, Cánovas's minister of war dismissed Blanco as head of the queen regent's military guard. Angered by humiliating criticism and slights, Blanco vowed to defend his military record.[32]

When Blanco left the Philippines, his replacement was General Camilo García de Polavieja. In a swift campaign Polavieja routed the insurgents, which produced great enthusiasm on the peninsula. Though military operations were still in progress, Polavieja asked to return to Spain because of an attack of hepatitis. Cánovas, with reluctance, replaced him. Polavieja's arrival in Spain set off cheering crowds and national celebrations. The queen regent gave the victorious general an especially warm public welcome, which raised the possibility that he might replace Cánovas. The popular general, a Conservative Party member, toyed with the idea of high office and during the coming months remained in the background of Spanish politics as a possible national savior. Since he had the queen regent's trust and public approval, every step he took was inspected for its political implications.[33]

Another political problem for Cánovas was that Sagasta and other Liberal Party leaders were increasingly critical of Weyler's Cuban campaign. To finance the Cuban war, Cánovas called the Cortes into session; this provided Liberals an opportunity to speak against the war. Just before the Cortes opened in May, Sagasta met several times with party leaders and backbenchers and informed them that he was ending the support he had given to the government when the Cuban insurrection had begun. Enormous Spanish sacrifices had failed to produce equivalent military results, and Sagasta doubted that treating the Cubans as enemies would bring permanent peace. At the door of the Cortes building, Sagasta told reporters: "After having sent no less that 200,000 men to Cuba, and having shed so much blood and spent more than a billion pesetas, the result is that [on one half of the island] our soldiers control no more territory than the land they stand on." Conservatives were outraged, especially since the American press printed Sagasta's remarks and Morgan used it in the Senate.[34]

Political cooperation collapsed after a fight erupted between Tetuán and Liberal Senator Augusto Comas in the Cortes hall. While arguing over Sagasta's statement, Tetuán angrily slapped the senator's face. Friends separated the two men and prevented a duel, but the Liberals demanded that Cánovas dismiss Tetuán because of his discourtesy toward Comas and the Senate as a whole. Cánovas refused, responding that the incident was an entirely personal event that had nothing to do with the ordinary proceedings of the Cortes. Filled with indignation, all Liberal Party members refused to return to the Cortes, which created a governmental crisis.[35] Cánovas used the Conservative majority to pass the financial bill without Liberal participation, and then he suspended the Cortes and resigned his ministry. During the ministerial crisis, the queen regent consulted leading national politicians of both parties, as well as Generals Martínez de Campos, Blanco, and José López Domínguez. When Sagasta met with the queen regent, he laid a new Cuban policy before her. He would dismiss Weyler and introduce insular autonomy. Blanco and López Domínguez also urged a political solution, but Martínez de Campos was not yet ready to see Weyler recalled. After two days of consultation, the queen regent reappointed Cánovas and his entire ministry, declaring that she had full confidence in the Conservatives and their Cuban strategy.[36]

Liberals were astonished that Tetuán was allowed to remain in the cabinet, and Sagasta increased pressure on the Conservative government by taking his Cuban reforms to the public. In cooperation with party leaders, Sagasta released on 24 June a "Manifesto to the Nation." He declared that the dissolution of the Cortes and passage of financial legislation without Liberal votes was an extraordinary event that required him to take his case to the people. On the key issue of Cuba, Sagasta declared that "all the efforts in the world [were] insufficient to maintain peace in Cuba by the bayonet alone." Military action should be combined with political and financial reforms and implemented by a captain general sincerely committed to a policy of reconciliation, an obvious rebuke of Weyler. Sagasta suggested as a basis of peace Maura's proposed autonomy reforms of 1893 and an enactment of a tariff satisfactory to the Cubans. Taking into consideration the uneasiness of Spanish bankers, Sagasta proposed dividing the Cuban debt between Spain and the island to provide a sound basis for public credit.[37] Segismundo Moret, a key Sagasta lieutenant, delivered a major speech in support of the manifesto that amplified the details of autonomy, comparing it to the status of Canada. Some Conservatives also joined in attacking the government's Cuban policy; Silvela urged Cánovas to withdraw Weyler and end the war.[38]

With the parliamentary system in disarray and growing Spanish opposition to the Cuban war, Cánovas took up the task of replying to McKinley's demand that Weyler follow "civilized" methods of warfare. Dupuy had made a preliminary response, using the standard retorts that American information was incorrect and that peace would come sooner if the U.S. government would curb the Junta. Cánovas adopted a more aggressive stance toward the Americans. Questioning American reports, he observed that exaggerations of suffering always appeared during wars, especially civil wars which generated greater fanaticism. For instance, although the United States had appropriated $50,000 to relieve American citizens in Cuba, Washington had spent only $6,000 on needy cases; this suggested that more imagination than reality entered consular reports. Cánovas assured McKinley that Weyler was attempting to end the war as quickly as possible, which was the truly humane approach. And Spain was only doing what other nations did in time of civil war; Cánovas cited the record of the Union during the Civil War, observing that Union generals had destroyed property, prohibited commerce, burned entire cities, and abolished constitutional rights. He quoted William Sherman and Philip Sheridan on Atlanta and the Shenandoah Valley, and he also mentioned that over twelve thousand men had died in Andersonville.[39]

Cánovas saw the "grossest injustice" in the U.S. charge that Spain was to blame for conditions in Cuba. Indeed, Gómez had started the destruction of property and had initiated a program of "abominable devastation," which had been approved by the New York Junta, composed of naturalized American citizens bent on arousing sympathy for the insurrection in the very "bosom" of the United States. By comparison with Gómez's program, Weyler's campaign amounted "to very little." Cánovas admitted that there had been some "unintentional neglect" of *reconcentrados* when the program started, but that was over. When the Cuban people first came from rebel areas where their food supply had been destroyed, they were "cadaverous and almost naked." As the rebellion was being gradually subdued, the Spanish authorities were providing food and public works and were sending some people back to their homes; thus, the cruel nature of the war was "every day becoming less bloody." To bring about a humane end to the war, the United States should cooperate with Spain in ending the "public and organized direction" that the insurgents obtained in the United States and without which the insurrection long ago would have collapsed.[40]

Four days after the prime minister turned back the American criticism, an anarchist assassinated Cánovas. The sudden loss threw Spanish politics into confusion; the queen regent named General Marcelo Azcárraga, the minister of war, to head the cabinet, but politicians saw the appointment as an interim solution. Cánovas had dominated the Spanish political system for nearly a quarter of a century, and despite the recent attacks on him, he was still the towering political figure of Spain. Azcárraga lacked the ability to unify Conservative Party members and to lead the nation. The first order of business for Conservatives was to coalesce around a new party leader. Martínez de Campos agreed to support the Azcárraga government if it could unite the various factions; otherwise he would back Silvela. Polavieja was inclined to place the Liberals in power. Other Conservatives sought power, and party members failed to rally behind a single leader; there was a growing realization that when the government returned to Madrid from vacation at the end of September, a change in ministry was likely.[41]

One of the problems that Conservatives faced was trying to decipher what Cánovas had planned for the future. Based on some Delphic remarks and fragmentary remembrances of close friends, many possible future courses seemed open; some of these suggested that Cánovas had been considering ending the Cuban war. Several confidants believed the fallen prime minister would have stopped fighting the Cubans if it meant war with the United States, which he considered to be folly, and they thought he would have changed course, perhaps in a dramatic move, to avoid an American conflict. Some said that if the island was still in rebellion at year's end, Cánovas had been prepared to end Weyler's campaign; he would have stolen the Liberals' thunder by offering complete autonomy. Others speculated that he would have resigned from politics, allowing the Liberals to fight an inevitable and disastrous war with the United States, and then returned as the savior of his nation. No one could say for certain what plan Cánovas had on 8 August when the assassin's bullet killed him.[42]

Whatever his innermost thoughts, Cánovas left the nation with a failed policy. Hints were no substitute for clear direction. His unrelenting support for Weyler in the face of limited results led to a growing discrepancy between claims for success and the actual situation. His own party was split, with Romero Robledo ardently behind Weyler and with Silvela calling for an end to the war. Moreover, the nation's top generals also offered divided counsel. The Liberal Party, withdrawn from the Cortes, had trumpeted an alternative program that was appealing to Spanish financiers. Confronted by growing opposition to the war, Cánovas never entered into meaningful discussion with the Cubans nor offered substantial reform that might have provided room for a negotiated settlement. By claiming that the Cuban insurrection was the handiwork of expatriates in New York City, Cánovas absolved Spain of all responsibility for the rebellion. This same reasoning, however, laid the groundwork for a confrontation with the United States, which held that the origins of the rebellion stemmed from Spanish misrule, which was starkly revealed in Weyler's military campaign. And Cánovas's last diplomatic note, no matter how clever, did nothing to ease relations with the United States. As

Spain mourned the loss of its leader, the country was on a collision course with the McKinley administration. Spanish attention was already turning with uneasiness to the arrival of Woodford, since it was feared that McKinley's new minister was carrying with him an ultimatum. On 8 August, Woodford was in London, conferring with other U.S. diplomats before making McKinley's policy known to Spain.

. . . .

CHAPTER 4

THE WOODFORD

. . . .

MISSION

. . . .

President McKinley's Spanish policy was expressed in Woodford's mission to Madrid. The specifics were delineated in Woodford's instructions, which remained in effect until the 1898 war crisis. Although there was considerable overlap between McKinley's and Cleveland's policies, McKinley was more sympathetic to the Cuban cause, more responsive to Congress, and more willing to pressure Spain to end the Cuban war and the horrors of reconcentration. For the first time, Washington fixed a deadline; the president wanted Madrid to stop the war or at least initiate steps that promised an early peace before 1 November. If Spain failed to alter its course, McKinley was considering, as a first step, extending belligerent rights to the insurgents. As Woodford prepared to present this firmer policy to the Spansh government, the death of Cánovas altered Spanish politics and slowed the McKinley administration's movement toward confrontation.

Shortly after Calhoun returned from Cuba, McKinley chose Woodford to be the new minister to Spain. He had earlier tried to select more experienced and talented people for the post, but without success. A few days after taking office, the new president asked in turn John W. Foster, Henry White, and Elihu Root to go to Madrid, all of whom refused. Foster, a former secretary of state and minister to Spain, told McKinley that he believed only the separation of Cuba from Spain would solve the problem, and since the Spanish would resist this, it "meant a war with the United States."[1] White, the nation's most respected career diplomat, wanted to be first secretary at the London embassy. McKinley offered to elevate the Madrid mission to an embassy in order to attract Root, one of the nation's most distinguished corporation lawyers, but Root declined because he did not know the Spanish language and was not a close friend of the president's. By June, McKinley had also offered the post to Jacob D. Cox, Seth Low, and Whitelaw Reid. The president was considering the consul at Barcelona, the librarian of the Library of Congress, and the president of Rochester University when Senator Thomas C. Platt of New York urged the appointment of Woodford.[2]

A New Yorker, Woodford had risen from private to general during the Civil War, and he had served one term in the House of Representatives and one as lieutenant governor of New York State. He had no diplomatic experience. He had favored the Cuban insurgents, and hardly was the appointment announced when the *New York Herald* published remarks that Woodford had made in 1870 at Cooper Union in support of the Cuban insurrection. Woodford's name also appeared on an 1897 list of members of the Cuban League, a pro-Junta organization, although he was not an active member, and he had recently made a small financial contribution to the insurgent cause. When the newspaper story broke, Woodford offered to give up the appointment if the publicity embarrassed the administration, but McKinley declined.[3]

Woodford's mission to Spain lasted a little over six months. It commenced and ended in an atmosphere of fear and apprehension. Many in Washington expected war with Spain soon, and there was fear that the Spanish people would mob American diplomats. Captain Tasker H. Bliss, designated as army attaché, left his family in the United States because the War Department anticipated hostilities and Bliss did not expect to remain in Spain long. Hannis Taylor predicted that Woodford would be in Spain less than a hundred days. When Woodford entered San Sebastián, Spain, Spanish officials warned of riots; and when he went to Madrid, there was fear that a mob would form and that rebellious Carlists would cut the rail lines between the capital and the French border. Clinging to the safety of France, Woodford's family stayed behind in Biarritz for six weeks. When the queen regent pointedly asked about his wife, Woodford decided to risk having his family—his wife and daughter and his wife's invalid niece—join him in Madrid.[4]

By November, Woodford was more hopeful of peace, and he felt safer in Spanish hands. He presented his wife to the queen regent and rented a house. On 5 December the Woodfords hosted a housewarming dinner for four ambassadors and two cabinet members.[5] But social life was tightly confined. Woodford moved within a narrow circle of legation employees and European diplomats. The legation contained three assistants—a secretary, an army attaché, and a navy attaché. The diplomatic corps was small, and Woodford apparently dealt only with the ambassadors of the six major powers and the papal nuncio. There is no indication that Woodford met with diplomats from lesser countries, such as Argentina, Brazil, or Mexico.

Woodford's contacts with the Spanish government and society were severely restricted. Although Woodford learned to speak some Spanish, he was only comfortable when talking with English-speaking people. Segismundo Moret, the minister of colonies, and the queen regent spoke fluent English, but Woodford met the latter only infrequently, on special occasions. The Spanish minister of state, Pío Gullón, did not speak English, and he did not attempt to cultivate Woodford. In addition, Woodford and Gullón each suspected the other of intentional deceptions. Beyond government officials, Woodford had few contacts. Madrid's social circles deliberately excluded the Woodfords from the salons, parties, and receptions that surrounded the court. There were a few English-speaking journalists, but Woodford kept them at arm's length on orders from the State Department and for fear that they might misconstrue what he said.

During the weeks before the outbreak of war, the Woodfords's sense of well-being rapidly deteriorated. The minister's wife broke down under the strain, and the naval attaché, Lt. George L. Dyer, escorted her and her niece to the French border. Woodford's daughter, "brave as [a] soldier," remained at his side to cheer him up and assist with the work until the legation closed. During the final days, Woodford confessed to Day that he was "tired, very tired, and [had] not even the strengthening that comes from [the] presence of old friends." He was a "little homesick" and was "living, working and eating, but not sleeping in the Legation." He added, "I do not sleep much anywhere." It was in this isolated, strained, beleaguered, and fearful atmosphere that Woodford conducted his diplomacy in Spain.[6]

McKinley's instructions to Woodford covered three issues: an indemnity of $75,000 for the Ruiz family, the collection of pending American property claims against Spain, and an early end to the Cuban war.[7] A lengthy 16 July memorandum located the cause of the rebellion in the "deeply rooted aspirations of the native Cuban elements toward more complete . . . self-government." Spain had failed to carry out its autonomy promise given at the end of the Ten Years War, and the 1895 insurrection had begun in "local and unorganized" uprisings that had engulfed the island. Two years of "mutual destruction and devastation" had rendered "Cuba worthless to the Cubans, should they prevail," and "equally worthless to Spain in the event of reconquest." Even if the war ended soon, the extensive destruction and slow process of recuperation would place a severe financial burden on Spain. The memorandum made no mention of the Junta's organizational and filibustering efforts.[8]

The United States had a direct interest in the war; it bore the burden of enforcing neutrality legislation, protecting American citizens and property on the island, and suffering the paralysis of profitable commerce. It also ran the risk of some unexpected incident that might "inflame mutual passions beyond control." Washington was no longer willing to follow a policy of "inaction." The American people wanted their government to be genuinely neutral toward both combatants. One year ago Congress had voted to recognize belligerency, and a recently passed Senate resolution was pending in the House of Representatives. With United States recognition of Cuban belligerency possible, the time had come for Spain to "put a stop to this destructive war and make proposals of settlement honorable to herself and just to her Cuban colony." If the Spanish government did so, "the United States [stood] ready to assist her and [tendered] good offices to that end."[9]

The president then took up direct intervention, since he could not "ignore the possibilities of duty hidden in the future." The "chronic condition of trouble and violent derangement" in Cuba disturbed American society, keeping up a "continuous irritation within our own borders," harming normal business functions, and tending to delay the return of prosperity. One could expect a nation injured by a neighboring conflagration to be passive for a "reasonable time" while authority was being reestablished. "The essence of this moral obligation [was] in the reasonableness of the delay . . . before alleging and acting upon the rights which it, too, possesse[d]." At issue was whether Spain had sufficient time "to restore peace" and the Spanish "measures of unparalleled severity which [had] received very general condemnation." "Assuredly Spain [could] not expect this Government to sit idle, letting vast interests suffer, our political elements disturbed, and the country perpetually embroiled, while no progress [was] being made in the settlement of the Cuban problem." The president wanted a solution "in conformity . . . with the feelings of our people, the inherent rights of civilized man, and . . . of advantage both to Cuba and to Spain." He did not propose how Spain was to achieve these goals.[10]

McKinley urged Woodford to state his views to the Spanish government courteously but firmly and as soon as possible, emphasizing "the self-restraint which this Government [had] hitherto observed until endurance [had] ceased to be tolerable or even possible for any longer indefinite term." "Unselfish friendliness" inspired the United States to have an accord "just and honorable alike to Spain and to the Cuban people." McKinley advised Woodford not to disguise the "gravity of the situation" nor to conceal the "president's conviction" that should this effort be "fruitless," his duty to the American people would be to make an early decision on future action.[11]

Given the determination Cánovas and Weyler had shown to suppress the insurrection, McKinley's instructions placed the United States on a collision course with Spain. Moreover, McKinley seemed to be asking the Spanish government to accomplish the impossible. How could Spain accommodate all of Washington's demands? What policy existed that would conform to the "feelings" of the American people, would be in accord with the "rights of civilized man," and would be "honorable alike to Spain and to the Cuban people"? Calhoun had just reported to the president that there was no obvious solution to the Cuban problem. Although Calhoun leaned toward autonomy, he also said that the insurgents would reject this. Woodford's mission, therefore, appeared to be the forerunner of direct intervention to end the Cuban war.

Representative Hitt explained McKinley's policy to Gonzalo de Quesada, the Cuban Junta's lobbyist in Washington. Hitt was familiar with Woodford's instructions and had discussed United States policy with Calhoun and Day. Hitt told Quesada that McKinley and Sherman wanted Spain to yield on Cuba so that it could be independent. Hitt assured Quesada that Woodford was about to enter negotiations with Spain that would provide the Cubans with "undeniable and unanswerable support." Testimony from Calhoun, Lee, and other American consuls, Hitt said, had strengthened the president's opinions, and Calhoun had stated to him the "impossibility of autonomy." Explaining to Quesada the recent failure of the House to take up the Senate resolution, Hitt said that Congress no longer had to pressure the president, as it had under Cleveland, since McKinley's administration was already committed to Cuban independence. The House leader was confident that the Cubans would soon see results.[12]

The State Department instructed Woodford to spend a week in both London and Paris before going to Madrid so that he could confer about Cuba with Hay, Porter, and Andrew D. White, the ambassador to Germany. Ambassador White would travel to Paris to meet Woodford. The American diplomats were to sound their respective governments, financial communities, and influential people about Cuban autonomy and even "complete self-government."[13]

When Woodford arrived in London, he began writing directly to McKinley; the letters, sixty-eight in all, were delivered unopened to the president. These letters constitute the best source of information about Woodford's mission. The early letters also reveal some of McKinley's thinking, since Woodford commented on items they had discussed while in Washington. From the letters it is apparent that McKinley was preparing to recognize Cuban belligerency and also was considering the possibility of annexation. Since the Cuban war was going against Spain, McKinley thought Washington could move slowly to gain its ends. The most compelling immediate issue was the plight of the Cuban people, and McKinley wanted Spain to adopt a method of warfare "consistent with humanity and the Christian spirit of this age."[14]

Reports from London, Paris, Berlin, and St. Petersburg were uniformly favorable to the United States. The English were mildly surprised that the United States had not done something sooner about Cuba, and they expected the island to become an American protectorate or possession. The British government would acquiesce in United States recognition of Cuban belligerency, but it might react adversely against forceful annexation; should annexation come as the logical progression of inevitable events, London would accept it. Britain's major concern was to protect its commercial and financial interests in Cuba. Lord Salisbury, the British prime minister, told Hay that England favored any policy that would return peace and prosperity to Cuba, and Hay concluded that England would not interfere "if it became necessary for [the United States] to adopt energetic measures for putting an end to the destruction and slaughter now going on [in Cuba]."[15]

The French government was also prepared to accept United States moves favorable to the Cubans. Since the French people had a large financial stake in Spain, holding about $400 million in Spanish bonds and having additional large investments in Spanish railroads, the French government was anxious to avoid any events that might depress bond prices. The French realized that Spanish bonds would rise in value if the nation cut its losses in Cuba, stopped its large military expenditures, and developed its resources at home and in North Africa. There was some sentimental French opinion favorable to Spain, but the year before, when Tetuán had attempted to gain European support against the United States, the French government had refused.[16]

The views from Berlin and St. Petersburg also encouraged Washington. Ambassador White cautioned that the German kaiser, Wilhelm II, was erratic and that therefore one could not predict with complete assurance what the German government would do; however, a German protest against recognition of Cuban belligerency seemed unlikely.[17] The American ambassador wrote from St. Petersburg that the Russians considered Cuba to be within a United States sphere of influence and that if the McKinley administration moved "reasonably, logically and firmly," there would be no Russian support for Spain.[18]

While Woodford was in London, the shocking news arrived of Cánovas's assassination, and the American diplomats speculated that the murder favored the Cuban cause. Spain's internal political troubles would exacerbate the growing debt problem and failed military policies. With Spain's ability to wage war decreasing, Woodford proposed that the United States do less and take more time to do it. "Time works in our favor," he wrote McKinley. "No harm can come to American interests by my moving very slowly." The United States should do nothing that might unite the Spanish people but rather allow them to "embarrass themselves" and "increase their [own] difficulties." "The current of events [was] setting towards the independence of Cuba" or toward some form of autonomy that would be practically the same as independence, and therefore the United States should "be patient and wait." Only one problem required American action—Weyler's inhumane warfare in Cuba.[19]

On 1 September, when Woodford crossed the Spanish border, the situation was tense. Americans feared that the Azcárraga government wanted to pick a fight with the United States, which would unite the Conservative Party and rally the public to support the ministry.[20] The Spanish, worried that the new American minister brought with him an ultimatum that would precipitate a crisis, requested that Woodford delay his arrival in San Sebastián, the summer capital, until after the bullfighting season so as to minimize the possibility of rioting in crowded streets.[21]

Woodford's mission began with a series of Spanish delays. It took almost two weeks to find a convenient time for Woodford to present his credentials to the queen regent, and Tetuán, on vacation, proposed a first formal discussion on 20 or 27 September. Since Woodford believed that delay favored the Americans, he was willing to wait. While doing so, he heard that the Spanish expected him to begin his mission by pressing financial claims and attempting to use them to embarrass the government. Worried that financial claims might lead to counterclaims resulting in prolonged litigation during which nothing would be done, he advised McKinley that he intended to set aside for the time being all claims in order to concentrate on the essential Cuban issue.[22]

While biding his time, Woodford met the British ambassador, Drummond Wolff, and explained at length Washington's policy. Woodford was in the midst of writing his first note to Tetuán, and the conversation with Wolff reviewed the points he was preparing for the Spanish. Woodford told Wolff of the heavy burden of the war on the United States: the investment and commercial losses, the imprisonment cases, and the cost of enforcing neutrality laws. The breakdown of sanitation in Cuban cities had resulted in more yellow fever along the American coast, and Cuban sugar was a "vital" import, since the United States produced only 10 percent of its needs.[23]

The American minister then took up Cuban conditions. He described the human suffering in reconcentration camps due to "the horrible and unchristian and uncivilized" method of warfare and asked whether the English people would put up with such conditions one hundred miles off their coast. The war was a stalemate, even though Spain had employed 250,000 men and $300 million to defeat an insurgent force of 40,000; continuation would turn the island into a "desert." Recent news that General Calixto García had captured Las Tunas, a provincial capital in eastern Cuba, after a fourteen-day siege indicated a weakening of Spain's position, since Weyler was unable to send a relief column.[24]

Finally Woodford turned to the future. Washington had no particular "remedy"; it wanted neither to annex Cuba nor to establish a protectorate. Rather Spain must find a means to end the struggle or put it on the road to a peaceful settlement by December, before Congress met. "For the sake of humanity and civilization . . . this cruel, useless and horrid warfare must stop." If Spain provided autonomy to Cuba such as Canada enjoyed, and if there was a "reasonable certainty of Cuban peace and prosperity . . . and protection of American interests," McKinley would be willing to use his good offices. Woodford warned, however, that "the insurgents might reject any suggestion of autonomy and mediation and insist upon absolute independence."[25]

Woodford's cautionary note about the insurgents was appropriate, since they played a critical part in any settlement. At the time of Cánovas's death, they were in the process of trying to buy their freedom. Since the Junta's financial proposals became known at the same time that the Woodford mission began, some observers saw the two initiatives as a combined effort to remove Spain from Cuba. When the insurrection had first begun, the Junta had attempted to sell Republic of Cuba bonds to raise money to buy arms and boats for filibustering expeditions. The early attempts had been disappointing. Receipts from a sale of bonds during the spring of 1896 reported only seven purchasers and netted less than $9,000. There were two major bond sale proposals later in 1896, and both fell through.[26] Having failed to raise money for arms, Estrada Palma proposed that sugar plantation owners be allowed to harvest and grind cane if they paid a tax to the insurgents; Gómez, however, categorically rejected the idea as contrary to his military strategy of strangling the island's economy.[27]

During the spring of 1897, Estrada Palma decided to offer bonds to Spain in exchange for Cuban independence. He turned for help to Samuel M. Janney, a banker, and John J. McCook. The financial plan envisaged the Republic of Cuba issuing $150 million in fifty-year bonds paying 4 percent per year in gold. The Mercantile Trust Company of New York would hold the Cuban bonds while Janney and McCook negotiated agreements with the Spanish and American governments. The American agents would offer Spain about $100 million for Cuba's freedom, and if they succeeded in getting Madrid to agree, the bank would turn over the purchase price in bonds to the Spanish government. The Cuban Republic would pay the interest and principal from customs receipts, and the U.S. government would guarantee payment. When all details were completed, the bank would give the remaining bonds to Janney and McCook as compensation. A provisional contract of 5 June 1897 outlined the plan, and one day before Cánovas was assassinated, Estrada Palma and Janney signed a contract.[28] McCook's and Janney's efforts to get Paris bankers to participate in the bond scheme led the French foreign ministry to conclude that the McKinley administration had initiated a delicate attempt to negotiate Cuban freedom. It thought the effort might interest French bondholders but expected the Spanish government to reject the proposal.[29] Another result of the Cuban bond scheme was that McCook became more closely involved with the State Department. He began visiting Day regularly and sending letters that set forth the Junta's view of Cuban developments. He warned of deteriorating Spanish control of the *voluntarios*, who might start anti-American riots, and he urged the McKinley administration to ready its fleet to protect American interests.[30]

The Cuban initiative gained scant attention in Spain, which focused its attention on Woodford's mission. The day Woodford presented his diplomatic credentials to the queen regent, Tetuán suddenly proposed an interview for 18 September. During the meeting Woodford read most of his instructions to Tetuán, and he later provided a copy of the parts he read. Woodford added that the United States expected Spain "during the coming month of October . . . to formulate some proposal under which [McKinley's] tender of good offices [would] become effective or . . . that peace in Cuba [would], by the efforts of Spain, be promptly secured." He explained to McKinley that he turned over his instructions to Tetuán because he could not summarize or rewrite them as well as they had been set down in Washington. [31]

Tetuán responded with the standard Spanish positions. He asserted that Spain was winning the Cuban war and expected to "crush the rebellion thoroughly before next spring." The insurgents' only hope came from the "sympathy and aid" they received from the American people, and he complained that the U.S. government was not doing enough to prevent filibustering expeditions. Woodford rejected these claims, declaring that there was no peace in sight and that if Weyler should militarily end the war, he would achieve a "peace of a graveyard, and not of a prosperous and happy country." The American minister insisted that the United States was fully discharging all of its neutrality obligations, and he did not want to hear more about the subject. The three-hour interview ended in polite affirmations of peaceful and friendly intentions. Woodford had expected Tetuán to use the 1 November deadline as an "apparent ultimatum" to consolidate Conservative power in Spain, but after the meeting the minister of state denied to the press that Washington had made an ultimatum.[32]

Woodford described to McKinley the weakened condition of the Spanish government. The Catholic church had recently excommunicated

the treasury minister for appropriating some church property, and Carlists were plotting a revolution. The ministry was having trouble raising
money, and Liberals hesitated to take power. Weyler had deceived the
government into believing that the insurrection was wearing down, and
Dupuy was reporting from Washington that the American government
would put things off for a while. Thus the Spanish cabinet pursued a
"hand to mouth policy," hoping that something favorable would turn up.
As a result, Woodford thought that "the chances [were] against . . . [a]
peaceful settlement" and that his only hope for success was to employ
McKinley's injunction to be "kind, just, persistent and unyielding." [33]

Woodford also decided to brief the press. He worried that Tetuán
would attempt to place the United States on the defensive by giving journalists a distorted report of their meeting. Accordingly, he provided an
American newspaperman with part of his instructions, which eventually
appeared in the New York press. At the same time he asked McKinley's
permission to release the material, on the basis that the American position was unassailable and should be used to isolate Spain. One way to
avoid war was to demonstrate that "our demands [were] just, our methods
conciliatory; and our purpose right." [34] Woodford also asked Tetuán for
permission to release the memorandum containing parts of his instructions. He was surprised and chagrined when both McKinley and Tetuán
objected. The president feared that Spain would decline his offer of assistance, and he wanted nothing done that might "prevent . . . full freedom of action." [35] Having been reprimanded for taking a journalist into
his confidence, Woodford delivered his message to the other European
diplomats. During October he met individually with the Russian, German, and French ambassadors. In conversations similar to the one he
had had earlier with Wolff, he explained American policy and described
his meeting with Tetuán. Woodford believed these interviews prevented
Spain from rallying European support to its cause. [36]

While Woodford was briefing the diplomatic community, Spanish officials were pondering his memorandum and Dupuy's analysis. Before
Woodford's first meeting with Tetuán, there had been considerable
Spanish apprehension that the American minister was going to make an
ultimatum. After the meeting, Tetuán informed the cabinet that Woodford had been friendly and courteous and that he had made no financial
demands. To the Spanish minister of state, the American position was
similar to that stated in Olney's note of 4 April 1896. Although the overall

situation was "more grave" than a year earlier, the United States still wanted a quick end to the war and tendered its good offices to that end.[37]

Dupuy confirmed Tetuán's optimistic view. From the perspective of Washington, Woodford had made the least demands one could expect. Dupuy predicted that McKinley would not recognize Cuban belligerency, although he warned that the president might give way to Congress under greater pressure. McKinley wanted nothing more than to see the Cuban insurgency end, since it represented a danger to the tranquility of the country and a challenge to his personal power. Dupuy recommended that Tetuán find out from Woodford just what McKinley wanted and how far he would go to get it. It was quite possible that Spain could meet the American position and still satisfy Spanish honor and interests.[38] The French minister in Washington sent a similar report to Paris, stating that McKinley would not recognize Cuban belligerency because the business community opposed it; but from Madrid, Wolff cautioned London that Spain was failing to take the Cuban situation seriously.[39]

With the crisis of Woodford's arrival over and the government hopeful that it could satisfy American demands, the Spanish leaders decided to change the ministry. The government was ending its summer season at San Sebastián, and on 29 September the queen regent returned to her Madrid palace. Instead of meeting with Azcárraga, as was customary, she sought out Polavieja, who told her that the military officers would accept Sagasta as head of a Liberal government. She then ended the Conservative ministry, and after further consultation with Spain's leaders, she asked Sagasta to establish the next ministry. Sagasta tried to include all the Liberal factions in the cabinet but failed to enlist Gamazo, Maura, and their followers. After being rebuffed, Sagasta chose Moret to be minister of colonies and on 6 October announced the formation of his ministry.[40]

Moret's inclusion in the cabinet signaled a major change in Cuban policy. He was the Liberal Party's most outspoken proponent of autonomy. Born in Cadiz in 1838, Moret had English connections through his family, and he had been educated in England. He had served six times in cabinet offices, including the foreign ministry, and was considered one of Spain's leading experts in foreign affairs. Opposing Cánovas on isolationism, Moret had attempted to align Spain with the Central Powers in order to minimize French influence. As early as 1891 Moret had spoken in favor of autonomy for Cuba and Puerto Rico, and during the summer of

1897 he had made the most important Liberal speech favoring autonomy. His force of character, distinguished past, position on the key Cuban issue, and close association with Sagasta made Moret the most important member of Sagasta's cabinet. The French ambassador described him as "the actual head of the new government."[41]

Sagasta chose Pío Gullón to be minister of state. Gullón was a member of the Senate and had only a limited knowledge of foreign relations; during the early 1870s he had briefly served twice in the ministry as a subsecretary. He had grown up in France and was considered pro-French. He had also once held a modest post in the colonial office. Much less influential than Moret within the Liberal Party, he brought to the cabinet a sense of patriotism modified by common sense.[42]

For the ministry of war, Sagasta named General Miguel Correa y García. It was an important appointment, since Sagasta needed someone who could maintain the respect of the army officers during the difficult days of changing military policy. Correa proved to be a mediocre appointment, and he later had difficulty attempting to defend Sagasta's policies. Like Gullón, Correa was not prepared to take new initiatives.[43]

More important than Correa was Sagasta's selection of Blanco to be captain general of Cuba. Blanco would have the difficult task of changing the military direction from Weyler's all-out warfare to Moret's political reforms. This was all the more difficult because of Blanco's recent failure in the Philippine campaign, which had placed him under a cloud. Polavieja, who had turned back the Philippine insurgents, had publicly charged Blanco with inefficient military organization and administration. Polavieja's criticism of Blanco had caused a sensation in Madrid, and in September Blanco had published a lengthy *Memoria* in defense of his command. Blanco was eager to prove his ability and willing to take the difficult Cuban assignment; he also was on record as favoring political reforms rather than relying on military means to end the Cuban rebellion. His post was especially difficult because many military officers in Cuba were loyal to Weyler, particularly the *voluntarios* who believed in giving no quarter to the rebellion. During the coming months, some of the most difficult and thankless political and military decisions would fall to Blanco.[44]

When the change in ministry occurred, Woodford speculated on what it meant for Cuba, and he revealed his underlying prejudices against the Spanish people. He took credit for helping to bring about the fall of the tottering Azcárraga ministry, believing that his friendly but firm meeting with Tetuán had undermined the Conservative idea of rallying the country against an American ultimatum. Yet he doubted that Sagasta would initiate fundamental reform in Cuba. He predicted that Sagasta would reject presidential good offices in favor of offering some form of indefinite autonomy with the promise of ending the rebellion in the near future. Woodford did not believe that Spaniards grasped the concept of "real autonomy as Englishmen and Americans" did. "We understand that personal freedom and local self-government are inherent, inalienable rights" while the "most liberal Spaniards" saw self-government as "a boon to be conferred and to be exercised under Spanish supervision." Under the veneer of Spanish courtesy existed "a disposition toward cruel methods . . . and a pride . . . which . . . repeat[ed] today the known mistakes of yesterday rather than admit an error and bravely correct it." By contrast, Woodford observed, the Cubans had been raised in America's shadow and understood and wanted self-government. Furthermore, by the time Spain granted reforms, the insurgents might be so strong that they would accept "nothing short of complete independence." Despite this pessimistic appraisal, Woodford sought to reassure the Spanish by moving his family from Biarritz to Madrid.[45]

In effect, the American position was gradually softening. Woodford had started his mission with a determination to set the Cuban war on the road toward termination before Congress met in December. Even as he was being selected, McKinley had demanded that Spain end its military measures associated with reconcentration horrors. The death of Cánovas, however, changed Spanish politics, and Woodford decided to go more slowly to take advantage of Spanish political currents, which were running in the direction of American goals. Although Woodford was skeptical of Sagasta's ability to provide self-government to Cuba, and although he expected the Cubans to reject anything less than independence, he was willing to be less confrontational. During the coming months these two ingredients, the quality of Spanish reforms and the insurgents' attitude toward the reforms, became the basis for Washington's decision on Cuban intervention.

CHAPTER 5

· · · · · · · · · · · · · · · · ·

SAGASTA'S CUBAN

· · · · · · · · · · · · · · · · ·

REFORMS

· · · · · · · · · · · · · · · · ·

S
agasta's government entered office committed to employing autonomy to solve the Cuban problem. It hoped to rally moderate Cubans and attract sufficient numbers of insurgents so that the war would diminish and eventually end in a negotiated settlement. But success also depended on holding the support of both Spaniards and Americans. At home the government had to check patriotic nationalists who wanted to crush the insurrection; abroad it had to prevent U.S. intervention. As Spanish and American policies became more complementary, a limited accommodation developed between Madrid and Washington. But Cubans rejected autonomy, and many Spaniards and Americans continued to doubt Madrid's ability to restore peace to the island.

On the peninsula Sagasta could count on the financial community and some business elements to support his efforts. Bankers and merchants worried about the Cuban debt of $400 million, the growing national indebtedness, and the financial ruin of waging a futile conflict against the United States. They hoped a Cuban settlement would provide a means of refinancing the enormous debt. But any solution that expanded Cuban trade with the United States would adversely affect Spanish producers and shippers of textiles and wheat.

A more dangerous source of opposition to Sagasta's program was the army. Sagasta ran a large risk that autonomy would appear unpatriotic and dishonorable. Slowing the war effort was certain to provoke accusations of failing to support the army and bowing to greedy Americans. Although Spain's ability to defeat the Cuban rebellion was declining, militant nationalists were unwilling to admit this. A retreat from Cuba, particularly under American pressure, was likely to touch off a political storm and perhaps even a military coup.

Sagasta's decision to recall Weyler and to alter the war effort was certain to rally patriots against the cabinet. The most serious threat would come from army officers; their discontent could be expected to attract Romero Robledo and his faction of the Conservative Party, the Constitutional Union in Cuba, and Carlists and Republicans who sought to wrap their movements in the flag of Spanish patriotism. Normally divided, these political elements might unite behind Weyler, and once joined, they might try to topple the ministry and to end the monarchy.[1]

Surprisingly, a recurring idea among Spanish nationalists was to enter a war with the United States and surrender the island to superior American forces rather than suffer a dishonorable loss to Gómez's rabble. Some businessmen also advocated a quick war as a means of ending the financial drain of the colonial war. After speaking to the queen regent, the French ambassador wrote, "This thought today haunts the mind of many political men of the country, and it would not be surprising that it would be realized if McKinley place[d] the Spanish in the position of having to choose by what means they must leave Cuba." More sober observers, however, held that war with the United States would be utterly disastrous, resulting in a national defeat of humiliating proportions and certain to lead to political chaos.[2]

Abroad, Sagasta's reforms had to satisfy three audiences: the Cuban insurgents, the McKinley administration, and the European capitals. If he succeeded in winning Cubans away from the insurrection, he could also hope to calm American interventionists. The odds for success were long, however, since after Weyler's devastating campaign, there were few Cuban moderates. Moreover, it would take time to woo centrist Cubans and to wear down determined rebels; and the Americans wanted a quick solution. If Spanish reforms did not satisfy the Cubans or the Americans, Sagasta could still attempt to use them to gain the support of the European powers.

To institute a new colonial policy, Sagasta relied on Moret, who immediately began drafting an autonomy law, counseling Blanco, and realigning Cuban tariffs. Moret also involved himself in Spain's relations with the European powers and the United States. There is no evidence that his diplomatic activities created problems with Gullón, the minister of state, who probably was unaware of much that Moret was doing. Moret worked hard to meet the deadline that Woodford brought to Spain. The Americans wanted a positive reply by 1 November, and Gullón and Moret delivered it 25 October; Woodford had asked for action before Congress met in December, and Moret produced a Cuban autonomy bill on 27 November.

As part of a peace package, Sagasta replaced Weyler with Blanco, who arrived in Havana in late October. Moret instructed Blanco to identify his administration with the people and to demonstrate that it was energetic, "popular and fruitful." The new captain general announced that he had come to initiate self-government and to affirm the sovereignty of Spain over the island. Publicly exuding optimism, Blanco reported that the Cubans received Madrid's new policies "with great enthusiasm." Privately, he held that the military situation was "bleak" and that the Spanish constitutional reforms were insufficient to end the revolt.[3]

The Spanish cabinet also approved a reply to Woodford's September meeting with Tetuán. Gullón and Moret based their response on the Liberal commitment to reform, and they sharply criticized Washington's failure to curb the Junta. The government declared that it had voluntarily undertaken a "total change of immense scope" in colonial policy as foreseen in the Liberal Party manifesto of 24 June. It promised "energetic and active" military operations but also a "humanitarian and careful . . . respect [for] all private rights." Madrid was prepared to extend to the Cubans "true self-government" under Spanish sovereignty, but it would retain control of foreign, military, and judicial affairs.[4]

Rather than accept U.S. presidential good offices, the Spanish government asked the McKinley administration to cut the "inexhaustible arsenal" of American supplies to the insurgents and to stop the Junta's organized "armed hostility and constant provocation against the Spanish nation." The United States could best cooperate in achieving peace by ending the "moral and material aid which [gave the insurrection] its only strength and without which it would have already been subdued." As for recognition of Cuban belligerency, the same conditions held as on 4 April 1896, when Olney had described the fiction of a rebel government; there was no "civil government, fixed territory, courts . . . , a regular army, coasts, ports, [or] navy." And the war was coming to an end; the Spanish army was completing the pacification of the western Cuban provinces, and Blanco would soon rally all men of "peace, liberty, autonomy and clemency."[5]

Having answered Washington, the Spanish cabinet attempted to satisfy American complaints about starving Cubans, American prisoners, and economic grievances. Moret ordered Blanco to break up the reconcentration camps and to conduct the war in a "humane and Christian" manner; the captain general was to send copies of all such orders to Dupuy so that he could inform the Americans. Dupuy urged Blanco to obtain as much publicity as possible when providing relief to the *reconcentrados*. Blanco signed a decree allowing some Cubans to return to their homes, and he promised "daily food and medical assistance" to those who remained in reconcentration camps.[6] Madrid began pardoning and releasing American prisoners in Spanish jails, starting with the *Competitor* crew members, and in early December, Gullón announced that not a single American remained in prison. By mid-December, Moret had satisfied all American claims resulting from Weyler's decree prohibiting the export of tobacco. And Moret also initiated reciprocal trade agreement talks to increase Cuban trade with the United States.[7]

The largest task, that of spelling out the details of Cuban autonomy, fell to Moret. On 25 November the queen regent signed three decrees: extending the provisions of the Spanish constitution to Cubans, establishing a Cuban electoral law, and providing an autonomy bill for the Cortes to pass. Self-government was to begin on 1 January 1898; the new insular administration would hold elections and was expected to convene a Cuban parliament about 1 April. Although Cubans were to have a major voice in trade matters, Sagasta's cabinet set initial tariff levels to satisfy Spanish business interests. As for the vexing Cuban debt, Moret put off apportioning it between the island and the mother country until there was a settlement of the war.[8]

These changes in Spanish policy were announced at about the same time that Weyler returned to Spain, and many watched closely, observing the extent of his public support. Although Weyler's arrival in Barcelona stirred a patriotic response, the general was unwilling to transform his popularity into a national coalition against Sagasta's government. Weyler realized that if he used his influence with army officers against Madrid, Martínos de Campos, Blanco, and others would oppose him. The army would divide, civil war might result, and Cuba most certainly would be lost. As long as Sagasta held Cuba, Weyler could be expected to bide his time. If military capitulation appeared likely, he might attempt to challenge Sagasta's leadership. Even though Weyler took no immediate action, unrest among military officers was growing. Correa was slowing down reinforcements to Cuba: under the Conservative government, Madrid had sent twenty to thirty thousand troops per month; the Liberal government furnished only six thousand during its first three months in office.[9]

Shortly after Weyler's return, *El Imparcial*, Madrid's most prestigious newspaper, carried an article on the high cost of the war and the difficulty of continuing it. The account, a criticism of Weyler, was probably inspired by the government. In a shocking exposé, the newspaper reported that of 200,000 troops sent to Cuba, only 114,961 remained on the island. How many had died was unknown, since many of the seriously ill had been repatriated to Spain. Of the soldiers remaining, 35,682 were detached from field units and 26,249 were ill, which left only 53,030 for actual combat. But even units supposedly fit for fighting contained sick soldiers who, although not in the hospital, were nevertheless unable to take the field. The conclusion was obvious; the army was too small to end the rebellion.[10]

At the same time that Moret was implementing Sagasta's Cuban policy, he began a round of conversations with the European ambassadors in Madrid in an effort to gain backing against the United States. In these talks, Moret took a pessimistic tone, perhaps revealing his inner feelings but possibly presenting a worst-case situation to find out what Europe would do to support Spain. Meeting separately with the French, Russian, German, English, and Austrian diplomats, he explained that McKinley's attitude toward Cuba was much harsher than that of Cleveland. Woodford's instructions did not explicitly recognize Spanish sovereignty over Cuba, as Cleveland and Olney had always done, and McKinley's position implied that Washington had the right to approve or disapprove a Cuban settlement. Moret surmised that McKinley wanted to participate in a Cuban settlement in order to obtain political and commercial advantages. Whatever the president had in mind, Moret warned that Spain would go to war rather than permit American participation in the exercise of Spanish sovereignty over the island.[11]

The December session of Congress worried Moret. He predicted that the House of Representatives would vot. to recognize Cuban belligerency and that McKinley would approve it. Moret believed that Sagasta's government would have to respond; the ministry could not afford to alienate public opinion by acquiescing in a flagrant and unjust American proclamation. Moret feared a rupture in diplomatic relations, which would result in conflict. He appealed to the English to use their influence in Washington to head off congressional action. At the foreign ministry, Gullón requested that the French and the Russian diplomats speak to Washington on Spain's behalf.[12]

The European response to Moret's and Gullón's pleas was discouraging. France and Russia were sympathetic but would not take any action in Washington unless all the powers agreed to do so, which did not appear likely. The French minister advised the Spanish to depend on their own resources and to provide as liberal reforms in Cuba as possible. St. Petersburg was even more discouraging; if Spain was on the point of war with the United States, Russia would take no step that the Americans might interpret as "contrary to friendly relations." After listening to Moret's pessimistic forecast, the Austrian minister told Vienna that the colonial minister was unduly gloomy.[13]

The Spanish government was also concerned about the large Cuban debt. During October and November, Moret explored several possible schemes for handling the debt. By chance, the Cuban Junta was also attempting a financial settlement of the war, and its activities spurred Madrid's interest and efforts. Spanish and Cuban proposals became confused with McKinley's policies and Woodford's mission. Legitimate investment interests soon competed with opportunistic entrepreneurs for recognition and government favor. The French government also took an interest in these schemes. The result was a cacophony of concrete proposals, trial balloons, and rumors. Nothing developed from these financial explorations; nevertheless, they are revealing of the various participants.

At the time the Sagasta ministry entered office, the Cuban Junta was attempting to use bonds to buy its independence from Spain, and Janney and McCook were trying to involve European financiers in the scheme. Madrid assumed that McCook, a friend of McKinley's, was acting on behalf of the president. In a casual conversation, Woodford spoke enthusiastically to Wolff about how American and British capital might jointly develop the rich Cuban agricultural and mineral resources that would provide a means of paying the Cuban debt; the British ambassador interpreted this as evidence of Washington's support for a financial settlement of the Cuban problem.[14] The assumption of a tie between McKinley and

McCook was probably incorrect; for instance, during the spring of 1898, McKinley asked Whitelaw Reid to find out to what extent McCook could speak for the Cuban Junta.[15]

McCook's attempts to form a syndicate of American and European financiers to assist the Cubans in buying their independence met some French interest and resistance. The French ambassador in Madrid, Jacques Reverseaux de Rouvray, encouraged bondholders in Paris to support Cuban autonomy rather than independence as a means of providing a favorable debt settlement. But by involving American financiers in a settlement, he thought Spain might gain Washington's cooperation in isolating the Junta. The Russian ambassador believed that a financial arrangement was the most logical way to end the war.[16]

Moret was wary of McCook's activities, and he attempted to counter them by taking up with Cuban autonomy leaders the possibility of creating a bank that would guarantee the Cuban debt. He proposed a syndicate of French, British, and German bankers; this would draw the European powers into a Cuban settlement. By excluding Americans, he would diminish Washington's role.[17]

Moret later tried to turn the Cuban financial scheme to Spain's advantage. When Dupuy reported that McKinley would accept only a financial arrangement satisfactory to Spain,[18] Moret proposed to Wolff that the English join an American-French syndicate. Moret also asked Reverseaux to encourage French financiers to present a plan to Madrid.[19] Wolff and Reverseaux discussed Moret's suggestion and agreed that any financial solution to the Cuban problem should originate in Madrid. They asked Moret to prepare a Spanish plan for the financial community to consider.[20]

Despite the widespread discussion, financial talks came to nothing; they failed in part due to Cuban and Spanish opposition. The Europeans, including Moret, wanted to tie a financial settlement to autonomy, but the Cubans would pay an indemnity only for independence. And Spanish patriots bridled at selling the nation's patrimony to American bankers.[21] By mid-November, talk of a financial solution had died down.

One means Moret had to soften Washington's posture was to convince Woodford of Madrid's good intentions. A few days after entering office, Moret asked Reverseaux to introduce him to Woodford at an embassy dinner. Instead, the French diplomat hosted Woodford, Gullón, and Moret at a breakfast, which also became the occasion for the Spanish to deliver their written response to Woodford's instructions. At the time of the breakfast, 25 October, Woodford was still convinced that the Spanish government would fail to solve the Cuban problem; he characterized the ministry as "evasive, procrastinating, full of hope and only positive in reiterations that the rebellion [was] . . . kept alive by American sympathy and active assistance." The Spanish note delivered at the French embassy breakfast did not alter his view. Nevertheless, two weeks later, Woodford described Moret as "honest and earnest." [22]

After becoming acquainted, Moret and Woodford had a long confidential talk that the latter described as "so direct, so free, . . . and so unreserved" that its confidentiality should be specially protected. Setting aside the usual diplomatic formalities, Woodford told Moret that McKinley was gratified by Spain's pledge to conduct a humane war but that the results were still to be seen. "An immediate change in the treatment of non-combatant Cubans would be an effective guarantee" of Madrid's promises. Woodford insisted that McKinley was doing his "full duty" in carrying out the nation's neutrality laws and that Spain must end its complaints if "thoroughly cordial relations [were] to be established and maintained" between the two governments. Moret convinced Woodford of his personal determination to see that the war was conducted in a humane manner; the colonial minister also promised that Blanco would "fully and loyally" carry out the government's instructions. Moret predicted that the autonomy decree under preparation would "enable the Cubans to govern themselves." In turn, Woodford pledged that "if the changes promised in the conduct of the war were carried out promptly and thoroughly," and if Madrid granted "the Cubans actual and honest self-government in local affairs, [he] would earnestly advise [his] Government to refrain from interference in Cuba for a reasonable time." Moret also proposed opening commercial treaty negotiations to promote "practically free reciprocal commerce" between Cuba and the United States, but Woodford wanted peace on the island before taking up trade issues. [23]

Moret had broken the ice; Woodford was gaining confidence in Madrid. The American minister confessed to McKinley that his faith had been "weak" in expecting Spain to carry out "humane methods of warfare, the just protection of American interests and the pacification of Cuba." He wrote: "Slowly but surely, I am coming to hope that we shall get the great ends for which you seek without war. . . . I [had] not hoped until recently that the new Ministry would go as fast or as far as they have gone and are going. Events have moved faster and more successfully than I dared expect." Whatever the outcome of its reforms, Woodford pointed out, the Spanish government was committed; if it attempted to turn back, it would break its pledges, which would justify or even "compel [American] intervention."[24] By early December Woodford was assuring the Spanish of McKinley's sincere desire for peace and explaining to Washington the good intentions of Spain. When he presented his wife to the queen regent, he relayed the president's goodwill; he described the queen regent to McKinley as "sensible" and "honestly trying to do the best she [could] under most difficult circumstances." At a housewarming dinner party that included Gullón and Moret, Woodford sought to "establish very cordial relations" and to encourage the Spanish ministry to move "ahead in the direction" desired by the United States.[25]

Woodford's conversion from skepticism to hope was mirrored by cautious optimism in Washington. When the Sagasta ministry assumed office, McKinley was pleased and willing to provide time for the Spanish to formulate and initiate Cuban reforms. McKinley was gratified by Weyler's dismissal, and Day noted that Washington's attitude changed from "aggression to expectancy."[26] The American press characterized Spain's 25 October note as "evasive," "sarcastic," "impertinent," and procrastinating. But McKinley let journalists know that he was pleased that the Spanish had replied so promptly; their response was conciliatory and greatly simplified the situation. Aside from Madrid's complaints about filibustering, the State Department thought the reply "put aside all complications."[27]

Dupuy predicted that the November off-year election results would influence McKinley's view of Spain's reforms. Although elections focused on local issues, providing no guidance on foreign affairs, politicians looked for evidence on how well the Republicans were doing. An important indication of voter sentiment occurred in Ohio, where Hanna had filled Sherman's Senate seat by appointment. The Republicans narrowly retained control of the state, allowing Hanna to continue in the Senate. But given the president's influence and Hanna's political machine, the close election outcome was considered a Democratic success. In addition, Republicans lost races in New York and Kentucky. McKinley commented that the polling results reflected local issues; Bryan, however, interpreted the election as reviving hope for silver. Washington's press decided that the election was a Democratic victory, which sharpened interest in the 1898 and 1900 elections.[28]

After the election, the McKinley administration continued to react positively to Spanish initiatives. Before publication of Spain's autonomy decrees, the *New York Tribune*, which was close to the administration, prepared its readers to accept Madrid's reforms. It predicted that Cuban autonomy would not equal that of Canada, but it pointed out that the Cubans were not as fit for self-government as the Canadians. Spain's offer of self-government would probably not satisfy the insurgents, but one could interpret the offer as initiating the start of negotiations for a final settlement.[29] Release of the *Competitor* crew in mid-November gratified American public opinion. A week later Madrid published Moret's autonomy bill. Washington's reception was mixed. Since the reforms fell short of true self-government, the press considered them insufficient to sway congressional opinion. But McKinley was convinced that Spain sincerely wanted to provide "real autonomy" to Cuba. Day informed the Spanish that McKinley was "impressed favorably" and that Madrid's efforts were improving public opinion. The Spanish government then released the remaining American prisoners and settled all the tobacco export cases. Dupuy recorded the change in Washington; his mission had not been "easier" since his arrival in May 1895. He predicted that the president's annual message to Congress would be "pacific and satisfactory" and that the forthcoming congressional session would not limit the president.[30] Thus, after Sagasta had been in office for only two months, Spanish-American relations had improved remarkably. Nevertheless, the growing accommodation between Madrid and Washington did not include the Cuban insurgents, who continued to reject autonomy, and the condition of the *reconcentrados* remained deplorable.

Skeptics existed in both the United States and Spain. Hannis Taylor launched a private effort to educate the American people about Spanish iniquities and to promote American intervention. After returning to the United States and meeting McKinley, Day, and Lee, Taylor published an article in the November issue of the *North American Review*. Since Taylor drew on his experience with Cánovas and Weyler, he was already out of touch with events in Madrid. Nevertheless, the Spanish government and European diplomats considered his article to be an unofficial statement of Washington's view and associated it with Woodford's mission. In a blistering attack on Spain, Taylor declared that Spanish sovereignty in Cuba was extinct. Spain's colonial government, unchanged since the sixteenth century, was responsible for the Cuban insurrection. Unjust economic tariffs had caused the 1895 revolt, and Spain was incapable of giving Cuba the control of its own finances. The Spanish government could not give self-government to the Cubans because that was something the

Spanish themselves did not have. The continuing war simply resulted in needless destruction, including American property, and the "endless strife" disturbed America's domestic politics and hampered the revival of economic prosperity. Taylor predicted that Sagasta and Blanco would alter nothing, since Spain's ruling classes—civil, clergy, and military—fundamentally opposed change. The Spanish nation would rather lose Cuba in a war with the United States than grant honest autonomy. Taylor advised Congress to pass a resolution of intervention in order to bring a speedy end to the Cuban impasse, even if it led to a short war with Spain.[31] Wolff characterized the article as brutal yet "undoubtedly correct."[32]

Taylor's caustic article created a sensation in Madrid. The Spanish government believed he was speaking for McKinley and had coordinated his efforts with Woodford to pressure the cabinet to sell Cuba through McCook's syndicate. Moreover, Madrid expected Taylor's article to encourage the insurgents to reject autonomy.[33]

Another skeptic was José Canalejas, a prominent Liberal politician and newspaper editor. Canalejas was the talented owner and editor of the *Heraldo de Madrid*, and he had served in several of Sagasta's ministries. Intelligent and capable, he was one of Spain's rising political stars. In June, when Sagasta had issued the Liberal manifesto favoring Cuban autonomy, Canalejas had strongly objected. He predicted the insurgents would reject autonomy and would consider reforms as a sign of Spanish weakness, which would encourage them to hold out for complete independence. At odds with Liberal policy, Canalejas temporarily "retired" from politics. During the summer his wife died unexpectedly, and he decided to travel to Cuba in his capacity as a newspaperman to see for himself what Weyler was doing.[34]

Although Canalejas was a private citizen, by October it was widely understood that he was serving as Sagasta's eyes and ears. Before leaving Spain, he visited the prime minister at his home in Avila, and while abroad he wrote two lengthy reports, one from Washington and the other from Havana. Romanones, the only biographer to use Sagasta's private papers, stated that the prime minister had in his files only three documents on Cuba, and two were letters from Canalejas. Romanones speculated that Sagasta had kept these because they painted such graphic pictures of the difficulties Spain faced; in the event of national disaster, Sagasta might have used them to convince the Spanish of the odds he had faced when he became prime minister.[35] It is quite likely that Sagasta also showed these reports to close advisers and prominent political leaders, such as Moret, Gullón, Martínez de Campos, and Polavieja. These reports also might explain Moret's pessimism in early December when he asked for the Austrian ambassador's help because war was imminent.[36]

Canalejas began his trip in a despondent frame of mind; his wife had just died, and he was deeply skeptical of Sagasta's reform program. Moreover, he distrusted the optimistic reports Weyler was sending from Cuba; he was determined to learn the truth about insular affairs. Departing from Madrid in late October, Canalejas spent over two months visiting Paris, New York, Washington, Havana, and the interior of Cuba. In Paris he discussed Sagasta's concepts of autonomy with Betances. Although Estrada Palma refused to meet with him in New York, the Junta arranged a meeting with a diverse group of expatriate Cubans, ranging from mild reformists to ardent insurrectionists. After touring the New York navy yard and harbor, Canalejas went to Washington, where he called on McKinley, Day, and Sherman. In Canalejas's honor, Dupuy held a dinner attended by the chief justice of the Supreme Court and four other justices, three cabinet officers including John Long, State Department officials such as Day, Foster, and John Kasson, General Nelson A. Miles, and Senator Stephen B. Elkins. Senator Elkins traveled twenty-four hours by train from West Virginia to make the dinner. A former secretary of war, Elkins spoke fluent Spanish, kept up on Cuban and Spanish affairs, and was a friend of the president's; he and Canalejas had a long conversation. After Washington, Canalejas met Blanco in Havana and then visited Matanzas, Santa Clara, and other parts of the island. During his trip in the back country, he was involved in firefights with the insurgents, and he made it a point to visit sick and wounded troops in military hospitals.[37]

Canalejas wrote Sagasta that after discussing the prospects for autonomy with many Cubans, he concluded that it would never succeed. Prominent Cubans who at one time had championed autonomy were now unwilling to take up the cause, and those in Madrid and Havana who spoke in favor of it carried no political weight.[38] As for possible war with the United States, American naval ships in New York harbor were far superior to Spain's gunboats; war with the United States, Canalejas warned, was unwinnable. Canalejas had found McKinley affable and outwardly committed to peace. American military officers, he decided, would not start a war for conquest and glory, but they were completely confident of being able to defeat Spain.[39]

In Havana, Blanco was optimistic, but the condition of the army was appalling. Canalejas was shocked by the staggering number of deaths and the fate of the sick and starving. The plight of the *reconcentrados* in Matanzas and Santa Clara was "horrible" and "frightful." "Priests and soldiers, radicals and conservatives," he wrote to Sagasta, "all agree that the war and reconcentration policy [had] led to the death of a third part, at the very least, of the rural population, that [was] to say, more than 400,000 human beings." If one added to this the number of *reconcentrados* who were about to die in the coming days and those in the military forces, both rebel and Spanish, who had already perished, the war had already "finished off more than 600,000 lives! What horror!"[40]

Canalejas was certain that Cuba was "lost." Autonomists were few, and Cubans who favored independence were increasing. The island's situation was "grave," since the army was miserable and had been abandoned as Cuba descended into anarchy. The plight of the soldiers in hospitals, the sick and wounded, was deplorable; makeshift hospitals, capable of accommodating hundreds, were filled with thousands. Canalejas laconically concluded that he had departed Spain with little hope, and he returned home with none. By the start of 1898, the pessimistic views that Canalejas had conveyed to Sagasta were circulating throughout Madrid. His newspaper reflected his findings, even if its columns did not carry the lurid details mailed to Sagasta.[41]

Another source of skepticism came from Lee and the American consuls in Cuba. A key to Washington's evaluation of Blanco's regime in Cuba was the condition of the *reconcentrados*. By late October, on the eve of Blanco's arrival in Havana, the tragic condition of these people was "frightful" and worsening. For instance, in mid-October the consul in Matanzas reported that the town's normal death rate was six per day, but on 10 October, sixty-two died, and this included only those names placed on the death roll; fifty-seven of these deaths were attributed to starvation. As many as half the people in interior towns had died. The local authorities were "powerless and unable to cope"; provincial "cities and towns [were] bankrupt" and unable to feed the "starving thousands." The State Department made certain that such shocking information reached Dupuy.[42]

When Blanco arrived in Havana, he was told that the American consuls had informed Washington that three hundred thousand *reconcentrados* had already died. He attempted to reverse Weyler's reconcentration program by opening zones of cultivation, providing food and public work, and allowing some people to work on private estates. He encouraged the formation of local civic associations to give food to the *reconcentrados*.[43] Lee was unimpressed by these efforts. Although Blanco was a kind, cultured, and courteous man, Lee observed that he was elderly and "physically and mentally incapable of discharging the duties of his great office." Lee had a higher regard for Blanco's secretary, Dr. José Congosto, a former consul in Philadelphia, who had ability and was "anxious to do all in his power" to cooperate with the American government.[44]

Day asked the consuls to report fully the results of Blanco's new orders, and November's consular reports were extremely discouraging. The daily death rate in Matanzas rose to over eighty, largely due to starvation. The consul recorded: "As I write this a dead negro woman lies in the street, within 200 yards of the consulate, starved to death; died sometime this morning, and will lie there, maybe, for days. The misery and destitution in this city and other towns in the interior are beyond description." In early December he reported a trip to the interior, where "two thousand rations were given out, for a few days only, to 8,000 persons. . . . One out of 4 [or 6] received the following ration: 2 ounces rice, ½ ounce [jerked beef], and sometimes a small piece of bread per diem," and this was discontinued after 11 December. The death rate was slowly decreasing in Matanzas only because there were fewer to die. The consul in Sagua la Grande reported that Blanco's orders had no effect whatsoever. In Santa Clara the death rate had climbed from 17 per month in January to 275 deaths during the first fifteen days of November and was continuing to rise.[45]

The condition of the *reconcentrados* in Havana was improving, Lee reported, primarily because private charitable committees were providing some relief. Lee first understood that Blanco had $100,000 for relief, but in early December he found out that there was only $12,500, which was insufficient to halt the distress and suffering. Lee estimated that in Havana Province, about half the *reconcentrados*, seventy-five thousand, had already died, and the amount of money Blanco had for each remaining needy person was about seventeen cents.[46]

Having witnessed Spain's failure, Lee proposed that charitable Americans privately donate food, clothing, and money to relieve Cuban suffering. The Ward Line could provide free transportation for relief goods, and the Spanish authorities could cooperate by removing all import duties. He recommended consigning the goods to the bishop of Havana, who was anti-Weyler. A few days later Lee suggested that the Catholic church in the United States help with relief; Americans could donate to their bishops, who could collect and ship the goods to Havana's bishop.[47]

McKinley quickly picked up on Lee's suggestion. On 1 December, Day told Dupuy that many people in Cuba were still dying from lack of food, medicine, and other necessities. The president felt strongly that charitable American people should be allowed to contribute money and goods and that the Spanish authorities should permit duty-free entrance and should cooperate in distribution. Day also suggested that Clara Barton and some members of the Red Cross be permitted to help in the distribution of Cuban relief supplies and to report the results to the American people.[48]

For a week Spanish officials argued among themselves over these requests. Dupuy strongly urged Havana and Madrid to accept American charity, since a prompt acceptance would have a favorable impression in Washington. Blanco did not think that American aid was necessary, adding that conditions in Cuba were improving daily. He opposed accepting help from a country that was already aiding the enemy; instead of charity, he suggested, the United States should stop sending "explosives." Moreover, receiving aid would look bad for his administration and would be resented by many people. Madrid, however, approved accepting charity, but it did not want Clara Barton and the American Red Cross in Cuba.[49] Responding to Blanco's negativism, Dupuy declared that the entire American and Cuban press believed that Spanish aid was inadequate. If Blanco could not document complete success in Spanish relief efforts, he should accept the "good intentions" of those wanting to help. Even the bishop of Havana was quoted in the press as saying that there was not enough food for the starving. More important, rejecting the request would create an American outcry against Spain; and Congress, which was about to meet, would be certain to pass a resolution harmful to Spanish interests. Grudgingly, Blanco accepted Dupuy's advice but insisted that the Americans give their charity to Dupuy to forward to Blanco for distribution, which Madrid approved.[50] Having settled the issue, Dupuy informed Day that Spain was grateful for the charitable feelings of the president and the American people and would allow all aid to be shipped into Cuba duty-free; Spain proposed that it be distributed by the bishop of Havana, who was engaged in relief work and knew where the need was greatest. Having witnessed the Spanish struggle over accepting American relief, Lee thought Blanco's "mental condition" was growing "worse," and he doubted that the general could "take the field."[51]

For autonomy to succeed, it had to win some support from the insurgents and weaken the armed rebellion. By December all the evidence pointed to complete rejection. From the start of the insurrection, the Cubans had opposed autonomy, and after Sagasta took power, there was no change. The Cuban rebel press ridiculed Sagasta as a hypocrite. Horrified at the thought of losing Cuba, convinced that Spain could not win the war, and pressured by the United States for an early settlement, the Spanish prime minister had grasped at autonomy. "Noble Cubans" were not about to solve the domestic and international problems of the "cruel Spanish" by accepting autonomy; Cubans wanted only independence. In early November, when Canalejas was on his way to New York, Estrada Palma published a strong rejection of autonomy, and a month later, when Canalejas was in Cuba, Gómez did the same, releasing an eloquent and patriotic letter.[52]

The Junta's rejection appeared in a new financial scheme to gain independence. Estrada Palma altered the Junta's financial and political policy in mid-November when he signed a second contract with Janney. The original contract, which offered to buy independence from Spain, remained in effect until 1 January 1898. The new agreement, in effect until 2 February 1898, provided $37.5 million in 4 percent gold bonds to secure U.S. recognition of the Republic of Cuba as an independent nation. These bonds were deposited in the Mercantile Trust Company of New York City, and the bank was to release them to Janney only after the last Spanish troops had left the island. The new Cuban nation would use customs receipts to redeem the bonds.[53]

At a December meeting of the Cuban assembly on the island, Andrés Moreno de la Torre, the secretary of foreign relations of the Cuban Republic, explained Estrada Palma's two-pronged financial strategy, one designed for Spain and the other for the United States. Cuba would benefit by an early end to the war, which would save many lives and stop the property destruction. The Cuban Republic needed to salvage as much as possible to ensure its future economic welfare. If the Cuban government could obtain recognition from Washington, Spain would have to end the war by granting Cuba complete independence. On the other hand, Cuba was also willing to indemnify Spain in order to end the war quickly. But Madrid should understand that the longer the war lasted, the greater the population loss and property destruction, and the clearer it became that Spain could not win the war, the less the Cuban Republic would pay. Moreno de la Torre insisted that any indemnity payment was not meant to cover Spain's Cuban debt. The Cuban Republic did not recognize this debt, and Spain must pay for all the costs of its war against Cuba.[54] There was no consideration given to anything less than complete independence in Moreno de la Torre's report. Thus, before autonomy was even initiated on the island, the Junta had rejected it.

With no settlement in sight, Lee was increasingly worried about the collapse of Spanish authority in Cuba. Madrid's reforms were opposed by Spaniards in Havana—army officers, government employees, and businessmen to whom Spain owed money. It was possible that these elements would start a second revolution against Spanish authority; that is, Weyler's supporters would rebel against Blanco. As Spanish military power declined, Havana's residents were arming themselves against the day when the insurgents would arrive. Lee heard that Congosto feared for his life. Some discontented people had passed out handbills denouncing Blanco and the United States; these had been promptly confiscated. There were rumors, probably originating with Spaniards and army volunteers, that anti-American riots might occur. If Congress passed a resolution recognizing Cuban independence, Lee believed war would result and Americans in Cuba would be in danger. Blanco and Congosto had assured Lee that the army would protect American life and property; nevertheless, Lee urged Washington to prepare to safeguard American interests. Ever since arriving in Cuba, Lee had suggested naval protection for Americans, and with conditions deteriorating, he reiterated more vigorously his belief that a ship should be ready to sail to Cuba on very short notice. In early December, Day responded, informing Lee that the naval commander at Key West had instructions to send a ship at once to Havana if Lee cabled a code letter "A." On 10 December, the *Maine* departed Norfolk for Key West.[55]

Thus, eight weeks after Sagasta entered office, the results were mixed. On the surface, Moret had provided many reforms for Cuba, cleared away irritating problems that troubled relations with the United States, and won Woodford's goodwill. Day and Dupuy were cooperating to provide Cuban relief, and McKinley continued to speak blandly of his desire for peace and his willingness to give Spain additional time. But in Cuba the issues were as intractable as ever. Canalejas, Taylor, and Lee shared a well-founded pessimism. The Americans and the Spanish fundamentally disagreed on the cause of the Cuban rebellion and therefore on the means to end it. The Cubans and the Spanish were nowhere near a settlement, and the condition of the *reconcentrados* was terrible. Although

Blanco's army was growing weaker, Spanish patriots would not hear of retreat.

In December, Congress would meet, and the president and legislators would have to decide Washington's course during an election year. In January, autonomy would begin, and Cubans would have to respond. Sagasta's government had offered its solutions; now it was up to Havana and Washington to provide their answers.

CHAPTER 6

. . . .

FAILURE

. . . .

OF CUBAN

. . . .

REFORMS

. . . .

At the start of December, Spanish-American relations were cordial and promising. When Congress convened, McKinley treated Sagasta's Cuban reforms favorably in his annual state of the union message. But six weeks later the outlook had changed completely. The root of the problem was the failure of autonomy to win support in Cuba. The island was threatening to descend into anarchy, which would require American military intervention.

McKinley devoted one-third of his annual message to Cuba, and he spoke to each of his audiences—the Spanish, Cubans, and Republican legislators. The president located the origins of the conflict in the Cuban desire for "liberty and self-control." Yet the Cubans carried on a cruel war. McKinley praised autonomy and sought an early end to the war through a peace "just and honorable alike to Spain and the Cuban people." The president drew a sharp distinction between the regime of Cánovas-Weyler and that of Sagasta-Blanco. The rebellion in Cuba had sprung from Spanish misgovernment. Weyler had pursued a "policy of cruel rapine and extermination that . . . shocked the universal sentiment of humanity." Reconcentration had "utterly failed" and was "not civilized warfare" but "extermination." But Sagasta and Blanco offered clemency, relief from starvation, protection of property, and self-government. The Spanish had released all American prisoners. McKinley advocated giving Spain "a reasonable chance to realize her expectations and to prove the asserted efficacy of the new order of things to which she stands irrevocably committed."[1]

The president sought to hold restless Republican legislators in line. He argued against congressional recognition of Cuban belligerency by quoting at length President Ulysses S. Grant on the attributes of government required for recognition, attributes that the Cuban Republic did not have. Besides, recognition of belligerency would give the Spanish navy legal authority to police sea lanes to prevent filibustering and would provide nothing tangible for the insurgents; Washington would have to enforce an "onerous code of neutrality." McKinley concluded that at this time, recognition of belligerency was "unwise" and "inadmissible." But he was not unalterably opposed to intervention. The president admitted that he had seriously considered intervening on humanitarian grounds but that Sagasta's reforms made this unnecessary. McKinley ruled out "forcible annexation" as unthinkable "criminal aggression," but he warned that if duty ever required the United States to "intervene with force," it would do so "without fault" and with the "approval of the civilized world."[2]

Overall McKinley's message was more favorable to the Spanish than the Cubans, and this slant was reflected in the response to the message. Congressmen viewed it through partisan eyes; Republicans approved it, and Democrats condemned it. Republicans pointed to the president's many successes, such as the removal of Weyler and the freeing of American prisoners, while Democrats questioned Spanish sincerity and called autonomy a fraud.[3] Dupuy informed Madrid that McKinley held the support of the majority of Republicans in Congress and that the message was a "serious blow to the insurgents." The Spanish minister was even more pleased when Hannis Taylor blasted the message. Although Estrada Palma publicly declared that he was satisfied, privately the Cubans criticized it.[4]

McKinley's words were acceptable to the Spanish cabinet. Gullón read the message with "great satisfaction," and Moret and Gullón said that they were "grateful." Nevertheless, the suggestion of intervention led Gullón to make a new appeal to France and Russia for assistance. And the president's criticism of Spain's military campaign enraged Weyler, who delivered an angry public protest to the queen regent and rallied antiministry politicians to his defense.[5]

With the message behind him, McKinley left Washington to be with his ill mother. While he was away, congressmen discussed the status of Cuba. Several senators gave press interviews, and two newspapers took a straw poll of congressional sentiment. These sources indicated that congressmen had little faith in autonomy and that the majority in the House of Representatives favored U.S. recognition of Cuban belligerency but not independence. The Republican House leadership, however, backed the president and opposed taking any congressional action. Even ardent Republican interventionists decided that the time was not ripe for agitating.[6] Sensing a political opportunity, Bailey caucused 101 Democratic House members, who voted unanimously for immediate recognition of Cuban belligerency. The Democrats realized that they could not force a House vote, but they could gain national attention and embarrass Republicans who favored immediate recognition. Bailey pointed out that if fifty Republicans would desert Reed and vote with the Democrats, they could pass the Senate resolution to recognize Cuban belligerency. Dupuy interpreted Bailey's posturing as advantageous to Spain, since wavering Republicans would now close ranks against the Democratic political attack.[7] Taking no formal floor action, Congress adjourned until the first week of January.

While Washington was quiet, diplomatic activity continued in Madrid. By 20 November the McKinley administration had completed writing a rejoinder to Madrid's 23 October note; sent by diplomatic pouch, the reply reached Woodford on 3 December. By then it was somewhat dated, since it had been drafted before Spain decreed autonomy and released the prisoners. Woodford decided to delay delivering the note, and he asked Washington if, in light of developments, the administration wanted to rewrite it. Ordered to present it immediately, Woodford decided to hand the note to Gullón just before Christmas, on 20 December, and without any fanfare. In complete contrast to his previous actions, when delivering his first note, Woodford this time said nothing to other diplomats or the press about the reply, and he allowed the Spanish to decide if any public announcement should be made.[8]

The new note made many of the points already stated in McKinley's annual message. But it extended to Madrid more understanding sympathy for the difficult task Spain faced in Cuba and indicated greater willingness to wait for results. McKinley assumed "an attitude of benevolent expectancy until the near future . . . [revealed] whether the indispensable condition of a righteous peace, just alike to the Cubans and to Spain, as well as equitable to American interests . . . [was] realized." On the other hand, the president had read with "pain and sorrow" Spain's criticism of his supposed failure to carry out the nation's neutrality laws. He explained at length his legal responsibilities and the extensive efforts his administration had made to honor them, and he concluded that the United States was "fulfilling every rightful obligation" of a friendly nation.[9]

The Spanish ministry showed more annoyance over this private note than over McKinley's annual message. The president's denigration of Cánovas's and Weyler's patriotic and military efforts was irritating, and the Spanish did not accept his assumption of the right to judge Spain's success or failure in Cuba, an assumption associated with a threat of forceful intervention.[10] Gullón took up the task of answering Washington; his response would take six weeks to reach the White House.

With McKinley's annual message and Woodford's 20 December note in hand, Gullón initiated another round of European talks in an effort to gain the support of the Great Powers. The Spanish wanted the Europeans to make a joint demarche in Washington to prevent American intervention in Cuban affairs, and they attempted to enlarge the Cuban issue to a European undertaking of protecting all Western Hemisphere colonial possessions against American aggression. But Europe's powers remained noncommittal. Most favorable to aiding Spain was the Austrian ambassador, who was close to the queen regent and whose country had the least to lose by arousing American hostility. Germany and Italy were lukewarm, but Gullón expected them to participate in a joint action if the other nations did. France, however, opposed any step, believing that a demarche in Washington would be "platonic" and counterproductive; achieving nothing for Spain, a demarche would instead arouse a hostile response in American public opinion. France, moreover, would take no action that Russia disapproved, and St. Petersburg warned against it. The Russians pointed out that McKinley was restraining the American public and that a demarche would hinder his efforts, particularly since the issue was so sensitive in American thinking. In addition, the Russians worried that if the Great Powers discussed Cuba with Washington, they would have to listen to American advice about Far Eastern events. Nevertheless, if all the powers agreed to a joint action, the Russian government would join to maintain European unity.[11] Significantly, Gullón did not involve the English in this round of talks.

While Gullón unsuccessfully sought European backing, Moret and the queen regent tried to get Woodford to advise McKinley to dissolve the Junta. Moret was playing his highest diplomatic card. Having set out in October to win Woodford's confidence, he now made a direct appeal from the throne. At the end of December, Moret asked Woodford to make a quick trip to the United States to carry a highly confidential message directly to McKinley. Woodford requested permission to return briefly to the United States, ostensibly to take care of personal business, but was told to remain in Madrid. He accepted the decision philosophically, reflecting that "the results must be wrought out in Cuba and by facts, rather than at Washington or Madrid and by negotiations."[12] Then, on 17 January, during a private social visit, the queen regent suddenly made a direct appeal to Woodford. Having received a promise of complete confidentiality, she asked that McKinley break up the New York Junta in order to end the flow of money and supplies to the insurgents. She argued that she had met all of McKinley's demands; she had changed the ministry, signed the Cuban autonomy decrees, and instituted relief for suffering Cubans. Now it was time for McKinley to demonstrate his friendship and give autonomy a "fair chance" by stopping the Junta from using American territory to make war on Spain. If he broke up the Junta, Americans and insurgents would know that they could "get [no] help; and their chiefs [would] accept autonomy and surrender; and this [would] stop the war; and the rebellion [would] be over and [she would] have peace."[13]

Woodford turned aside the queen regent's request. He explained that in a democracy, the executive was accountable to the public. He stated, "I believe that the majority—the large majority of the American people think that the war in Cuba should be stopped at once and that the president should do all that may be necessary to stop it." It would be extremely difficult to close down the Junta, since the United States had a free and constitutional government. "All men in the United States . . . [were] free to do and say what they like[d], so long as they did not levy open war against a friendly power." The queen regent interjected: "They do levy war. . . . They raise money; they buy guns; they send them to Cuba and if there were no Junta in New York there would be no rebellion." She added, "All Europe [would] approve this action." Woodford responded that the United States "accept[ed] the responsibility of doing what . . . humanity and justice and American interests require[d] on our side [of] the ocean even at the possible risk of meeting disapproval of [the] European powers." He assured her that McKinley would do what he thought "right and just towards Spain and Cuba and the United States." Disappointed, the queen regent broke off the interview.[14]

There could be no doubt that Moret was behind the extraordinary appeal, since the next day he called at Woodford's house and discussed the meeting, making an identical request for McKinley to "show the Cuban rebels that they had better accept autonomy and give up their struggle." Having had time to reflect, Woodford now responded that Americans believed that government was derived from the consent of the governed; in the case of Cuba, the Cuban people had the right "to decree their own independence, [and] they [had] the moral right to achieve that independence if they [had] the physical power to do so and . . . the United States [could] not interfere to keep a people under monarchical rule, who [were] seeking to establish a republic." Moret questioned the democratic principle, asserting that the great majority of property holders and educated people in Cuba wanted autonomy. He said that a relatively few guerrillas in the mountains were able "to maintain indefinite warfare" because "they were supplied with guns and powder from the United States." Should these few people "be permitted to keep the Island in perpetual disorder" when one act by the president could "restore order and give peace?"[15]

Woodford countered that the problem was not the U.S. democratic principle but rather the Spanish government's inability to end the war. Pointing to the fragility of Spanish politics, he noted that Spaniards in Cuba and even army officers resisted Cuban autonomy, while there were rumors in Madrid of conspiracies and mutinies against the Liberal government. Moret insisted that the army would be kept under control and that the political opposition—Weyler, Carlists, Romero Robledo, Socialists, and Republicans—would not overthrow Sagasta's government.[16]

In commenting to McKinley on these extraordinary interviews, Woodford ruminated: "So long as there is hope that Marshal Blanco may succeed, by autonomy combined with military measures, in securing peace, the Liberal Ministry is safe here. When it becomes clear that he cannot succeed or that the United States must intervene, the Queen will have to choose between losing her throne or losing Cuba at the risk of a war with us. Sagasta and Moret are patriotic Spaniards. They wish peace. I believe that they have done and are doing all they can. If they fail and have to choose between war with us or the overthrow of the dynasty, they will try to save the dynasty." [17]

Woodford did not attempt to counsel McKinley on how to respond to the queen regent's dramatic appeal, and the president never had to. The pace of events moved so quickly that by the time McKinley received the diplomatic pouch containing her plea, the *Maine* was already riding at anchor in Havana harbor. Washington had intensified its level of intervention—but not against the Junta. Nevertheless the exchanges between the queen regent, Moret, and Woodford went to the heart of the matter. Spain defined the rebellion in terms of an external attack sustained by American aid; the insurgents were lower-class subjects who mattered little in the island's political, economic, and social life. For Madrid, Washington's cooperation in suppressing the rebellion was the key to success.

Woodford's scattered replies were also on target. The president of the United States could not join with Spain in crushing the Junta in the face of overwhelming public sentiment in its favor. American public opinion, which included important politicians and civic leaders, championed Cuban freedom. The public took as fundamental the right of people to govern themselves rather than be ruled by a monarch. The fact that Spain lacked the strength to end the rebellion and wanted Washington's assistance gave credence to the Cuban cause. And, as Woodford noted, the Spanish political community was itself divided and unstable.

Instead of cooperation between Madrid and Washington to curb the Junta, as Moret had hoped, Cuban events were driving the two nations farther part. The continued plight of the *reconcentrados* and evidence that autonomy lacked support made conflict more likely. The Spanish cabinet became more bellicose; it increased preparations for war, sent more troops to Cuba, and increased purchases of supplies and ships. [18]

One of the troubling problems of Spanish-American relations was providing relief for starving *reconcentrados*. In mid-December, Day asked Dupuy to place the Red Cross in charge of distribution, since the organization would obtain a better response from Americans and would do a good job. Just before Christmas, Day warned Dupuy that American press reports of Cuban starvation and criticism of Spanish authorities might provoke a political reaction when Congress returned to Washington. Blanco, supported by Gullón, described newspaper reports as exaggerated and asserted that conditions in Cuba were improving. But Dupuy accepted Day's view that relief was a political act, and he argued that it demonstrated American sentiment for the new Cuban government and against the insurrection. Dupuy obtained Spanish permission for Lee to receive and distribute money and goods in cooperation with Spanish authorities. On Christmas Eve, McKinley made a national appeal for charity. His sincerity was evident: he anonymously donated $5,000 to start the program, a gift that remained unknown until after his death. The president also formed a Central Cuban Relief Committee, chaired by Stephen E. Barton, to collect and forward contributions to Cuba.[19]

The initial response of private charity was disappointing. By early January the State Department had received just over $7,000, which included the president's gift. On 8 and 12 January, the Central Cuban Relief Committee appealed for donations, presenting lurid accounts of Cuban suffering, particularly the plight of innocent women and children. Contributions swelled, and the committee rapidly expanded relief operations. Clara Barton went to Cuba in February and reported appalling conditions in reconcentration camps. But Lee calculated that the amount of money needed to support the *reconcentrados* exceeded anything private charity could be expected to provide. He estimated that it would take about $20,000 per day to feed the remaining two hundred thousand *reconcentrados*. Only peace, he concluded, could feed, clothe, and house the unfortunate.[20]

A realization of the limited prospects for private charity came at the same time that evidence was accumulating that many Cubans and Spaniards rejected autonomy. The Junta made its position clear; in late December it trumpeted its refusal in a publication entitled "A Birthright for a Mess of Potage."[21] And Gómez declared that he would die fighting for independence rather than accept autonomy. He decreed that anyone urging the acceptance of autonomy would be court-martialed and sentenced to death. Blanco sent an envoy, Lt. Col. Joaquín Ruiz, to treat for peace based on autonomy, and Gómez arrested, tried, and executed Ruiz. The Spanish interpreted this as a sign that Gómez was desperately trying to hold together his troops in the face of an enticing settlement. The Spanish also announced that some Cuban officers and troops had accepted amnesty and surrendered their guns. While the American press and consuls in Cuba claimed that autonomy was failing, Blanco continued to hold that a negotiated settlement with Gómez was possible.[22]

Blanco encountered resistance from many Spaniards and army officers in Cuba who opposed autonomy. On Christmas Eve a crowd gathered in the central square of Havana and shouted: "Viva Weyler! Abajo Blanco! Abajo la autonomía!" Some went to the office of *El Diario de la Marina*, a Havana newspaper favorable to autonomy, and shouted, "Vivan los voluntarios!" Congosto described the incident as a drunken riot that was easily handled by the police and that had little political significance. There was no suggestion that the crowd was anti-American. Another indication of Spanish thinking occurred the day before the autonomy government took office, when some Spanish officers told Lee that they considered the new regime to be a farce.[23]

During the morning of 12 January, a much more serious antiautonomy riot broke out in Havana. This time hundreds and perhaps thousands of rioters, led by Spanish army officers, mobbed three Havana newspapers favoring autonomy: *Reconcentrado, Discusión,* and *El Diario de la Marina.* Police disbursed the rioters, but they reunited and for several hours dominated the streets. They cried: "Viva España, Viva Weyler, Abajo Blanco," and "Abajo la autonomía!" During the riot, Congosto sent twenty-five soldiers to protect the American consulate. Lee heard later that a few rioters shouted anti-American slogans, but basically the riot was not anti-American.[24]

Moret and Blanco considered the riot part of a larger plot to unseat the Liberal government in Madrid. Twice before, the last time in 1895, military officers had toppled Sagasta's government by attacking newspaper offices. One way to show dissent in the Spanish political system was to attack the press that advocated a particular policy. Immediately after the Havana riot, Romero Robledo petitioned the queen regent to reopen the Cortes. Moret interpreted this as an attempt to unite the opposition against Sagasta in order to end his ministry and to replace Blanco with Weyler. Moret speculated that at the bottom of the intrigue were Carlists who intended to overthrow the monarchy. In Havana, Blanco drew much the same conclusion. Moret wanted Blanco to banish the officers who had led the riots in order to shore up the government and save the monarchy. Blanco requested a strong public statement of Madrid's support, which he received, and he released it in an attempt to convince wavering Spaniards that he had the complete confidence of the government. But since the antiautonomy forces had considerable backing in Cuba and Spain, Blanco acted with prudence as well as energy in order to retain control.[25]

In a few days the excitement died down and calm returned to Havana. Blanco reinforced the city's garrison with ten thousand to twelve thousand Spanish troops, which were more reliable than the insular volunteers, and he exposed officers who wanted the return of Weyler. But plotting continued, and Blanco and Moret expected renewed rioting at any time, the latter warning that if the Sagasta government fell, the United States would promptly annex Cuba. Moret mused that Blanco had failed to take sufficient steps against the key military officers; he should have jailed the ringleaders and sent them to prison in Fernando Po. Moret considered Blanco a strong soldier, upright and generous, but one who was inclined to take cautious half measures and was not sufficiently suspicious of those around him.[26]

The Spanish government was especially concerned about the impact of the riots in the United States. The press, particularly the *New York Journal*, featured the events, while Congress showed renewed interest in Cuba, and the McKinley administration considered a naval visit to Havana. The Junta rejoiced, and moderate Cubans favorable to autonomy were disillusioned. Dupuy initially reported that the administration was little affected, but he soon warned that "the change of [public] sentiment [had] been so abrupt, and our enemies, influenced by it, so numerous," that another troubling event could sway the administration.[27]

A few days later Dupuy concluded that Spain had lost "much ground"; the McKinley administration now lacked "confidence in the future." He attributed the change to Lee's reports, which were circulating in Washington. During the riot, Lee had offered to Congosto two American cruisers from Key West to restore order. Afterward, Lee concluded that the riot had ended the hope for autonomy, and reliable sources said that even Blanco privately believed autonomy had failed. After Blanco restored order in Havana, Lee advised Washington against sending a ship. As Lee saw it, Spaniards were fighting Spaniards, and the arrival of a gunboat would only unite them against the Americans. Time favored the United States; the riot had weakened Spain, and influential Spaniards would increasingly look to Washington to pacify the island.[28]

Symptomatic of the change in Washington was a visit to Dupuy by a well-informed newspaperman who said that McKinley believed autonomy had failed. Allegedly, the president expected serious disorders throughout Cuba and had decided to send naval ships and to land troops to protect the consulate if necessary. The journalist asked Dupuy how Spain would react if McKinley did this. The Spanish minister responded that such action would mean war, since Spain would never submit to an invasion. The interview indicated to Dupuy the fragile nature of Spanish-American relations; it was a warning to Madrid and Havana of the consequences of renewed rioting. Gullón, upset by Dupuy's reports, pressed him to explain to Day that autonomy was succeeding; moreover, given Lee's prejudicial views, Dupuy should ask that Lee be transferred from Havana at the earliest reasonable time.[29]

The administration responded to the Havana riots by increasing naval preparedness. Since 15 December, Captain Charles D. Sigsbee, the commander of the *Maine*, had been at Key West on ready alert to leave for Havana on Lee's request. In addition, the Navy Department was moving the fleet to the Gulf of Mexico for naval exercises. During the previous two years, Cleveland had suspended these routine winter maneuvers for fear of raising Spanish suspicions, but the McKinley administration had decided to resume them, arguing that normal exercises showed that conditions in Cuba were improving. The navy organized its ships into fighting groups rather than dispersing for trips and port calls, and it later credited its farsightedness.[30]

The day of the riots, Adee wrote to Day that the uprising signaled the end of Spanish authority in Cuba, and he proposed that the American naval squadrons in the Atlantic prepare for immediate action in the event of an emergency. The Navy Department instructed its squadron commanders to retain in service all men whose terms of enlistment were due to expire. This order, dated 11 January, may have been backdated to give it the appearance of being unrelated to events in Havana.[31] The cabinet on 14 January discussed assisting Lee with naval force. Long considered Spain to be doing everything the United States could ask for, but he recognized that an unforeseen incident might arise at any moment. After the cabinet meeting, Long ordered the North Atlantic squadron to move from Hampton Roads to the Gulf of Mexico for battle exercises, and he prepared a second ship at Key West for Lee, directing that the ships at Key West sail to Havana if the cable was cut.[32] The *Washington Star*, which had a reporter in Havana, did not think that the navy's actions were sufficient. Since it took six hours for a ship to sail from Key West to Havana, the "dirty work" would be done by the time a ship got there. The newspaper advised the navy to station a ship in Havana harbor.[33]

On 18 January, Day asked Lee to report on the condition of the Spanish army within Cuba. A week later, Lee estimated that the Spanish army consisted of eighty-five thousand troops, fifty-five thousand fit for duty and scattered across the island and thirty thousand in hospitals. In addition, nine thousand Cuban volunteers were in Havana. The army was poorly equipped and of low morale. It had few horses and artillery, bad food and poor clothing, and no training, and the soldiers had not been paid for eight or nine months. The troops had been conscripted in Spain and sent to the interior of Cuba without training or acclimatization; many did not even know how to use their guns. Lee then suggested how United States forces, in cooperation with the Cubans, could take the island.[34]

The riot also touched off congressional action. When Congress reopened after the holidays, there was little interest in Cuba. The day after the riot, however, Senator Frank Cannon, silver Republican of Utah, introduced a resolution, which passed, asking the president to explain what the government was doing "to protect the lives, liberty, and property of American citizens now dwelling in Cuba."[35] On 18 and 19 January, House members had an opportunity to speak on Cuba for three hours while the consular appropriation bill was under consideration. Democrats made several attempts to amend the bill to add recognition of Cuban belligerency. As expected, Speaker Reed ruled the amendments out of order, but Democrats appealed his rulings and, during the debate on the rulings, discussed Cuban affairs. The Democrats charged the House Republican leaders with stifling debate and preventing a vote on Cuban recognition. One Democrat predicted that in the coming election, the Democrats would meet the Republicans "on the stump and all over this country . . . and the people [would] condemn [them]."[36]

Republicans were uneasy. Representative David G. Colson, Republican of Kentucky, said that he would vote this time to sustain the chair but that the American people wanted recognition of Cuban belligerent rights, and if the Foreign Affairs Committee did not act soon, he would vote against the speaker. Hitt calmed Republicans by promising early presidential action. He pointed to the failures of Cleveland and the many successes of McKinley, and he argued that Spain deserved more than two weeks to test autonomy. But grave times were coming to Cuba; the Spanish government was tottering from insurgent pressure without and Spanish riots within. American citizens and property were imperiled, and Hitt reminded the House that McKinley had promised in his annual message to intervene if necessary. Hitt called on all Americans to rally behind the president as he faced decisions involving the protection of American interests. Adams declared that Congress should not act on the basis of newspaper stories; it needed accurate information, and he informed House members that Day was preparing the consular reports for submission to Congress. When the House received Day's report, Adams said, it would be time to act.[37]

Washington interpreted Hitt's and Adams's speeches as foreshadowing intervention. The *Washington Star* considered Hitt's remarks as promising intervention as soon as it was certain that autonomy had failed. The Cuban Junta was buoyed by Hitt's speech, and Lodge assured Quesada that McKinley was only waiting for the chance to intervene decisively. Dupuy, however, explained Hitt's "verbosity and extreme views" as necessary to hold the Republican majority together despite the "painful impression" his speech made in Spain.[38]

Worried that McKinley was accepting Lee's position on autonomy, Dupuy attempted to counter the trend by talking frankly to Day. The day after Hitt's speech, Dupuy told Day that he was extremely pessimistic and thinking of resigning. Lee's conduct—openly calling autonomy a failure and advocating American annexation of Cuba—was "reprehensible." And Long was readying the U.S. fleet for war and sending it to Key West while Hitt revealed that the United States was preparing to intervene. Dupuy predicted that Spain would have to respond by sending its fleet to Cuba, and there was certain to be an incident. In actuality, Dupuy declared, autonomy was an "unqualified success!" (The exclamation point was supplied by Day.) The only thing that kept the insurrection alive was the insurgents' belief that the United States would intervene. Washington should make it clear that even if American lives and property were endangered, it would not send a ship to Havana. Once the Cubans understood that, the insurrection would collapse and there would be peace by 1 May.[39]

Day reported Dupuy's appeal to McKinley, who was unmoved. Instead, the president, worried about the protection of American life in the event that Spanish authority collapsed, wanted to send the *Maine* to Havana. If an unforeseen incident led to the loss of American lives, Congress and the press would hold him responsible for failing to take precautionary measures. And on 21 January, Lee again asked Washington to send a ship, suggesting that it arrive early in the morning before the city was fully awake in order to minimize popular feeling.[40]

McKinley faced the problem of easing a ship into Havana harbor without creating an emotional response. Lee had once suggested an American ship might time its arrival when a foreign gunboat was already in Havana harbor. Thus the American ship would blend in with other foreign naval vessels. On 21 January, McKinley queried Lee on how many foreign naval vessels were in Havana harbor and learned there were none. Three days later Day sounded out Dupuy about a naval visit. He said that

McKinley believed friendly visits should be resumed, particularly since Spain was successfully pacifying Cuba. The president thought it best to have a ship call when calm prevailed and there was no excitement over protecting American citizens. Dupuy responded that visits should not have been discontinued in the first place. Day hurried Dupuy's comment to the White House, where McKinley called in Long, Miles, and Justice Joseph McKenna, the former attorney general. Day then called Dupuy to the State Department and informed him that the *Maine* had been ordered to Havana. Day described the port call as a friendly courtesy, expressing the cordial relations that existed between the two countries.[41]

When Lee learned of the ship's impending arrival, he suggested a week's delay to allow the excitement to die down but was told that the *Maine* was already under orders. The following morning, 25 January at 11:00 A.M., the ship entered Havana harbor. Sigsbee delayed his arrival to make certain that all Havana was awake to witness his call. Despite predictions of trouble in Havana, the *Maine*'s visit did not provoke any anti-American outburst. But in Madrid, Gullón was angered that Woodford had not told him of the ship's visit until twelve hours after the *Maine* dropped anchor.[42]

On Capitol Hill, Republicans and Democrats alike warmly greeted news of the *Maine*'s visit. Members of the Senate Foreign Relations Committee were uniformly positive, with some saying that it should have been done years age. Foraker suggested sending the entire fleet. House members also approved, and some attributed Hitt's speech and the need to keep the Republicans in line as the reason for the visit. Legislators appreciated the political nature of the visit but also understood that if Lee or any other American had been injured in anti-American riots, the president would have come under heavy criticism.[43]

Dupuy advised Gullón and Blanco to regard the visit of the *Maine* as a sign of friendship, providing moral support for the government's reform program. Accepting this counsel, Gullón described the visit as strengthening the "cordial friendship" between the two countries. He told Woodford that the Spanish government would also show its amicable disposition by directing royal naval ships to visit American ports.[44] The Spanish press, however, considered the *Maine*'s visit an unfriendly act that would encourage the Cuban insurrectionists. In Havana, Sigsbee detected an undercurrent of Spanish government hostility despite the official courtesies, but hundreds of Cubans enjoyed visiting the ship.[45]

Two days after the *Maine* dropped anchor in Havana harbor, the annual diplomatic dinner took place at the White House. After dinner, McKinley made certain that Dupuy sat at his small table, together with the ambassadors from England, France, and Germany. After coffee, the president referred to the recent votes in Congress, telling Dupuy that he was pleased by the "discipline of the Republicans" in the House. Dupuy should be "satisfied and confident," McKinley continued, since "our position" had greatly improved during the past year. The president made no reference to the *Maine*.[46]

To a certain extent McKinley's observation was true. The previous March, there had been fear that Congress would force the Cuban issue, but Reed had prevented this. Then, in December, many had expected the House to pass the Senate resolution recognizing Cuban belligerency. McKinley's annual message, the charity drive, and the *Maine* visit had calmed Congress. On the surface, it appeared that the congressional situation was under control.

Beneath the calm exterior, however, the American and Spanish perceptions about Cuba were as far apart as ever. Spanish officials asserted that autonomy was succeeding and would end the insurrection in a short time if only the United States would take a firmer stand against the Junta. The Spanish wanted time for their reforms to take effect. In contrast, the Americans considered autonomy a failure. McKinley was following a "go slow" policy in part to support Spain but also because his diplomatic agents, both in Madrid and in Havana, thought that the final outcome of Spanish reforms would be the end of Spanish sovereignty in Cuba. Moret's futile attempt to obtain American cooperation in destroying the Junta highlighted the gulf that divided Madrid from Washington. One problem that bothered the McKinley administration was the possible collapse of Spanish authority on the island. As the United States attempted to feed the starving Cubans and protect American lives, the government was assembling its navy only hours from Cuba's ports.

Government officials, both Spanish and American, were fearful of some unexpected event that might dramatically alter the situation. The most likely possibility was anti-American riots in Havana. It was also conceivable that Sagasta's cabinet would fall and pro-Weyler forces form a government, with the promise of increased military operations in Cuba. And Congress was not above taking some action which would spark a crisis. Under the circumstances, both nations were prudently stepping up naval preparations.

William McKinley, 9 July 1898, after Cervera's defeat
(Library of Congress)

William R. Day in his State Department office
(Library of Congress)

Stewart L. Woodford (*The American-Spanish War*
[Norwich, Conn.: Charles C. Haskell and Son, 1899])

Fitzhugh Lee
(Library of Congress)

Máximo Gómez
(Library of Congress)

Tomás Estrada Palma (*The American-Spanish War*
[Norwich, Conn.: Charles C. Haskell and Son, 1899])

María Cristina of Austria, queen regent of Spain
(Library of Congress)

Práxedes Mateo Sagasta (Alvaro
Figueroa y Torres, conde de
Romanones, *Sagasta o el político*
[Bilbao: Espasa-Calpe, 1930])

Segismundo Moret (Rafael Pérez
Delgado, *1898: El año del desastre*
[Madrid: Tebas, 1976])

Ramón Blanco y Erenas
(Library of Congress)

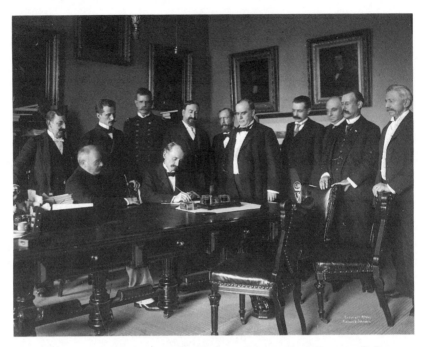
Reenactment of the signing of the peace protocol, 12 August 1898
(Library of Congress)

CHAPTER 7

. . . .

TWO SHOCKS

. . . .

THE DE LÔME LETTER AND

. . . .

THE *MAINE* DISASTER

. . . .

During the first part of February two unexpected events, the publication of the de Lôme letter and the sinking of the *Maine*, jolted Spanish-American relations. The astonishing incident of the de Lôme letter was settled quickly through diplomatic channels, but it deepened American suspicion of Spain. The catastrophic sinking of the *Maine* aroused much greater public passion. Both of these sensational episodes took place while the condition of the *reconcentrados* remained deplorable, and there was a growing belief that Spanish reforms were ineffective. Time was running out as both Madrid and Washington considered war more likely.

During the first part of February, Cuban news was depressing. On 1 January, Blanco established an autonomist government composed entirely of anti-Weyler Cubans. Expecting the centrist regime to appeal to moderates, the Spanish hoped to end the war quickly through negotiations. Blanco sent General Luis Manuel de Pando y Sánchez into the field to fight as well as to talk to the Cubans, but Calixto García checked Pando's advance into the interior, and no negotiations followed.[1] Blanco also made an inspection tour of ten towns. To Moret he reported the success of pacification, the high spirit of his troops, and the large public support for autonomy. But in a private letter to Sagasta, Blanco painted a dismal scene, "The administration [was] in the final stages of disorder; the army, tired and anemic, fill[ed] the hospitals, without the strength to fight nor hardly to lift its weapons; more than 300,000 *reconcentrados* [were] dying or starving, perishing of hunger and poverty in the towns; the countryside [was] demolished, [and the people were] frightened, obliged to abandon their homes and properties, grieving under the most dreadful tyranny, without any recourse to alleviate their terrible situation other than to join the ranks of the rebels."[2]

Blanco's depressing report was as bleak as that of American naval officers and businessmen. Captain George A. Converse of the *Montgomery* visited the port of Matanzas, where the effects of reconcentration were among the worst in Cuba. Converse discovered that starvation had spread from the poor to the rich and now threatened the few Americans living there, who had food for only two more weeks. Burial records showed that since December 1897, 59,000 had died in the province. He estimated the number of people starving at 98,000 out of a total population of 253,000. In the port city there remained 14,000 *reconcentrados*; food relief for them consisted only of nine hundred servings of rice per day. Given the critical situation, Converse urged Washington to send aid immediately.[3]

American businessmen also witnessed the breakdown of Cuban society. Edwin Atkins, who supported Spanish sovereignty, described the pitiful state of *reconcentrados* in the neighborhood of his sugar plantation. About 1,000 lived in crowded, disease-ridden quarters where the death rate was high. Although he was providing some food for widows and orphans, he predicted that if the situation was not cleared up by June, "the mortality . . . [would] be very great." C. F. Koop, a Boston tobacco merchant, was in Cuba from 6 January to 12 February. He testified to the Senate Foreign Relations Committee that Cuban business was at a standstill and that everywhere women and children were begging for food. Of 35,000 *reconcentrados* in Cárdenas, 26,000 had died; no American aid had reached the town. In some towns, up to 80 percent of the *reconcentrados* had died, and he calculated the island's total deaths at 500,000 to

600,000. The Spanish policy was genocide, and he predicted that Spanish officials would never allow American aid to reach the needy.[4]

Sigsbee also sent a distressing report on Cuban deaths, and together with Lee, he urged Washington to increase the American naval presence in Havana harbor by adding a torpedo boat, which would keep in touch with the rest of the fleet in case the cable was cut. When Long asked if the *Maine* should leave Havana harbor because of sanitary conditions, Lee assured him that current health risks were minor. Lee and Sigsbee thought the *Maine* should not depart until another ship had replaced it, preferably a large battleship. Lee wrote, "We are masters of the situation now and I would not disturb or alter it." [5]

Dupuy interpreted the situation quite differently. He informed Madrid that the purpose of the *Maine*'s prolonged stay was to calm Congress and the security market. The ship's presence had been effective, since Congress had refused to increase appropriations for "fortifications, armament, and munitions." If the *Maine* were relieved, Dupuy understood that a small cruiser would replace it. Surprisingly, he heard that the McKinley administration had rejected Lee's view that autonomy had failed and was regaining its "faith and confidence" in Spanish reforms.[6]

Despite Dupuy's upbeat view, Spain's hold on Cuba was increasingly difficult to maintain. In Cuba, the new autonomy government made few inroads in insurgent ranks, and the military stalemate continued. In Spain, army officers were restive, Weyler was more active, and Carlists were threatening. With no end to the insurrection in sight and wary of military opposition to reform, the Sagasta ministry decided against additional Cuban reforms and faced the probability of an American war.[7]

The immediate issue that Gullón faced was completing a reply to the State Department's 20 December note. His answer, delivered to Woodford on 1 February, reflected the changing mood in Madrid. He sharply criticized the McKinley administration and championed Spanish patriotism and military honor. Gullón rejected the McKinley administration's condemnation of Cánovas and Weyler. He asserted that all ministries and military officers, whether Conservative or Liberal, acted out of the "most zealous patriotism." Spanish troops had a brilliant and splendid history, and the Madrid cabinet did not accept Washington's tarnishing of any of its military actions in Cuba. Gullón was offended by Washington's comparison of the heroic exploits of the Spanish regular army to the "incredible excesses" of the Cuban insurgents. The Spanish minister rejected the idea that the United States had the right to decide how much time

Spain should have to bring peace to Cuba. After all, Washington had no license to intervene, and Spain would resist American interference with all its strength. Gullón asserted that the war was being conducted in the "most modern and humane conditions"; its objective was to establish a free Cuba, "autonomous, ruled by a government of her own . . . [and] subject to the immutable sovereignty of Spain." To facilitate this end, McKinley should do as Cleveland had done and vigorously enforce neutrality. For it was the Junta that was "creating a state of hostility" between the United States and Spain, and Washington should promptly suppress the "conspiracy . . . [and] completely discourage the seditious and restless elements which [were] . . . sustaining the rebellion."[8]

Woodford was astonished and dismayed by Gullón's blast, which ran counter to the plea for friendly cooperation made only two weeks before by the queen regent and Moret. The American diplomat conjectured that the Spanish ministry was responding to the failure of autonomy and the likelihood that the rebellion would continue into the approaching rainy season. Once the May rains started, Spanish offensive military operations would stall, and then there would be no foreseeable end to the war. Since the Spanish government would make no further concessions and would "insist upon [its] own time to crush the rebellion," Woodford advised McKinley to delay responding to the queen regent's appeal for cooperation.[9]

The only remaining Cuban reform that might improve Spanish-American relations was the establishment of a reciprocal trade agreement. As early as October, Moret had suggested applying the provisions of the Dingley Tariff of 1897 to Spanish-American trade, and in December he had urged Blanco to send a Cuban negotiator to Washington. The Spanish government believed that opening Cuban markets to the United States would go a long way toward relieving American pressure for intervention. Furthermore, a treaty negotiated by Cubans would provide proof of their new political status, and the promise of freer trade with the United States could be expected to build support in the Cuban business community. When the autonomy regime took office in January, Blanco picked Manuel Rafael Argulo, a prominent Cuban businessman, to negotiate.[10]

The McKinley administration also wanted to enter trade negotiations and asked that they take place in Washington under the supervision of John Foster, McKinley's reciprocal trade treaty negotiator. Woodford predicted that lower tariffs would deliver the Cuban market to American business and open the Spanish market on equal terms with French and English traders. Woodford sent his correspondence on trade negotiations to Washington to facilitate talks, but after reading Gullón's 1 February note, he was less certain about the commitment of the Spanish to liberalizing trade. The election of a new Cortes was scheduled to take place in March, and he gathered that the cabinet did not want to alienate peninsular businessmen with the vision of lower tariffs. Except for Moret, the Spanish government appeared hesitant and "inclined to conciliate [public] opinion and go slowly."[11]

The more rigid Spanish diplomatic position was accompanied by increased military preparations in response to the American naval buildup in the Gulf of Mexico. The Spanish considered the *Maine* and the *Montgomery* to be vulnerable in Cuban harbors; they worried more about the growing fleet stationed in Key West, the Dry Tortugas, and Portuguese waters. Rear Admiral Pascual Cervera y Topete was painfully aware of America's overwhelming naval superiority and the poor state of preparedness of the Spanish fleet. His ships had guns that didn't operate, they lacked sufficient coal and the ability to resupply, and he had no war plans; he did not even have adequate maps of the Caribbean. Despite Cervera's repeated warnings of disaster, the Spanish government expected war. On 7 February, Moret alerted Blanco that war was probable; and the minister of marine, Segismundo Bermejo, predicted war by April. To prepare, the Spanish government stepped up the purchase of guns, munitions, and ships. As for soldiers, on 4 February the Spanish government announced an increase from five thousand to fifteen thousand in the troops it planned to send to Cuba.[12]

Associated with a stiffening diplomatic and military posture was a new round of Spanish pleas for European diplomatic support. For Gullón the key had become Great Britain. Characterizing the British ministry as a "sphinx," he worried about the British government's "cold reserve." The Spanish minister sent a list of questions to his London ambassador in an attempt to discern the British relationship with the United States and the orders of British naval officers. He also wondered whether British interests in Gibraltar, the Canary Islands, and its Western Hemisphere colonial possessions explained England's relationship with the United States.[13]

Mystified by London, Gullón looked to Paris to rally European support for a demarche in Washington. The Spanish made several approaches to the new French ambassador, Jules Patenôtre, and to Gabriel Hanotaux, the French foreign minister. Appearing despondent, Moret told Patenôtre about the American naval buildup and Cuban difficulties; the French ambassador advised him to provide McKinley with commercial enticements that would enable the president to resist congressional pressures and thereby delay intervention. In Paris, León y Castillo pleaded with Hanotaux for French leadership of a European demarche but received the standard response: Europe was not ready to act as a unit, war did not seem likely, a demarche in Washington would have "little chance of success," and Austria should take the lead.[14]

Despite Spain's weak position in Europe, Woodford reported rumors in Madrid that the Great Powers believed Spain had done all that could be expected in Cuba and now was entitled to sufficient time to crush the rebellion. If the United States should intervene, the powers would come to Spain's aid.[15] Such rumors were almost certainly generated by the foreign ministry.

Troubled in Cuba and Europe, Spain unexpectedly suffered a stunning blow through the publication of the de Lôme letter. Sometime in December, after McKinley's state of the union address, Dupuy de Lôme wrote a private letter to Canalejas in Havana. Dupuy's style was unguarded; urbane and arrogant, he derided many targets with a cynical, sarcastic wit. He ridiculed Blanco's military efforts, Cuban autonomists and insurgents, British journalists and politicians, and Spanish-American relations. What caught the nation's eye were the insulting characterizations of McKinley and the contemptuous treatment of trade negotiations and autonomy. Referring to the state of the union message, Dupuy decried McKinley's blunt attacks on Weyler and Spain. He described the speech as a bid "for the admiration of the crowd" while the president kept "on good terms with the jingoes" of the Republican Party. Accordingly, the president was "weak" and a "would-be politician." Trade talks would be "advantageous" for Spain, Dupuy wrote, "even if only for effect"; Madrid should send to Washington a prominent negotiator who could "carry on a propaganda among the senators and others in opposition to the junta and to try to win over" the Cuban expatriates. Similarly, Dupuy described autonomy as a means of diverting American attention from Spanish to Cuban officials; he had no faith in it, since military rather than political means would determine the outcome in Cuba.[16] The unflattering portrayal of McKinley was in itself enough to end Dupuy's usefulness; but the duplicitous description of the trade talks and the disparaging treatment of autonomy put Spanish sincerity in doubt.

The means by which the Junta obtained the letter are unknown. Horatio Rubens, the Junta's spokesman, claimed that while in Havana, Canalejas unsuspectingly hired a Cuban patriot, Gustavo Escoto, as a temporary employee to help with his mail. Supposedly, Escoto saw the letter, realized its importance, stole it, and hurried it to New York to hand to the Junta for its disposition. This account portrayed Escoto as a Cuban patriot and removed the crime as far as possible from the Junta's door. But on the day the letter was published, Rubens wrote Quesada that he assumed all the risks of the release. There was no question as to the letter's authenticity, since he had gotten it from Quesada's files. Thus it appears that Quesada had the letter in Washington, and Rubens decided how to release it for maximum effect while protecting the Junta. Estrada Palma was conveniently out of New York.[17]

Before releasing the letter, Rubens made an English translation that heightened the insulting language. He then offered the letter with translation to many newspapers, hoping to get a conservative journal to publish it, since he wanted the most credible distribution. The *New York Herald* showed interest but refused to print it until Dupuy had admitted that it was authentic. The first news that Dupuy had of the letter's impending publication was an inquiry from the *Herald*. William Randolph Hearst's *Journal* was not as fastidious about authenticity, and with Rubens's permission it scooped the other newspapers.[18]

Publication of the letter on 9 February created a sensation. There was widespread feeling that Dupuy must go because of his disrespect for the president. And many picked up on the duplicity and insincerity of Cuban reforms, drawing the conclusion that the United States would never be able to negotiate a settlement with the treacherous Spanish. To many newspaper editors, the time had come for American intervention; conservative journals, however, stressed that the letter did not change the facts of Cuba and that therefore there was no reason to alter the administration's policy.[19]

Circulation of the letter was a personal shock for Dupuy. The morning of 9 February, Rubens, accompanied by McCook, called on Day at the State Department and showed him the original. Adee did not at first believe that Dupuy could have made such an error; he also criticized Rubens's translation, which the *Journal* had used. But after examining the handwriting, Adee decided it looked authentic.[20] Day consulted McKinley. To make certain the letter was authentic, Day took the original to Dupuy. When he arrived at Dupuy's house, Jules Cambon, the French minister, was already there. As soon as the news had broken, Cambon had hurried over to see Dupuy, who had explained to Cambon that Canalejas was a prominent Liberal politician who aspired to head the party. Sagasta, Dupuy said, had sent him to the United States and Cuba to assess the situation. Dupuy had been completely frank with Canalejas, thus the unreserved nature of his private letter. Dupuy had already cabled Madrid that he was prepared to retire. When Day arrived, Cambon stepped into an adjoining room. The meeting between Day and Dupuy was short. After Day left, Dupuy bitterly described to Cambon his upsetting interview. When Day had shown him the original letter and asked if he had written it, Dupuy retorted haughtily that as a diplomat he did not have to answer such a question. Since the letter was private, however, and since he was responding as a private person, he admitted writing it, and he asked Day to give his personal regrets to McKinley. When he read Rubens's English translation, he angrily denounced the traitors who had worded it so badly. Incensed, he told Day that he would not take advantage of a stolen private document. He asked what one might find in Day's private letters if one published everything Day had received from friends. Dupuy lashed out at the American public, which for the duration of the Cuban war had quenched its thirst on public outrages and private injuries. Dupuy then declared to Day that he had sent his resignation to his government. After dismissing Day, Dupuy told Cambon that he felt "relieved"; he had been doing a thankless job for nearly two years, and his compatriots only criticized him for weakness.[21]

Confirmation of the letter's authenticity set off a week of intense negotiations. McKinley and Day met with McCook and Rubens; the president was irritated not only at Dupuy but also at Rubens, who had created a sensation by publishing it instead of bringing it to the State Department. The cabinet met, and the McKinley administration decided that Dupuy would have to resign; in addition McKinley asked that Spain disavow Dupuy's statements and express its "pained surprise and regret" over the minister's "reprehensible allusions" to the president and the American people.[22]

The Spanish government was stunned by Dupuy's indiscretion. It searched for ways to undo the embarrassing damage in Washington without appearing to bow to any American demands that the Spanish public might find objectionable. Dupuy's initial telegram to Gullón admitted using words "humiliating to the President" and stated that his diplomatic position might be "untenable," but Dupuy left the decision of his status to the government, asking only that it adopt a policy "without considering [him] in any way." He did not resign, as he had told Day, but rather permitted the cabinet to dismiss him if it became necessary. After speaking to Day, Dupuy sent a second telegram explaining that he had claimed the right to express private opinions, much as American officials did, but that he now considered his diplomatic situation so changed that he could no longer "continue here." [23]

Gullón and Sagasta called Canalejas to the foreign ministry to learn what he knew. After the meeting, Canalejas told waiting journalists that he had never received the letter and was surprised by Dupuy's language, which was out of character. While in Washington, Canalejas said, Dupuy had always been respectful and even laudatory of McKinley.[24] These comments undoubtedly reflected what Gullón wanted the McKinley administration to hear.

The Spanish cabinet decided to treat the affair as "absolutely personal." Gullón distanced the government as far from Dupuy as possible by accepting his resignation and maintaining that the letter was strictly private and known only because of a theft. Gullón picked up Dupuy's resignation before Woodford had a chance to request it so as to appear to act without any American pressure. In accepting Dupuy's resignation, however, Gullón commended Dupuy's zealous duty under difficult circumstances and his personal "sorrow" at losing Dupuy's services.[25]

Moret and Blanco were acutely aware of the damage done to autonomy and the treaty negotiations. Blanco played down to Cubans the political importance of the letter, but he privately admitted to Moret that by jeopardizing Spanish sincerity, Dupuy had prejudiced autonomy. Moret held that the commercial treaty negotiations were urgently needed now to satisfy Cuban autonomists and American officials of Spain's commitment and sincerity.[26]

Moret was anxious to find a means of repairing the damage done to Spanish credibility. He devised a plan to go on a special mission to Washington to complete a trade treaty. With the queen regent's support, Moret asked Sagasta to provide him with full negotiating powers so that he could conclude a treaty while in Washington. Sagasta turned down the idea. To provide sufficient authority would require convening the Cortes, which was made up of Conservative Party members, many of whom opposed lower tariffs. In addition Sagasta was in the midst of preparing new elections; calling the Cortes would delay them and keep the Cortes under Conservative control. Sagasta also worried that Moret's mission to Washington might fail, leading to another setback for his government.[27]

Spain's initial efforts to distance itself from the de Lôme letter did not satisfy the McKinley administration. When Woodford arrived at the foreign ministry to ask for Dupuy's recall, the Spanish cabinet was in an extraordinary morning session discussing the affair, so Woodford waited several hours. When Gullón finally emerged from the meeting, he said that the Spanish government had accepted Dupuy's resignation. Woodford was initially satisfied, since he did not know the language of Dupuy's letter and did not have complete instructions from Washington.[28]

Dupuy's resignation, however, was not enough for Washington; McKinley expected Madrid to repudiate Dupuy's statements. More fully informed, Woodford now demanded a specific statement regretting and disclaiming Dupuy's language. Gullón was willing to strike his initial words of commendation from the acceptance of Dupuy's resignation, but he considered the dismissal to be a sufficient apology. In an effort to break the impasse, Moret called on Woodford and asked him exactly what was needed to end the incident. The American minister explained that Dupuy not only had insulted the president but also had characterized Spain's reform program as insincere. Woodford could not continue to do business with a government that refused to disavow such words. He asked how the queen regent would feel if on the one hand he held confidential meetings with her and on the other hand he took a hypocritical attitude toward her. If the ministry failed to repudiate such views, Woodford threatened, he would resign.[29]

When the government reconsidered Woodford's demand, the queen regent urged a positive response. The cabinet turned over to Gullón the task of writing an apology that would satisfy the Americans. The foreign minister did it by reasserting Spain's commitment to political reforms in Cuba. Gullón declared that the Spanish government's acceptance of Dupuy's resignation repudiated his language; moreover, the government solemnly and sincerely proposed to persevere with firmness in attaining "political and tariff" reforms in Cuba. For her part, the queen regent accepted Dupuy's resignation without the usual glowing words of commendation. McKinley considered these actions sufficient.[30]

During the de Lôme affair, Woodford had met frequently with Gullón, Moret, and the queen regent. As a result of these interviews he had an opportunity to better understand the politics of the Spanish cabinet. The ministry was divided, Woodford reported, with Gullón believing that Spain had "gone as far as [it could]" and that "war [was] preferable to further concessions" to the United States; the majority agreed with him. Moret held a minority view that peace could be kept, and he was more broad-minded and flexible; the queen regent sympathized with him. Sagasta was an "opportunist," inclined to act only when necessary. As a whole the ministers believed that Cuban autonomy was ineffective, and they were "seriously considering the contingency of war in order to save themselves, and possibly the Dynasty, from [being] overthrown here in Spain." The ministers "want[ed] peace, if they [could] keep peace and save the Dynasty. They preferr[ed] the chances of war, with the certain loss of Cuba, to the overthrow of the Dynasty." There was only one glimmer of hope: although Madrid would make no more concessions to the United States, it might grant some through the new insular government.[31]

The Spanish government quickly named a new minister, Luis Polo de Bernabé. His father, an admiral, had served in Washington as Spanish minister during the Ten Years War. The younger Polo was a career diplomat. His first post had been Washington; after that he had been stationed in The Hague, Paris, Lisbon, Rio de Janeiro, and Cairo before returning to Madrid in 1894 as head of the commercial and consular office. Polo was knowledgeable about current Spanish-American relations. Since his rank was not up to that of the Washington post, the assignment carried an automatic promotion. After Dupuy left and before Polo arrived, Juan Du Bosc, the first secretary, was in charge of the legation.[32]

In the United States, the congressional reaction to the de Lôme letter was limited but extremely significant. Three senators introduced resolutions about American intervention, Cuban independence, and the war in Cuba. Debate on these resolutions was perfunctory. The House passed a resolution asking for the costs of patrolling against filibustering; a resolution was introduced to give Dupuy his passports; and another opposed accepting Dupuy's resignation. Then on 14 February, Lemuel F. Quigg, Republican of New York and a known interventionist, reported out of the Foreign Affairs Committee a resolution requesting the administration to furnish all consular information on the *reconcentrados* and the status of autonomy. The resolution had unanimous committee support, which showed the president's approval. Since it was understood that the consular reports would provide Congress with the basis for intervention in Cuba, McKinley had taken an important step toward war. Quigg's resolution passed immediately by voice vote.[33]

The diplomatic controversy over the de Lôme letter lasted a week and was a public relations triumph for the Junta. Rubens made all of his points: Madrid's offer of autonomy was insincere, Spanish officials still believed in military subjugation of the Cuban people, the trade negotiations were cosmetic, and the American people were anti-Spanish. But Rubens irritated McKinley, who was unhappy that the Junta had chosen to have the *Journal* trumpet the diplomatic blunder rather than bringing the letter first to the president for a quiet resolution of the affair. At the same time the McKinley administration handled the unexpected dispute well. Day obtained the facts, Woodford got a Spanish apology, and McKinley kept Congress under control. McKinley's decision to take another step toward release of the consular reports suggests that the de Lôme letter, together with Gullón's 1 February note, had moved Washington one step closer to confronting Spain. The Spanish government also handled the de Lôme letter well; it found a means of satisfying Washington while respecting national sensitivities against kowtowing to the Americans.

Within hours of the settlement of the de Lôme controversy, the *Maine* blew up in Havana harbor. During the early evening of 15 February the ship's forward magazines, which were beneath the crew's quarters, exploded, causing a large loss of life—264 sailors and 2 officers. Lee and Blanco hurried to the port, where the Spanish and Cubans did everything possible to rescue the remaining American sailors. The news reached Washington by 1:00 A.M.; both Long and McKinley were awakened to learn of the tragedy. By morning, Lee believed that it would be impossible to determine the cause of the explosion, but he was "inclined to think it was accidental." Sigsbee was more cautious; after all, any accident reflected on his command of the ship. He advised Long that "public opinion should be suspended until further report."[34]

During the following weeks the national tragedy dominated American thinking. The shocking loss of American life fired public excitement and patriotism, and it directly linked the United States to the revolutionary events taking place in Cuba. Fueling American assumptions of Spanish brutality and duplicity, it sparked calls that the crime be avenged and justice be done.

Two explanations of the explosion developed: either the cause was internal and accidental, or it was foul play, probably an external mine. The possibility of a torpedo attack was quickly ruled out because of the shallow mooring. Generally speaking, those who favored a peaceful settlement of the Cuban problem believed it was an accident, whereas those who wanted direct and immediate intervention in Cuba suspected foul play.[35] The position taken by informed opinion was that an internal explosion based on spontaneous combustion in the coal bunkers probably had destroyed the ship. Since 1895, the navy had had thirteen ship fires associated with spontaneous combustion. Coal bunker fires were particularly dangerous. Ship construction placed coal at the sides of the ship and munitions in the middle, with a metal bulkhead dividing them; in the event of an attack, the coal was expected to serve as a buffer, absorbing the shock from shells, mines, or torpedoes. This made it even more unlikely that an underwater mine had set off the *Maine*'s munitions. An undetected fire, however, could heat the bulkhead separating the coal from the powder and cause an explosion. As a result, many naval officers, explosive experts, nautical engineers, and ship architects told reporters that they believed an accidental fire had triggered the *Maine* disaster. At the same time, other naval officers, particularly senior officials, were reluctant to admit that there were defects in the design of modern ships or in the procedures followed to minimize accidents. Roosevelt, for instance, immediately wrote that the *Maine* had been "sunk by an act of dirty treachery on the part of the Spaniards," although this would never be proven and the explosion would go down in history as an accident.[36] Predictably, the press divided over the possible cause of the explosion. While sensational journals trumpeted the treachery theory and provided imaginative details on how the deed might have been done, the conservative press published information on the long record of coal bunker fires and accidents.[37]

The congressional response was emotionally intense and threatening. Perhaps as many as nine out of ten congressmen believed that the Spanish were responsible for the catastrophe. Only a few conservative legislators pointed to a lack of information. The Senate Foreign Relations Committee held a day-long special closed session; emerging from the meeting, most members stated that the issue was too grave for comment, but several said that Spain needed to convince the American people of its innocence. Many congressmen called for a thorough and prompt investigation, although large numbers believed that the actual cause of the disaster would probably never be known.[38]

McKinley and Long thought that the explosion was accidental, but the president decided to take no stand until after learning the results of a naval inquiry. After conferring in the morning with McKinley, Long told waiting journalists that although the catastrophe excited "suspicions," it was most likely an accident. He repeated Sigsbee's appeal that "judgment should be suspended until a full investigation [was] made." After a cabinet meeting, members told waiting reporters that the disaster was probably accidental. The White House staff shared with journalists the telegrams coming from Havana, which helped to calm the press.[39]

That evening McKinley met with Senator Charles W. Fairbanks, Republican of Indiana, a friend and leading conservative. McKinley was careworn and in a serious mood. He told Fairbanks that "his duty was plain"; he would resist interventionist pressure for an "avenging blow" and wait for the facts, which the public should know. He would continue to prepare for war while hoping to avert it. The nation, he vowed, would not "be plunged into war until it [was] ready for it."[40]

One way to calm the nation was to employ naval procedures to determine the cause of the explosion. Navy Department regulations required a court of inquiry to investigate; the unruffled atmosphere of naval proceedings, resulting in a judicious report, promised to quiet the nation and to settle the public division over the cause of the disaster. Less than forty-eight hours after the accident, Long created a court, presided over by Captain William T. Sampson. Despite the emotionalism and international sensitivity of the *Maine* affair, routine methods were followed in selecting the members of the court, which consisted of five naval officers—three members, a judge advocate, and an ensign in charge of diving operations. The court was to go to Havana to examine the wreck and to take the testimony of the officers and men. There was no special technical expertise associated with the court, such as a munitions expert or naval architect. Long's swift appointment headed off an attempt by some legislators to create a congressional joint committee to investigate the disaster. Some members felt that the navy could not be trusted to investigate its own failures, but the overriding sentiment of Congress was to support the navy and not to question its integrity.[41]

The investigation took place under difficult conditions. The harbor water was muddy and visibility was poor. Deep mud hampered divers attempting to move on the harbor bottom, and they risked snarling and cutting their air hoses in the wreckage of twisted steel. The explosion had blown out the sides and deck of the ship, making it hard to piece together where various remnants originated. As a result, divers constructed only a fragmentary description of the ship. Nevertheless, the responsibility for providing a factual basis on which to judge the *Maine* explosion fell to the divers and the ensign who directed them.[42]

Unlike the de Lôme letter, the *Maine* disaster did not generate intense diplomatic activity. Blanco, having done everything in his power to aid the stricken Americans in the harbor, offered his condolences. Du Bosc appeared at the State Department at 3:00 A.M. on 16 February to share his cables with American authorities and to express his sorrow. Both the Spanish government and the queen regent gave formal expressions of sympathy, and Du Bosc conveyed these in person to McKinley.[43]

The only diplomatic matter that immediately arose was jurisdiction over the ship and the investigation. Since the accident had occurred on a naval ship, the United States claimed the right to investigate the wreckage, even though it rested in Spanish waters. The police authority for the harbor was Spanish, and just as the American navy automatically opened a court of inquiry, the Spanish also began an investigation. Within hours, Moret urged Blanco to gather all facts favorable to Spain.[44] Given the overlapping jurisdictions, the Spanish government proposed a joint investigation, which Washington quickly rejected. Widespread American suspicion of foul play made a joint investigation politically unacceptable. As a result, the Americans and the Spanish conducted separate inquiries, although they coordinated diving operations and worked together to police and protect the wreckage.[45]

Although outward calm returned to Washington, these two extraordinary events deeply embittered Spanish-American relations, which were already moving toward a crisis. The episodes—a purloined letter and an unexplained explosion—were seemingly unrelated; nevertheless, the de Lôme controversy magnified the significance of the *Maine* disaster. The former generated American suspicion of Spanish duplicity, insincerity, and hostility, and these attitudes were projected on the *Maine* tragedy. In both instances, Americans were the injured party, and the public mood became vengeful.

Both Washington and Madrid handled these difficult dramas well. They settled the de Lôme affair in a week, and within two days the government directed the *Maine* disaster into routine investigative channels. If at the end of Washington's inquiry, the American naval court had concluded that the *Maine* had exploded as a result of spontaneous combustion, which was what McKinley expected, both episodes might have faded into the background of Cuban developments.

But even if these dramatic events had been successfully set aside, the United States and Spain were still on a collision course. The McKinley administration understood that Gullón's 1 February note meant that Spain was unwilling to make any further Cuban reforms; instead, Madrid had adopted a defiant nationalistic and patriotic stance. The Spanish cabinet was aware of the consequences; it considered war likely. The more strident line taken in Madrid had its counterpart in Washington as the McKinley administration readied the consular reports. Washington was preparing to intervene, not because of the de Lôme letter and *Maine* explosion but because Spain appeared to be unable to end the war and suffering in Cuba.

CHAPTER 8

. . . .

BACKDROP FOR

. . . .

DIPLOMACY

. . . .

D uring the weeks following the *Maine* disaster, the
United States and Spain moved closer to war, and
both prepared for it. From the start of the naval investigation of the *Maine* wreckage, the court of inquiry suspected an external explosion had caused the disaster. In theory, the court operated in
secret, and the results were not to be known until the end of the investigation; in practice, there were constant leaks. Lee regularly gleaned information in Havana, which he forwarded to Day, and much the same
news appeared in reputable journals within twenty-four hours. The public outwardly displayed patience, but this cloaked an intense emotional
involvement in the catastrophe and a deep-seated conviction that the time
had come to settle the Cuban issue. Most Americans expected the
McKinley administration to solve the Cuban problem; if necessary, they
were prepared to fight Spain to free Cuba. Just before the naval court
completed its report, Senator Redfield Proctor, Republican of Vermont,
heightened the emotion by dramatizing the deplorable condition of *reconcentrados* and Spain's futile efforts to end the insurrection. Spain's attempts to counter the naval court and Proctor's accusations had no influence on American opinion.

News about the *Maine* came quickly; the naval court opened hearings on 21 February, and the next day Lee tersely reported that the divers had found evidence suggesting an external explosion. Lee advised Americans living in Havana to consider leaving, and the American newspapers carried the story.[1] Within a few days the idea that an accident had caused the sinking of the *Maine* gave way to the common belief that a mine had ignited the ship's magazines. By the end of February, the press reported that an American diver had found some bottom plates of the *Maine* twenty feet above their normal position; this strongly suggested that the explosion had originated under the ship.[2] Accordingly, the nation's attention turned from the cause of the explosion to who had set off the mine. Lee did not think that Blanco and his entourage were responsible; rather private individuals, perhaps even Spanish officers, might have managed to place guncotton at a point where the ship swung against it. The press accepted the idea that Blanco was not directly involved, but it held that Spain was responsible for the well-being of ships in its harbors; if the Spanish were unable to protect visiting battleships, they were unworthy to govern the island.[3]

To counter repeated American leaks, Spanish officials announced that their investigators were finding evidence of an internal explosion, and Du Bosc insisted to reporters that there were no mines in Havana harbor. But Lee told Day that the Spanish investigation was a farce; their divers were not making a serious attempt to explore the wrecked ship.[4]

As soon as the McKinley administration learned that the cause of the disaster was external, it searched for an appropriate policy. If evidence developed that the Spanish government had set off the explosion, war was inevitable. But what if the Spanish government was not implicated? McKinley's cabinet initially thought Spain should pay a large indemnity; failure to do so would be grounds for a military assault on Cuba. Long confided to his diary that for the first time, war seemed possible. Day, normally quite reticent, told Cambon that if there was an exterior cause for the *Maine* tragedy, particularly if it turned out that Spanish authorities had berthed the ship at a point in the harbor where mines existed, nothing could stop the American people from ending "such a barbarous and inhumane situation."[5] When Lee stated that he doubted Blanco and his subordinates were behind the explosion, Long told journalists that now there was no reason for war. The following day Alger explained to newspapermen that Long spoke only for himself. The *Washington Star* concluded that McKinley wanted neither to excite the public nor to dispel apprehension, since the situation was fluid.[6]

With war possible, both the United States and Spain sped up military preparations. In late 1897 the Navy Department had begun moving its ships into the Gulf of Mexico for winter maneuvers. During January, Roosevelt became convinced that if Spain was successful in buying naval ships, it might obtain a fleet larger than the United States. He calculated Spain's Atlantic strength at seven ironclads, which he considered equivalent to the American squadron. When the *Maine* sank, Roosevelt jumped to the conclusion that Spain had achieved naval superiority in the Atlantic. He urged Long and others to expand the U.S. fleet, but Long was unconvinced.[7]

Spanish attempts in early March to buy ships and move some to Cuban waters provoked an increase in America's naval buildup. On 5 March the McKinley administration learned that the Spanish were negotiating to buy two cruisers being built in England for the government of Brazil, one of which was nearly complete. The Brazilian government needed money and was considering selling both to Spain; the Brazilians, however, preferred to sell the ships to the United States.[8] A related vexing problem was Spain's preparations to send several torpedo boats and other gunboats to Cuba. The torpedo boats, smaller and faster than armored ships, were designed to attack large ships, and American naval officers considered them a major threat.[9]

On Sunday, 6 March, McKinley called Joseph G. Cannon, Republican of Illinois and chairman of the House Appropriations Committee, to the White House to obtain funds to preempt Spain. They decided to ask Congress for $50 million, surplus in the treasury. The following day Cannon introduced an appropriation bill for $50 million for national defense and on Tuesday reported it to the House floor. Within hours, both the House and the Senate unanimously passed the bill.[10] There was no Senate debate, but House members spoke in favor of it for four hours, which gave them a chance to show their patriotism. Speaker Reed's clerk noted in his diary, "Before it was over it seemed as though a hundred Fourths of July had been let loose in the House."[11]

Passage of the $50-million bill was a political and diplomatic triumph for McKinley. In two days he had demonstrated to Spain the unanimous support of Congress, which had shown its confidence in him by providing that the money be spent at his discretion. And the nation had sufficient wealth that no new taxes or borrowing was required. The stark contrast between American political cohesion and financial resources and Spanish party factionalism and national debt was stunning. Moreover, the

Americans quickly purchased the Brazilian cruisers as well as supply ships, coal, guns, and ammunition; American dollars froze Spain out of the international ship market. Some Americans interpreted the $50-million appropriation as more likely to bring peace than war, since it was a warning to the Spanish of American power and commitment.[12]

Nevertheless, the Spanish flotilla of three torpedo boats, three destroyers, and one armed merchant ship departed Spain for Cuba by way of the Canary Islands. The news provoked alarm and indignation in the United States. Since the ships would not be needed to fight Cubans in the countryside, Americans considered the move a menace aimed at the United States. Roosevelt believed Washington should consider the approaching ships as an act of mobilization, and Captain Sampson urged Long to "destroy them at once."[13] To the navy's consternation, the flotilla continued to sail slowly westward.

Some of McKinley's thinking about Spanish-American relations was revealed on 10 March, when Catholic Archbishop John Ireland joined the president, Day, and Vice President Garret A. Hobart at the White House, where they spent the evening reviewing the Cuban situation. Ireland learned that McKinley was convinced that an exterior explosion had sunk the *Maine* and that Spain had already lost Cuba. Desiring peace, the president feared that prolonging the Cuban war would provoke a rupture with Spain. The McKinley administration did not wish to annex the island because it did not want two Cubans voting in the Senate. McKinley was considering the idea of providing Spain with financial compensation to give Cuba its independence.[14]

As McKinley and the nation closely followed the *Maine* inquiry and prepared for war, Senator Redfield Proctor was touring Cuba in an attempt to see for himself the conditions on the island. When he returned in mid-March to Washington, he delivered a dramatic speech to the Senate, creating a national sensation and measurably moving the country toward intervention. There were several reasons Proctor had such a large impact on public opinion. He was a self-made millionaire, one of the wealthiest members of Congress, and he therefore influenced the business community, which still opposed using force in Cuba. Proctor also projected an image of calm and detached judgment; he rarely made speeches and was not regarded as a demagogue. When Proctor spoke, he was believable. Proctor was considered a Republican insider, since he had served as secretary of war during the Harrison administration and was a friend of McKinley's. Journalists believed the White House had prompted Proctor's trip to Cuba. This was repeatedly denied, but newspapermen winked at the denials.[15]

Actually Proctor was sympathetic to the Cuban cause and curious about events on the island, which he had visited before. He also had an eye out for potential investments. In early 1898 he decided to visit the island. Before leaving Washington he called on McKinley, Day, and Alger and received special consideration. Alger furnished an army officer to accompany him, and Day asked Lee to welcome and assist him. Admiral Montgomery Sicard, the commander of the North Atlantic Station, hosted Proctor at Key West and supplied a special naval escort for the boat ride to Havana.[16] During his two-week visit, Lee introduced the senator to Blanco, the members of the naval court of inquiry, Sigsbee, and Clara Barton. Barton and her aids escorted him to several sites to observe the distribution of charitable goods. The senator toured the western half of the island, including the towns of Matanzas and Sagua la Grande. He made a point of visiting reconcentration camps and hospitals. While in Cuba, Proctor wrote two letters to Day, letters that showed he was visiting the island in a personal capacity. Proctor was complimentary of Lee, Sigsbee, and the efficient work of Barton and her staff in distributing American relief to needy Cubans. After traveling outside Havana, however, the senator became sharply critical, comparing Cuban conditions to St. Bartholomew's massacre and the Inquisition.[17]

On returning to the United States, Proctor spoke guardedly to the press. In private he described the terrible conditions in Cuba to many friends, including McCook, who urged him to inform the Senate and the press. Senators also asked him to speak out. So Proctor prepared a statement; before releasing it, he showed it to Day and McKinley, who raised no objections. Since the senator had again conferred with McKinley, journalists were more convinced than ever that he spoke for the administration. Rubens drew the same conclusion: the speech was "most significant" because Proctor delivered it with McKinley's approval.[18]

Proctor's speech was, above all, credible. He approached the topic as a skeptic who disbelieved what was in the American press and the propaganda of the Cuban Junta. "[He] went to Cuba with a strong conviction that the picture had been overdrawn; that a few cases of starvation and suffering had inspired and stimulated the press correspondents." He took with him a few pictures provided by the *Christian Herald*, photos that he assumed were "rare specimens." He did not believe that two hundred thousand from a population of 1.6 million had died from starvation and disease.[19]

And the senator was authoritative; he based his report on conservative and informed testimony obtained from American officials and important members of Cuban society. Proctor carried with him many letters of introduction from American businessmen, which gave him access to Cuban business leaders. "[His] inquiries were entirely outside of sensational sources. They were made of our medical officers, of our consuls, of city alcaldes (mayors), of relief communities, of leading merchants and bankers, physicians and lawyers. Several of [his] informants were Spanish born." He also talked to one American who was serving in the insurgent army. Having met with Blanco, Proctor decided against direct contacts with Gómez.[20]

Proctor examined several aspects of the Cuban situation: the condition of the *reconcentrados*; hospitals; the military situation; race relations; and the political future of the island. His most dramatic testimony described the pitiful condition of the remaining *reconcentrados*. Havana looked much as he remembered it, but when he toured outside the capital city, everything was "changed." Every town was surrounded by a trench, barbed-wire fence, and blockhouses. The country people, who had once been self-sufficient farmers, had been herded inside the trenches of the fortified towns, which had become "virtually prison yards." "Every man, woman, and child, and every domestic animal, wherever [Spanish] columns have reached," was under guard within these fortifications. Outside the towns there were no domestic animals or crops. "The Spanish [held] . . . just what their army [sat] on." "It [was] neither peace nor war. It [was] concentration and desolation. This [was] the 'pacified' condition of the four western provinces." Only a few sugar mills continued in operation, and he understood they did so because Spanish soldiers guarded them and the owners paid taxes to the Cubans.[21]

About four hundred thousand people had been herded into fortified towns. Driven from their farms and homes, they now lived in makeshift huts of about fifteen feet by ten feet without furniture and with little clothing after a year's wear. "The commonest sanitary provisions [were] impossible. Conditions [were] unmentionable in this respect. Torn from their homes, with foul earth, foul air, foul water, and foul food or none, what wonder that one-half [had] died and that one-quarter of the living [were] so diseased that they [could] not be saved. . . . Little children

[were] still walking about with arms and chest terribly emaciated, eyes swollen, and abdomen bloated to three times the natural size. The physicians [said] these cases [were] hopeless."[22]

Proctor visited the Los Pasos hospital in Havana. There he saw "400 women and children . . . lying on the floors in an indescribable state of emaciation and disease, many with the scantiest covering of rags—and such rags!—sick children, naked as they came into the world; and the conditions in the other cities [were] even worse."[23]

The military situation in Cuba remained a stalemate. Out of more than two hundred thousand soldiers Spain had sent to the island, only about sixty thousand remained fit for duty. The others either had died, had returned to Spain in ill health, or were in military hospitals. Spanish soldiers were quite young and untrained. The senator saw no military drills, and no one he talked to had ever seen one. The Spanish troops lived in barracks in the fortified towns. By day they searched for insurgents, and they nearly always returned to their barracks at night. They had little equipment.[24]

According to an American insurgent field officer, the Cubans had about thirty thousand men under arms. Although they had sufficient guns, they had very few cartridges, sometimes only one or two per soldier. The Cubans held the eastern part of Cuba, which everyone called Cuba Libre, and they operated in small bands throughout much of the rest of the countryside. Reportedly four small contingents were in Havana Province.[25]

On the political future of Cuba, Proctor differed from most other commentators. He described the racial and cultural differences of Spaniards, Cubans, and blacks, concluding that there was more racial harmony in Cuba than in the United States. In addition, many well-to-do Cubans had been educated in England, France, or the United States and were capable of self-government. The Cuban people would never accept autonomy under Spanish rule. Even officials of the new autonomy government believed it would not work. "You do not have to scratch an autonomist very deep to find a Cuban." The business community unanimously wanted peace but considered it "too late for peace under Spanish sovereignty." Men of affairs, however, were divided about the future. "Some favored a United States protectorate, some annexation, some free Cuba." If the Cubans were free and at peace, they would create a stable and prosperous society. "The conditions for good self-government [were] more favorable" than for continuous upheaval.[26]

Proctor concluded with some advice to the nation. He urged no particular policy on the McKinley administration; the president and the American people should define that. He personally opposed annexing the Cubans because of their different language and cultural background. Rather he wanted to define the central issue for the United States, which was not "the barbarity practiced by Weyler nor the loss of the *Maine*, . . . but the spectacle of a million and a half of people, the entire native population of Cuba, struggling for freedom and deliverance from the worst misgovernment of which [he] ever had knowledge." [27]

Proctor's speech had an immediate and profound national impact; it especially moved the business community, religious organizations, and legislators. Before 17 March many business journals and spokesmen had been wary of the Cuban problem because they feared the consequences of a war with Spain. After the speech they joined the rest of the nation in support of American intervention to end Spanish rule in Cuba. The *Literary Digest* summed up the reversal: "With very few exceptions, the most conservative of newspapers now express the opinion that Senator Proctor's careful statement of conditions in Cuba . . . makes intervention the plain duty of the United States on the simple ground of humanity. . . . The situation in Cuba is actually intolerable." The *Wall Street Journal* stated: "Senator Proctor's speech converted a great many people in Wall Street, who have heretofore taken the ground that the United States had no business to interfere in a revolution on Spanish soil. These men had been among the most prominent in deploring the whole Cuban matter, but there was no question about the accuracy of Senator Proctor's statements and as many of them expressed it, they made the blood boil." [28] The *Literary Digest* also found that with few exceptions, the religious press had become insistent on changing the conditions in Cuba, peacefully if possible but through war if necessary. For instance, a leading Baptist journal in Boston, the *Watchman*, declared, "Our right to intervene in Cuba, on the ground of self-interest and humanity, is, to our way of thinking, indisputable." [29]

The timing of Proctor's speech was part of the reason for its effect on Congress. It intensified the clamor for action only days before the *Maine* report reached Washington. Moreover, the public was divided over what to do about the *Maine*; although everyone believed there had been an external explosion, there was no evidence that Spanish officials were responsible. Proctor's speech established a position that united the nation. His advice to look beyond the *Maine* to the Cuban struggle for self-government against Spain's barbarous rule rallied the people. For instance, Russell Hastings, an old McKinley family friend, wrote: "Senator Proctor's report seems to have solidified all elements and the *Maine* disaster sinks into insignificance. When this true knowledge *comes* to every household of the inhuman barbarity of the Spanish Government. You, as the head of the Government and the Nation must at once put a stop to such barbarity and the quicker the better." [30]

Proctor's speech served McKinley's purpose well; the president confided to Charles G. Dawes, comptroller of the currency and a close friend, that he did not want to intervene in Cuban affairs because of the *Maine* tragedy but rather on the "broader grounds" of Cuban suffering. Dawes noted in his diary that the president's policy was "being assisted by events." [31] Although there is no evidence that McKinley prompted Proctor's speech, Rubens's private comment that the president had approved the speech was probably close to the truth.

But Proctor's speech also threatened McKinley's control of the government by igniting an emotional demand for immediate action. Congress became belligerent, intolerant of delay, and saw Spanish procrastination in diplomatic exchanges. And McKinley now feared that the *Maine* report would stampede Congress into voting for war. Reed and some conservative Republican senators considered adjourning Congress so that McKinley would have a free hand for diplomacy. Bailey denounced the idea, and McKinley let it be known that he wanted Congress in session so that it could receive facts and, if necessary, declare war. Day confessed to Dawes that war would "be difficult to avoid." [32]

On Saturday evening, 19 March, four naval officers delivered to Long a summary of conclusions of the naval court. This was the court's first official report and preceded the arrival of the complete document by five days. There were no surprises. The next morning McKinley examined the account with Long, Day, and Bliss, and the following morning Reed called on the president. These meetings decided the means of releasing the *Maine* report to the Spanish government and the best way to inform Congress. Day cabled the conclusions to Woodford to give to the Spanish government, and two days later Day informed Polo de Bernabé. [33]

In an effort to establish a governmental consensus, McKinley began meeting with large numbers of congressmen; for the first time he reached beyond the Republican leadership to include influential Democrats and Republicans who championed immediate recognition of Cuban belligerency or independence. He also met frequently with cabinet officers. The legislators and officials entering the president's office strongly urged him to end the Cuban problem. McKinley asked for time to pursue a diplomatic solution; he described the essential issues as relief for the Cuban people and an end to Spanish rule on the island rather than quick justice for the loss of the *Maine*. The president worried that if he asked Spain for a large financial indemnity, Madrid would request arbitration, which would delay a decision. As he talked and listened, the president stitched together a plan of action that he believed Congress would accept and that would free Cuba. He decided to request $500,000 from Congress for immediate relief of the *reconcentrados*. Large-scale relief would require Spain to cooperate to alleviate Cuban suffering and to end the strife that had caused the suffering. If Spain balked, McKinley would use military force, and "his conscience and the world [would] justify it." On 24 March, only hours before the complete *Maine* report arrived at the Navy Department, the press outlined the president's program: (1) send the *Maine* report to Congress immediately; (2) before the end of March, send the consular correspondence to Congress and ask for $500,000 for Cuban relief; and (3) if Spain failed to succor its people and to end the war, send a message to Congress on 20 April detailing the horrible conditions on the island and declaring that the United States must intervene on humanitarian grounds.[34]

That evening the *Maine* report, nearly four hundred pages long, arrived in Washington. The next day the president and his cabinet studied it for five hours. McKinley also consulted Republican and Democratic legislators. He decided to forward the report to Congress on Monday, 28 March, and to treat the *Maine* disaster as one more example of Spain's inability to rule Cuba. The president drew up a brief transmittal note stating that he was sending the report to the Spanish government, that he expected Spain to do what was honorable between friendly nations, and that he would inform Congress of Spain's response. In the meantime, he asked the legislators to give the report "deliberate consideration."[35]

Despite all of McKinley's efforts, when the *Maine* report became public, there was an impassioned outcry for immediate action. The details were convincing. Navy divers had found the bottom outside plating and the keel of the ship, frames 17 to 25, as much as thirty-four feet above their normal position. The court concluded that this could have resulted only from a mine explosion under the bottom of the ship at about frame 18.[36] Emotions ran so high that McKinley set aside his request for $500,000; legislators made it clear that they would vote for relief only if it was coupled with recognition of the Cuban Republic and forceful intervention.[37]

The clamoring for intervention in the United States helped to unify the Spanish people, but basically Spain remained politically divided, financially exhausted, and militarily unprepared for war. As 1898 began, Sagasta was trying to strengthen his control of the government. When he had assumed power in October, the Conservative Party dominated the Cortes; elected in 1896, the Cortes had 276 Conservatives and only 109 Liberals. To obtain a Liberal majority, Sagasta needed to hold national elections. On 26 February, the queen regent proclaimed elections for 27 March and 10 April and scheduled the new Cortes to meet on 25 April. As a result, Spain was reorganizing politically as the war crisis developed.[38]

The Spanish government was also preparing for elections in Cuba. The autonomy regime was getting ready to elect its first insular Cortes. In Cuba, as in Spain, the central government controlled the election. Moret and Blanco carefully picked the candidates to ensure a legislature that contained a majority of Liberal Party autonomists. They gave Conservatives some seats but diligently excluded all supporters of Weyler and Romero Robledo. Thus, Cuban self-government was illusory as Madrid continued to dominate insular domestic politics.[39]

Sagasta also had to cope with a weak economy. By the spring of 1898, the three-year Cuban war had drained the treasury and undermined the economy. August Belmont, who represented the Rothschilds, estimated that Spain might raise $5 to $10 million through domestic subscriptions. Paris bankers thought that Madrid had the potential of borrowing up to $50 million. The value of the peseta was dropping against foreign currencies, and the possibility existed of a financial collapse if Spain entered a war against the United States. The falling peseta led to rising food costs, and there were bread shortages in some Spanish towns. Higher food prices and a lack of jobs resulted in street demonstrations and riots.[40]

On top of economic difficulties, a war with the United States was likely. The cabinet was alarmed by the increasing number of American ships stationed near Cuba, Portugal, and the Philippine Islands and by the American efforts to improve coastal fortifications. Washington was playing a "double game"—talking peace while preparing for war. Sagasta, Moret, and Gullón considered war with the United States to be utterly hopeless, and Admiral Cervera repeatedly warned against it. On the other hand, much of Spain's press, particularly the military journals, was belligerent, and these factions pressured the government to stand up to American humiliations. There was a popular belief that the army and navy would fight well against the Americans. Even Weyler joined in belligerent braggadocio by describing how a Spanish army might invade the United States. Since Sagasta's government needed the support of military officers and was anxious to prevent other political factions from seizing the flag of Spanish patriotism, it did not publicly contest militaristic assertions.[41]

The bellicose national mood was aggravated by leaks from the *Maine* investigation. The Spanish were dumbfounded that the American investigators believed a mine had caused the disaster, and the government realized the grave implications. Du Bosc cabled on 25 February, "Alarming reports from Cuba . . . that the catastrophe . . . was caused by a submarine mine have stirred up the greatest agitation until even the most important and conservative men have lost their heads." Gullón characterized McKinley and his government as "inclined to incomprehensible apprehensions"; holding Spain responsible was "incredible." He insisted to the European governments that the explosion had been accidental. In mid-March, Blanco confirmed that the American court would declare that the *Maine* had sunk because of an "internal and an external explosion." Polo and Moret urged Blanco to make the Spanish investigation as complete and convincing as possible and to ready the Spanish investigation for release at the same time as the American report.[42]

With war more likely, Madrid's one means of checking American naval superiority was to purchase a fleet. When Congress passed the $50-million bill, a financial panic swept Madrid as Bank of Spain stock plunged and "deep pessimism" spread throughout the stock market. Woodford commented that the news "stunned" the Spanish. The government watched helplessly as the Americans bought the Brazilian ships and other vessels. Moret alerted Blanco to the war "panic" in Madrid and warned that if Spain did not improve its position in Cuba, McKinley had decided to go to war in May. Moret urged Blanco to redouble his efforts to defeat the insurgents; given the "grave circumstances," Blanco must be prepared "for all eventualities."[43]

Gullón vented his frustration to the conde de Rascón, Spain's ambassador to England. Under pretext of naval maneuvers, Gullón wrote, the United States had assembled a squadron of ships in the Dry Tortugas, which was only eight hours from Cuba. The ships had arrived in mid-January for two to three weeks and were still there in mid-March. Washington was posting other ships to Lisbon, and when and in what direction they would depart was unknown. A small squadron was also in the Far East; without doubt, it was aimed at the Philippine Islands. The Americans had also sent officials to buy and contract for ships, supplies, and munitions in Great Britain and every other place available. In the face of these extreme provocations, Spain's policy was to be "firm, correct and very prudent" in order "to avoid a dreadful conflict" with the United States.[44]

Just after Congress passed the $50-million appropriation, Polo arrived in Washington. His mission lasted only six weeks. He brought with him instructions from Gullón to adhere strictly to the tone and content of the 1 February note. At the start Polo attempted to do this, but swiftly moving events soon led him to assume a greater role in shaping Spanish diplomatic policy and providing political guidance to Blanco. Throughout, Polo was suspicious of American intentions and skeptical of finding a diplomatic solution. Polo served Spain well, and after the war he continued to fill diplomatic appointments with distinction.

As Polo took charge of the mission, Du Bosc wrote a final report on his brief tenure in charge of the legation. He predicted an "inevitable" war by 1 May. Du Bosc considered McKinley to be a peaceful man, and those Republican leaders closest to him and who had supported his election, such as Hanna, Allison, Reed, and Cannon, shared the president's view. But politicians were anticipating the fall elections. The Republicans had recently lost various municipal elections, and the prospect of a national election defeat would convert them from peaceful to aggressive ways. The same senators who yesterday had said that "war [was] a crime and not possible," now said, "We hope war can be avoided." McKinley's indecision, Du Bosc predicted, would eventually crystallize into American intervention in Cuba. Americans believed that Spain could not end the insurrection, and McKinley thought that if he applied enough pressure, Spain would allow the United States to intervene in Cuban affairs without a war.[45]

Polo began his mission with a round of calls on Sherman, Day, McKinley, and Alger. Although McKinley's welcome was warm, Polo and Day traded sharp words. When Day remarked that the impending *Maine* report posed problems, Polo coldly replied that he did not understand why, since the sinking of the *Maine* was a purely internal American affair. Disparaging Spanish military activity on the island, Day acidly observed that without pressure, the insurgents were unlikely to accept autonomy.

He accused Madrid of attempting to buy ships and arms to fight the United States rather than the insurgents. And he warned Polo against sending the Spanish torpedo boats from the Canary Islands. Many people, Day noted, held that Spain was seeking a war with the United States in order to lose Cuba honorably to a stronger power. By contrast, he explained, the United States had appropriated $50 million as a defensive measure. Polo countered that the Spanish increase in armed forces was designed to end the Cuban war quickly. The problem was not a lack of Spanish military effort but rather the failure of the United States to curb the Junta. He flatly denied that Spain wanted war with the United States, which would be a "crime against humanity and civilization," and he said that the Spanish would fight the United States only to defend against American intervention. As for ship movements, Polo pointed out the extremely threatening positions of American ships, which were a major irritant to Spain. Gullón read Polo's reports with satisfaction and congratulated him on ably representing the Spanish viewpoints.[46]

A week after Polo arrived, Proctor delivered his speech to the Senate. Polo attempted to convince Washington that Proctor's account was overdrawn, but to no avail. Polo knew that Day was compiling consular information about the *reconcentrados* to submit to Congress, and he asked Blanco for recent facts about the *reconcentrados* to forward to the State Department. Blanco pictured an improving situation as a result of the $150,000 spent by Spain and $50,000 by the United States. Relief supplies entered duty free, and the American Red Cross participated in distributing goods. But he admitted that much remained to be done: "Warfare, which always leaves profound ravages, demands much time and assiduous labor to repair the evils." Blanco's analysis was in part substantiated by American reports; only a few days after Proctor's speech, Lee commented that relief efforts were "progressing most satisfactorily." When asked about greatly increasing American aid, Polo assured Day that the Cuban authorities would admit much larger quantities of relief goods. Proctor's moving speech, however, overwhelmed all Spanish efforts to convince the United States that conditions were improving on the island and that greater cooperation was possible.[47]

More worrisome for the Spanish were Proctor's statements that military operations were without effect and that autonomy had failed. These struck directly at the Spanish means of pacifying the island. Polo asked Blanco for facts to counter Proctor's "misinformation" and "exaggeration"; he told Gullón that Proctor and the pressure of Congress had persuaded McKinley to submit the entire Cuban issue to Congress. "All [was] to be feared," since the American government would "pretend to intervene in Cuba in the form of official aid for *reconcentrados*." [48]

On 22 March, Day discussed the *Maine* conclusions with Polo and two days later provided the complete report. He assured Polo that the *Maine* situation could be settled amicably. It was more important, Day explained, to solve the *reconcentrado* problem. McKinley expected to calm public opinion by asking Congress to vote a large sum of money for relief. Polo responded that the McKinley administration should not act until it had considered the results of the Spanish investigation of the *Maine*, and he asked for time for Madrid to study the American report. [49]

In Spain, the press and the government rejected the American findings. *El Correo Militar*, for instance, sneered that the ship had sunk because of the "ineptness and laxity of the crew." Since there was no Spanish responsibility, the government should not pay a single peseta in indemnity; any payment would imply Spanish culpability. [50] On 27 March, the cabinet released the conclusions of the Spanish inquiry, which denied that an external explosion had caused the *Maine* disaster. Arguing through a series of negative statements, the Spanish investigators noted, "No column of water was seen to rise, nor the water to be agitated, nor to dash against the sides of near-by vessels; nor was any shaking felt on the shore; nor were there subsequently seen dead fish floating." The harbor contained an abundance of fish; on previous occasions, when harbor repairs had required underwater explosions, there had always been many dead fish. The bottom of the ship was buried in mud and could not be examined, but the sides of the ship had obviously been blown outward, which proved there had been an internal explosion. The Spanish court complained that its investigators had been unable to carry out a thorough examination of the shipwreck because American officials had refused to cooperate in a joint endeavor. It concluded that a complete investigation based on the recovery of the wreck would undoubtedly demonstrate that the explosion had been internal. The Spanish government believed that discrepancies between the two official reports should be settled through arbitration. [51]

With the release of the conflicting *Maine* reports, nationalistic passions ran high in both countries. And Washington and Madrid continued to color their views of each other through long-held perspectives. To the McKinley administration, the facts were clear: Spanish misrule justified the Cuban rebellion, military operations were ineffective, autonomy had failed, Cuba was lost, and there was no end in sight as the rainy season approached. Up to late March, McKinley had restrained Congress. After Proctor's speech and the *Maine* report, there was little time left for the McKinley administration to find a peaceful way to remove Spain from Cuba. From Spain's point of view, the American government was playing a perfidious "double game" of talking peace while preparing for war. Ominously, Washington was stationing ships in threatening positions around the globe. Dupuy had been right: McKinley appealed to the peace faction while keeping a door open for the jingoes. The president was weak, and likely to join the interventionists. But the Spanish government continued to hold on to Cuba. Leaving the island was certain to arouse sharp public disapproval, and opponents might attempt to overthrow the government and even the monarchy. Sagasta's cabinet preferred to take a nationalistic stand against American intervention rather than risk igniting a civil war. Nevertheless, faced by the prospect of a Spanish-American war, Moret searched for a means to peacefully resolve the Cuban crisis.

CHAPTER 9

. . . .

FAILURE

. . . .

TO SOLVE

. . . .

THE CRISIS

. . . .

As Spain and the United States moved toward war, both nations attempted to find a peaceful solution. In Washington, McKinley led the search; in Madrid, it was Moret. The McKinley administration's objective was to separate Cuba from Spain. To save face for Madrid, the United States was initially willing to allow nominal Spanish sovereignty over the island. But the threat of force was always evident, and as emotions rose, war itself became an acceptable means. Spain wanted to retain the island. Its fading hopes clung to autonomy, and it sought more time to solidify the new regime. Ironically, faced by war, Madrid looked to the autonomous government to deal with the insurgents and to do what Spain could not: cut the tie between the mother country and its colony.

At the beginning of March, Woodford asked McKinley a series of questions that highlighted the need to be more aggressive in solving the Cuban problem. With the Cuban rainy season starting about 1 May, he asked if Spain could be expected by that time to reduce the rebellion to the extent that the American people would consider it practically ended. If not, would the public accept five more months of Spanish military inactivity? If the rebellion was still active by 1 April, what could the American government do during April to "prevent the famine, the sickness, the danger of yellow fever epidemics and all the suffering that must be in Cuba during the . . . rainy season"? If the United States intervened about 1 April, had McKinley given sufficient warning in his December message and the diplomatic note of 20 December "to justify effective action" that would "be approved by the sober judgment of our people and the final judgment of history"? Woodford's questions were apt; Cuban developments were stalled, and time was running out. Unless the president was willing to accept another rainy season, he had to use a more forceful hand.[1]

During the first part of March, McKinley explored several possibilities: the purchase of Cuba, Spanish suzerainty, and the recognition of Cuban independence. None of these worked out, but McKinley showed the greatest interest in purchasing Cuba. He discussed the possibility with senators in late February, and at the time of the $50-million defense appropriation, the president sounded congressmen about linking military funding to an appropriation of $300 million to purchase the island. Legislators were unenthusiastic; why should they pay for Cuba when Spain was about to lose the island? A few days later the president confided to Ireland that he would like to purchase Cuba for $300 million, and the Catholic archbishop conveyed this to Cambon, but there was no response from across the Atlantic. In early March, McCook reiterated to Day and McKinley the Junta's long-standing offer to give Spain $100 million in Cuban bonds for the island's independence, with payment guaranteed by the United States. For the first time McKinley was sufficiently interested that he made inquiries into McCook's authority to represent the Cubans. Later in March, Gómez raised the ante by announcing that he favored paying $200 million for Cuban independence.[2]

Woodford also thought that purchase was a promising solution. On 18 March he received a State Department status report that convinced him that Spain's cause was hopeless. Day characterized Blanco's military efforts as "barren." Despite Blanco's good-faith effort to promote autonomy, only a few insurgents had accepted it, and Spaniards as well as rebels opposed it. The financial and productive resources of the island continued to decline, and the condition of the *reconcentrados* worsened daily. From the centers of reconcentration came the same "appalling tale of misery, suffering, and death." Relief was helping, but it was "painfully insufficient to meet the situation."[3]

After reading this dismal report, Woodford concluded that the logical solution was the sale of Cuba to the United States. In confidence, he presented his ideas to Moret. Given the failure of Spanish military efforts and autonomy, Woodford asserted that only the United States could restore peace and prosperity to the island. On undertaking his mission to Spain, Woodford reflected, he had opposed American annexation of the island; now he believed it was the only possible solution. Woodford was against involving banking syndicates because they would arouse suspicion about trusts and corruption and make it difficult for the United States to control the island. An American protectorate would be unwieldy; only direct U.S. ownership would establish peace and provide the necessary authority to govern. To avoid war with the United States, Spain should sell Cuba. Moret was skeptical. He did not believe the Spanish public would tolerate selling the island, and he also wondered if the American people would approve annexation. And would Washington be willing to assume the Cuban debt?[4]

The sale of Cuba also came up in other talks. American financiers made an offer to Moret to assist the Cubans in paying the island's debt in exchange for independence; Moret curtly rejected their approach. Woodford informally suggested to a Spanish businessman, Ramón García, who was in touch with Moret and Sagasta, that Spain sell the island. For a few hours Woodford thought that the queen regent seriously considered his suggestion, but she then changed her mind. Years later, the queen regent's court biographer wrote that an unofficial agent of the president had approached her with a proposal to buy Cuba for $300 million, with $1 million for bribes. The queen regent reported the offer to Sagasta and other Spanish politicians, and they unanimously advised against it. Although all the evidence demonstrated a strong Spanish opposition to selling the island, nevertheless Woodford believed that Moret and the cabinet would come to see the advantages of the proposal. Woodford was so confident of his reasoning that he asked McKinley for authority to treat if Spain made an offer, but the president never provided any instructions.[5]

McKinley also examined a plan of Cuban suzerainty. Oscar Straus, a former American minister to Turkey who was in touch with McCook, suggested to McKinley that Cuba assume a position of suzerainty toward Spain, much as Egypt did toward Turkey. In this way Spain would retain nominal sovereignty over the island, but the Cubans would be completely independent, as in the Middle Eastern example. This would satisfy Spain's honor and Cuba's national aspirations. Under such a settlement Cuba might pay an initial indemnity to Spain, loaned or guaranteed by the United States, and make a nominal annual payment from customs, which would imply the continuation of Spanish sovereignty. If the United States took part in the original financing, Straus pointed out, it would have the right to intervene on the island later should this become necessary. Since an initial indemnity and annual payment conformed to the Junta's contract with McCook, the Cubans should willingly accept such a settlement. McKinley was intrigued. On 19 March he examined suzerainty at length with Straus. On reflection, however, McKinley told Straus that although he liked the idea, he thought it would be hard to get the Junta members to agree, since they were "even more difficult than Spain to deal with." The president also did not think congressional jingoes would approve such a settlement.[6]

Another possibility was recognizing Cuban independence. In early March, McKinley discussed recognition with Reid, who advised against it. Reid did not believe that the Cubans possessed the attributes of nationhood, and he counseled the president against doing anything before the Cubans achieved an important military success, such as securing a port.[7]

The McKinley administration was also considering some of the knotty questions that would be raised if it used military force in Cuba. An American invasion might result in Cuban hostility, since there was no understanding with the Cuban Republic. If the United States ended up acquiring the island, international law indicated that it could be held accountable for the island's debts. Since the French held many Cuban bonds, refusal to honor the debt might provoke French hostility. International legal precedents suggested that to avoid the debt, the United States should disclaim all responsibility for it, deny any intention of annexing the island, and recognize Cuban independence.[8]

While McKinley and Woodford were searching for a means to remove Cuba from Spain, Moret was attempting to gain time for autonomy to succeed. At the beginning of March, Moret informed Woodford that Blanco had several complaints about the Americans: the captain general suspected that an American naval visit to Santo Domingo involved a liaison with the insurgents, he was fuming over the antics of sensational newspaper correspondents and was threatening to expel some of them from Havana, and he accused Lee of being openly proinsurgent and wondered if Washington would recall him. Woodford satisfied Moret that the naval visit had nothing to do with Cuba and that Washington was as embarrassed by sensational journalists as Havana.[9] The transfer of Lee was another matter. The press learned that Spain wanted Lee recalled, which provoked a national outcry and ringing congressional statements of support. McKinley strongly defended his consul general, and Moret accepted the inevitable, advising Blanco to drop the idea of removing Lee.[10]

Moret tried to influence Woodford through a prominent Spanish businessman, Ramón García, who had lived in the United States for many years and was married to an American. García was in the tobacco trade and thus was knowledgeable about Cuba. During several social meetings initiated by García, the influential businessman explained the Spanish point of view. Spain would never willingly sell or cede the island to the United States. Spain needed time to implement autonomy and would be unable to end the rebellion by the onset of the rainy season. García pointedly asked if the "United States [had] ever set any time limit for the suppression of the rebellion." Woodford responded negatively, but he urged García to have his government end the insurrection before the Cuban rains began.[11]

Despite the lack of diplomatic progress, Woodford turned optimistic as he and Moret attempted to find a means to settle the Cuban issue. On 19 March, Woodford, with Moret looking on, cabled McKinley for the general terms he wanted in a settlement. Woodford thought the Spanish government would offer a plan before 15 April "without compulsion and upon its own motion." Although Moret continued to insist that Spain would not cede Cuba, Woodford was convinced that the Spanish realized Cuba was lost and were only posturing while seeking a means to leave the island "and yet save Spanish honor."[12]

Woodford's request for terms arrived in Washington a few days before the *Maine* report, and McKinley spelled out what was needed to keep the peace. He asked for "full reparation" for the ship and the "certainty of prompt restoration of peace in Cuba." Unless Spain provided peace, ended starvation, and restored commerce, McKinley would "lay the whole question before Congress." Fifteen April was "none too early" to accomplish these ends.[13]

Armed with the president's program, Woodford told Moret that it was now up to Spain to suggest how to accomplish these ends. Moret arranged a meeting with Gullón on 23 March, when Woodford laid out

McKinley's demands. Since the State Department had not yet responded to Spain's 1 February note, Woodford decided to use the meeting to present American thinking on the entire Cuban situation. In a long, well-rehearsed exposition, Woodford described the situation in Cuba: the large loss of life, the horrors of reconcentration, the failure of military operations and autonomy, America's loss of property and commerce, and the destruction of the *Maine*. Gullón steadfastly defended Spanish accomplishments; he praised Blanco's efforts, which would succeed were it not for the Junta, and predicted that autonomy would be installed by the start of the rainy season. But Gullón also interjected a new idea. He asked for a delay until 4 May, when the Cuban parliament would convene and could arrange a peace. Woodford replied that Washington would accept no more delays.[14]

After Woodford departed, the Spanish cabinet met for several hours, and then Sagasta conferred with the queen regent. The cabinet believed the *Maine* situation should be settled through arbitration. As for the 15 April deadline, the cabinet backed Gullón's position that it was up to the Cubans to make peace, which required waiting for the insular elections in late April and the convening of the island's assembly in early May.[15] Sagasta also took the Spanish case to Madrid's press. The prime minister told journalists that there was a great distance between the words and the deeds of McKinley. The Spanish government questioned Woodford's repeated statements that McKinley wanted peace when it saw the United States preparing for war. Since neither McKinley nor Woodford paid any attention to Spanish viewpoints, it was the American government that was jeopardizing the peace that Spain so ardently desired.[16]

During Woodford's interview with Gullón, the minister of state had become suspicious that Woodford was exceeding his instructions. His criticism of Spain differed markedly from Day's statement to Polo that the *Maine* affair could be settled amicably. Gullón therefore requested Polo to investigate. Polo asked Day if Woodford's meeting with Gullón indicated a change in Washington's policies, and Day replied that Woodford had no new instructions. Day discussed the Madrid meeting in generalities; unwittingly, his denial and vagueness suggested that Woodford was acting without authority and was not keeping Washington informed. Certain that Woodford had exceeded his instructions, Polo asked Day to keep him fully in touch so that Washington and Madrid could act together. Day's agreement to inform Polo further undercut Woodford. Polo's report increased Gullón's suspicion of Woodford and Gullón's determination to resist him.[17]

Both Moret and Gullón fashioned responses to McKinley's program. The day after Woodford's meeting with Gullón, Moret said that the Spanish government was considering a means of meeting McKinley's demands. Speaking unofficially, Moret sounded Woodford on employing an armistice to end the Cuban fighting. Madrid was prepared to enforce an "immediate armistice or truce" on its army "provided the United States [could] secure the acceptance and enforcement" of a similar truce by the insurgents. Then Spain would empower the insular assembly with "all [the] necessary authority to negotiate and conclude" a comprehensive peace. Woodford asked what would happen if the autonomy government was unable to arrange a permanent peace with the insurgent government before 15 September, when the rainy season would end and Spanish military operations could be expected to resume. In such a case, Moret replied, the Spanish and American governments could "jointly compel both parties in Cuba to accept such settlement" as Spain and the United States approved. The two nations could agree to the details by 15 September. In effect, Moret was proposing that Spain and the United States cooperate to impose a solution on the Cubans. The next morning, however, Moret amended his remarks by noting that the insular government could do nothing that would "diminish or interfere with the constitutional power vested" in the central government.[18]

Woodford seized on Moret's trial balloon and advised McKinley that the plan had several important advantages. An armistice would immediately end the war; once ended, it would never be resumed. When the autonomy government treated with the insurgents, Spain would be recognizing the Cuban Republic, and the final result would be Cuban independence or American annexation. The proposal also invited direct American involvement in the island's affairs. Yet Woodford also recognized the difficulties; Cuban negotiations would incur delay, and the outcome was uncertain. As for Moret's last-minute proviso about the Spanish constitution, Woodford considered it unimportant. There was more significance in Spain's yielding further concessions after it had declared it would never do so. Woodford optimistically concluded that the Spanish government was searching for a way to get rid of Cuba and that McKinley could now keep the peace and get almost all that he wanted.[19]

Spanish flexibility was far less apparent in two official notes Gullón prepared in response to McKinley's demands. Gullón criticized Washington's sending the *Maine* report to Congress before receiving the results of Spain's investigation; by submitting it to a popular assembly without any corrective explanation, the McKinley administration was inviting a "national enthusiasm" rather than a resolution of differences. An "elementary sense of justice" required a careful discussion in a calm atmosphere in order to reconcile differing positions. Unresolved differences could be submitted to new investigations or settled by impartial judges. As for Cuba, Gullón reiterated that peace should be left to the insular parliament. Woodford asked Gullón if the Spanish government would be willing to enter into an armistice with the insurgents. Gullón responded that he would have to consult the cabinet but that he personally "feared that such armistice [was] impossible."[20]

Given the discrepancy between Gullón's combative and negative stance and Moret's cooperative peace feelers, Woodford returned to the colonial minister for clarification. Moret repeated everything he had said before. Reassured, Woodford proposed to McKinley that he be empowered to ask Gullón two questions: (1) did Gullón's formal notes and clarifying statements mean the same thing as Moret's proposals; and (2) if so, would Spain provide an armistice throughout the rainy season if the insurgent government did the same? If Gullón agreed, Woodford believed that "peace [could] be secured."[21]

McKinley's cabinet discussed Gullón's suggestion to turn peace making over to the autonomous government. The president was inclined to try it, but some cabinet members asked what would happen if the insurgents rejected a truce and refused to cooperate. How could the American government compel Gómez to stop fighting and to negotiate? Out of these discussions and Woodford's request for instructions came a plan that Day initially discussed with seven conservative senators. He wanted their advice and support before sending it to Woodford. Day explained that McKinley was considering asking Spain for three things: to concede an armistice, to negotiate with the insurgents on establishing autonomy, and to accept presidential arbitration if Spain reached no agreement with the Cubans. The senators pledged to support these propositions.[22]

But in the uproar over the *Maine*, this plan fell far short of meeting the expectations of most legislators. House Republicans, no longer willing to accept Reed's stifling authority, threatened to join the Democrats in voting for war. As legislators placed pressure on McKinley, he was forced to toughen his position. On 28 March, the *Maine* report arrived on Capitol

Hill and was directed to the appropriate House and Senate committees; Congress adjourned for the day. The surface calm was deceptive, since many felt that McKinley's laconic message accompanying the report did not adequately express national outrage. Given the rising clamor for retribution for the *Maine* and for removal of Spain from Cuba, congressmen were eager to vote. In the Senate, five members introduced resolutions on Cuba; the most important was Foraker's, which later became the basis for Senate action. Foraker called for Cuban freedom, recognition of the Cuban Republic, the immediate withdrawal of Spain, and authorization to use force to implement the resolution. Eleven House members offered Cuban resolutions to recognize Cuban independence or to declare war; most significantly, Republicans submitted all of them.[23]

Aroused House Republicans considered revolting against the leadership in order to bring the Cuban issue to a floor vote. The evening of 29 March, an informal group of forty-six dissatisfied Republicans met to voice their discontent with Reed, Hitt, and McKinley and to determine how to bring the Cuban issue to the floor as a Republican measure. The group attempted to find a common ground. They wanted their party to assume leadership of the Cuban issue and to dispel the idea that business dictated the party's policies. They agreed that Spain must leave Cuba, but they turned down voting an immediate declaration of war. Having failed to decide on how to proceed, they decided to speak to other House members and to reconvene the next evening.[24]

The next morning, 30 March, the Republican revolt spilled over into a House floor debate. Bailey introduced a resolution recognizing the independence of the Republic of Cuba. When Reed ruled the resolution out of order, Bailey appealed the procedural decision and attempted to open a debate. Reed produced an obscure precedent that he employed to quash floor action. During the procedural maneuvering, Adams moved about the floor promising Republicans that if the president did not produce a satisfactory diplomatic outcome by 4 April, the Foreign Affairs Committee would report a joint resolution recognizing Cuban independence. When the Republicans voted to sustain Reed's ruling, Democrats taunted them for breathing fire the previous evening and making a "humiliating surrender" the next day. The Democrats managed to get into the *Congressional Record* a statement that the Republicans had delivered "their solid vote . . . in opposition to any recognition of freedom for the Cuban patriots."[25]

During the day, McKinley met with a stream of worried Republicans and attempted to provide the assurances they wanted. House members were told that the president had sent an ultimatum to Spain to accept an armistice in Cuba. Many legislators objected to the American plan, however, since they saw it as forming an alliance with Spain to impose autonomy or some other settlement on the Cubans. An armistice was acceptable to them only as a means of hastening Spanish withdrawal from the island. McKinley assured visitors that Cuban independence was the only acceptable solution. If Spain did not make a favorable reply within a day or two, he promised to turn the Cuban issue over to Congress and accept its decision. Reed also promised House members that they would have an opportunity to vote on Cuba. Senator William E. Chandler, Republican of New Hampshire and an ardent Cuban supporter, observed the sharp change in McKinley's policy. A week before, the president had favored a settlement based on Cuban autonomy with some measure of Spanish sovereignty. Asked what he would do if the insurgents refused, the president had replied that they could "take care of themselves." But as a result of the House revolt, McKinley now wanted an armistice with negotiations leading to independence.[26]

That evening, 115 House Republicans attended a second informal meeting on Cuba. This time Republican leaders, such as Adams and Grosvenor, were present. During the discussion it appeared that over half of those present favored immediate intervention in Cuba; the disagreement was not over what to do but how long to wait. Michigan representatives reported an unsatisfactory visit to McKinley; they were still not certain what the president would do if Spain refused his ultimatum. Adams assured the group that they would have a chance to vote on Cuban independence, and Grosvenor told them that if needed, he would call a House Republican caucus on Cuba. With the understanding that a diplomatic decision was only hours away and that Congress would take up the Cuban issue by 4 April at the latest, the meeting broke up.[27]

The next day, Democrats again managed to bring up the Cuban issue. Taking the floor to speak on a naval appropriation bill, Bailey called for Republicans to recognize the Cuban Republic as a means of preventing war. He objected to the president's attempt to force the Cubans to purchase their independence; just give them recognition, Bailey said, and they would win their freedom. James H. Lewis, Democrat of Washington, accused McKinley of joining the nation's financial interests in an effort to stick the Cubans with a $200-million debt that would benefit the banks. Grosvenor asserted that Cuba would be free and gain its freedom "by the intervention of the United States." During several partisan exchanges, Bailey got off the best shot when he taunted the Republicans who wanted to vote for Cuban independence, calling them Reed's "caucus of reconcentrados."[28]

Behind the intense congressional interest in Cuba was the approaching national election. Many Republicans were afraid that the Democrats would capture the popular Cuban issue and at the same time tar the Republicans with the monied interests. Senator Knute Nelson, Republican of Minnesota, wrote James J. Hill: "A popular war might do more than anything else to relieve the country from the night mare [sic] of the free silver question. The success of Bryanism, Populism, and free silver would inflict infinitely more damage on this country than a short, sharp war with Spain." Lodge wrote that if the Republicans refused to go to war, Bryanites would win "a sweeping free silver victory" in the coming elections. Alger, urging a senator to tell McKinley "to declare war," said of the president: "He is in danger of ruining himself and the Republican party by standing in the way of the people's wishes. Congress will declare war in spite of him. He'll get run over and the party with him." Elihu Root sent McKinley a letter that circulated through the cabinet; he urged the president to get out in front and unite the nation as it entered a war. Without presidential leadership, the risk was "destruction of the President's party, ... [and] the elevation of the Silver Democracy to power." In the wings, Bryan declared: "Humanity demands that we shall act. . . . The sufferings of [Cuba's] people cannot be ignored unless we, as a Nation, have become so engrossed in money-making as to be indifferent to distress."[29]

Day repeatedly warned Woodford of the congressional mood. On 28 March he pressed Woodford for a "prompt answer on [the] armistice matter," and a day later he cautioned that feeling was "intense" and that it was of the "utmost importance" that "definite results" be achieved by 31 March. "There [was] profound feeling in Congress, and the gravest apprehension on the part of most conservative members that a resolution for intervention [might] pass both branches in spite of any effort which [could] be made. Only [an] assurance from the President that if he fail[ed] in peaceful negotiations he [would] submit all the facts to Congress at a very early day prevent[ed] immediate action on the part of Congress."[30]

Day also impressed on Polo the gravity of the situation. On 29 March he said that if Spain did not accept McKinley's plan, the president would not be able to prevent a break in relations. Congress had the authority to declare war, and the president was unable to resist the bellicose currents any longer. Despite the grave circumstances, Polo predicted that Madrid would reject the American plan; it had earlier turned down presidential arbitration because it involved U.S. intervention in Spain's internal affairs. Moreover, Polo did not understand how McKinley would be able to require the insurgents to respect an armistice. Day said the president could do so because the insurgents were dependent on the United States and could do nothing without the support of the American people; if the Cubans refused to cooperate, they would alienate public opinion, and the president would be free to side more openly with Spain. Polo acidly agreed that American support of the insurgents was crucial; without it, the rebellion would be over.[31] The next day Polo warned Gullón: "Congress converted into a madhouse. No [Spanish] concession would satisfy the partisans of a declaration of [Cuban] independence and war."[32]

The congressional rebellion stiffened and hurried McKinley's diplomacy. In a series of telegrams, the president escalated what Washington expected from Spain. On 26 March he separated the issue of the *Maine* from Cuba. About the ship, McKinley noted that the United States held the Spanish government responsible for the "protection to persons and property" within Havana harbor and relied on its "sense of justice . . . [to] dictate a course of action . . . [conforming] to the friendly relations between the two countries."[33] As for Cuba, McKinley asked for peace and relief for the sick and starving. Madrid's reforms had failed, and the existing misery on the island "shocked and inflamed the American mind." The United States did not want the island. To bring peace, McKinley asked Spain to end reconcentration, to provide for the people until they could support themselves, and to propose to the Cubans "full self-government, with reasonable indemnity." The president offered to mediate, if desired by Spain and the insurgents. A second telegram sent the next day spelled out a three-point plan. First, there should be an armistice until 1 October, during which Spain and the insurgents would negotiate peace through the "friendly offices" of McKinley. Second, Spain should immediately end reconcentration so that the Cuban people could return to their farms; Spain and the United States would cooperate in providing relief for those who were needy. Woodford was to obtain a third point if possible: if a satisfactory peace was not agreed on by 1 October, the United States should be the "final arbiter between Spain and [the] insurgents." If Spain adopted these steps, McKinley would use his "friendly offices to get [the] insurgents to accept [the] plan." In reply,

Woodford asked what "full self-government" and "reasonable indemnity" meant. On 28 March, Day answered: "Cuban independence."[34]

As in the United States, the mood in Spain was nationalistic and belligerent. *El Heraldo de Madrid* called for the government to champion the truth and to defend Spain's rights in the face of American duplicity, humiliation, and lies; to do otherwise would be moral suicide and intolerable. The Spanish government agreed. Under intense pressure, Sagasta, Moret, and Gullón met with the queen regent and declared their intention to uphold Spanish national pride. Sagasta assured journalists that Spain would stand behind its *Maine* report.[35]

With McKinley's instructions in hand, Woodford delivered the statement on the *Maine* to Gullón and asked for a meeting with Sagasta to discuss Cuba. The meeting took place the afternoon of 29 March and lasted a little over one hour; Gullón and Moret also attended, the latter serving as an interpreter. Woodford read McKinley's demands but did not leave a written note, thereby attempting to avoid the sense of an ultimatum. While presenting the armistice proposal, Woodford gave categorical assurances that McKinley could get the insurgents to adhere to it. He ended by insisting that the Spanish cabinet respond in forty-eight hours. Sagasta replied that reconcentration had been inherited from the previous ministry and that his government was providing relief and was willing to work with the United States in furthering the relief effort. Thus he could fully satisfy this request. Sagasta also believed the two governments could reach an honorable settlement on the *Maine*. As for an immediate end to the fighting in Cuba, Spanish domestic politics made it impossible for his cabinet to request an armistice; if the insurgents asked for one, however, the Spanish would promptly comply. Sagasta was prepared to empower the Cuban parliament to propose an armistice, and he hoped the United States, which had waited so long for peace, would accept six more weeks of delay. Sagasta expected Blanco's military operations to make further inroads on the insurgency by that time. The prime minister complained about being asked to reply in forty-eight hours, but he agreed to do so. When the meeting ended, Woodford was optimistic that the Spanish government would meet McKinley's demands.[36]

Sagasta assumed the task of framing a written response to McKinley's proposals. He began a series of conferences with cabinet ministers, other political leaders, and the queen regent. Moret threatened to resign if Spain did not respond positively. He believed an armistice would provide several months of delay during which the new Cuban regime could gain strength. Moret had queried Blanco about an armistice, and the response from Cuba was that the Spanish army officers would accept an armistice if agreed to by the insurgents and if it assured insular autonomy. Sagasta favored Moret's approach. But the other cabinet ministers, led by Gullón and Correa, opposed an armistice; they could not accept Washington's intervention and an ultimatum that violated Spain's national honor. Accordingly, Sagasta wrote a majority reply, which the cabinet reviewed and amplified but basically accepted. The Spanish cabinet met with the queen regent and explained the somber implications of its response; they expected war, and Spain could not count on any European military support. Sagasta also made a brief statement to the press.[37]

On the afternoon of 31 March, Sagasta, Gullón, and Moret met again with Woodford. The colonial minister read the reply in English. Woodford asked if there was anything else the Spanish wanted to say; there being nothing to add, the meeting ended after half an hour. Sagasta's formal reply was in four parts. The Spanish government offered to arbitrate differences over the *Maine*. It had requested Blanco to revoke reconcentration in Cuba's western provinces, which he had just done. The Spanish government had granted an additional three million pesetas for relief, and it was cooperating in distributing increased levels of American relief. As for ending the fighting in Cuba, the Spanish cabinet had decided to turn this issue over to the insular government, with the understanding that the insular government would not exceed the powers reserved by the Spanish constitution. Since the Cuban parliament would not assemble until 4 May, the Spanish government in the interim would accept a suspension of hostilities if the insurgents requested one and if Blanco approved the conditions and duration. There was no response to McKinley's offers of mediation and arbitration.[38]

Gullón explained to Polo that if the American government really wanted to avoid a war with Spain, it would have the insurgents request a suspension of hostilities. Polo replied that even if Spain agreed to all of McKinley's demands, this would not satisfy Congress, which had gone mad. The situation was "grave." Polo added, "Everything [was] to be feared from the Congress, as it had arrived at a condition of true insanity." Even McKinley had been surprised by the congressional rebellion. "If there [was] war it [would] be the responsibility of Congress, and not of [McKinley.]"[39]

Spain's press supported Sagasta's stand. *El Correo de Madrid* approved

Spain's rejection of the armistice, which amounted to "outside intervention" impinging "on Spain's national honor and affect[ing] the integrity of the nation." It was preferable "to succumb with glory than to live with a stigma of humiliation and cowardice." *El Heraldo de Madrid* was apoplectic in its denunciation of the armistice proposal and warned, "To abandon Cuba in the midst of a rebellion offended the nation's dignity; to give it to the Yankees . . . would be even more humiliating." *El Imparcial* intoned, "It is better to weep over lost loved ones than to live in shame and dishonor." [40]

Woodford was keenly disappointed. Spain's reply turned, as he had "feared, on a question of punctilio"; Spanish pride prevented the cabinet from offering an armistice. Yet Woodford went on to explain that if the Spanish government offered an armistice, it "would cause [a] revolution here." "The army [was] still the controlling factor in Spanish politics, and the attitude of the army constitute[d] the real danger." The ministry had sounded Spain's most important generals and gone as far as it could go; it was determined to "save the dynasty." Despite this appraisal of Sagasta's predicament, Woodford still remained hopeful. The cabinet knew that Cuba was lost, and it had gone much further than it had said it would only a month before. Public opinion was steadily moving toward peace, "but Spanish pride remain[ed] and common sense [came] late." [41]

At the White House on the evening of 31 March, McKinley was surrounded by close associates as he waited for Spain's reply. Hobart, Day, Alger, and Bliss were joined by Senators Allison, Aldrich, Spooner, and Hanna. Adee was on hand to decode. When they heard Sagasta's response, all agreed that it was unsatisfactory. The news quickly spread; Spain's reply was unacceptable, and the president would send a message on Cuba to Congress on 4 April. One cabinet member told waiting journalists that he had "little faith . . . in promises made by Spain" and therefore could not put "any confidence [in] her latest proposals." There was some talk of delivering a twenty-four-hour ultimatum to Madrid in an effort to see if the Spanish would back down, but the general feeling was that war could no longer be avoided. McKinley had no additional diplomatic initiatives to offer and expected nothing more from Spain. [42]

Spanish-American diplomatic efforts to solve the Cuban problem had ended. Washington and Madrid were unable to reconcile their differences. The *Maine* disaster had injected intense emotionalism into the Cuban question. Although Washington and Madrid tried to minimize and isolate the *Maine*, the incident compelled Washington to toughen the

U.S. stance, and it bolstered Spanish determination to resist American lies and pressures.

Timing was also important. The McKinley administration had long held that by 1 April there should be visible progress toward a settlement, which should be in place by 1 May. The Republican House revolt tightened this schedule by only a few days; nevertheless, McKinley was left with no leeway. Washington's unyielding deadline clashed with Madrid's attempt to shift the unpalatable Cuban decision to Havana's new parliament. Given Spain's constitutional restriction, however, one wonders how this new body could have in a few months brought the peace that had eluded Madrid for three years.

Moret attempted to use an armistice to bridge the one month that separated Washington and Madrid. Each side, however, perceived the armistice differently. The Americans considered it to be a means of easing Spain out of the island; the Spanish saw it as a way of strengthening autonomy in order to preserve Spanish sovereignty. An armistice was probably a moot issue anyway. The American government had neither the political will nor the physical ability to force the Cuban army to ask for an armistice, and the Spanish cabinet also lacked the political strength to require the Spanish army to request one.

Had there been no emotionalism over the *Maine*, would McKinley's diplomacy have fared any better? Probably not. The differences over Cuba were as large as ever. Time had run out, and neither Washington nor Madrid had any new proposals to offer. Only one remote possibility remained for a peaceful outcome. The Great Powers and the pope were about to enter the diplomatic field to seek a delay in American intervention and to halt the fighting in Cuba.

CHAPTER 10

. . . .

SPANISH

. . . .

SUSPENSION OF

. . . .

HOSTILITIES

. . . .

War seemed inevitable when the European powers and the pope entered the crisis. In response to their efforts, McKinley postponed his message to Congress, and the Spanish authorized a suspension of hostilities. But the Cubans were not a part of these last-minute efforts, and the fundamental differences that divided the three protagonists remained.

Although the McKinley administration was committed to sending a Cuban message to Congress on 4 April, the deadline was extended two days. The pressure on McKinley decreased on 1 April when it was learned that the Spanish torpedo boats had gotten only as far as the Cape Verde Islands and were not yet ready to cross the Atlantic. Moreover, Day and John W. Griggs, who had replaced McKenna as attorney general, needed time to draft the presidential message. The White House notified congressional leaders that it would delay the Cuban message until 6 April, which Congress accepted.

During the first week of April the Great Powers and Pope Leo XIII took a larger role in attempting to find a peaceful solution to the crisis. When the signs of American intervention had first appeared during the Cleveland administration, Spain had sought diplomatic support from the European powers. The European foreign offices had expressed varying degrees of sympathy, but until April 1898 they had rebuffed Spain's repeated entreaties to enter the controversy. The European nations were divided and unwilling to antagonize the United States over Cuba.

Madrid found the greatest sympathy in Paris and Vienna. The French historically had a close association with Spain, shared a common border, and held much of the Spanish debt. They were also concerned about American expansionism; after Cuba, what would be Washington's next target in the West Indies? In Austria-Hungary, the Hapsburg monarchy wanted the queen regent to retain her throne, and Vienna held a prominent position in Madrid through Ambassador Viktor Dubsky, who was the doyen of the diplomatic corps and on good terms with the queen regent. Austria-Hungary also felt freer to organize and lead a European coalition to support Spain because it had no New World possessions and little American commerce. But Vienna had little influence in Washington, and neither Austria-Hungary nor France was willing to act alone.

The other European powers were even more cautious. Great Britain, second only to France in importance to Spain, was pro-American. The Sagasta ministry watched England carefully not only because of extensive commercial relations but also because of its large Atlantic fleet, Gibraltar, North Africa, and Suez. Without British participation, the other European states refused to act, and London would do nothing unless the United States approved it in advance. Britain displayed such cordiality toward Washington that the Europeans suspected the existence of a secret Anglo-Saxon alliance.

The other European powers were more distant from the controversy. The German government chose a neutral policy even though the kaiser, Wilhelm II, was outspokenly pro-Spanish and friendly to the queen regent. The German chancellor and foreign minister, Prince Bernhard von Bülow, was determined to keep on good terms with Washington. American commercial interests far outweighed those of Spain, and the chancellor was wary of allowing London to obtain special influence in Washington. At the same time he did not want to appear too remote, which might drive the Spanish into closer relations with France. The Russian government assumed a cold and distant attitude toward Spanish troubles;

it played a largely negative role by functioning as a brake on French impulses to help Spain. Russian influence in Washington during the crisis was negligible, since its ambassador was absent. The Italian government was unimportant in both Washington and Madrid.[1]

Pope Leo XIII became involved because he wanted to help the queen regent. The Vatican historically had close ties to Catholic Spain. In addition, the pope had a fatherly protective feeling for the pious young widow on the Spanish throne. He was godfather to her son, and he feared a disastrous war might topple the monarchy.[2]

Prince Otto von Bismarck, the ex-chancellor of Germany, made the first recommendation for papal diplomatic involvement. In February 1898 he suggested that Spain might avoid war by asking the pope to arbitrate the Cuban affair. Sagasta sharply rejected the proposition on the grounds that Spain would not submit Cuba to arbitration. Terming Bismarck's proposal "absurd," Sagasta asserted Spain's sovereign right to complete freedom of action over all its territories; Madrid's press applauded Sagasta's stout declaration.[3]

In early March the queen regent began to take an active part in Spanish diplomacy. Up to this time Moret had dominated foreign policy, in part because of his close association with Woodford. But the queen regent had kinship ties and personal relationships with the crowned heads of Europe, and she acted in the realm of Spanish-European relations. Gullón continued to play a lesser role, tending to assert Spanish patriotism rather than to attempt to find solutions. Sagasta also remained in the background of foreign affairs, devoting his energies to keeping together the cabinet, the Liberal Party, and the nation.

With war clouds gathering, the Spanish government was still trying to obtain European support. Paris and Berlin agreed to send gunboats to Manila harbor to show their interest as the American naval buildup proceeded in the Pacific, but no nation would take the diplomatic lead for a demarche in Washington. When the $50-million bill caused a war scare in Madrid, the queen regent began personal diplomacy. She begged the Austrian ambassador to carry her case to Emperor Franz Josef I. With tears streaming down her face, she told Dubsky that in all her years in Spain and through many difficulties she had never once asked for special consideration from the emperor, but now she feared for her son's throne. Franz Josef responded warmly, and for the remainder of the crisis, Austria-Hungary took a leading role in working to advance and coordinate European steps.[4] The queen regent also asked Queen Victoria to influence Salisbury, and she pressed the French ambassador to help Spain. But Cambon warned Hanotaux that the "American national spirit" would not tolerate outside intervention and that the time had not yet come for a friendly European initiative in favor of peace.[5]

Two weeks later, when McKinley announced that he was submitting the *Maine* report to Congress, Gullón appealed to all nations with which Spain had diplomatic relations, asking for understanding and help. He expected the *Maine* report, accompanied by a message on Cuba, to provoke congressional resolutions leading to war. Convinced of Spanish rectitude, Gullón notified the Great Powers that if McKinley acted unilaterally, Spain would ask for their counsel and mediation to prevent a war that might affect all of Europe.[6]

As usual, the European response disappointed Madrid. Berlin, St. Petersburg, and Rome were sympathetic but noncommittal. Even the Austrians and the French hedged their desire to help Spain. Vienna suggested that Madrid wait until both the American and the Spanish reports on the *Maine* were available, at which time the European powers would learn what differences existed; then the Spanish could propose arbitration. Moreover, Vienna wanted assurances that London would cooperate. Paris was more accommodating and asked the English and Russian governments if they were willing to join in a friendly representation to Washington. London agreed to speak to Washington about the Spanish situation but advised that a joint European demarche was premature because McKinley opposed it. The Spanish and the Americans should be left to work out their differences. At the end of a round of consultations, Hanotaux observed that France would participate in a demarche only if all the Great Powers took part and if the McKinley administration welcomed it in advance. At the same time, he encouraged Madrid to delineate those points separating Spain and the United States to see if mediation might be possible.[7]

Among the sympathetic responses Gullón received to his circular appeal was the one penned by Cardinal Mariano Rampolla del Tindaro, the Vatican secretary of state. McKinley's lack of good faith in handling the *Maine* dispute had upset the cardinal. Since the Vatican had no diplomatic representative in Washington, Rampolla suggested that Madrid rely on France, which had a Republican government and therefore was closer to the United States. Despite the rebuff, Gullón asked Dubsky to tell the papal nuncio, Giuseppe Francisca Nava di Bontifé, that Spain was willing to arbitrate differences with the United States and would welcome the pope as a mediator.[8]

The next day Francisca Nava informed Rampolla that all the European chancelleries had turned down Gullón's circular appeal. At the same time, the Austrian, German, and Russian ambassadors had encouraged Gullón to suggest that the pope arbitrate the Cuban problem; the Spanish government appeared willing to accept mediation by the pope. Gullón had not directly approached Francisca Nava, but the Spanish foreign minister wanted European intervention that might take this form. Francisca Nava speculated that the German and Russian envoys looked to the Vatican because they wanted to prevent France from assuming a more prominent role in Spanish affairs.[9]

The pope responded on 27 March by asking Archbishop Ireland to go to Washington to do what he could to maintain peace. Rampolla contacted Ireland through Archbishop John J. Keane, who was on assignment at the Vatican. A close friend of Ireland's, Keane cabled the archbishop to try to get the United States to agree to arbitrate the conflicting *Maine* reports and to abstain from intervening in Cuba. Keane warned Rampolla that Spain would have to be more forthcoming about the *Maine*. Since it was evident that an external explosion had sunk the ship, Spain should accept the responsibility and blame the deed on vicious individuals. Rampolla passed this idea to Madrid, and Keane informed Ireland that the pope was using his influence in Spain.[10]

Ireland, unusually well connected in Washington, was a good choice for the assignment. A chaplain during the Civil War, the archbishop of St. Paul was a lifelong champion of the Union and the Republican Party. Energetic, enthusiastic, and able, Ireland was a friend of McKinley's and had campaigned for him in 1896 in a region that was politically important. Minnesota was also significant because the chairman of the Senate Foreign Relations Committee, Cushman K. Davis, came from there. As a result of being educated in France, Ireland was well known to Jules Cambon, the French ambassador in Washington. An ambitious church leader who longed to become a cardinal, Ireland was also wary of the many pitfalls of the assignment. The Vatican wanted him to use his influence with McKinley to keep the peace, but this might run counter to American public opinion and the Protestant majority, and Ireland was determined to avoid identifying American Catholics as pro-Spanish and unpatriotic. Thus Ireland's mission began with conflicting purposes:

Rampolla wanted to restrain American jingoism, and Ireland sought to please the Vatican but to do nothing that might embarrass patriotic Catholics.[11]

Arriving in Washington on 1 April with vague instructions and limited information, Ireland called on McKinley to offer his help. The president warmly greeted him, explained the American diplomatic demands that Spain had rejected only hours before, discussed the difficult congressional situation, and welcomed any assistance Ireland could give. The president provided no new initiatives; he emphasized the importance of an armistice but did not expect Ireland to produce any results in Madrid. The archbishop then visited Capitol Hill and called on Cambon.[12]

Ireland's first report to Rampolla ended up in a diplomatic controversy that set back the mediation scheme. The archbishop wired that McKinley "ardently wishe[d] for peace and help to obtain it." The pope and Rampolla tied this message to another from Madrid. Supported by the queen regent, Dubsky, Woodford, and Josef von Radowitz, the German ambassador, had asked the nuncio to request the pope to recommend a suspension of hostilities. Putting together the information from Washington and Madrid, the Vatican thought that the American government favored papal mediation. Rampolla, therefore, informed the Spanish government that McKinley was "well disposed to accept the offices of the Pope," and the cardinal asked if the cabinet would welcome a papal request for an armistice that "would save the national honor." Sagasta's government decided on a conditional acceptance of McKinley's alleged initiative: Spain would order a suspension of hostilities if the United States first accepted the pope's mediation and also accompanied the truce with a withdrawal of its ships from Cuban waters, which would discourage the insurgents.[13]

On 3 April, Gullón explained the Spanish reply to Woodford, who was surprised by Gullón's reference to McKinley's offer. Woodford had encouraged the nuncio, but he had heard nothing from Washington. He doubted that McKinley had suggested papal mediation and thought there was some confusion. Nevertheless, Woodford believed that the Spanish offer met Washington's requirement for an armistice, and he urged McKinley to accept. The allegation that McKinley had requested papal mediation became public knowledge when Gullón informed journalists of Spain's conditional acceptance.[14]

When the news reached Washington, McKinley emphatically denied that he had asked the pope to mediate or that he would accept papal mediation. Day assured Woodford that the president negotiated with Spain only through him and that McKinley had made no overture to the Vatican. Moreover, the United States would not reposition its fleet at Madrid's request. If Spain was to provide an armistice, it must be immediate and result in Cuban independence.[15]

The American denial angered both Woodford and Gullón. Woodford complained to Sagasta that Gullón had deliberately misled him again, much like Gullón had during the de Lôme affair; since he could not trust the minister of state's word, Woodford would no longer deal with him. If the Spanish government had a message to give Woodford, the cabinet should write it out and sign it. This emotional outburst limited Woodford's effectiveness for the rest of the time he was in Madrid.[16] At the same time, Gullón was stung by Washington's denial and Spanish criticism and demanded that his ambassador to the Vatican, Rafael Merry del Val, determine who had erred. Rampolla denied that he was at fault, implying that the pope was responsible for mixing up and misconstruing several messages on the same topic. On the other hand, Francisca Nava criticized Gullón for making too much of Rampolla's telegram and then going public. Interestingly, neither Madrid nor the Vatican accused Ireland or McKinley of causing the error. Nevertheless, Ireland noted that McKinley was now more reserved toward him.[17]

Despite the angry charges and finger pointing, the queen regent and Moret continued to support papal mediation. Moret also prepared Blanco to accept a suspension of hostilities. Pointing out that a cease-fire was difficult to arrange, Moret doubted that McKinley could impose an armistice on the insurgents or that he had adequate time to get the Cubans to act; therefore, Washington expected Spain to take the lead. Moret had proposed to the cabinet that the autonomy government initiate the first step, but everyone vacillated. The public was growing anxious; Moret noted, "No one wants war." From differences over how to proceed hung "this most grave conflict." Correa was part of Moret's frustration; he argued that any suspension of hostilities should last for only a few days in order to allow the insurgents to surrender their arms, and he vowed to resign from the cabinet if Madrid ordered an end to the fighting against the wishes of the Spanish army.[18]

Meanwhile in Washington, Ireland was meeting with senators and diplomats to rally support for McKinley's three-point plan to prevent war: armistice, negotiations, and presidential arbitration. Because the president did not want the archbishop to appear frequently at the White

House, he designated Senator Elkins as a contact. To get the peace process moving, Ireland and Elkins decided to appeal to Polo to use his influence in Madrid. On 3 April the three men met at Elkins's home and exhaustively reviewed the situation. During the talks Polo vehemently objected to having McKinley arbitrate a final settlement. In the end, Ireland and Elkins agreed to wave presidential arbitration if Spain conceded an armistice. They believed that conservative senators would support this modification in McKinley's plan. Ireland promised to have the Vatican urge Spain to offer an armistice, and Polo said he would inform Madrid of Ireland's efforts in Washington. After the meeting Ireland asked Cambon to employ French influence in Madrid.[19]

When Elkins told McKinley of Ireland's progress, the president was unenthusiastic and little interested. He believed Vatican involvement came too late to change Spain's position. A few hours later, it was learned that the pope had asked Madrid to grant an armistice, but McKinley was still unimpressed, since he did not think the insurgents would agree to it. Elkins retorted that if the Cubans refused to cooperate and the result was a Spanish-American war, then the United States should annex Cuba, Puerto Rico, and the Philippine Islands as an indemnity for the war. At McKinley's request, Elkins made this threat to McCook; Elkins also warned him that the only way the Cubans would gain their independence was through making common cause with the United States. McCook doubted that the Cubans would accept an armistice, but he promised to pass on Elkins's stern warnings to the Junta. Polo told Madrid that the administration had contacted Estrada Palma and was placing pressure on the Junta to cooperate.[20]

Both Woodford and Ireland obtained assurances on 5 April that the Spanish ministry was considering a suspension of hostilities. Francisca Nava told Woodford that the queen regent was ready to accept the holy father's request to order a suspension of hostilities, which would take effect as soon as the insurgents agreed to it and would last until 5 October. During the cease-fire the Cuban autonomy government would negotiate with the insurgents to bring about a permanent and honorable peace. Rampolla cabled Ireland that the queen regent had consented to place the "honor of the Spanish army and the vital interests of the monarchy" in the pope's hands by granting an armistice. Rampolla asked Ireland to do his best to get Washington to recall the American navy from Cuban waters, which would bolster the Spanish government, given the "difficult" public opinion.[21]

After consulting Day, Ireland replied that the president could not recall the navy because of the threatening nature of Congress. But if Spain granted a "definite and unconditional" armistice, the fleet would no longer be needed in Cuban waters; since there was danger from yellow fever during the summer months, Washington could be expected to move the fleet. Spain would have to trust the American government to reassign the ships. Ireland assured Rampolla that the McKinley administration was attempting to get the Cubans to accept an armistice and that these efforts were expected to "bring results." McKinley's message to Congress would oppose recognition of Cuban independence; the president's stand would probably lead to extended congressional debate and thus would delay passage of a resolution. As soon as Spain acted, Ireland promised, McKinley would inform Congress. In a follow-up telegram, Ireland added Cambon's view that U.S. ships stationed in Key West were in an American harbor and not Cuban waters and that Spain could not expect to have a nation move its ships from its own harbors.[22]

On 5 April a peaceful outcome began to seem possible. The Spanish authorities were ending reconcentration, and Spain appeared to be receptive to an armistice. But additional time was needed. Although McKinley's message was scheduled for delivery the next day, Congress was not planning to consider it until two days later, and congressional deliberation might last for several days. During this time the European powers could make an appeal to Washington for restraint, which might calm the atmosphere and provide even more time. Taking all these elements together, there might still be time to bring about a cease-fire.[23]

McKinley decided to use the Great Powers to gain support. The Europeans were eager to make a gesture in favor of peace, and on 5 April, Day set the diplomats in motion. He told British Ambassador Julian Pauncefote, the dean of the diplomatic corps, that the United States would welcome a European collective appeal in the interest of peace in order to calm public opinion. Using an Austrian draft furnished by Pauncefote, Day edited it to suit his needs. Pauncefote then assembled the diplomats, who approved the message and cabled their respective foreign offices for instructions. They planned to deliver the joint note on 6 April, but St. Petersburg's response was tardy; the note was dated 6 April, but the demarche took place at noon the next day.[24]

The collective note was brief, and McKinley responded with a prepared rejoinder. The six diplomats appealed to America's "humanity and moderation" and hoped that "further negotiations" would keep the peace and reestablish order in Cuba. The president replied that he shared their hopes but pointed to Cuba's "chronic" disturbances, which injured American interests and troubled its "tranquillity" while "shocking its sentiment of humanity." He welcomed the efforts of the European powers to keep the peace and trusted that they appreciated America's "earnest and unselfish endeavors" to end a situation that had become "insufferable."[25] The impact of this polite exchange of views was minimal. The McKinley administration could point to Europe's backing for further negotiations, but Congress was unmoved. The Spanish were deeply disappointed that the intervention of the Great Powers, which they had sought for so long, was toothless.[26]

While Day was orchestrating Europe's diplomatic initiative, McKinley obtained an additional delay for his message to Congress. On 4 April, Lee asked Washington to postpone taking any action that might result in war so that the consuls and other Americans, estimated at about one thousand, would have time to leave the island. The State Department sent a copy of Lee's request to Davis to alert the Senate Foreign Relations Committee and another copy to Spooner, who was the White House contact with the conservative senators supporting McKinley.[27]

Washington's residents were greatly excited on the morning of 6 April; everybody expected the president to send his Cuban message to Congress. A crowd estimated at ten thousand waited at the Capitol. But in the morning, Lee again appealed to Day for a delay: "If message can be withheld until Monday 11th can arrange everything. If sent before will have trouble here." McKinley huddled with Day, Griggs, Long, and Alger and then called for Senators Davis, Lodge, and Frye and Representatives Adams, Nelson Dingley, Jr., and Joe Cannon. Surrounded by these administrative and legislative leaders, McKinley dramatically declared that he was postponing his message. Asserting that he did not want to endanger the lives of American citizens in Cuba, he announced that he would not send his message to Congress until 11 April. The president said nothing about Spain's expected armistice or the Great Powers's collective action, which was hours away. Since Long argued against additional delay—reasoning that Congress would take several days to act, during which time Americans would have ample time to leave the island—it appears that the president's diplomatic purposes were a tightly held secret.[28]

Congress was surprised and upset by the delay, but the weight of Lee's request carried the day. A rump session of dissident Republicans, about fifty strong, met to discuss how to force the issue. They considered voting with the Democrats to adjourn until McKinley's message arrived, but since an army appropriation bill had to be passed, they decided to complete the business before the House and adjourn until 11 April.[29] The next day some disgruntled representatives used the army appropriation bill to condemn McKinley's vacillation, Republican ties to big business, and Spanish misrule. Representative William Sulzer, Democrat of New York, characterized McKinley as "weak and wabbling" and the House leadership as "impotent." Spanish government was "one long, unending, hideous carnival of crime, of public plunder, of rapine, of official robbery, of cruel, torturing death—a frightful big black blot on the pages of civilization." John J. Lentz, Democrat of Ohio, labeled Hanna, McCook, McKinley, and Wall Street as the peace party that was manipulating the Cuban situation to aid Spanish bondholders. Defending McKinley, Grosvenor insisted that the administration would yield no more and that peace would come only if Spain granted independence to Cuba. After acting on the army appropriation bill, Congress took an Easter recess until 11 April.[30]

One essential component of peace was Cuban compliance with an armistice. The Cuban position was well known: the Junta would accept an armistice if it was preceded by recognition of the Cuban Republic and independence. Gómez had vowed to stop fighting only to allow Spanish troops to leave the island. Nevertheless, the Junta feared that a Spanish-American war might result in American military occupation and annexation of the island. The McKinley administration tried to use this threat to get the Junta to accept an armistice. The probable channel was Elkins and McCook. The Junta learned on 4 April that McKinley was preparing to intervene without recognizing Cuban independence and two days later that the president wanted them to accept an armistice and negotiate a settlement allowing some form of Spanish sovereignty. The Cuban reply was vitriolic. In several press interviews Rubens categorically denounced these ideas. He lambasted "peace-at-any-price" financiers who wanted to seize Cuba to pay for the war and to provide an indemnity for the *Maine*. The United States might annex or sell the island as well as Puerto Rico and the Philippines, but Rubens reminded reporters of Cuban sacrifices in blood and treasure and vowed that Cubans would not be treated as cattle and passed along as property when the title of the land changed hands. They would rather die fighting than be "sold like slaves." Either the United States recognized Cuban independence when it intervened or it faced a rebellion. If the United States landed armed forces on the island without recognizing the Cuban government, Cuban patriots would consider it a declaration of war against the revolution and would resist the United States as bitterly as they had Spain.[31]

Rubens's heated outbursts embarrassed other Cuban leaders. Quesada and Estrada Palma, who had been called to Washington, feared that Rubens's tough talk would lessen congressional support; although they criticized his performance, they held firm to recognition and independence. Testifying before the House Foreign Affairs Committee, Estrada Palma explained that the Cubans considered themselves already free of Spanish control and that they would resist any attempt "to compel them to pay a new allegiance to the sovereignty of Spain." As for an armistice, if the United States first recognized Cuban independence and the Republic of Cuba and if Spain then offered an armistice, the Cubans would accept an armistice as a means to bring peace to the island. Gómez made a similar statement in Cuba. In effect, the Cubans were unmoved, and they turned the initiative back on McKinley; if he wanted their cooperation, he would first have to recognize them.[32]

One of the Cubans' problems affecting their negotiating ability was the loose nature of their organization. The Cuban government, which met infrequently, was not in session in April when the negotiations for a cease-fire were under way. The Junta in New York had no cable connection with Gómez. Estrada Palma wrote letters to Gómez, but he could never be certain that they would reach their destination or how long they would take. Gómez often communicated through proclamations and press releases. Estrada Palma had no authority to agree to an armistice that would halt the Cuban army; only Gómez could do that. Atkins understood the communications problem, and in mid-April he arranged, through Polo, for a telegraphic link between Estrada Palma and Gómez. But his efforts to bring the Cubans into the negotiations came too late. As a result, during the last-minute Spanish-American diplomatic activity, the Cubans were unable to consult rapidly and fully; of necessity, they clung steadfastly to their basic commitment to independence and recognition.[33]

As McKinley tried to restrain Congress, to elicit a Spanish armistice, and to moderate the Cuban stance, the Spanish government began giving ground. Polo announced on 5 April that he had made a mistake about the repeal of reconcentration in Cuba; instead of the decree covering only the western four provinces of the island, Blanco had actually ended reconcentration throughout the island.[34] But the Madrid government remained divided. Correa and the conde de Xiquena, the minister of production, gave an extraordinary press interview in which they criticized Moret and rashly spoke of fighting the Americans in Cuba and on the peninsula. They predicted that if the Spanish ministry failed to uphold the nation's honor and rights, it would face civil war at home. Their dissension led to speculation that the ministry was about to fall, but Sagasta denied to journalists that a ministerial crisis existed.[35] At the same time, the queen regent was encouraging a papal request. Her majordomo assured Francisca Nava and Dubsky that the Spanish cabinet would accept a Vatican offer. Woodford added his support by promising that if Spain approved, McKinley would prevent hostile congressional action. But when the nuncio went to the palace to arrange the details with the queen regent, he was astonished to learn that she had given an assurance without cabinet approval and wanted him to persuade ministers to accept it.[36]

On the evening of 6 April the cabinet, still divided, met at the palace to discuss what to do about a papal appeal for peace, which was expected at any hour. While the cabinet was in session at six o'clock, Woodford had a special messenger give Gullón a letter that criticized the ministry for its delay and asked that it proclaim an armistice by midnight. Woodford mistakenly believed that McKinley had delivered his message to Congress at noon. Woodford had waited anxiously all day for news of a Spanish proclamation and thought that a few hours still remained for the Spanish cabinet to act before Congress began to debate. Instead of encouraging the cabinet, however, Woodford brought its deliberations to a halt. The ministers had assembled to consider a papal plea for peace; instead they got an American six-hour "ultimatum." If they ended the fighting now, it would appear that the Spanish had bowed to American pressure. Accordingly, Gullón wrote Woodford a laconic reply that stiffly declared that the Spanish position of 29 March was unchanged, and the ministers left the palace before the pope's appeal arrived.[37]

Hours later, Francisca Nava carried the papal request to Gullón, who was still fuming over Woodford's letter. Together the two men went to Sagasta's home. The prime minister did not want to respond until he had heard from Blanco, and he pessimistically predicted that the Spanish army in Cuba would oppose a cease-fire. Nevertheless, he telephoned three other ministers to come to his house for an informal midnight meeting to consider the pope's appeal. After a general discussion it became clear that Gullón, Correa, and Alejandro Groizard, the minister of justice and grace, opposed conceding a suspension of hostilities; only Moret approved. Sagasta promised Francisca Nava an early official response, and the next morning Gullón told the nuncio that the Spanish cabinet had decided to postpone action. He explained that on the one hand Woodford had presented an ultimatum and that on the other hand McKinley had delayed his message until 11 April. It was unclear just what policy the American government was following, and therefore the cabinet was waiting for clarification.[38]

The diplomatic community was appalled by Woodford's blunder. Rampolla called it an "unpardonable indiscretion"; Dubsky said it was an "indescribable" act. Cambon thought that Woodford had destroyed the chance for peace; if the Great Powers and the Spanish government had acted simultaneously on 7 April, the one calling for continued negotiations and the other proclaiming a suspension of hostilities, Cambon thought that during the next four days McKinley could have calmed American public opinion and pressured the Cubans to accept a diplomatic settlement.[39] Cambon's analysis seems overly optimistic, given the mood of the nation, Congress, and the Cubans.

The Spanish government became more cooperative as developments appeared to favor its position. On 7 April, Woodford retracted his "ultimatum," and the Great Powers made their joint appeal to McKinley. The Spanish also observed the growing rift between the insurgents and the McKinley administration. And Ireland kept insisting that Spain's failure to act was hampering McKinley's efforts to keep the peace, warning that the president was "provoked" by Madrid's holdout, which was undermining him.[40]

With circumstances improving, the cabinet considered a formal reply to the pope's appeal. On the evening of 7 April the ministers assembled at Sagasta's home. Having stood up to Woodford and received the plaudits of the public, they were more united but at the same time were unwilling to alter their stance. The cabinet decided to accept the pope's appeal, with conditions. Gullón explained to Francisca Nava that the cabinet appreciated the pope's efforts on behalf of peace and would accede if the Vatican could guarantee three things. The United States must accept mediation first, not deny it as on 3 April; the United States must agree to withdraw its ships from Cuban waters; and the United States must give assurances that the Cubans would accept a suspension of hostilities. Francisca Nava realized the Spanish conditions were a rejection.[41]

Some cabinet ministers explained to Madrid's waiting journalists that the papal effort had failed because of the United States. In the first place, they were unable to understand how papal involvement, which had begun as a gesture on behalf of Spain, resulted in Vatican pressure to end the fighting in Cuba. But they doubted that any step Madrid took would have a positive effect on Washington, since the Americans were determined to start a war. If McKinley was unable to keep Congress in line, what hope did the Spanish government have of influencing it? Why should Spain make unpopular concessions to the United States when a collision was coming anyway? Rather it was the duty of the government to uphold Spain's honor and to rally the nation to meet the threat.[42]

The nuncio carried Gullón's conditional acceptance of the pope's appeal to Sagasta. Appearing quite worried and thoughtful, the prime minister explained that he did not dare suspend hostilities in Cuba. Ending the fighting might cause a popular uprising and, even worse, perhaps a rebellion within the ranks of the Spanish army or the Cuban volunteers. Besides, he did not believe that the Cuban insurgents would honor a suspension of hostilities. The Spanish government had originally accepted the Vatican's offer because it had mistakenly believed that McKinley had asked for papal mediation. After the American president denied this and stated that he remained committed to turning the Cuban issue over to Congress, Spanish-American relations remained unchanged, and the Americans were following their usual negative and belligerent course. The only positive news was the demarche of the Great Powers and the delay until 11 April, which provided some time to think. Nevertheless, Sagasta promised to reconsider and told the nuncio not to take Gullón's answer as final.[43]

Francisca Nava and Dubsky met on 8 April to see what might be done, and they also talked to the queen regent's majordomo. At her request they decided to organize a Great Power appeal to the Spanish government, much like the one just carried out in Washington. The nuncio set out to get support from leading politicians, such as Silvela, Gamazo, and the brother of Alejandro Pidal, and Dubsky used his position as doyen to convoke the envoys of the major powers at the German ambassador's house.[44] Since the Russian ambassador could not be located, Patenôtre volunteered to inform him. It was well after midnight before the diplomats agreed for all to assemble that morning at the home of Gullón and each to make an identical statement: "It seems to us that under the circumstances the Spanish government should accept the advise of the Holy Father and decree a suspension of hostilities which can bring peace to

Cuba without damaging the honor of the Spanish army." The envoys decided to act individually instead of collectively because there was insufficient time to obtain additional instructions from their home offices.[45]

On 9 April at ten o'clock, the six diplomats assembled at Gullón's house. It was apparent that he expected them and had decided how to handle their demarche. Although the envoys were to make separate statements, Gullón chose to treat them as a group; this made their gathering appear similar to the one in Washington. Instead of listening to each in turn, Gullón turned to Dubsky. After the Austrian had read the prepared statement, Gullón asked what would happen if Spain granted a suspension of hostilities and the Cubans refused to honor it. The diplomats replied that Spain would have done everything it could for peace and would have won the sympathy of the world; at the same time, the Cubans would have lost it.[46]

Gullón carried the message to the palace, where Sagasta and the queen regent were waiting. Correa soon joined them, and he reluctantly agreed to support an end to the fighting. Correa later explained that if Spain had turned down the request, it would have been completely isolated from the rest of the world. The European powers understood national honor and would not advise anything detrimental to Spain. He could have resigned, but his replacement would have faced an extremely difficult position. If the United States made no further concessions, such as withdrawing its ships from Cuban and Philippine waters, then the Great Powers should ask the United States to dissolve the Junta and end its moral support of the rebels. Moreover, during a cease-fire, Spain could continue to build up its forces in Puerto Rico, the Canary Islands, the Balearic Islands, and on the peninsula. Correa failed to mention that Martínez de Campos had come out in favor of conceding a suspension of hostilities. With Correa won over, Sagasta assembled the entire cabinet, which authorized Blanco to decree an immediate suspension of hostilities for as long as he thought prudent to arrange and facilitate peace in Cuba.[47] Gullón immediately informed the waiting diplomats and cabled Spain's diplomatic posts, explaining that it was now up to the United States to withdraw its fleet and use its influence on the insurgents. The queen regent also asked that McKinley moderate his message to Congress, which would help calm Spanish public opinion.[48]

In sum, by ordering a suspension of hostilities, the Spanish government hoped to gain European backing. It expected McKinley to soften his message to Congress, to withdraw his ships, and to get the insurgents to stop fighting. If the president failed to do so, Madrid wanted the Great Powers to side openly with Spain and to pressure Washington to end its support of the Junta.[49]

The Spanish public was divided over the ministry's announcement. There were riots and street demonstrations in Madrid, Barcelona, and Valencia. In Madrid, working-class demonstrators denounced the United States and shouted: "Viva España! Viva el ejército!" Republicans and Carlists denounced the decision, and Don Carlos left Venice for Brussels, presumably threatening to return to Spain to lead an uprising. The military press was outraged; for instance, *Correspondencia Militar* trumpeted rebellion, calling on the military to topple the government of "imbeciles and cowards." The more moderate press, such as *El Imparcial*, criticized the powers for pressuring Spain to give an armistice and not forcing the Cubans to do so as well. It opposed having the Spanish army surrender in the face of Gómez and García, which was dishonorable and unacceptable. Spain should extend a truce only to accept the surrender of the rebels and to allow its fleet to reach Cuba so as to defend against the Americans. But there was also support for Madrid's decision. Silvela, Pidal, Gamazo, and some business and religious journals backed the government. Ever since Spain had granted autonomy and provided tariff authority to the insular government, the business press had become less interested in Cuba's fate. Some high church officials also approved the government's decision and urged transferring the island to the United States, which would protect church property. Most important, during the turmoil, Spanish troops loyally suppressed Madrid's street demonstrators; Moret termed the military support "admirable."[50]

Although Europe's diplomats were congratulating themselves on their accomplishment, the Great Powers had really demonstrated their weakness. They had done nothing in Washington without the approval of the McKinley administration; and in Madrid the queen regent, Moret, and Sagasta had used them to bring Gullón and Correa around.

Even though Madrid had authorized a suspension of hostilities, it had little chance of preventing a Spanish-American war. Madrid, Washington, and the Cubans disagreed over the meaning of a cease-fire. Their opposing views were evident even in the words used—*armistice* by the United States and *suspension of hostilities* by Spain. The diplomats considered the verbal distinction to be minor, but to Correa and the Spanish military it was critical. A *suspension of hostilities* represented a unilateral Spanish decision with no recognition extended to the opponent; an *ar-*

mistice implied the right to fight, equal status on the battlefield, and a cease-fire negotiated with a recognized political entity. The Spanish cabinet had agreed to end the fighting not because it had lost Cuba but because it hoped to improve Spain's relations with the Great Powers. Spain was still committed to defending Cuba from American aggression. To the Americans, a cease-fire acknowledged the failure of Spanish arms and reforms and foreshadowed an inevitable withdrawal from the island. The Spanish proclamation was expected to result in negotiations, recognition of the insurgents, and accommodation of their demands. And Washington expected to play a part in the final settlement. The Cubans viewed the offer of a cease-fire quite differently. Deeply suspicious of Spanish and American purposes, they had no intention of ending the fighting during the rainy season when their forces had the military advantage. Instead, they insisted on independence and recognition of their Republic. Thus Madrid, Washington, and the Cubans were still in fundamental disagreement. But now that Spain had agreed to stop fighting, attention turned once again to Washington and Havana.

CHAPTER II

· · · · · · · · · · · · · · ·

DESCENT

· · · · · · · · · · · · · · ·

INTO WAR

· · · · · · · · · · · · · · ·

S ince Madrid authorized a suspension of hostilities less
than forty-eight hours before McKinley was to deliver
his message on Cuba to Congress, attention was immediately directed to how Spain's decision would affect his message and
Congress. The results quickly disillusioned Madrid; the announcement
of a suspension of hostilities produced no discernible effect on the White
House, Congress, or the Cuban insurgents. Europe's diplomats were
frustrated by the McKinley administration's failure to respond, yet they
were unwilling to do anything for Spain. In Washington the most important question was whether to recognize the Cuban Republic, and once
that was resolved, Congress quickly empowered the president to use force
in Cuba.

At first, hopes for peace ran high when Spain agreed to a suspension
of hostilities; diplomats were euphoric. Woodford predicted a final Cuban settlement by 1 August and asked that "nothing . . . be done to hu-
miliate Spain as [he was] satisfied that the present Government [was]
going and [was] loyally ready to go, as fast and as far as it [could.]" Ireland
thought that the cease-fire would enable McKinley to delay congressional action, since the president could tell Congress that the Cuban war
had ended, that Spain would now try by ever greater concessions to win

over the Cubans, and that if these failed, she would sell the island. He was certain that McKinley would get the insurgents to cooperate. Cambon expected more time for Spain to strengthen the autonomy government.[1]

News of the suspension came to the president by way of the Vatican to Elkins, who immediately telephoned the White House. That evening McKinley, Elkins, Fairbanks, McCook, and Charles Emory Smith of the *Philadelphia Press* discussed the favorable events. After leaving the White House, Elkins joined Polo and Ireland, who cabled Rampolla that "the armistice [was] producing an excellent impression" and peace was certain. Polo heard that McKinley was modifying his message to Congress and that the administration had asked Estrada Palma to come to Washington.[2]

Easter Sunday, 10 April, was a day of discussion and decision for the McKinley administration. The president spent the entire day with cabinet members, congressmen, and others in an effort to determine how best to respond to the Spanish initiative. Day was among the first to arrive and the last to leave late that night. The president met with his cabinet for six hours, three before lunch and three after dinner. He called in members of the House Foreign Affairs Committee and the Senate Foreign Relations Committee, and he dealt with the Junta through McCook and with Polo through Day.[3] Out of these protracted sessions came his decision to deliver his message to Congress as approved by the cabinet on 4 April, with a short additional statement about the Spanish action.

One of the difficulties facing McKinley was the steadfast demand of the Junta for independence. Speaking to reporters and testifying before the House Foreign Affairs Committee, Quesada scorned and rejected the Spanish offer. Since the Spanish proclamation said nothing about leaving the island, the Junta considered the cease-fire to be a trick to get through the rainy season and to force some type of home rule on the Cuban people. The Cubans would continue to fight, asserted Quesada, and Gómez would put to death any treasonous person who dared to consider an armistice. A McKinley emissary asked Rubens if the Cubans would accept a cease-fire if the president changed his message to make a reference to Cuban independence, and Rubens rebuffed the offer. Despite the strong stand, the Cubans were wary of McKinley. Quesada asked the Mexican government to organize a Latin American demarche in Washington in favor of Cuban independence, much as the European nations had done on behalf of Spain. The Mexican government, not wanting to become involved in the Cuban question, politely refused. McCook explained that the Cubans did not trust Spanish promises and preferred to place their future in congressional hands rather than rely on McKinley. The Junta expected Congress to declare war and to recognize Cuban independence. If Congress declared only war, the United States would expel the Spanish forces from Cuba and then grant the Cubans independence. If Congress did nothing, McCook thought the Junta would probably attempt to pay Spain up to $200 million for independence.[4]

Blanco also faced the problem of trying to get the Cubans to cooperate. He turned to Polo for help because he understood that the McKinley administration was acting as a mediator between Spain and the insurgents. Polo urged Blanco to decree a suspension of hostilities in general terms as soon as possible in order to get the maximum effect in Washington. Blanco should simply express the desire of the queen regent and the Spanish government for peace and amity on the island; he could fill in the details later. Blanco quickly complied with a two-point declaration that the Spanish troops were to cease fighting twenty-four hours after learning of the suspension of hostilities, with details of the duration and execution of the cease-fire to be determined.[5]

Polo then took Blanco's request to Day and asked for his help in fixing and implementing the terms of a cease-fire. This was the test of Moret's policy. Would the United States cooperate with Spain and use its influence to get the Cubans to end the fighting? Without consulting McKinley, Day replied that he had nothing more to add to what Woodford had already presented: that the armistice should begin immediately and should last until 1 October and that if the Spanish and the insurgents failed to negotiate a peace, the president should arbitrate a settlement. Day's set response angered Polo, especially his reassertion of presidential arbitration; this had earlier been set aside by Ireland and Elkins. Confronted by the angry Spaniard, Day took the dispute to McKinley and several hours later told Polo that the president "decline[d] to indicate . . . any suggestions as to the particular measures to be taken by Spain to secure peace in Cuba" other than what he had "already done in his communications through Mr. Woodford and the Spanish Minister in Washington." Day handed Polo an official memorandum to this effect, which made the Spanish minister even angrier because he had approached Day in an "extremely confidential and personal" way. Moreover, Day asked that Blanco say nothing about autonomy in his proclamation, which led Polo to exclaim that the Americans wanted everything from Spain but gave nothing in return. Polo spilled out his bitter feelings to Elkins, who got Day to withdraw the memorandum.[6]

Frustrated by his failed attempt to concert Spanish-American efforts to end the fighting, Polo cabled Blanco that he should authorize a suspension of hostilities for six months. Polo advised against making any reference to autonomy, since the insurgents would be less likely to cooperate. Polo hopefully predicted that once there was peace, the Cubans would come to accept home rule.[7]

At the same time, the British and French ambassadors advised Polo to write a memorandum that would state Spain's case. The ambassadors were upset that the American government and press were ignoring Spain's many efforts to keep the peace. So Polo spent the afternoon writing Day a long note in which he reviewed all that Spain had done: established autonomy, abolished reconcentration, aided the *reconcentrados*, assisted the *Maine* survivors, publicly expressed horror over the *Maine* tragedy, showed a willingness to accept arbitration, and promulgated a suspension of hostilities.[8] Several days later when Polo's note reached Madrid, Gullón, Sagasta, and the queen regent strongly approved it. Nevertheless Gullón chided Polo for his displays of temper and for delivering a note without consulting Madrid. Gullón's inadequate and fruitless policy was contained in an instruction that asked Polo to continue to impress on Day the military and political successes of Blanco and the decline in insurgent prospects.[9]

In essence, the Spanish and the Cuban positions on the future of the island remained poles apart. Spanish officials believed that Cuba should remain under the royal crown; and Cubans demanded independence and recognition of their republic. The suspension of hostilities failed to break the impasse. It was here that the United States, Spain, and the Cubans ended their diplomatic efforts.

As McKinley and Day struggled unsuccessfully with the Cubans and the Spanish, the president was trying to put together a consensus within the American government. McKinley wanted more time to see what effect the Spanish proclamation would have. His cabinet quickly decided to retain the Cuban message that it had already approved, but it then wrestled for hours over what to say about Madrid's proclamation. During the evening session, McKinley gained cabinet approval to ask Congress for a delay.[10] But after the cabinet session ended, the president was unable to convince Republican legislators. McKinley met with Senators Davis, Aldrich, and Lodge; Jonathan P. Dolliver, Republican of Iowa and a member of the House Foreign Affairs Committee, may also have been present. The president probably consulted other legislative leaders as well. The legislators strongly opposed further delay. They argued that the Spanish cease-fire would not bring peace to Cuba and that a delay would divide the party and bring about an election defeat in the fall. They urged McKinley to turn the Cuban issue over to Congress and to accept the results of its deliberations.[11]

McKinley reluctantly gave in. At the close of his original message, he simply declared that the Spanish government had directed Blanco "to proclaim a suspension of hostilities . . . in order to prepare and facilitate peace," a development that should have the "just and careful attention [of Congress] in the solemn deliberations upon which [it was] about to enter." And the president still held out a prospect for peace: "If this measure attains a successful result, then our aspirations as a Christian, peace-loving people will be realized. If it fails, it will be only another justification for our contemplated action."[12] In this way, late at night on Easter Sunday, McKinley ended his efforts to keep the peace; the responsibility had moved from the White House to Capitol Hill.

But McKinley's message did not exclude a peaceful settlement. Although his message on Cuba had been designed to obtain congressional authority for military intervention, there was still a lingering hope at the White House and among peace advocates. McKinley thought that the threat of force might bring further Spanish and Cuban concessions. Faced by overwhelming American military power and a war it could not possibly win, the Spanish government might agree to leave Cuba. To prevent American troops from occupying the island, the Cubans might settle for something less than immediate independence.[13]

The most controversial part of McKinley's message was its opposition to recognizing the independence of Cuba and the Cuban Republic. This issue focused on future Cuban-American relations rather than on the Spanish-American controversy. The majority of legislators favored Cuban independence, and most of them wanted to recognize the Cuban Republic. Day and Griggs, who wrote the president's message, based their opposition on international law, the status of American troops in Cuba, American economic claims, and the rights of intervention. Quoting from legal authorities, Day and Griggs argued that U.S. recognition of a nonexistent Cuban Republic would provide Spain with a casus belli and would justify European support. They were against recognition because invading American soldiers would come under the jurisdiction of

Cuban sovereignty and law; carried to an extreme conclusion, recognition would cause American troops to enter Cuba as allies, under the command of Gómez. There were economic interests as well; the McKinley administration wanted to hold the Cubans responsible for damage done to American investments, and Cuban sovereignty would diminish American rights. A nonrecognition policy also would give the United States the right to hold the island of Cuba in "trust" until it secured peace, established a government, and sealed future relations with a treaty. Premature recognition would prevent a means of "dictat[ing] the peace and control[ling] the organization of an independent government in Cuba." [14]

Besides these legal and political reasons, McKinley's Spanish policy also favored nonrecognition. As long as the United States did not recognize the Cuban Republic or the island's independence, Spain could hope to retain some element of sovereignty over the island, and a means of Spanish-Cuban accommodation might yet be found short of war. Indeed the Spanish cabinet was heartened by the news that McKinley opposed recognition, and it thought that nonrecognition might goad the Cubans into seeking an agreement with Spain. Moreover, nonrecognition could be expected to provide additional time for diplomacy; since Congress was divided between those who strongly favored recognition and those who stood by the president, extended congressional debate would delay legislative action. Thus the threat of American forceful intervention, a nonrecognition posture, and extensive congressional wrangling might keep the peace. [15]

On Monday morning crowds gathered once again at the Capitol to hear the president's message. Clothed in spring colors and Easter finery, the people appeared to be attending a festive occasion rather than a prelude to war. As the administration's legalistic, stilted, and florid message of over seven thousand words droned on, many were disappointed by the president's failure to capture the emotions of the occasion; House members clapped only briefly and in a perfunctory manner. [16]

Moreover, many considered the president's logic flawed and his arguments unconvincing. His message provided a historical account of Cuban troubles as well as a legal defense of his opposition to recognition. It evoked the horrors of reconcentration and the massive loss of civilian lives. Yet it noted the end of Weyler's destructive campaigning, the abolition of reconcentration decrees, and the months of Spanish-American cooperation to aid the unfortunate victims, aid that had "now extended through most if not all of the towns where suffering exist[ed]." The tragic

Maine disaster illustrated the "elements of danger and disorder" that existed on the island and was "a patent and impressive proof of a state of things in Cuba that [was] intolerable." Yet Spain had offered to arbitrate the differences between the two investigative reports, and to this the president had "made no reply." The message described three years of fighting which had degenerated into a stalemate. The prospect was for continued bloodshed until a state of "physical exhaustion of the one or the other party, or perhaps of both" concluded the strife. Yet the queen regent had directed Blanco to proclaim a suspension of hostilities "in order to prepare and facilitate peace"; and if the attempt succeeded, "then our aspirations as a Christian, peace-loving people [would] be realized." Overlooking these contradictions, McKinley declared that he had "exhausted every effort to relieve the intolerable condition of affairs." Therefore, American intervention was justified because neither the Spanish nor the Cubans were able or willing to end the "barbarities, bloodshed, starvation, and horrible miseries" on the island; to provide American citizens in Cuba "protection and indemnity for life and property"; to end the "very serious injury to [American] commerce, trade, and business"; and to stop the "constant menace to our peace [that] entails upon this Government an enormous expense." Accordingly, he asked Congress to approve the use of force to pacify Cuba and to place a "hostile constraint upon both the parties to the contest as well to enforce a truce as to guide the eventual settlement." [17]

Turning to relations with the Cuban Republic, the president cited as precedent Andrew Jackson's refusal to recognize Texas and Ulysses Grant's rejection of the Cuban government during the Ten Years War. Instead of recognition, McKinley asked Congress for authority "to use the military and naval forces of the United States as may be necessary . . . to secure a full and final termination of hostilities between the Government of Spain and the people of Cuba" and to establish "a stable government, capable of maintaining order and observing its international obligations." [18]

At the same time that McKinley's message went to Congress, the State Department released the Cuban consular correspondence. The next day the nation's newspapers carried large excerpts from the reports, which contributed to the public insistence that Spain leave Cuba. The arrival of Lee in Washington and his testimony on Cuban conditions added to national indignation. During a sensational congressional hearing, Lee declared that he believed Spaniards had deliberately sunk the *Maine*. At the time of the explosion, he said, the electric lights had dimmed in Havana, which indicated that someone, probably a Spanish official, had used an electrical device to explode the mine. Lee was certain that Blanco had had no knowledge of the attack.[19]

McKinley's message was criticized even within his own cabinet. Long found it illogical; since Spain had met all of America's demands, McKinley's conclusion did not follow. Long thought that McKinley was losing his ability to think clearly due to loss of sleep and intense pressure. Alger, who favored intervention, wished the message had more "ring." Lyman Gage, the secretary of the treasury, and James Gary, the postmaster general, who were both opposed to war, did not like the message.[20]

The congressional response was mixed. Senate and House conservative Republicans approved it; Senators Elkins, Fairbanks, Platt of Connecticut, Spooner, Aldrich, Allison, Hoar, Hanna and Speaker Reed voiced support. Most members of the Senate Foreign Relations Committee, however, were disappointed; Foraker thought the president should have asked for a declaration of war. Davis, Lodge, Platt of New York, and Chandler were among the disappointed. Many legislators were surprised to learn that McKinley had never asked Spain to give independence to Cuba and were astonished that the president proposed using force against the Cubans as well as the Spanish.[21]

Washington's diplomatic community lined up behind the president, although with reservations. Given the state of public excitement, the diplomats thought the president was "relatively conciliatory" and "peaceful." Had he been more moderate, an angry Congress might have immediately passed a declaration of war. The diplomats were quite disappointed that McKinley said nothing about their collective demarche. All in all, they believed that McKinley had successfully stymied the jingoes and created discord in Congress, thereby gaining time.[22] Ireland put the best face on it; although "the message seem[ed] to be war-like, its meaning [was] peace," which was "certain." McKinley had adapted himself to the feelings of Congress in order "to steer it towards peace." He had set the *Maine* issue on the "path of arbitration," asked for time "to get acquainted with the effects of the armistice," and "weaken[ed] the party for war."[23]

Surprisingly, Pauncefote was upset by the message; he strongly objected to McKinley's statement that the civilized world approved America's stand. The British ambassador thought the Great Powers should make it clear to the American people that the European nations did not approve using military force, which would be an unjustified "act of aggression"; the Great Powers should draw attention to Polo's 10 April note, which Pauncefote believed formed the basis for a peaceful resolution of the Cuban dispute. Pauncefote was also alarmed by the House debate, which he believed threatened all European possessions in the Caribbean.[24]

Pauncefote used his position as dean of the diplomatic corps to hold a meeting on 14 April at the British embassy to consider a second European demarche. He proposed to the assembled envoys that they deliver to the State Department a joint note denying European approval of American armed intervention and supporting Polo's memorandum as a reasonable basis for peace. The diplomats were surprised by Pauncefote's bitter criticism of the United States. The German ambassador, Theodor Ludwig von Holleben, was willing to consider another demarche, but he asserted that any new gesture would be meaningless without a joint European naval demonstration; he also belittled giving a note to Day, since McKinley had ignored the first one. Instead Holleben suggested that the six diplomats ask their foreign ministers to call in the American envoys and give them identical notes. This would demonstrate Europe's moral disapproval and have a greater impact on European public opinion. Having agreed to accept Pauncefote's views and Holleben's method, Cambon rendered the British draft into French, and each diplomat sent a similar request to his home office.[25]

The European foreign offices, except for Vienna, responded negatively; London, Berlin, and Paris objected to delivering a moral rebuke, which the United States would deeply resent and which would not prevent war. Arthur J. Balfour, acting for Salisbury, believed that unsought advice would undermine rather than support McKinley, and Britain did not want to appear to be taking sides in the Spanish-American controversy. Bülow held that a second demarche would be too late to succeed. Hanotaux considered the idea counterproductive, since a demarche would inflame American public opinion. Rebuffed, Pauncefote suggested dropping the moral condemnation and simply declaring that Polo's note provided a basis for peace, but even this was turned down. Thus, what Madrid had long sought, a European step favorable to Spain, foundered.[26]

The Spanish greeted McKinley's message with outrage, pessimism, and street demonstrations. Sagasta's cabinet declared to the press, "The certain knowledge of its rights, united with the resolve to maintain them in their entirety, inspire[d] the nation . . . to defend energetically the sacred interests which [were] the patrimony of the Spanish race." Rejecting Washington's assertion that it had the legal right to intervene in Cuba, the cabinet maintained that Spain had gone to the limit to keep the peace. To defend Spanish rights, the queen regent opened a public subscription to buy arms.[27]

The Spanish press fulminated over McKinley's message. *El Imparcial* accused the United States of insulting behavior, injustice, and false, ignoble, and ungrateful acts. It called on the government to rally and unite the people to defend Spanish honor. *El Correo Militar* accused McKinley of lies and villainies and reviled the United States for "vomiting" humiliation over Spain for three years. The message provoked "disgust . . . great pessimism . . . [and] widespread unity . . . in public places, political circles, streets, and cafes."[28] Newspaper invective was accompanied by street demonstrations; erupting in Madrid, Barcelona, Valencia, and Zaragosa, these were largely led by Republicans and Carlists, who claimed to be Spain's true patriots. The Carlist newspaper, *El Correo Español*, called for Spaniards to unite against the regency if the government agreed to the "dishonorable loss of Cuba." When Carlist leaders traveled to Majorca to talk to Weyler, it appeared that national outrage might forge an alliance against the monarchy.[29]

One reason the Spanish public was so belligerent was the misinformation circulating about the relative strengths of the Spanish and the American fleets. It was widely known that the American navy was larger than the Spanish, but the general public was told that Spanish sailors were better trained and disciplined. Newspapers carried articles about how the Spanish navy would devastate American commercial shipping, blockade ports, and win some naval battles. In the long run, most conceded, the United States would win the war and take Cuba; in the short run, however, Spain would have the satisfaction of bloodying the American nose. For example, Admiral José María Beránger, the minister of the navy under Cánovas, boasted that the Spanish navy would defeat the Americans because Spanish destroyers were superior, Spanish sailors were better trained and disciplined, and torpedoes defended Cuban ports. *El Correo Militar* contended that the Spanish fleet would ravage American shipping in the North Atlantic and close the Mediterranean. And there was even some self-deception among senior Spanish naval officers; one told French officers in Paris that because American vessels were poorly armed and the sailors badly trained, the Spanish navy would give the Americans "hell for at least a year."[30]

But Spanish indignation and braggadocio were ignored in the United States. After McKinley's message was read in Congress, the House and Senate both introduced joint resolutions that authorized armed intervention, but the resolutions differed on recognizing Cuban independence, the Cuban Republic, and the use of armed force. The House resolutions, conforming more closely to the president's request, "authorized and directed" the president "to intervene at once to stop the war in Cuba" in order to secure "permanent peace and order" and to establish "by the free action of the people . . . a stable and independent government of their own." To this end the House "authorized and empowered" the president "to use the land and naval forces of the United States." The House resolutions did not recognize either Cuban independence or the Cuban Republic, and the president might intervene without employing force, thus keeping the door open to negotiation.[31]

The House debate was short and heated; the rules committee limited floor debate to just forty minutes. Republicans had settled their differences in caucus; before reporting the resolutions to the floor, the Foreign Affairs Committee met with sixty Republicans who agreed to support the measure. When the House took up the resolutions, Republican ranks were solid. The limit on debate, however, caused a minor scuffle on the floor; while attempting to separate members, someone hit the chief page on the jaw.[32]

When order was restored, Hugh A. Dinsmore, Democrat of Arkansas and the leading Democrat on the Foreign Affairs Committee, and Adams debated the resolutions. Dinsmore opened with a condemnation of Spanish misrule and then attacked the Republican failure to recognize the Cuban Republic. Cuban accomplishments warranted recognition, which would convey legal and economic status that would further the Cuban cause. Dinsmore suggested that the McKinley administration opposed recognition for financial reasons; was an attempt being made to honor Spanish bonds by making the American government liable for Spain's debts? And if the United States declared war without Cuban recognition, wouldn't the insurgents be Spanish subjects and wouldn't America find itself at war with them? He also warned against forcing the Cuban people to accept a carpet-bag government.[33]

Adams answered that the so-called Cuban Republic did not meet the requirements of international law; it had no capital, civil administration, port, or ships, and it was surrounded by the Spanish army, which was still attempting to quell the rebellion. At the close of debate, a Democratic substitute resolution for recognition was defeated 191 nays to 148 yeas, with 16 not voting; then the majority resolution was passed, 325 yeas to 19 nays, with 12 not voting.[34]

In contrast to the swift action by the House, the Senate took four days to debate its resolutions and define its position. The Senate resolutions were more pointed. The Foreign Relations Committee majority introduced a set of resolutions that affirmed the Cuban people to be "free and independent." It was the duty of the U.S. government to "demand" that "Spain at once relinquish its authority and government in the Island of Cuba and withdraw its land and naval forces," and to this end, Congress "directed and empowered" the president "to use the entire land and naval forces of the United States." There was no mention of recognizing the Republic of Cuba. Four senators from the Foreign Relations Committee, led by David Turpie, Democrat of Indiana, and Foraker, reported a minority resolution stating that the U.S. government recognized the Republic of Cuba.[35] Much of the debate that followed turned on the Turpie-Foraker amendment.

During the debate several senators offered additional resolutions. Frye attempted to set aside the recognition controversy by simply empowering the president to intervene to bring peace. Conservatives rallied in support, which divided the senators into three groups: those who favored recognition, those who opposed, and those who wanted to take no position. Senator Henry M. Teller, silver Republican of Colorado, sponsored a resolution to deny annexation. Under this resolution, the United States disclaimed "any disposition or intention to exercise sovereignty, jurisdiction, or control" over Cuba and promised after pacification "to leave the government and control of the island to its people."[36]

Nearly half the senators spoke on the resolutions. They repeatedly justified intervention as a humanitarian and Christian duty to end Spanish barbarism, cruelty, and hypocrisy and to avenge the crime against the *Maine*. They pointed to the loss of American trade and investment and praised the Cuban rebellion against tyranny. As one after another spoke, it became apparent that the majority favored recognizing the Cuban Republic; many saw it as a means of assuring the cancellation of Spanish debts. Those who opposed recognition cited international law; they also condemned Cuban attacks on American property and Cuban destruction of crops, which had contributed to the large loss of civilian lives.[37]

During the debate McKinley let it be known that he favored the House over the Senate resolutions and that he was considering vetoing any resolution that recognized the Cuban Republic. His stance contributed to a lingering feeble hope that the Cuban insurgents might change their attitude and at the last moment cooperate with Spain in ending the war. Estrada Palma speculated that McKinley refused to recognize the Cuban Republic because he planned to occupy the island and then hold a plebiscite to determine if the people wanted independence or annexation.[38]

The Cubans, however, were more interested in finding their salvation in Congress than in Madrid. Cuba's lobbyists, Janney and McCook, worked hard to get Congress to recognize the republic. One of their successes was the Teller amendment. Although Teller was an expansionist, he opposed forceful acquisition of Cuba. Sympathetic to the Cubans and a longtime proponent of recognition of belligerency, he believed that eventually the Cubans would willingly join the United States. After the Spanish-American War began, Estrada Palma gave $2 million in 6 percent Cuban bonds to Janney as payment for securing the Teller amendment. Since Cuba's bonds were discounted to about half their value, this represented an award of about $1 million. Janney and McCook shared the bonds and were expected to pay those people who had assisted them, which may have included some members of Congress. Polo claimed to have proof that some representatives who favored recognition stood to profit from Cuban bonds, but there is no indication that Teller received any money. The Cuban Republic redeemed the bonds at par in 1912.[39]

After four days of debate, the Senate on 16 April took a series of votes. Davis first had the senators vote on recognition of the Cuban Republic, and by 51 to 37 they approved it. The division was largely partisan, with Democrats overwhelmingly in favor. Eleven Republicans, however, supported recognition; only 2 Democrats opposed it. The Senate then adopted the Teller amendment by voice vote. Frye attempted to delete the words recognizing the independence of Cuba, but his motion was defeated 55 to 33. Davis then brought to a vote the House resolutions, which were roundly defeated. The Senate sent its resolutions to the House, which voted them down, 178 to 156.[40]

Given the impasse, Congress formed a conference committee composed of six members: Representatives Adams, Dinsmore, and Joel P. Heatwole, Republican of Minnesota, and Senators Davis, Morgan, and Foraker. On 18 April the conference committee labored throughout the day and late into the night. As the hours ticked away, it became apparent that Reed was able to keep the House Republicans united and that McKinley's conservative forces were gaining strength in the Senate. At

2:00 A.M. on 19 April, the committee reached agreement; the House conferees accepted the Senate resolutions with the Turpie-Foraker amendment deleted. Thus Congress defined Cuba as independent but did not recognize the Cuban Republic. Legislators, who had been singing patriotic songs in the Capitol corridors, hurried to the chambers, where senators passed the compromise 52 to 35 in a nearly straight party vote and the House voted 311 to 6 for the conference report. It was all over by 2:45 A.M.[41]

Legislators understood that the resolutions allowed no possibility of further negotiation and that the compromise was the equivalent to a declaration of war. Spooner thought the result was "absurd" and "insulting" to Spain; Congress gave "legislative notice to Spain to quit her own property . . . [and it] precluded all possibility of arrangement, except by war." Chandler gave up on recognition only because "*the main battle was won*"; war was inevitable.[42]

McKinley and those around him watched the congressional debates with growing despair as all possibility of a peaceful settlement ebbed away. Those who had hoped that Congress would divide and debate at length were surprised by the swift House recognition of Cuban independence. Before Congress voted, there was still some talk of peace. Woodford suggested a Cuban plebiscite; Day thought a prompt Spanish military withdrawal from Cuba followed by a plebiscite would prevent war. McKinley fretted that Spain would consider the 13 April House proceedings as cause for war and dreaded the coming Senate debate; Bellamy Storer, an old Ohio friend, recorded that the president's spirits were good but that he still hoped for peace and as a result the atmosphere in the White House was "heavy and dark." Long considered McKinley "worn and overwrought" and was "anxious" for his "physical endurance." George B. Cortelyou, McKinley's secretary, scorned the "spirit of wild jingoism" that possessed Congress and the "party politics [that were] playing too prominent a part in this great crisis." He also worried about the "great strain" the president was under and noted McKinley's "haggard" face as the president worked until one and two each morning. Yet White House mail was running about 90 percent in favor of McKinley's efforts to keep the peace.[43]

After Congress voted, there was criticism of its hasty and ill-considered action; Long and Woodford believed that if Congress had provided more time, the president would have achieved Cuban independence without a war. McKinley probably believed this as well. Nevertheless, when the resolutions reached the White House, McKinley waived a ten-day waiting period and on 21 April signed them. Surrounded by cabinet members Day, Alger, Griggs, Bliss, James Wilson, and Smith and congressional leaders Elkins, Frye, and Cannon, the president gave his consent. Elkins commented that the resolutions were virtually a declaration of war; and while the men were still in the cabinet room, Polo's notification of a break in diplomatic relations came. With no further news from Spain, McKinley on 22 April ordered a naval blockade of Cuba, which started the war. Congress then passed a joint resolution setting 21 April as the official beginning of the conflict.[44]

Although many believed that war might have been prevented if Congress had not acted so rashly, there was no evidence that the Spanish and Cubans were ready to take additional steps to keep the peace. If anything, just before the war started, the Spanish were stiffening their position. Then the insulting congressional language directed at Spain and Sagasta's government aroused Spanish patriotism and anti-Yankee passion. Madrid's press reflected the national outrage. *El Imparcial* was infuriated that the American government held Spain responsible for sinking the *Maine*, which the newspaper ascribed to negligence. It was astonished that McKinley took no account of the actions of the Great Powers and papal mediation, and it castigated American policy toward Cuba as having three points: the removal of Spain, the descent of the island into racial violence and anarchy, and American annexation to restore law and order. The newspaper applauded the Spanish government for championing national honor, and it welcomed the sympathy of the European powers. *El Correo de Madrid* accused the United States of three years of duplicity, trickery, and slander and demanded that Sagasta's government stop making repugnant concessions to Washington and instead defend the nation's dignity, honor, and sovereignty in Cuba. *El Correo Militar* urged Spain to go to war knowing the nation championed the right and had the sympathy of the world. Spain would become synonymous with heroism, and if there was justice in the world, Spain would prevail.[45]

The general public joined in excoriating the United States and championing Spanish nationalism. Street demonstrations, some ending in riots, occurred in Barcelona, Valencia, Málaga, Granada, Orense, and Valladolid. Riots continued for six days in Valencia, and in Málaga an angry mob stoned the American consulate and tore the escutcheon off the balcony. Crowds shouted: "Viva España! Muerte a los Yanquis! Abajo el armisticio!"[46]

With war imminent, the Spanish government gained political support. Sagasta convened the Cortes on 20 April. The evening before, he had given a patriotic address to Liberal Party members. Sagasta had explained his efforts to keep the peace, described the aggression of the United States, noted the support of Europe's diplomats, and pledged the government to defend its territory. Party members hailed his defense of Spanish policy, and the next day the queen regent's message, modeled on Sagasta's remarks, received loud cheers in the new Cortes. Only the Spanish stock market registered a decline.[47] A few days after the war started, Sagasta called for a vote of confidence. The queen regent asked the advice of important politicians and the nation's military leaders. Newspapermen, waiting outside the palace, interviewed each departing person. All but two, Weyler and Romero Robledo, supported Sagasta's policies and opposed a change of government. Several, however, thought that Sagasta should replace Moret, who had been overly partial to peace, and Moret considered stepping down, since his policy of concessions had failed.[48]

The Cuban leaders were equally firm. Bartolomé Masó, the president of the Cuban Republic, rejected Blanco's proclamation of a suspension of hostilities; the United States had forced it on Spain, and the suspension had been prepared without any Cuban involvement. Blanco's proclamation changed nothing; Cuban military forces would continue to fight until Spain recognized Cuban independence and evacuated the island. Gómez made a similar declaration. *La Independencia*, a newspaper published in Manzanillo, Cuba, had only contempt for Spanish groveling at the feet of the United States in the effort to impose autonomy on Cuba. It predicted that a Spanish-American war would make Cuba independent.[49]

Given the effort that went into obtaining a Spanish suspension of hostilities, it did little more than uncover the militancy of both Spaniards and Cubans. Madrid's proclamation set off a flood of domestic opposition, and the Cubans never wavered in resisting a cease-fire. Sagasta's government had gone as far as it could. With no prospect for a truce in Cuba and faced by a patriotic backlash in Spain, it could only respond to Washington's rejection of cooperation and outpouring of congressional hostility with increased determination to defend the nation's honor. Nevertheless, by showing flexibility, Spain gained moral stature in Europe while the United States lost sympathy.

Although the suspension of hostilities failed to check Congress, the closing hours demonstrated McKinley's desire for peace. He fought for more time, he attempted to dampen the war fever, and he applied pressure on the Cubans to cooperate. The president reluctantly turned the decision for war over to Congress when it became apparent that further delay would split his party and end his control of the government.

McKinley's message to Congress was full of contradictions. It had been drawn up with two purposes: to provide a historical account and to set administration policies, but the actual events did not always support the political goals. Yet the discrepancies mattered little. More important, the decision for military intervention raised the issue of future relations between Cuba and the United States. When McKinley refused to recognize the Cuban Republic, he began to involve Washington in the island's domestic politics and to move toward establishing a protectorate.

CHAPTER 12

· · · · · · · · · · · · · · · ·

PRELIMINARIES

· · · · · · · · · · · · · · · ·

TO PEACE

· · · · · · · · · · · · · · · ·

The Spanish-American War was short; it lasted only sixteen weeks, from 21 April to 12 August. Both the United States and Spain wanted a short war and had limited objectives, which encouraged early peace negotiations. The McKinley administration was determined to remove Spain from Cuba and Puerto Rico and to minimize European influence in the region. After the Manila Bay victory, the United States became interested in Pacific acquisitions. The Spanish government hoped its armed forces would uphold Spanish honor by bloodying the Yankees, but it expected to lose Cuba. To prevent the insurgents from taking vengeance on Spanish subjects, Spain anticipated ceding the island, together with its debt, to the United States. Madrid did not want to lose any other colonies, and it continued to seek European backing.

The Cuban Republic stood on the sidelines during the war. Washington held the Junta at arm's length, never consulting it about peace objectives or negotiations, and initial military cooperation on the island rapidly broke down. Quesada encountered the McKinley administration's frosty attitude in May when he attempted to deliver a letter from Gómez to McKinley. Day would not see him if he came on "official" business; Adee refused to take the envelope because it was addressed to "The Secretary of State"; and Quesada was called back to the State Department because it was discovered that there was a covering letter addressed to "The Secretary of State." Frustrated, Quesada asked Day if he would deliver Gómez's letter to McKinley; the secretary of state replied that he would hand it to the president, who might or might not take it. Two months later Quesada asked Alger and Griggs about recognition of the Cuban Republic, and the latter, though cordial, replied that recognition was "useless" for now.[1]

The peace negotiations stemmed from America's three military victories: Dewey's success in Manila Bay on 1 May, the sinking of Cervera's fleet on 3 July, and the capitulation of Santiago de Cuba on 16 July. These American triumphs brought an early end to the war. In the eyes of the Spanish, the naval defeats were bitterly disappointing, yet the army defended Santiago de Cuba tenaciously, inflicting many casualties. And as Spain predicted, American troops suffered heavy losses from tropical diseases.[2]

The war also ended quickly because the United States successfully employed psychological warfare. The Naval War Board used an intelligence-gathering operation to disseminate misinformation, thereby frightening the Spanish with imaginary attacks. At the start of the war, both Spain and the United States established intelligence-collecting services. Polo relocated in Montreal, Canada, and took charge of relaying information to Madrid about American military moves. Du Bosc also collected information, and Canada eventually jailed him for spying.[3] Before leaving Spain, Lt. George Dyer recruited a spy who apparently was a double agent. Lt. William S. Sims in Paris and Lt. John C. Colwell in London were at the heart of a European-wide U.S. navy intelligence network that collected information about Spanish ship and troop movements. Colwell and Sims also provided many reports on Spanish politics. Sims volunteered to circulate misleading information, and the naval war board used him to plant fabrications about naval targets and ship movements through French agents who had access to important Spanish officials, including León y Castillo. The naval war board frequently released fake reports in American newspapers, and these articles found an echo in the European press.[4]

The most successful hoax of the naval war board was a phantom fleet under the command of Commodore John C. Watson; this fleet was always on the verge of implementing "Roosevelt's Plan" to cross the Atlantic to attack Spanish ports and colonial holdings such as Cádiz, the Canary

Islands, and Ceuta. Although Spanish officials suspected that Watson's fleet was a trick, they nevertheless directed scarce military resources to peninsular and colonial coastal defenses and decided against sending Spain's few remaining gunboats to relieve the siege of Manila. More important, many frightened Spaniards fled coastal cities for fear of imminent bombardment, particularly after Cervera's fleet sank off Cuba.[5] Thus by mid-July the actual battles, as well as fear of peninsular attacks and additional colonial losses, especially Ceuta and the Canary Islands, provided the backdrop for Spain's decision to end the war.

Another reason the Spanish-American War was short was the desire of the European powers to end it quickly. When the war started, they had accepted American intervention in Cuba. But Dewey's victory in Manila Bay suddenly gave a global dimension to the conflict. England, France, Germany, and Russia were interested in the fate of the Philippine Islands, and they also worried about Watson's fleet. The longer the war lasted, the more likely that the United States would attack other Spanish colonial outposts. What if the Americans actually took the Canary Islands, Ceuta, a Moroccan port, or the Balearic Islands? Overnight, Europe might find American bases established in African and Mediterranean waters and a military buildup of naval and land forces. France in particular was wary, and even London showed some concern, leading both to encourage the peace process.[6]

Dewey's triumphant victory in Manila Bay stunned the Spanish. Admiral Patricio Montojo lost his entire fleet without sinking an American ship or even causing the death of an American sailor. Street demonstrations broke out in Madrid and eighteen provincial cities; one crowd went to Sagasta's house and called for the end of his government and the dismissal of Moret. The government used the army to keep order in the streets. Some Carlists and Republicans were arrested; others fled. Sagasta's government entered a crisis of confidence, and during the next two weeks Sagasta began exploring a change of ministers, particularly the idea of dropping Moret and Bermejo. During this time, Silvela delivered to the Cortes several speeches that were critical of the government but that also served the government by asking the Spanish people to realize that Cuba was already lost; moreover, Silvela was not prepared to assume power.[7]

During the crisis, Sagasta offered to step down in place of Gamazo and Eugenio Montero Ríos. Working together, they could command a majority in the recently elected Cortes, but they were unable to reach agreement on the composition of a cabinet. So on 16 May, Sagasta obtained the queen regent's approval to form a new ministry. He dismissed the unpopular members, Moret and Bermejo, and he also dropped Gullón and Xiquena. Gullón had been complaining of exhaustion and asking to be relieved. Sagasta's political challenge was to strengthen his ministry by bringing in Gamazo, who was respected for his administrative talents and energy and who headed a large block of Liberal Party members. Gamazo wanted to become prime minister when the aging Sagasta stepped down, and he had grown impatient waiting for the retirement. While outside the government, Gamazo had freely criticized Sagasta for drifting with the tide of events and failing to take control, and he particularly denounced Moret, his rival for the party leadership. By bringing Gamazo into the cabinet, Sagasta hoped to end the attacks. Gamazo, however, took the ministry of production portfolio; this was the least political cabinet position. He continued to distance himself from Sagasta, criticizing the prime minister's performance and maneuvering to replace him. The exchange of Moret for Gamazo, however, did not set back peace prospects. Gamazo had opposed entering the war, blamed Sagasta for not finding a way to end the war, and once within the cabinet, pressed for an early peace.[8]

More important for the diplomats was the appointment of a new foreign minister. Sagasta considered León y Castillo for the post, but after calling him to Madrid to offer him the position, Sagasta agreed to León y Castillo's request to return to the Paris embassy. The Spanish diplomat argued that the end of the war would come through a peace worked out in Paris and expected his close relationship with Hanotaux to prove valuable in the coming negotiations.[9] Sagasta then selected Juan Manuel Sánchez Gutiérrez de Castro, the duke of Almodóvar del Río and an advocate of peace. A member of the Cortes and respected for his expertise in budgetary matters, Almodóvar had limited foreign policy experience. Socially prominent, he had cultivated Madrid's diplomats. Educated in England and known to Salisbury, he was initially considered a pro-English selection. Sagasta, as usual, entrusted his new foreign minister with extensive authority in foreign affairs while he worked to hold together the domestic political elements.[10]

Madrid applauded the change in naval ministers. Bermejo had a reputation as a poor administrator, and the Manila Bay defeat was attributed to his failure to provide defenses for the port. The public respected his replacement, Captain Ramón Auñón y Villalón, who had commanded a battleship and was considered a good manager. Despite the loss of Moret, the new cabinet was able and leaned toward an early peace.[11]

The Spanish government also faced serious economic troubles. Inflationary food prices, trade disruption caused by rioting in interior cities, temporary food shortages in some towns, and economic depression contributed to widespread discontent. When the war started, Spanish bonds dropped to 29 percent of issue value. Worse yet, the Spanish government was unable to borrow money from France. It attempted to float a new loan backed by income from the tobacco monopoly, but French bankers refused to extend more credit until the Spanish sued for peace.[12]

The first hint of peace terms originated in Madrid. After Dewey's victory and during the cabinet crisis, the queen regent suggested to Patenôtre that if the United States offered peace in exchange for Cuba, the Spanish government would accept. Gullón told the French ambassador that although the cabinet did not agree on peace terms, he thought it would be willing to trade Manila for Cuba.[13] Madrid's trial balloons ended when Spanish forces won their only naval victory of the war. On 11 May the USS *Winslow*, a small torpedo boat that was part of the fleet blockading Cuba, entered Cárdenas harbor. Shells from Spanish shore guns and a gunboat disabled the torpedo boat, killing one American officer and four sailors. News of the successful repulse stiffened Spanish determination to continue the war by raising hopes that Cervera's fleet, which had not yet engaged the Americans, might win a victory. Eight days later Cervera successfully reached the harbor of Santiago de Cuba, which buoyed the Spanish mood. A stronger Spanish stance was reflected in a suggestion made to Wolff by a person close to the queen regent: Spain wanted to retain sovereignty over Cuba, although it would accept some American intervention on the island, and it was willing to cede a coaling station in the Philippine Islands. Salisbury did not think the suggestion was significant enough to relay to Washington.[14]

London and Paris, however, were interested in getting the peace process started, and Dewey's victory encouraged them. The British asked Washington to formulate its requirements for peace, and the French tried to open direct negotiations between León y Castillo and Porter. The initial inquiries encouraged the McKinley administration to clarify its goals.

Joseph Chamberlain, the British minister for colonies, first expressed London's interest in peace negotiations. On 8 May at a dinner party, he casually asked Hay if the United States would end the war if England could get Spain to evacuate Cuba. The question prompted the McKinley administration to formulate its aims. Moore, appointed assistant secretary of state when Day replaced Sherman at the start of the war, had talked informally with other government officials about American objectives. When Chamberlain's inquiry arrived at the State Department, Moore, without further consultation, wrote out four American objectives with a supporting rationale. First, Spain should evacuate and deliver Cuba to the United States, which would establish order, and agree to protect Spanish citizens and their property. Second, Spain should cede Puerto Rico to the United States, thus removing the Spanish flag from the Western Hemisphere and ending the possibility of future conflicts. Third, the United States should consider Puerto Rico a war indemnity and not request a financial settlement. Since Spain had no money and there were unpaid American claims arising from the Cuban insurrection, the United States might assume these claims against the value of the island. Fourth, Spain should retain the Philippine Islands but should cede a coaling station there or in the Caroline Islands; the Navy Department should decide the location. Since the United States did not yet occupy the islands, Moore suggested that Washington might trade its military power over the archipelago for the evacuation of Spain's army from Cuba, thereby saving the lives and money needed to take Cuba.[15]

The next day Moore gave his four-point program to Day, who liked it and in turn reviewed it at a cabinet meeting. Alger objected to giving up the Philippine Islands, but Day thought one port in the Philippines was enough, since the administration would have its hands full governing Cuba. Despite the Teller amendment, Day expected a lengthy period of military rule over the island. There was no indication of how McKinley regarded Moore's draft.[16] While Moore's points were under discussion, Salisbury asked if the McKinley administration was interested in European mediation to end the war. Day responded that if McKinley believed it was necessary, he would ask for it; the president was anxious to end the war but thought another American naval victory was needed to bring Spain to terms.[17]

The European diplomatic scene was shaken on 13 May when Chamberlain, in a Birmingham speech, warmly endorsed Anglo-American friendship and even suggested an alliance. Referring to the possibility that England take part in the Spanish-American War, Chamberlain said, "Terrible as war may be, even war itself would be cheaply purchased if in a great and noble cause the Stars and Stripes and the Union Jack should wave together over an Anglo-Saxon alliance." The Spanish were astounded that the English, presumably neutral, threatened such a hostile stand. Madrid later rebuffed all British suggestions of mediation, since it considered London too pro-American and also eager to profit from a redistribution of colonies at the end of the war. Relations between Spain and Britain deteriorated into a quarrel over Gibraltar, which continued for several months after the Spanish-American War ended.[18] Chamberlain's speech also alarmed the European powers, which saw England taking advantage of continental pro-Spanish feeling to link the European powers with a losing cause while identifying its own fortunes with the victor. A press battle erupted in Europe as the continental nations criticized England and proclaimed their neutrality.[19]

Late in May the question of American peace terms came up again. Hay asked for guidance on McKinley's thinking and at the same time advised the president against making peace until the United States had a firm grip on the Philippine Islands and Puerto Rico. McKinley's reply, closely following Moore's four points, set off a flurry of European diplomatic activity over starting peace talks and the possibility of mediation. On 3 June the president cautiously responded to Hay, noting that Spain would have to evacuate Cuba and deliver the "title and possession of the island to the United States," which would hold Cuba until a stable government was established. The United States would protect the lives and property of Spanish subjects as long as it held the island. Spain need not pay a monetary indemnity but instead should "cede Porto Rico," and the United States would assume American citizens' claims that resulted from the Cuban insurrection and present war. Spain could retain the Philippine Islands, "except for [ceding] a port and necessary appurtenances," and it should also cede "an island in the Ladrones with a harbor, as a coaling station." The president emphasized that these terms were transitory; "further sacrifice and loss of life [and] prolongation of the war [could] change this materially."[20]

McKinley's answer quickly made the diplomatic circuit. Pauncefote got wind of it and sent a paraphrase to Salisbury, suggesting a secret contact with Spain and perhaps British or Great Power mediation to end the war. When Hay confided McKinley's terms to Salisbury, the British prime minister offered to inform Austria, proposing that Franz Josef advise Spain to take advantage of McKinley's "liberal disposition." Hay asked for instructions.[21] Day and Moore were unwilling to elevate McKinley's tentative scheme into an American overture to Spain; they were particularly worried that any step taken by London would result in "European intervention." McKinley responded that an American offer to Spain was "premature" and might be "misinterpreted" as a sign of weakness; he was also wary of European actions, which might commit the president and result in loss of flexibility. But these cautions came too late; Salisbury had already informed Austria, explaining to Hay that he had acted in response to Pauncefote's original telegram and that the Austrians had replied that the Spanish government was not yet ready to make peace.[22] Meanwhile Pauncefote spread the news in Washington to his French, German, and Austrian diplomatic colleagues, who informed their home offices. On 6 June, McKinley's ideas appeared in an unattributed article in the *New York Times* and later showed up in the Madrid press.[23]

In mid-June, McKinley's views on the Philippine Islands changed. He explained to Hay that a final peace settlement would have to take into consideration the Philippine insurgents. Therefore Hay should alert the British that it was difficult to say what the future of the islands would be. Spain also worried more about the Philippines and in mid-June asked Britain and other European powers to take temporary possession of Manila to protect the lives of the residents from an insurgent attack. Salisbury rejected the suggestion as going beyond the role of a neutral during wartime.[24] Although these British-American exchanges produced no direct negotiations, they clarified American thinking, and Madrid was alerted to McKinley's views.

The London-Washington exchanges corresponded with Paris-Madrid attempts to get peace negotiations under way. Dewey's victory also started the French thinking about ending the war. A few days after the battle, Hanotaux asked Porter whether the United States was considering annexing the Philippine Islands. Without instructions, Porter responded that the American government opposed annexation in general and would not take the islands. Hanotaux passed this reply to León y Castillo, who saw in the conversation the possibility of future peace talks developing in Paris. Hanotaux was interested in bringing the Spanish and Americans together and found support in St. Petersburg for taking a role in ending the war. Nevertheless, Hanotaux decided that the two nations were not yet ready to make peace.[25]

In early June, Hanotaux and Porter discussed possible peace terms. León y Castillo had recently returned from Madrid as a result of the cabinet reorganization, and on 2 June, Porter asked Hanotaux if the

Spanish ambassador brought any news. Hanotaux replied that the Spanish army was not yet ready to make peace because it wanted to show its prowess in battle. Nevertheless, Hanotaux followed up Porter's initiative with questions about possible peace terms. Porter assured him that the United States was still opposed to annexing the Philippines. Its sole desire was the independence of Cuba, and it would not assume Spain's debts covering the island. Hanotaux countered that if the United States took over Cuba's debt, it would obtain rights of intervention and that paying Spain's debts would be cheaper than continuing the war. Porter was impressed by these arguments.[26]

After another conversation with Hanotaux, Porter on 7 June informed the State Department of his talks. Assuring Day that Hanotaux was close to León y Castillo and trusted in Madrid, Porter explained that the French foreign minister was willing to use his good offices to promote Spanish-American negotiations because the war depressed Spanish bonds, injured French commerce, and threatened a wider war. Since Hanotaux believed Spain would fight to the bitter end, he was willing to use his position to pressure Madrid to end the war quickly. Hanotaux suggested that Spanish pride could be assuaged if the war ended with a Cuban plebiscite to determine the government the people wanted. A new government could assume Spain's Cuban debts, and the United States might guarantee Cuba's debt payments and withdraw from the Philippine Islands. Porter guessed that León y Castillo advanced these ideas. Porter requested authority to engage in peace talks, and León y Castillo asked, through Hanotaux, for proof that Porter spoke for Washington. A week later, and after another talk with Hanotaux, Porter cabled for permission to open negotiations and instructions as to what to say.[27]

Day replied to Porter's appeals in much the same language previously sent to London. McKinley would not make any peace proposals and believed that negotiations were premature and liable to misinterpretation by Madrid. The president did not want to be bound by arrangements made abroad and would not accept foreign intervention of any kind. If León y Castillo had authority to negotiate peace, Porter was allowed to accept his proposals without any discussion and to forward them to McKinley. Porter carried Washington's reply to Hanotaux, who countered that León y Castillo had "full powers" to negotiate, was prepared to make peace proposals, and had wide discretion to discuss them but was unlikely to do so until the American government provided Porter with similar credentials.[28] Efforts to start peace talks in Paris died out, since Porter had no power to treat. León y Castillo continued to hint that he had a Spanish peace plan, but he never revealed it. When Hanotaux left the foreign ministry post in favor of Théophile Delcassé, the new minister was less inclined to intervene on Spain's behalf.[29]

Additional military defeats were needed to pressure Spain to sue for peace on American terms. American and Spanish attention was focused on the developing siege of Santiago de Cuba. On 19 May, Cervera's fleet safely entered the well-defended harbor, and ten days later, the American Flying Squadron blockaded the port. On 22 June, American soldiers began disembarking on beaches east of the port, and Cuban insurgents helped to encircle the city to prevent Spanish forces from reinforcing it. The battle for Santiago de Cuba and Cervera's fleet was under way.

The Spanish government nervously watched the growing hopelessness of Cervera's situation. It faced a dilemma. If Cervera's fleet remained in port and helped to defend the city, the siege would last longer, but when the city surrendered, the fleet inevitably would be lost. If the fleet sailed and engaged the blockading ships, the Americans would probably win, since they had a superior force. A battle, however, held some hope that the Spanish might sink some American ships and perhaps free some of their own. Spanish public opinion favored chancing a battle. Moreover, some Spanish politicians calculated that if Cervera sailed, the outcome would be decided sooner, thereby setting the stage for an earlier end to the war and limiting additional Spanish losses. Gamazo wanted to seek peace after the battle for Santiago no matter what the outcome. Sagasta prepared for impending defeat and the opening of peace talks by suspending the Cortes on 24 June; this silenced the daily attacks by government opponents in the chamber, particularly the Carlists. Then on 30 June the government released figures showing the high cost of the Cuban war: 2,161 combat deaths, 53,440 dead from disease, over 8,600 wounded, and a financial expenditure of 1.554 billion pesetas.[30]

In this atmosphere Sagasta turned control of Cervera's fleet over to Blanco, encouraging him to send Cervera to sea. Ordered repeatedly to depart, Cervera on 3 July left the safety of Santiago de Cuba. Within hours, all his ships were destroyed; American casualties were one dead and one wounded. The disastrous naval defeat was another cruel blow to Spain's hopes for gaining military honor. McKinley cautiously appealed to the Spanish government to begin peace talks. On 6 July, one day before Congress voted to annex the Hawaiian Islands, McKinley issued a short proclamation calling for religious thanksgiving for the success of American arms. His last sentence contained an appeal for God's intervention to bring peace.[31]

Cervera's defeat was a harsh blow to Spain's national spirit. Initially the population remained calm; only a handful of demonstrators, mostly Carlists, took to Madrid's streets and cried for a change in government. Rather than being angry, the public was disheartened and, with each passing day, increasingly opposed to continuing a war that promised only additional catastrophic defeats. But the threat of Watson's fleet off Spanish coasts was now believable, and panic developed in some ports as many people fled to the safety of interior towns. The Spanish cabinet recalled a small fleet that had set out for the Philippine Islands and had gotten as far as Suez, but these few ships could not provide a serious defense against American naval power or inspire confidence in coastal areas. It was clear that Americans controlled the seas, completely isolating the remaining Spanish forces in Cuba, Puerto Rico, and the Philippines. Since Spain could not send food and munitions to its embattled forces, the United States was certain to prevail on every front.[32]

Despite the hopeless condition of Spain's colonial armies, Sagasta's government faced resistance to opening peace negotiations. The cabinet was divided; Sagasta, Almodóvar, and Gamazo wanted peace. Sagasta wrote that he did not know how the war would end but that he knew it must stop. But Correa, reflecting army opinion, opposed surrendering without a battle. After all, the Spanish had anticipated losing Cuba to the United States, but in the process the army intended to inflict substantial casualties on invading American forces. The army had had some initial successes in defending the approaches to Santiago de Cuba, and General José Toral's entrenched troops were expected to give a good account of themselves if the Americans tried a direct assault. Since Correa and the army in Cuba wanted to continue the war, Sagasta feared that if he made peace, the dissatisfied and humiliated officers and soldiers, about one hundred thousand strong, would threaten the government when they returned to Spain. Weyler, Romero Robledo, Carlists, and Republicans were championing the army and criticizing the government for inadequate military preparations, and they could be expected to try to make the most of military unrest. Until the army was ready to accept peace, Sagasta did not believe that he had sufficient political authority to impose it.[33]

In an attempt to break the impasse, Sagasta asked Blanco to assess the political situation in Cuba and the depth of military commitment to continue the war. Blanco reported that the Cuban people overwhelmingly sympathized with the Americans, and as the invasion strengthened, Cuban support for them was increasing. Peninsular Spaniards for the most part were unpatriotic and consulted their own personal and business interests first. Only a minority of autonomists were still loyal to Spain. On the other hand, the army was completely loyal, intact, high-spirited, and ready to fight on. The army had valiantly defended Santiago de Cuba, and it opposed surrendering territory it had defended so decisively. There were sufficient munitions and food to continue fighting for many months; and Blanco predicted that Americans would pay a heavy price for their eventual victory.[34]

Blanco's reply led to a cabinet crisis. Sagasta wanted to sue for peace, but Correa backed the army, and he threatened to resign. With the government divided, Sagasta offered his resignation to the queen regent, reasoning that if the army wanted to continue the war, it should provide the governmental leadership for the nation. Sagasta's offer placed the queen regent in a difficult situation. She too wanted peace, but since the start of the war, she had tried to be the most patriotic of all, steadfastly supporting the nation's armed forces. A change to military government would prolong the war. Some support for Sagasta and the queen regent came from Polavieja, the most likely military candidate to form a government, since he showed no interest in taking up the task. And Weyler also did not step forward during the crisis. Thus the queen regent rejected Sagasta's offer to resign and encouraged him to persist in finding a means to get the generals to agree to end the war. Time was running out; the Spanish government feared Watson would attack Tangiers or some other Moroccan port.[35]

Sagasta also had to deal with Spain's beleaguered forces in Santiago de Cuba. Toral's besieged troops faced overwhelming odds. After Cervera's defeat, General William R. Shafter, the commander of the American troops, asked Toral to surrender the city; the alternative was a naval bombardment that would take many civilian lives or a frontal attack that would lead to heavy military casualties. Hopelessly outnumbered and outgunned and short of food and munitions, Toral took Shafter's offer seriously and sought conditions favorable to the city's population and his command. On 12 July, Toral told Blanco that the American navy had bombarded the city and that the army had tightened its encirclement; on the other hand, Shafter had offered to transport Toral's troops to Spain, and Toral asked for instructions.[36]

Strengthened by royal support and advice, both Sagasta and Correa appealed to Cuba's army commanders to consider ending the war. With the queen regent's assistance, Sagasta made a strong case for cutting Spain's losses. Control of the seas, Sagasta reasoned, would allow the Americans to tighten the blockade of Cuba, to dominate the Philippines, and to attack Puerto Rico, the Canary Islands, the Balearic Islands, and some peninsular cities. Defeat on all these fronts would lead to domestic disorder and possibly the destruction and ruin of Spain. This could be avoided if the government ended the unequal and disastrous war. Spain could still negotiate a peace that would be acceptable and honorable to the army; this would not be the case if the army had to surrender Cuba due to hunger. Blanco and his generals, who loved the nation and its institutions, could show their discipline by accepting the government's resolve to make peace. Using a different approach, Correa praised the army and the glory it had won at Santiago de Cuba; it did not need additional battlefield laurels. But lacking food and munitions, Spain's valiant soldiers would soon have to surrender Santiago de Cuba, and there was no honor in defending thankless people who rebelled and sought independence. Correa reminded the army officers that military honor also involved the duty to obey and submit to the will of the government. He promised that the government would pay and discharge the troops on arrival in Spain.[37]

Blanco took two days to poll eighteen generals about Madrid's desire to seek peace and the fate of Toral's troops. After consultation, he replied that the army wanted to continue the war. It had not yet sacrificed enough to demonstrate its military honor, and his command opposed surrendering the island, which had been acquired and held by so many brave Spaniards. Nevertheless, the generals agreed to accept and obey the government's decisions and would not be an obstacle to implementing them. Blanco added that if the government decided to sue for peace, he wanted to be relieved of his command. Committed to defending the island to the point of death, he had urged others to fight on and criticized those who had refused; it was inappropriate for him to take part in surrendering the island to "greedy" Yankees. Blanco also asked Madrid for permission to surrender Santiago de Cuba. The Spanish garrison was in an "unequal and disadvantageous position," and the Americans had offered "liberal" terms: repatriating troops to the peninsula in neutral ships and allowing officers to keep their swords in exchange for an oath not to fight the Americans again.[38]

In Madrid, Sagasta's government prepared to contain the public shock of the fall of Santiago de Cuba and the initiation of peace talks. To end newspaper criticism and limit Carlist agitation, the government on 15 July suspended constitutional guarantees and instituted press censorship. The resolute action indicated that the cabinet was united and felt strong enough to govern during the difficult times ahead.[39] The same day it authorized Toral to capitulate. In reporting the surrender, Blanco noted growing antagonism between the Cuban insurrectionists and the American army. A Cuban rebel envoy had asked for a conference with Blanco, and he had sent General Peralta y Pérez de Salcedo to parley with the insurgent.[40]

When the news of Toral's surrender reached Spain, the newspapers were not allowed to comment on it. But editorials just before censorship showed military dissatisfaction. *El Correo Militar* blamed the government rather than the Americans for Spain's naval defeats and the impending loss of Santiago de Cuba. *La Correspondencia Militar* predicted that the Spanish army would deal a severe blow to the invading Americans; on the other hand, it criticized the government for inadequate preparation and lack of foodstuffs, which would eventually require the army to surrender.[41]

Having suspended Spanish constitutional guarantees, Sagasta polled Spain's major political figures about peace talks. The consensus was to save as much of the empire as possible within the demands of the victorious Americans; only Romero Robledo opposed suing for peace.[42] McKinley's list of requirements was well known; yet by bringing the war to a speedy conclusion, before an invasion of Puerto Rico and while Manila and Havana still held out, the Spanish hoped to minimize American demands.

As the war neared its end, Spain's weakened political and economic condition was evident. The restoration monarchy was in disarray. The government reeled from one ministerial crisis to the next; public dissatisfaction was seen in the streets; and Sagasta had to act cautiously to prevent direct military rule. Surprisingly, during this time of troubles, the monarch was an element of stability. Sagasta, a tired and dispirited fox, and the Austrian-born queen regent, bent on saving a throne for her son, managed to keep Spain together. Vulnerable, Spain could hope for little more than the survival of its governing system and a minimum of colonial losses.

But Madrid could take some comfort in knowing that the United

States and Spain agreed on some peace terms. The McKinley administration disdained the Cuban Republic and was pledged to protect Spanish nationals and their property. It was considering a long-term stay on
the island to ensure domestic order and to aid economic recovery. The
McKinley administration, however, was unlikely to accept the island's
debt, it wanted Puerto Rico, and its Philippine goals were unclear.

CHAPTER I 3

. . . .

THE PEACE

. . . .

PROTOCOL

. . . .

W hen peace negotiations began, the general positions of both sides were known. The McKinley administration wanted to remove Spain from Cuba
and Puerto Rico; it did not expect a financial indemnity, and it rejected
the Cuban debt. It wished to treat directly with Spain, opposing European interference. But there were uncertainties about the future of the
Philippine Islands and Cuba. The United States had the military initiative. It was poised to invade Puerto Rico and to assault Manila, and Watson's fleet menaced Spain's other colonies and coasts.[1]

Spain could accept many of Washington's positions. The Spanish government was prepared to cede Cuba, and it wanted American protection
of Spanish subjects and property. Spain was relieved that the United
States did not expect a financial indemnity. It also was wary of conducting
peace negotiations through a third government, which might expect compensation for its efforts. The Spanish government, however, worried
about the Cuban debt and wanted to keep the Philippine Islands and
Puerto Rico, the latter still untouched by the war. Although on the defensive, the Spanish government had some military assets that it hoped to
trade. Its army occupied most of Cuba and the Philippine Islands including Manila. It could fight a defensive war for many months and inflict

many casualties, and tropical diseases would erode American forces. Madrid hoped to barter its military potential for retention of Puerto Rico and the Philippines. At the same time, the Spanish government realized that prolonging the war would inevitably diminish its military position and increase American demands; therefore the cabinet was anxious for an immediate cease-fire.[2]

To initiate peace talks, Spain had to open a direct channel of communication with the United States. The Spanish cabinet had repeatedly turned aside British offers to act as a go-between. Anglo-Spanish relations were poor and getting worse, and the British might ask for the Canary Islands.[3] France was more attractive. Hanotaux had been sympathetic and helpful, and although Delcassé had recently replaced him, one of Spain's most experienced diplomats, León y Castillo, was in Paris. Since Washington had balked at the attempt to open direct talks between León y Castillo and Porter, Spain decided to ask the French government to act simply as a carrier in relaying messages. This was logical: when the war had begun, the French embassy had taken charge of Spanish interests in Washington. During the war, French diplomats had effectively handled Spanish blockade shipping cases and provided services for prisoners of war. Therefore, on 18 July, Almodóvar asked the French government to permit Cambon to deliver a Spanish message to McKinley and to arrange, on behalf of Spain, a suspension of hostilities that would precede the final peace negotiations. Almodóvar explained that Spain wanted peace because the American naval blockade imposed suffering on the Cuban people and prevented food shipments to the army, placing it in an inferior position.[4]

The request for Cambon's services met with an unexpected eight-day delay, which frustrated Spain's desire for a quick cease-fire. Delcassé would not authorize Cambon to represent Spain until the French president and cabinet approved it, and he also wanted Cambon's advice. Since the French president was ill and residing outside Paris and Cambon was on vacation in New England, it took three days for the French government to consent to Almodóvar's request.[5] On 22 July, Almodóvar sent Madrid's message to Cambon in code, believing that Cambon could decode it with a key that remained in the Spanish legation. Cambon was unable to find the decoding key, so he suggested that León y Castillo decode the message in Paris and Delcassé relay it in French code to Washington. This mix-up added three more days of delay. By the time Cambon had Madrid's message translated into English and was ready to deliver it to McKinley, an American army had landed in southern Puerto Rico, and one of Spain's objectives had been lost.[6]

Although the French government was supposed to act only as a post office, Cambon and Delcassé began to counsel the Spanish government and to assist in presenting Madrid's views to Washington. The French officials wanted the war to end as quickly as possible in part because of Spain's predicament but also because they wished to keep American armed forces out of the eastern Atlantic and North Africa. The fate of the Canary Islands, Ceuta, and Morocco was important to France. Accordingly, Cambon and Delcassé pressed Madrid to accept Washington's demands in order to end the war quickly. The French position emerged with Cambon's initial communication, which warned Madrid to have no illusions; to obtain an armistice, Spain must agree to McKinley's terms.[7]

Almodóvar's first message to McKinley sought peace based on a new status for Cuba. The cause of the war, Almodóvar reasoned, was Spain's refusal to grant Cuba independence, which was undeserved; U.S. intervention had then required Spain to defend its possessions and honor. Having suffered calamitous military losses in an uneven struggle, Spain was no longer willing to persist in a conflict that brought hardship to both nations as well as suffering to the Cuban people. Spain was prepared to end the war in Cuba and to search for other means to settle the dispute. Almodóvar asked McKinley to define a "political status in Cuba" that would end the strife and pacify the island.[8]

Almodóvar also met with the diplomats in Madrid to explain the Spanish position. Spain hoped the United States would annex Cuba and protect Spanish and other foreign subjects and their property from anarchy and racial violence. The Cuban people, Almodóvar observed, were largely illiterate and not ready for self-government and independence. The Spanish were prepared to surrender Havana without a battle, a military concession that was the equivalent of an indemnity of war. Accordingly, Spain hoped to keep Puerto Rico and the Philippine Islands. Cambon quickly warned that the United States did not want to annex Cuba and that Spain should be prepared to lose Puerto Rico.[9]

On 26 July, Cambon delivered Almodóvar's note to McKinley. Accompanied by Eugène Thiébaut, the first secretary of the French embassy, who served as translator, Cambon was ushered into the White House library where McKinley and Day were waiting. Cambon explained that he came as a representative of the Spanish government rather than as the French ambassador. After Thiébaut read Almodóvar's note, Cambon asked for permission to speak, which McKinley granted. Cambon congratulated the president on the government's military success, "the greatest military victory in the history of the world," observing that there were no higher honors to be gained by continuing the war. He asked McKinley to display "his Christian and generous humanity" by granting Spain "liberal and honorable terms." Day pointed out that Almodóvar's note mentioned pacifying only Cuba, and he asked if Spain sought peace just on the island or on every front. Cambon assured him that Spain desired a comprehensive peace. While Day and Thiébaut prepared a press release on Spain's initiative, McKinley and Cambon stepped to the library window, which overlooked the Washington Monument. Cambon appealed to McKinley by referring to the American and Spanish mothers whose sons were now in Cuba. Cambon hoped that the president reflected on the four thousand American soldiers afflicted by typhoid and yellow fever. McKinley thanked Cambon with emotion, and the French diplomat believed that the initial impression of Spain's message was "favorable." The meeting ended with the understanding that McKinley would take Spain's request into consideration and consult his cabinet; when his answer was ready, he would reply formally through Cambon.[10]

Throughout the remainder of the day and into the next, McKinley met with his cabinet officers. Alger and Long joined the president in the afternoon, and Bliss, Smith, and Wilson arrived after dinner; discussions continued until midnight. Sometime during the evening, McKinley wrote a note to himself on Executive Mansion stationery: "Tuesday evening. As a condition to entering upon negotiations looking to peace, Spain must withdraw from Cuba and Porto Rico [sic] and such adjacent islands as are under her domination. This requirement will admit no negotiation. As to the Philippines, I am of the opinion, that with propriety, and advantage they can be the subject of negotiation and whenever the Spanish gov't desire it, I will appoint commissioners to that end. WmK." Cortelyou believed that this note showed that McKinley's ideas dominated the cabinet discussions, since at the end of the consulting process he had achieved his goals. But McKinley's note followed long-accepted positions on Cuba and Puerto Rico and left the Philippine issue open, which conformed to the cabinet view.[11]

Newspapermen interviewing McKinley's cabinet officers reported a wide-ranging discussion. There was consensus on freeing Cuba, annexing Puerto Rico, and refusing all Cuban and Puerto Rican debt. The cabinet members also agreed on the means to negotiate: the administration would state precise minimum terms in the form of an ultimatum and stick to them. The cabinet wanted to avoid making flexible demands that invited haggling with Spain and that might lead to lengthy negotiations and indecisive exchanges. Spain would have to accept or reject American terms; if it turned them down, it would bear the onus of continuing the war. And if Spain continued to fight, some cabinet officers talked about a monetary indemnity and coaling stations in the Canary Islands and the Mediterranean.[12]

The difficulty was defining American policy toward the Philippines. The *New York Times* noted, with some exaggeration, that nine cabinet members offered nine different opinions, ranging from complete annexation to total withdrawal. An additional problem was that cabinet opinions were not deeply held and fluctuated as news from the islands arrived. Cabinet members also complained that they lacked information about the islands and wanted to hear more from Dewey. Initially, Griggs and Wilson argued for keeping all the islands. But when Wilson learned of Philippine opposition, he thought the fewer islands, the better. Alger at first wanted all of them, but he was increasingly absorbed by army scandals and less interested in annexation. Smith thought of taking Luzon and having a protectorate over the other islands. Bliss favored commercial expansion, seen in a coaling station and a free-trade zone at Subic Bay. Day and Long thought a naval station at Manila was sufficient. Gage was the contrarian; he wanted nothing. McKinley also asked the advice of Hay, who thought that the United States should protect the islanders and prevent any other power from ceding or leasing the archipelago. Britain, Hay added, believed the United States should retain the islands; if they were to be sold, the British wanted an option to buy. From various comments, reporters gathered that McKinley wanted to retain an American presence in the Philippines but not in all the islands. He was not worried about how the European nations might react to American annexation. The president held that insufficient time had elapsed for the American people to conclude what to do, and he hoped that when the time came for a decision, public opinion would crystallize sufficiently to allow him to act decisively.[13]

A troubling problem was coming to terms with the Philippine nationalists. Cabinet members worried about returning the islands to Spain, which would then suppress the rebels who had fought beside the American army. Would the American public stand by as Spain quelled the Philippine patriots? The United States might promote independence under a government led by Aguinaldo and provide military protection for it. But were the Filipinos ready for self-government, and how well would Washington be able to work with Aguinaldo, who was already assuming a threatening position? Finally, the United States might oppose Emilio Aguinaldo and his independence movement and annex the islands. Some cabinet members thought that the United States could provide the islanders with better government than either Spain or Aguinaldo. But would the islanders submit to U.S. rule? And with the Republican Party divided over annexation, would the Senate approve a treaty?[14]

From these lengthy cabinet discussions McKinley devised a set of peace terms. Moore prepared a draft note that reflected administration thinking. It placed the blame for the war on Spain, pointed out the heavy cost of the war, and set forth American demands. For the Philippines, Moore wrote three alternative proposals, followed by two additional drafts; this illustrated the government's difficulty in deciding what to do. The cabinet reviewed Moore's draft for over five hours, with discussion centered largely on two problems, Cuba and the Philippines. Despite the Teller amendment, the administration was uncertain about Washington's future relations with the island. Responding to Spain's willingness to cede Cuba to the United States, Moore first wrote that the island was "distracted and prostrate" and would need "aid and guidance"; therefore, the United States would "receive the delivery of the title to and possession of the island, for the purpose of restoring order there and establishing stable government" to protect the lives and property of its inhabitants. The cabinet rejected this language in favor of looser terminology. The United States, it declared, did not share Spanish "apprehensions" over "premature independence" but was prepared to give "aid and guidance" to the island. Spain must relinquish "all claim of sovereignty over or title to Cuba" and immediately evacuate the island. The United States would not demand a "pecuniary indemnity" but would assume the claims of American citizens arising from the insurrection and war. This vague language did not spell out where Cuban sovereignty went after Spain relinquished it. Presumably the Cuban people were to become sovereign, yet the United States assumed responsibility for aiding and guiding the island.[15]

The other problem the cabinet wrestled with was the future of the Philippine Islands. Moore's premise was that the United States had taken "practical possession" of the Philippines, long the scene of insurrection. Of his three drafts, one stated that the United States would not require the cession of the islands but would establish on one island a "naval station" over which the United States would have "exclusive title and jurisdiction." In another attempt, Moore wrote that the United States would acquire a naval station and relinquish the islands only with "satisfactory [treaty] guarantees for the maintenance of order, the preservation of the rights of their people, and the freedom of commerce." A redraft of this paragraph spelled out that the United States would "require satisfactory guarantees of complete amnesty to all persons in the Philippines for political offenses against the Government of Spain since the arrival in the islands of [Dewey's] naval forces." In a third effort, Moore declared that the president was "prepared to appoint commissioners to treat with [Spanish] commissioners . . . as to future disposition [of the islands]." [16]

None of Moore's drafts survived cabinet scrutiny. As the members labored over the issues—obligations toward the insurgents, sufficient territory to support a naval station, and Senate attitude toward cession— Long received from Dewey a telegram stating that Philippine soldiers were threatening the American army. Troubled by the news and the lack of complete information, the cabinet decided to put off a decision. It adopted language that fit McKinley's idea of leaving the options open: "the United States [was] entitled to occupy, and [would] hold the city, bay, and harbor of Manila pending the conclusion of a treaty of peace which [should] determine the control, possession, and government of the Philippines." [17]

Since the decision on the islands was pushed into the future, the cabinet discussed the role of the commissioners who would negotiate the treaty. It was understood that McKinley would appoint people of high quality who would be sensitive to doing justice to the Philippine nationalists yet would also be conscious of the expansion of American power. None of them should be hostile to annexing foreign territory. [18]

The remaining points were less controversial. The United States wanted as a war indemnity an island in the Ladrones, Puerto Rico, "and other islands now under the sovereignty of Spain in the West Indies." This wording suggested that the McKinley administration was interested in acquiring the Isle of Pines, a large island lying off southwest Cuba. Spaniards and Cubans considered this island a part of Cuban jurisdiction, but Americans contested its ownership with Cuba for the next two decades. McKinley's cabinet concluded that if Spain accepted these terms, the United States would name commissioners to settle the details of a peace treaty; there was no mention of an early armistice. [19]

During the four days that the McKinley administration was hammering out its peace proposals, the French and Spanish governments were attempting to speed up the process. Both worried that the McKinley administration would delay talks in order to continue military operations; to facilitate the exchanges, Delcassé urged Almodóvar to authorize Cambon to negotiate on Spain's behalf. He also encouraged the Spanish to prepare concrete terms to offer the United States. Since Madrid was pleased with Cambon's initial presentation of Spain's case, Almodóvar accepted Delcassé's advice and provided Cambon with negotiating authority and Spanish views.[20]

The Spanish foreign minister explained that the war with the United States began over separating Cuba from Spain. Now the Spanish government was willing to conclude the war on any Cuban settlement that satisfied the United States—"absolute independence, independence under the protectorate, or annexation to the American Republic," preferring the latter as a better guarantee of Spanish lives and property. But the war had involved other Spanish colonies, and Spain wanted to preserve as much of these territories as possible. Madrid accepted the principle of claims derived from "military operations," which constituted "temporary occupation," or possibly war "expenditures." Indemnification, however, should be "in reasonable proportion and measure." Almodóvar asked Cambon to press to retain Puerto Rico and the Philippine Islands and to insist on an immediate suspension of hostilities. Once the two nations agreed on the fundamentals for peace, there should be an armistice; negotiations for a final peace treaty could follow. Spain opposed holding an international conference and would consider bilateral talks at a neutral site.[21]

On 30 July both sides were ready for a second meeting; McKinley had a set of proposals embedded in a formal note, and Cambon had authority and instructions to represent Spanish interests. The meeting lasted over two hours. Day read the note, which Thiébaut translated, and then Cambon and McKinley examined each proposal. During the conference, Long, Admiral Montgomery Sicard, and Adee were summoned. Cambon complained that the American proposals were too "harsh." He repeated Spain's fear of Cuban independence and its desire to cede Cuba to the United States. McKinley responded that there was no advantage in American acquisition. He intended to give Cuba an "absolutely independent government, but not until it showed itself able to carry out all its responsibilities, both domestic and foreign." Cambon quickly replied that in that case the United States would never leave the island. Cambon urged the United States to accept Cuba as its indemnity and to permit Spain to keep Puerto Rico and all of the Ladrones, pointing out that the United States had withdrawn its troops from Mexico City at the end of the Mexican War. Day interrupted to assert that it would be difficult to find in all history a nation that did not ask for a pecuniary indemnity. And McKinley categorically refused to modify the American position.[22]

The most difficult issue was the future of the Philippine Islands. Cambon objected to the loose language on sovereignty, which implied that the issue was to be settled at the peace conference. The implication that sovereignty was negotiable threatened to end the current talks. McKinley insisted that the United States should derive some advantages from its victory in Manila Bay and the sacrifices made in sending a large army there. He assured Cambon that the United States "did not want to trouble anyone, and that everyone would profit, including Spain, . . . from the new battles the United States would undertake on behalf of civilization." Over Day's objections, McKinley agreed to change one word in the note; he approved substituting *disposition* for *possession*, which Cambon believed softened the issue of sovereignty. The clause now read that the treaty of peace would "determine the control, disposition, and government of the Philippines." When Day left to change the wording of the note, McKinley and Cambon had a relaxed and intimate exchange. McKinley explained how important it was to satisfy public opinion and the Senate in order to conclude a peace treaty. Cambon concluded that the president did not want to acquire all the Philippines, just an "establishment," but that McKinley was unwilling to "disappoint the American public."[23]

A final item concerned Spain's desire for an immediate armistice. Day suggested it should begin when the peace commissioners first met, but McKinley thought that hostilities could end as soon as Spain consented to American terms and authorized Cambon to sign preliminary articles. When the meeting was over, McKinley was "highly satisfied" and "very hopeful" for an early peace. Cambon was impressed by McKinley's earnest and sincere demeanor, whereas McKinley appreciated Cambon's eloquence and depth of feeling. Because of leaks and rumors, McKinley released to the press on 2 August a verbatim set of American terms.[24]

When Washington's proposals reached Madrid, the Spanish government considered them to be "extremely harsh"; the cession of Puerto Rico was "completely unjustified," as was the loose language on the Philippines and the American demand to occupy Manila. Patenôtre coun-seled Almodóvar that some U.S. presence in the Philippines could prove useful. If the Americans withdrew completely, Spain would have to enter a costly colonial war to defeat the insurgency. The nation was war-weary, bankrupt, and without a fleet. Under the circumstances, a joint Spanish-American agreement that satisfied the inhabitants might be the best pos-sible solution for Spain. Almodóvar rejected this logic. He preferred a guarantee of Spanish sovereignty, with commissioners empowered only to negotiate political reforms for the islands. On the other hand, the Cuban settlement and lack of monetary indemnity were satisfactory. Despite misgivings, Almodóvar urged the cabinet to accept the Amer-ican package.[25]

Sagasta's cabinet considered the Puerto Rican and Philippine propos-als for over four hours. Aware that Puerto Rican subjects were welcoming American troops and helpless to prevent the loss of the island, the gov-ernment nevertheless wanted to show the Spanish people that it had done everything possible to keep the island. Cabinet members were also troubled by the indeterminate wording on the Philippines. Any residual American presence would limit Spanish sovereignty, yet they realized the heavy cost involved in regaining control of the islands. The government decided to offer the United States other territory, such as Pacific islands, in exchange for Puerto Rico and to request clarification of the American language governing the Philippine settlement. It also approved a French suggestion to ask the McKinley administration to hold the final peace conference in Paris.[26]

Armed with new instructions, Cambon on 2 August met again with McKinley and Day. When Cambon told McKinley that the Spanish would like to keep Puerto Rico and cede other territory instead, the pres-ident did not even reply; he just smiled. McKinley, however, did try to clarify his thinking on the Philippines. He assured Cambon that his ad-ministration had decided nothing prejudicial either to Spanish or Amer-ican interests. Cambon speculated that the approaching national elec-tions affected the Philippine issue. Republicans entered the war, Cambon reasoned, to prevent the Democrats from winning the fall elections. Now the Republicans did not want to risk public disapproval by returning the Philippines to Spain. Cambon predicted that McKinley would press Spain hard before the elections and that afterward the president would be freer to do as he wanted and less inclined to demand as much from Spain. A new problem arose when Day stated that acceptance of the peace terms required the "immediate evacuation" of Spanish troops from Cuba and Puerto Rico. Cambon objected to this as an additional American demand, since an armistice implied that each side would keep its troops in place until a peace treaty was completed. Cambon speculated that the spread of yellow fever among American troops was pressuring Washington to remove Spanish soldiers so the government could reassign its troops to a healthier climate. After a lengthy discussion, Day modified the American position to having the right to demand immediate Spanish evacuation even though the United States did not expect to request it. In a more positive gesture to Spain, the president agreed to hold the final peace negotiations in Paris rather than Washington and suggested that each country send five negotiators. The president considered this concession a "token of his good will."[27]

During the discussion Cambon was again impressed by McKinley's straightforward and frank exchanges. The president explained his "lack of confidence" in the Cubans and his desire to place the government of the island "under the direct control of the United States." McKinley was somewhat "embarrassed" by the Teller amendment's declaration of American disinterest. And Cambon was convinced that McKinley sincerely believed American terms were "generous." Cambon warned that if Madrid rejected these "generous" provisions, the result would be "more devastating" and "more humiliating" for Spain.[28]

Despite the candor and openness, Cambon thought the president was difficult to deal with; McKinley was responsive to public pressure and therefore weaker than Cleveland. When one negotiated with McKinley, it was as if one was treating "with the politicians who fill his Cabinet, with the Senate, with the press, [and] with an electoral body aflame for glory and profits." Yet, Cambon concluded, historians would regard Cleveland as "without distinction" while McKinley would be "known as the energetic genius who enlarged the United States, presided over the revolution which gave them the world, and ended the last vestiges of division between the North and the South."[29]

After Cambon departed, McKinley optimistically believed that Spain would capitulate to American terms in a few days. Day was also "full of confidence." Symptomatic of Washington's buoyant mood was Long's curtailing of fleet operations; indeed, the navy secretary left Washington to take a vacation.[30]

But the American demand for immediate evacuation of Spanish troops raised a new problem for Spain. If the United States insisted, Spain would have to give up what little military advantage it had; it would have to cede the islands before the peace conference even began. With American troops occupying Manila as well, the Philippines would be at the mercy of the Americans. This news came while Sagasta was consulting with Spain's prominent political and military leaders in an effort to prepare for peace. The result was the emergence of constitutional questions and a call for reconvening the Cortes. Some Spanish cabinet members and outside politicians cited constitutional grounds for opposing troop withdrawals. According to article 55 of the constitution, the monarch could not "alienate, cede, or exchange . . . Spanish territory" or "ratify treaties . . . which . . . bind Spaniards" without the approval of the Cortes. In addition, Silvela and Tetuán wanted to reopen the Cortes to debate the issues. Almodóvar argued that the cabinet could set aside article 55 because the constitution also provided extraordinary powers to act in an emergency. And Sagasta opposed convening the Cortes, which was certain to complicate the peace process. The cabinet decided to combine these ideas into a new negotiating position: it accepted all of Washington's points with the stipulation that the withdrawal of Spanish troops and final settlement terms be subject to the approval of the Cortes. Almodóvar was certain that Washington would reject this conditional reply. Depressed by Spain's humiliation and sick at heart over ceding Puerto Rico, he considered the United States a "reckless superpower" that was imposing "cruel" conditions on Spain.[31]

The Spanish foreign minister took up the distasteful task of acceding to Washington's demands while adding Madrid's constitutional reservation. Almodóvar addressed a long note to Day. In it he continued the debate begun in the first exchange over responsibility for the war, charging the United States with starting a war that Spain reluctantly accepted in defense of its rights. Given that the Cubans lacked the ability to govern the island, Spain would relinquish sovereignty and withdraw its troops with the understanding that the United States would provide "guidance" and protect Spanish residents and Cuban natives loyal to the mother country. Spain's agreement, however, was "subject to the approval of the Cortes," a reservation that applied to all other terms and was similar to U.S. Senate approval of treaties. In like manner, the Spanish government agreed to cede Puerto Rico and an island in the Ladrones. Pointing out that the Spanish flag still flew over Manila and the Philippine Islands and characterizing American intentions as "veiled," Almodóvar asserted that Spain did not "*a priori* renounce [its] sovereignty . . . over the archipelago." Agreeing to leave to the negotiators only the "reforms" to be made, Spain acceded to Washington's language on the Philippines. Having accepted Washington's terms, the Spanish government was prepared to suspend hostilities and name commissioners to settle the details of a peace treaty.[32]

On 9 August, Cambon carried the Spanish reply to the White House. When Thiébaut finished reading Almodóvar's note, there was a long silence; it was evident that McKinley and Day were displeased. Breaking the silence, McKinley said that he had asked for and expected Spain to cede Cuba and Puerto Rico. Instead of a "categorical acceptance," the Spanish government had invoked the need for Cortes approval. He could not accept this stipulation. During the long discussion that followed, McKinley said several times: "We cannot *stand* this." Day wanted to return the Spanish note, and Cambon refused to take it back. Cambon tried to convince McKinley and Day that the need for Cortes approval compared to that of the American Senate, and he insisted that Spain had agreed to every American point. The meeting was about to end when Cambon asked McKinley what Spain could do to show its sincerity. McKinley suggested drafting a protocol that specified the American demands and spelled out the appointment of peace commissioners to negotiate a treaty at Paris and other commissioners to arrange the withdrawal of Spanish troops. The protocol would be a "preliminary document" to facilitate ending the war; it would not need Cortes or Senate approval, which would apply only to ratification of a final treaty. Cambon grabbed at the idea. That evening while Moore and Day drafted a protocol, Cambon warned that it was "time to end the war. . . . Day's patience [had] worn thin. . . . McKinley's idea of a phased and orderly withdrawal of Spanish forces . . . [was] preferable to [Spanish] capitulation."[33]

On 11 August, Cambon sent a copy of the protocol to Madrid, pointing out that Day had shown greater flexibility in drafting it. The demand for the "immediate" withdrawal of Spanish troops remained in the document but was modified by a procedure that delayed evacuation, since Spain would have ten days to name commissioners and thirty additional days before the commissioners met to work out the details of withdrawal. Day also promised that as soon as Spain signed the protocol, the United States would send provisions to Cuba.[34]

Sagasta's cabinet quickly agreed to the protocol and empowered Cambon to sign for Spain. The Spanish government was grateful for Cambon's able defense of its interests. It asked only that when the armistice took effect, the United States take measures to see that the Cubans abided by the cease-fire.[35]

The protocol was signed on 12 August. When Cambon received his instructions, he once again asked McKinley for a meeting, which the president set for 4:00 P.M. Cambon and Thiébaut joined McKinley and Day in the cabinet room. Moore, Adee, and Thomas Cridler from the State Department and Cortelyou, Benjamin F. Montgomery, O. L. Prudent, and Carl Loeffler from the president's staff witnessed the ceremony. As the president watched, Cambon and Day signed the protocol; Cridler attached the seal of the United States. Then Alger, Brigadier General Henry C. Corbin, and Acting Secretary of the Navy Charles H. Allen entered the room, and McKinley signed a proclamation ending hostilities with Spain. The military representatives quickly left to send the cease-fire order. But the order arrived in the Philippines too late to prevent a successful American assault on Manila, which jolted the Spanish government. Madrid bitterly assessed this final defeat, which jeopardized its claim to the Philippines. Nevertheless, Almodóvar hoped that Washington's attitude toward the islands would not change as a result of a battle that had taken place after the armistice had been signed.[36]

It is noteworthy that no Cuban or Puerto Rican was present at the ceremony concluding the war. The entire peace negotiation took place without Spain or the United States consulting the Cubans. And on the island, the American armed forces looked with contempt on Cuban troops. While Americans were fraternizing with Spaniards in Santiago de Cuba, Cuban soldiers were not even allowed in the city. General García was angered and embittered. Only on 13 August did the War Department ask Estrada Palma to honor the armistice. The Cuban leader agreed, and he cabled President Bartolomé Masó and the military commanders "to cease hostilities." An uneasy and uncertain cease-fire began. After three and a half years, the Cubans ended their struggle against Spain, but Washington had imposed a truce on the island that threatened their national aspirations.[37]

Ending the war had not been easy for either the Spanish or the American government. Spain suffered crushing military defeats and national humiliation. Even as it sued for peace, it endured military reverses. And the price of peace was high: complete capitulation to American terms. But Sagasta had managed to bring the government through the disastrous war and threats of army coups and Carlist uprisings.

The peace protocol defined much of America's foreign policy at the close of the century. In ending Spanish rule in the Western Hemisphere, the United States rejected any European role; it excluded an international conference as well as Great Power mediation. The United States held unquestioned authority in its geographic sphere. The American government took different stances toward the Atlantic and the Pacific. The McKinley administration never attacked Spanish colonies in the eastern Atlantic or Mediterranean Sea. It steered clear of the Canary Islands, Fernando Po, Tangiers, Ceuta, and the Balearic Islands. In effect, the Atlantic Ocean still existed as a barrier, with Europe held at arm's length from the Western Hemisphere and with American restraint exhibited toward North Africa and the Mediterranean. The Pacific Ocean was different. Dewey's victory was followed by an army expedition to the Philippines and an assault on Manila. The Americans took Guam and annexed the Hawaiian Islands. Clearly the Far East was more attractive. The question was not one of taking Pacific naval bases and coaling stations but of determining how much to acquire. McKinley's cabinet contained a spectrum of views, but only one in nine wanted nothing. Overwhelmingly, the McKinley administration favored expansion.

The fashioning of Pacific expansionism revealed the dynamics of foreign policy formulation. The United States was unmoved by European interests. Spain's physical possession of and historic claim to the islands were of no consideration; and the United States was certain that it could administer the islands better than the Spanish or the native inhabitants. More important were domestic politics. The McKinley administration wanted to obtain something substantial and satisfying from Dewey's victory. And the extent of what it took depended on the national mood, the approaching November election, divisions within the Republican Party, and a judgment over what the Senate would accept in a treaty. McKinley explained the American situation well; he wanted something of value in the Philippines, and he hoped that when the American people crystallized their attitude toward the islands, they would provide him with sufficient political support to act decisively. McKinley would get the American people what they wanted.

Cambon fully understood the fundamentals of negotiating with McKinley; one had to deal with the president, the cabinet, Congress, the press, and greedy special interests. Cambon disparaged this system; he believed it revealed a weak president, one who bowed to domestic pressures rather than ruled the nation. To Cambon, an unflinching Cleveland was preferable. Yet McKinley adhered more closely to the American political system than Cleveland. The Democratic president had divided his party and lost an election; the Republican chose a course that united his party and was destined to win the next election.

CHAPTER 14

. . . .

CONCLUSION

. . . .

The Spanish-American War was inevitable and necessary: inevitable given the irreconcilable political positions dividing the Cuban, Spanish, and American
people, and necessary to bring an early end to the Cuban-Spanish colonial war. Spanish misrule and Cuban nationalism had caused the colonial
revolution. Once the revolution was under way, *peninsulares* and wealthy
Creoles advocated concentrating the peasantry in fortified towns and destroying crops in order to isolate and end the rebellion. The Spanish
knew reconcentration would be costly in lives and human misery; nevertheless, Cánovas and Weyler adopted this strategy. But it failed to end the
rebellion. Sagasta's reforms, which aimed to rally moderates, attract insurgents, and satisfy *peninsulares*, had unrealistic expectations for success.
The reforms came too late and were only halfway measures. Few autonomists remained, and Madrid tightly controlled the new insular regime
by selecting the executives and manipulating the insular legislative elections. This was not the Canadian model Moret had promised. Sagasta
delayed giving Cubans control over tariffs to avoid offending peninsular
businessmen, and Blanco did not abolish all reconcentration until April.
The Spanish government also waffled on the role of military power in
ending the insurrection, courting military officers by giving lip service to
defeating the insurgents. When these tardy, limited, and contradictory
measures faltered, the Spanish government unrealistically blamed the
failure on American support of the New York Junta. The Spanish ascribed Washington's aggressive behavior to decades of American interest
in acquiring the wealth of Cuba.

A major problem for Sagasta was the military presence in peninsular politics. Cánovas had better relations with the army officers than Sagasta, and when the Cuban war started, military discontent with Sagasta surfaced, leading Cánovas to take charge of the government. Sagasta's criticism of Weyler generated more army dissatisfaction. When Sagasta dismissed Weyler and began winding down the war, army officers led riots in Havana, which foreclosed further reforms. In effect, the military held a veto over Sagasta's Cuban policy. Sagasta presided over a weak government; if he broke with the ranking officers, the army might upset his government, and a "dishonorable" settlement in Cuba might result in a peninsular rebellion ignited by returning officers and soldiers. Nevertheless, with reforms stymied and American pressure mounting, Moret suggested an armistice, which Sagasta's cabinet reluctantly and belatedly adopted. But the Spanish public angrily denounced the armistice, and the Cubans rejected it. Sagasta's government reassured the public that a suspension of hostilities was a means of gaining time to shore up autonomy, to improve Spanish defenses, and to allow Cubans to surrender. The government could make no further concessions. Indeed, to satisfy the military, to rally the nation, and to fend off Carlists, Madrid needed to demonstrate its patriotism. As cabinet ministers acknowledged, it was better to enter a war with the United States and risk the consequences than to surrender Cuba ignominiously and face a civil war at home.

Whereas the Spanish made some attempts to end the colonial war and to prevent an American conflict, the Cubans were inflexible. Given the danger of exchanging Spanish rule for American control, Cuba's revolutionary leaders showed little imagination in trying to avoid U.S. domination. Naturalized citizens, the Junta members manipulated their adopted country in their efforts to gain independence, but in the process they irritated Cleveland and McKinley. The Cuban revolutionary army willfully destroyed American property while the Junta outfitted illegal filibustering expeditions, lobbied Congress, and released the de Lôme letter. Perhaps the Cubans mismanaged American government relations because of poor leadership and weak organization. One of Martí's objectives had been to avoid American imperialism; had he lived, he might have pursued a different course. But leadership devolved on Gómez and Estrada Palma. Gómez was not known for compromise; his stubbornness kept the revolutionary forces in the field despite a staggering cost in lives and property. Although Estrada Palma was respected for his devotion to the anti-Spanish cause, he lacked Martí's political stature and had no authority to speak for Gómez. Poor communications made it difficult for these leaders to consult on policy. The result was inflexibility as the Cubans adhered to one position that all could agree on: independence from Spain at all cost.

For Washington, the turning point in Cuban-American relations came during the month before the outbreak of the Spanish-American War. When the McKinley administration realized it would have to fight in Cuba, it wanted complete control. It did not wish to form an alliance with the Cubans or place invading American soldiers under Cuban jurisdiction, legally subservient to Gómez. In the closing hours, the McKinley administration pressured Estrada Palma to accept an armistice in order to prevent a Spanish-American war. The Cubans balked. Distrusting the McKinley administration, they condemned its coercion and threatened to turn Cuban soldiers against invading American troops. The price of Cuban cooperation, Estrada Palma said, was the immediate recognition of Cuba's independence and of the Cuban Republic; McKinley refused to pay it. Rather than cooperate with McKinley, the Junta relied on Congress. Estrada Palma managed to get the Teller amendment passed, but this did not bring diplomatic recognition. Once the war began, McKinley cut the Cubans out of wartime decisions and peacemaking negotiations as he prepared to use the army to govern the island.

One wonders what might have occurred if the Cubans had attempted to cooperate. They might have respected American property and obeyed the neutrality laws; when they obtained the de Lôme letter, they might have taken it to the State Department rather than spread it across the front page of the *Journal*. Most important, they could have helped the McKinley administration to establish an armistice in Cuba in order to prevent a Spanish-American war. A policy of cooperation would have required a gamble on gaining independence, but antagonizing the McKinley administration and allowing an invasion was also full of risks.

One of the major points of disagreement among Cubans, Spaniards, and Americans was the status of the Cuban war. Cubans and Spaniards denied that the Cuban-Spanish war was a stalemate and therefore questioned the timing and purpose of American military intervention. But the facts favor a stalemate. By 1898, both the Spanish and the Cubans were war-weary, and the scale of military operations had diminished during 1897. Spain had about sixty thousand effective troops. It held all the major cities and ports, controlled the seas, and could resupply food and munitions. Its army, however, did little to pursue the rebels, preferring to defend the garrisons. The Cubans had up to forty thousand soldiers, held the eastern mountainous third of the island, and had small units functioning in central Cuba and to a lesser degree in the western part of the island. The Cuban army was poorly armed. Lacking artillery and sea power, it was not strong enough to lay siege to an important city or port or to assault and take major Spanish-entrenched fortifications. It had taken only one provincial capital, Las Tunas, in eastern Cuba. One should keep in mind the difficulties Americans later faced in assaulting Santiago de Cuba. If the Cuban army was about to triumph, why did Estrada Palma and Gómez continue to offer Spain money to recognize the island's independence? And if the rebels were about to take the cities, why was there no panic or flight among the *peninsulares* or wealthy Creoles? In fact, the breaking point was not in sight. Had the United States not ended the stalemate, the Cuban and Spanish death toll and property destruction would have continued to mount.

Related to the military situation in Cuba were the repeated stories that the Spanish, who would not surrender the island to the insurgents, preferred to end the colonial war by losing Cuba to the American army. Thus, Spain courted a war with the United States to provide an honorable means to withdraw from Cuba. The evidence does not support this. Sagasta's ministry worked hard to avoid a war, and after war began, Spanish officers showed no inclination to surrender. They fought against overwhelming odds and were the last element in Spain to give up.

For American historians, the major issues have been determining the reasons the United States went to war and the role McKinley played in the events. One important element was the support the American people gave to the Cuban struggle for independence. Public approval of national aspirations of downtrodden people was part of a pattern of nineteenth-century American thinking, as seen in the country's response to Greeks, Hungarians, Irish, Armenians, and others. American involvement in the Cuban uprising was more intense; the revolution included naturalized American citizens, it featured filibustering, it affected business, it involved domestic politics, and it raised national security considerations. During the conflict, Americans expressed their sense of morality, justice, and fair play as well as their self-interest and prejudices. They opposed military tyranny and cheered on an oppressed minority seeking self-rule. They were shocked by the loss of innocent lives and human misery and were disgusted by deliberate property destruction, all of which confirmed their prejudice against the Spanish. Americans needed no great debate to decide the issue; it was axiomatic that corrupt and cruel Spain should leave Cuba. Fundamental to American thinking was the realization that the United States had the military power to stop the conflict. And Congress reflected the public mood well; it sympathized with Cuban aspirations, thundered against Spanish outrages, and advocated intervention.

But one important element of American society, business, was slow to accept intervention. Business interests directly affected by the Cuban revolution were divided over what to do. Investors, fearing Spanish reprisals on property if war came and distrustful of Cuban insurgents, lobbied to keep the peace. Merchants, watching their trade collapse, petitioned for intervention. From 1895 to 1898, the American government protested the losses, but it did not go to war to stop property destruction or to restore trade. The general business community wanted the McKinley administration to settle the Cuban issue, but it was not until Proctor's speech that the business community finally came to support the use of military force. The change did not alter the McKinley administration's policy. The president pursued his diplomacy in response to developments in Cuba and Spain. He was aggressive during the summer of 1897, moderate during the fall, skeptical and more inclined to intervene by February 1898, and reluctant in April. None of McKinley's changes in direction coincided with business fluctuations. And when it came to defining peace terms, Moore drew up a package of administration objectives without consulting the business community.

One area of business that advocated American intervention was the sensational press. Some historians have interpreted William Randolph Hearst's drive to dominate New York City journalism as causing the public hysteria that galvanized the nation to intervene. But sensational journalism had only a marginal impact. Hearst played on American prejudices; he did not create them. Although he and other sensationalists supplied many false stories, they did not fabricate the major events that moved the United States. Calhoun, American consuls, naval officers, Red Cross officials, and Proctor gave eyewitness accounts of Cuban wretchedness, and they were not on Hearst's payroll. Hearst published the de Lôme letter, but he did not make it up. Hearst charged that Spaniards had sunk the *Maine*, yet he did not write the naval report that propelled the nation toward war. Had there been no sensational press, only responsible editors, the American public nevertheless would have learned about the terrible conditions in Cuba, would have wanted Spain to leave, and would have considered Proctor's speech, the *Maine* report, and the consular reports as justification for using military force.

Another aspect of American interest in the Cuban conflict evolved from national security issues. The McKinley administration was interested in an Isthmian canal, Caribbean naval bases, coaling stations, and the Hawaiian Islands. It wanted to diminish Europe's presence in the New World. But none of these considerations caused the United States to fight Spain. To the contrary, as late as March 1898, McKinley would have been satisfied if some form of suzerainty had succeeded in ending the revolution and keeping the island under Spanish sovereignty.

Much more significant was a series of unexpected and shocking events that fanned the flames of public emotion, embittered officials, and narrowed the choices for McKinley and Sagasta. The first surprise was the 12 January riot in Havana, which slowed Spain's reform program and led to the visit of the *Maine*. Dupuy de Lôme's letter undercut the Spanish government and fueled American suspicion and patriotism. One week later, the *Maine* explosion vastly increased hostility toward Spain. And Proctor's speech convinced the most conservative and timid that it was time for Spain to leave. When the navy's investigation concluded that a mine had caused the explosion, the public was united and prepared for war. Accused of the *Maine* explosion and seared by congressional condemnations, the Spanish angrily asserted their integrity and fulminated over American hypocrisy and injustice. McKinley and Sagasta desperately worked to control these escalating crises, but both found conciliatory approaches unpopular and the target of opposition politicians. It is sobering to realize that during a time of international tension, a string of unexpected and reinforcing events could provide such a strong impetus for war.

These unanticipated events raise an important question: might the war have been avoided had even some of these episodes not taken place and had skilled diplomats managed them better? If the *Maine* hadn't blown up or Dupuy hadn't written to Canalejas, would there have been a Spanish-American war? Such questions cannot be answered definitively. There probably would have been a war, since the Cuban-Spanish-American conflict sprang from fundamental and not accidental differences. Americans believed in Cuban independence and wanted an end to the suffering and destruction on the island. Even before the January riot, Day was preparing the consular reports for release, and McKinley expected them to do what Proctor's speech actually did. The inadvertent happenings of early 1898 heightened tensions, impeded concessions, and made U.S. intervention overwhelmingly popular. Without these events, however, the Cubans would have fought on, the Spanish government would have held on, and the United States probably would have intervened.

Related to the unexpected was the amateur nature of Washington's diplomatic service. McKinley's foreign affairs administration was based on inexperienced personnel. The president had never held a diplomatic post and had never traveled outside the United States. He relied on his cabinet for advice, yet none of its members had diplomatic experience. Sherman was senile, and Day was new to both Washington and foreign affairs; Hay was the only cosmopolitan figure in the senior ranks of the administration. McKinley first obtained advice from Calhoun, who based his recommendations on a short visit to Cuba. Woodford had no diplomatic experience, knew nothing of Spain or Cuba, and had no Spanish language capability. And Archbishop Ireland, with conflicting loyalties, was an important player in the last-minute negotiations.

McKinley's most important diplomatic advice came from Woodford. The president gave him great authority, since negotiations were largely carried out in Madrid. Although Woodford worked diligently to serve the president, his lack of experience and expertise inevitably colored his mission. During eight months in Spain, Woodford learned the basic facts of Spanish politics, but he never fathomed the depth of Spanish national feeling. He drew close to Moret, with whom he could speak in English. Since Moret was the most flexible cabinet member, Woodford came to believe that the government was more pliable than it was. He erroneously interpreted Sagasta's reforms and Moret's flexibility as evidence of Spanish movement toward withdrawal. Operating from American pragmatic logic, Woodford reasoned that if Washington exerted enough pressure, the Spanish would sell Cuba rather than risk an unwinnable war. When the Spanish cabinet balked at further concessions and insisted on upholding its national honor, Woodford characterized its stand as mere "punctilio." He did not understand that the Spanish could not bargain away four hundred years of Cuban ownership for $100 million or any other sum. Thus McKinley's reliance on Woodford led to serious errors of judgment.

One of the most important aspects of American intervention was domestic partisan politics. During the 1890s, American politicians were not inclined to treat foreign crises through bipartisan cooperation. When

Cleveland was president, Republican legislators passed Cuban resolutions designed to impress voters and embarrass the White House. When McKinley became president, Democratic congressmen attempted to use the same tactic. Party divisions ran deep because of passionate disputes over money, tariffs, big business, and labor unions. The acute rivalry put a premium on winning elections and the struggle between the executive and legislative branches for control of policy. The 1896 presidential race augmented partisanship, and Republicans considered the elections of 1898 and 1900 to be crucial.

The battle for party ascendancy was intense in Congress. In 1897, Republicans narrowly organized the Senate, but silver Republicans were partial to the Cuban cause, and the Foreign Relations Committee, though Republican, was overwhelmingly pro-Cuban. In the House, Reed was the bulwark against Democratic moves, but his mastery depended on the Republican rank and file. Several times Democrats managed to bring the Cuban issue before the House and to record Republicans voting to put off action. Reed's *reconcentrados* made good politics for the coming election.

At the start of the McKinley administration, the president and Republican legislators were not too far apart. The latter were willing to give diplomacy a chance, and McKinley held in his arsenal of diplomatic threats a congressional resolution for intervention. In January he began preparing consular reports to release as a means of triggering a congressional resolution, and he intended to employ this weapon by April if Spain did not break the deadlock in Cuba. Up to mid-March, the president was in control and prepared to act forcefully.

But McKinley was more flexible and pragmatic than the legislators. His overriding concern was ending the Cuban-Spanish conflict; the means were secondary. The Cubans could win independence, or Spain could defeat them, or autonomist moderates could establish control, or the United States could purchase the island. The final option, direct military intervention, was the least desirable, although U.S. naval power promised a quick war with minimum American losses.

The series of inadvertent happenings in February and March galvanized public opinion and panicked many Republican politicians. In defense of the legislators, many of them held deep convictions about Cuba and were as inflamed by the events as the general public. They did not need to be prodded by constituents or told by sensational newspapers that Spain should leave Cuba. It was surprising that McKinley, who listened carefully to legislators, was caught off balance by a Republican revolt that threatened a declaration of war. The House rebellion launched a struggle between the McKinley administration and Congress for control of Cuban policy. The conflict was based in part on Woodford's misleading advice to the president. At the time that Proctor made his speech and the *Maine* report arrived in Washington, Woodford concluded that Spain was moving toward an accommodation; continued American pressure and a little more time, Woodford advised, would free Cuba without a war. Prodded by Congress and acting on Woodford's erroneous judgment, McKinley stepped up the pressure but delayed for a few days in the vain hope that Spain was about to end the struggle in Cuba. By 1 April, McKinley had concluded that war was inevitable. Then a cease-fire appeared possible, and the president held off Congress for several more days. Only on 10 April, when he could no longer persuade Republican legislators to provide more time, did he cede the decision for war to Congress. It is ironic that Congress, filled with prejudice against Spain and impelled by partisan political considerations, was closer than Woodford or McKinley to the reality that American military intervention was the only way to bring the Cuban-Spanish impasse to a quick end.

The president's resistance to congressional pressure and ultimate surrender made him appear more committed to peace and a weaker leader than he was. As the news from Madrid fluctuated, the president followed a course of zigs and zags that led to confusion over his intentions and doubts about his resolution. Obviously the president preferred peace to war, and he softened his stand in November when Sagasta promised reforms and again in early April when a cease-fire seemed at hand. The president's final attempts to restrain Congress were commendable; it was unfortunate for McKinley's reputation that many misjudged his performance, some critics finding him irresolute in the face of Spain and others with respect to Congress.

McKinley worked hard to define the reason for using military force in Cuba. Cleveland had set the tone by warning Spain that humanitarian considerations could cause American intervention. McKinley adopted this view and held it consistently through April 1898. The president sought to minimize the Dupuy de Lôme affair and the *Maine* report. He approved Proctor's speech, attempted to manipulate Cuban relief into a cause for intervention, and then released the consular reports. Obviously, it was better to blame Spain for inhumane conditions that required American intervention than to act because of domestic political pressures. But in the end, it was these pressures that brought about military intervention. Republican legislators made war on Spain not to obtain control of Cuba but to retain control of Washington.

In dealing with the Cuban nationalists, McKinley pursued illogical means and objectives. Moved by the suffering of *reconcentrados* and sympathetic to Cuba's aspiration for independence, he began by deciding that there should be no Cuban settlement that did not satisfy the insurgents; in effect, he gave the Cubans a veto over his negotiations with Spain. Yet he never made an effort to establish an understanding with Estrada Palma and Gómez or to open consultations with them other than to receive information from McCook, a financially interested party.

Since the Cubans were pledged to accept no settlement short of total independence, the president's consideration of other possible solutions is difficult to understand. Either he did not believe that the Cubans meant what they said, or he thought that he could bend them to his way of thinking. For example, the president repeatedly offered mediation, but he never discussed with the Cubans what might be negotiated. He explored purchasing the island but did not ask the Cubans how they might regard American ownership. McKinley seemed to have two separate positions on Cuban goals: with respect to Spain, the Cubans should not settle unless satisfied; with respect to the United States, the Cubans should accept whatever was offered.

Part of this confused situation was McKinley's rejection of the Cuban Republic. The president wanted the Cubans to have independence, but he yoked independence to American guidance. Clearly the path of Cuban-American relations was strewn by both sides with suspicion and distrust, and it is not surprising that the path led to American military control of the island and to the Platt amendment.

By contrast, McKinley's relations with the Spanish government were carefully designed, although flawed. After determining the situation in Cuba, the president took a strong stand against Weyler and was considering using force to end Spain's "uncivilized" warfare. He responded sympathetically to Sagasta, believing Liberal reforms were moving in the right direction. Washington, in an effort to prevent any appearance that the United States was dictating to Spain, never suggested a specific solution to the Cuban problem. Offers to purchase Cuba were made discreetly, and the armistice plan first appeared in Madrid. McKinley pressed Spain to provide a solution acceptable to both the Cubans and the Spanish; unfortunately, no such means existed. The president made it clear that he would not accept a stalemate in Cuba, and he prepared the navy for war. But he erroneously believed that increased pressure would bring the Spanish government to find a way to avoid a catastrophic war.

In the end, military force cut the Gordian knot that bound Cuba to Spain and led to American expansion. The war changed American foreign affairs by creating a new diplomatic and political situation. Successful naval battles and land campaigns heightened American nationalism and turned attention to expansionism. Each victory shifted power from Spain to the United States. The war concluded with the McKinley administration's imposing a peace protocol on Spain. The reasoning behind the protocol defined much of American foreign policy. The McKinley administration removed Spain from the Western Hemisphere and kept the European powers out of the settlement. At the same time, the United States took no steps to gain Spanish colonies in the eastern Atlantic or the Mediterranean Sea. The Atlantic Ocean continued to serve as a barrier between the hemispheres. The status of Cuba was a vexing issue. A continuum of possibilities ran from complete independence through limited American control to immediate annexation. The McKinley administration rejected the extremes. Despite a widespread American belief in free Cuba, the McKinley administration's thinking was more closely aligned with Madrid than the Junta. It shared Spain's belief that the Cubans were not ready for self-government and could not be trusted with sovereign power. Fearing that Cuban soldiers might initiate a racially inspired vendetta against Spanish *peninsulares*, wealthy Creoles, and American interests, Washington was determined to impose order, to protect lives and property, and to aid the *reconcentrados*. It mattered little that this violated Cuban sovereignty. The United States expected many years to pass before the Cuban people would be ready for self-government, and during the transition period, McKinley planned to control the island through a protectorate.

Although the United States annexed Puerto Rico, Guam, and the Philippine Islands, these territories played no part in starting the war and were not important in ending it. Washington annexed Puerto Rico to remove Spain from the Western Hemisphere. It was interested in Pacific naval bases and coaling stations. The transforming event was Dewey's smashing victory. Within days, McKinley was seeking to exploit the success, and Americans were reconsidering the reach of American military power, foreign trade opportunities, and the Christian mission. Given the limited prior involvement in the Pacific, however, there was confusion over what advantages to obtain from Dewey's triumph. The Philippine independence movement further complicated the decision. Uncertainty over what to do about the Philippines showed up in the divided American cabinet and the loosely worded protocol that kept options open. At the end of the war, McKinley was probably honest when he told Cambon that he was undecided about the Philippines. He apparently did not intend to annex the entire archipelago. If he secretly had wanted the islands, he would have sped up the military campaign in the Philippines and delayed the cease-fire a few hours until the army had successfully assaulted Manila.

Neither McKinley nor Sagasta wanted the Spanish-American War, but the leaders could find no way to prevent it. Cubans and Spaniards held irreconcilable differences. The internal politics of the Cuban, Spanish, and American people limited diplomatic flexibility and prevented a negotiated solution. The Spanish-American War was inevitable. And to save lives, it was necessary to quickly end the colonial war; only the United States could do that. Although short, the war had far-reaching consequences that profoundly affected each of the participants. The Spanish endured national humiliation and entered a period of intense soul-searching and regeneration; the Cubans exchanged a vicious and corrupt colonial rule for an insensitive and overbearing protector; and the United States confidently assumed the burden of aiding and guiding reluctant subjects, believing that it could do a better job than Spain.

APPENDIX

. . . .

Protocol of Agreement between the United States and Spain, Embodying the Terms of a Basis for the Establishment of Peace between the Two Countries
Signed at Washington, August 12, 1898

Protocol

William R. Day, Secretary of State of the United States, and His Excellency Jules Cambon, Ambassador Extraordinary and Plenipotentiary of the Republic of France at Washington, respectively possessing for this purpose full authority from the Government of the United States and the Government of Spain, have concluded and signed the following articles, embodying the terms on which the two Governments have agreed in respect to the matters hereinafter set forth, having in view the establishment of peace between the two countries, that is to say:

Article I.

Spain will relinquish all claim of sovereignty over and title to Cuba.

Article II.

Spain will cede to the United States the island of Porto Rico and other islands now under Spanish sovereignty in the West Indies, and also an island in the Ladrones to be selected by the United States.

Article III.

The United States will occupy and hold the city, bay and harbor of Manila, pending the conclusion of a treaty of peace which shall determine the control, disposition and government of the Philippines.

Article IV.

Spain will immediately evacuate Cuba, Porto Rico and other islands now under Spanish sovereignty in the West Indies; and to this end each Government will, within ten days after the signing of this protocol, appoint Commissioners, and the Commissioners so appointed shall, within thirty days after the signing of this protocol, meet at Havana for the purpose of arranging and carrying out the details of the aforesaid evacuation of Cuba and the adjacent Spanish islands; and each Government will, within ten days after the signing of this protocol, also appoint other Commissioners, who shall, within thirty days after the signing of this protocol, meet at San Juan, in Porto Rico, for the purpose of arranging and carrying out the details of the aforesaid evacuation of Porto Rico and other islands now under Spanish sovereignty in the West Indies.

Article V.

The United States and Spain will each appoint not more than five commissioners to treat of peace, and the commissioners so appointed shall meet at Paris not later than October 1, 1898, and proceed to the negotiation and conclusion of a treaty of peace, which treaty shall be subject to ratification according to the respective constitutional forms of the two countries.

Article VI.

Upon the conclusion and signing of this protocol, hostilities between the two countries shall be suspended, and notice to that effect shall be given as soon as possible by each Government to the commanders of its military and naval forces.

Done at Washington in duplicate, in English and in French, by the Undersigned, who have hereunto set their hands and seals, the 12th day of August 1898.

William R. Day
Jules Cambon

NOTES

· · · · · · · · · · · · · · · · ·

CHAPTER I

1. There are many good accounts of Cuban social and economic changes.
See especially Pérez, *Cuba between Empires*, 4–163, and "Toward Dependency
and Revolution"; Scott, *Slave Emancipation in Cuba*, 201–78; Le Riverend, *Historia económica de Cuba*, 481–500; Carreras, *Cuba*, 216–36.

2. Weigle, "Sugar Interests and American Diplomacy," 177–92; Atkins,
Sixty Years in Cuba, 48–51, 109, 138; Healy, *Drive to Hegemony*, 14–18.

3. Baker, "Imperial Finale," 152–66; Serrano, *Final del imperio*, 10–17;
Lewis, *America's Stake in International Investments*, 266; U.S. Department of War,
Census of Cuba, 528–29.

4. Baker, "Imperial Finale," 148; Atkins, *Sixty Years in Cuba*, 143–45. The
literature on Martí is extensive; an excellent offering is Abel and Torrents, *José
Martí*; see also Foner, *Spanish-Cuban-American War* 1:xviii–xxxiv, 1–4.

5. American historians often locate the sources of the Cuban revolution in
the capricious tariff changes and economic dislocations of the 1890s. For a longer
view, see Poyo, "Cuban Separatist Thought in the Emigré Communities"; see
also Pérez, *Cuba between Empires*, 93–94.

6. Camacho, *Estrada Palma*, 111–24; Pérez, *Cuba between Empires*, 93–94.

7. Poyo, *"With All,"* 114–15; Pérez, *Cuba between Empires*, 97–112; Camacho,
Estrada Palma, 124–28; Foner, *Spanish-Cuban-American War* 1:147–50; True,
"Revolutionaries in Exile," 101–4. When the war was over and Cuba held elec-
tions, Gómez threw his support to Estrada Palma, who became Cuba's president.

8. Poyo, *"With All,"* 115–16; Le Riverend, *Historia económica de Cuba*, 490–
93; Foner, *Spanish-Cuban-American War* 1:98–102; U.S. Department of War,
Census of Cuba, 713. Fears of banditry and anarchy had a historical basis; see
Pérez, "Vagrants, Beggars, and Bandits," 1092–1121.

9. Pérez, *Cuba between Empires*, 125–37; Pérez, "Insurrection, Intervention,
and the Transformation," 229–33; Foner, *Spanish-Cuban-American War* 1:21–6.

10. Pérez, *Cuba between Empires*, 16–17; Estrade, *Colonia cubana de París*,
102–16, 142–54.

11. Poyo, *"With All,"* 119–21; Auxier, "Propaganda Activities of the Cuban

Junta," 286–305; True, "Revolutionaries in Exile," 104–19; Corzo Pi, *Estrada Palma,* 45–53. A good example of the Junta's lobbying is Estrada Palma's letter to Richard Olney, 7 December 1895, explaining the causes and development of the Cuban war. U.S. Congress, Senate, Committee on Foreign Relations, *Affairs in Cuba,* 1–42. Many prominent people associated with the Junta through the Cuban League of the USA. A list of members and one of contributions exist in the Wm. Bourke Cochran Papers, New York Public Library, New York City.

12. Foner, *Spanish-Cuban-American War* 1:128–47.

13. Benton, *International Law and Diplomacy,* 42; Foner, *Spanish-Cuban-American War* 1:108–9, 144–47; True, "Revolutionaries in Exile," 188, 198.

14. A good overview is found in Payne, *Spain and Portugal* 2:463–90.

15. Ibid. 2:490–510; see also Carr, *Modern Spain,* 1–15.

16. Varela Ortega, *Los amigos políticos,* 401–28; Artola, "El sistema político de la Restauración," 11–20.

17. Varela Ortega, *Los amigos políticos,* 135–203.

18. There are many accounts of Cánovas's life. A thorough treatment is Fernández Almagro, *Cánovas.*

19. There are no good biographies of Sagasta. The best is by Romanones, a friend and Liberal Party member who had access to Sagasta's private papers, which have since disappeared. Romanones, *Sagasta.* An official parliamentary biography, which contains many of Sagasta's speeches, was prepared by Nido y Segalerva, *Práxedes Mateo Sagasta.* An anecdotal biography by an admirer is Rivas Santiago, *Sagasta.* See also Kern, *Liberals, Reformers, and Caciques,* 13, 41–44; Payne, *Spain and Portugal* 2:491–96; Ramos Oliveira, *Men of Modern Spain,* 110–11.

20. Payne, *Spain and Portugal* 2:496–500; Payne, *Politics and the Military,* 44–65; Baker, "Imperial Finale," 130–47.

21. Fernández Almagro, *Historia política de la España* 2:181–212; Baker, "Imperial Finale," 44–70, 353–70; Serrano, *Final del imperio,* 75–89.

22. Serrano, *Final del imperio,* 70–72. The author provides an excellent survey of Spanish public opinion on pages 90–127.

23. Ibid., 1–17; Fernández Almagro, *Historia política de la España* 2:191–206; Meléndez Meléndez, *Cánovas y la política exterior,* 327–73.

24. Payne, *Spain and Portugal* 2:501–3; Baker, "Imperial Finale," 32–40; Carr, *Modern Spain,* 22–29; Kern, *Liberals, Reformers, and Caciques,* 82–83; Pérez, *Cuba between Empires,* 18–38.

25. Fernández Almagro, *Cánovas,* 519–28; Payne, *Politics and the Military,* 66–72; Varela Ortega, "Aftermath of Splendid Disaster," 317–18. For Martínez de Campos's letter to Cánovas and other documents, see volume two of O'Donnell y Abreu, *Apuntes del ex-ministro de estado duque de Tetuán.*

26. Foner, *Spanish-Cuban-American War* 1:73–97; Fernández Almagro,

Cánovas, 528–39; Serrano, *Final del imperio*, 26–29; Payne, *Spain and Portugal* 2:511–12; Baker, "Imperial Finale," 195–97.

27. The exact number of deaths resulting from reconcentration is not known. Estimates in 1897 and 1898 were exaggerated, and by early 1898 the number was widely believed to be 400,000, which was one-fourth of the island's population. For example, in March 1898 the American minister told the Spanish prime minister that 400,000 had died in Cuba; the Spanish leader did not dispute the figure, since his sources reported a similar loss. An American census report in 1899 concluded that Cuba had lost over 200,000 people during the revolution. By comparing the Cuban death rate for the years 1890 to 1893 with the death rate for 1895 to 1898, the army demographer calculated that there was an increase of 208,210 deaths, which he attributed to conditions in Cuba resulting from the insurrection. Since more than 12 percent of the island's population was not covered by this survey, he projected an even larger number of insurrection-related deaths, perhaps as many as 235,000. U.S. Department of War, *Census of Cuba*, 717–19. Regardless of the exact number of deaths, the important point was that Cubans, Spaniards, and Americans believed the death toll was extremely large and growing. Pérez, *Cuba between Empires*, 55–56; Foner, *Spanish-Cuban-American War* 1:110–18; May, *Imperial Democracy*, 127. Throughout this text, I assume a death toll of 200,000. The reader should keep in mind that in 1898 the accepted figure was 400,000.

28. See two draft memoranda, apparently prepared by the conde de Rascón for Tetuán, 15 April 1896 and 15 April 1897, Estado, legajo 8663, AHN; Baker, "Imperial finale," 212–17.

29. Baker, "Imperial Finale," 218–19.

30. There is a wealth of material on U.S. imperialism at the turn of the century. A good bibliography exists in Beisner, *From the Old Diplomacy to the New*; Pletcher provides a bibliographic essay in "Caribbean 'Empire,' Planned and Improvised."

31. See, among others, Abrahamson, *America Arms for a New Century*.

32. For an economic interpretation, see LaFeber, *New Empire*. For contrary views, see Holbo, "Economics, Emotion, and Expansion," and Pletcher, "Rhetoric and Results."

33. Morgan, *From Hayes to McKinley*.

34. Jones, *Presidential Election of 1896*.

CHAPTER 2

1. *Cong. Rec.*, 54th Cong., 1st sess., 24–25, 105, 219, 272, 403, 482, 514, 577–78, 607, 725, 810, 815, 1020, 1086, 1376, 1552, 2148–49, 2281, 2294.

Morgan was an ardent southern expansionist, favoring a Nicaraguan canal, annexation of Hawaii, and intervention in Cuba. He chaired the Foreign Relations Committee when the Democrats controlled the Senate. A concurrent resolution is an expression of congressional opinion; a joint resolution has the status of law and requires presidential action.

2. Ibid., 1065–68, 1317, 1967–80, 2054–67, 2105–23, 2163–69, 2241–58.

3. Ibid., 2244–48.

4. Ibid., 2163–69, 2206–13, 2249–51.

5. Ibid., 2257.

6. Ibid., 2256.

7. Ibid., 2342.

8. Ibid., 2343–44.

9. Ibid., 2354–59.

10. Ibid., 2587–94.

11. Ibid., 2826–27.

12. Ibid., 3541–55, 3574–3600.

13. Ibid., 3627–28.

14. McWilliams, *Hannis Taylor*, 21–32; Eggert, *Richard Olney*, 170–74.

15. "Arrest, Imprisonment, etc., of Julio Sanguily," in U.S. Department of State, *Papers Relating to the Foreign Relations of the United States, 1896*, 750–846 (hereafter cited as *Foreign Relations*).

16. "Maltreatment of José M. Delgado," ibid., 582–631.

17. "Seizure of the *Competitor* and Trial of Americans Found on Board Thereof," ibid., 711–45.

18. "List of Claims against Spain . . . January 22, 1897," and "Citizens of United States Arrested in Cuba," ibid., 710–11, 746–50.

19. Olney to Cleveland, 25 September 1895, microfilm 59, Olney Papers; Cleveland to Olney, 29 September 1895, in *Letters of Grover Cleveland*, 410–11. During October 1895, Olney and Cleveland considered sending an army major to Cuba, but the secretary of war thought a senior officer should be chosen; nothing more came of this. Cleveland to Olney, 6 October 1895, and Olney to Cleveland, 8 October 1895, microfilm 59, Olney Papers.

20. Atkins, *Sixty Years in Cuba*, 156–58, 213–14, 218; Weigle, "Sugar Interests and American Diplomacy," 208–19; *Diary of William L. Wilson*, 78–79.

21. *Diary of William L. Wilson*, 35–36.

22. Born in 1851, Enrique Dupuy de Lôme was Spain's youngest career ambassador. He was a member of the Conservative Party, and Cánovas chose him for the Washington assignment after the Cuban war began. A short biography is found in García Barrón, "Enrique Dupuy de Lôme"; Dupuy to Tetuán, 20 March 1896, Política, legajo 2416, AMAE.

23. Olney to Dupuy, 4 April 1896, in *Foreign Relations, 1897*, 540–44.

24. Readnour, "Fitzhugh Lee," 223–24; Eggert, "Our Man in Havana";

Millis, *Martial Spirit*, 53. Eggert criticizes Lee for taking a personal financial interest in Cuba and attempting to influence events toward his own views. But Lee's positions proved to be sound, as Eggert admits, and the general was courageous enough to describe events in Cuba as he saw them rather than to report what Olney and Cleveland wanted to hear. As for taking an economic interest, consuls in the 1890s expected to engage in business activities at their posts; salaries were low, consular affairs were slow, and promoting business opportunities was part of the reward for overseas service.

25. Readnour, "Fitzhugh Lee," 226–34.

26. Cleveland to Olney, 16 July 1896, microfilm 59, Olney Papers; Cleveland to Olney, 13 July 1896, in *Letters of Grover Cleveland*, 446.

27. A good example of Madrid's views is found in Tetuán to Dupuy, 22 March 1896, Política, legajo 2416, AMAE.

28. Dupuy to Tetuán, 10 April 1896, ibid.

29. Tetuán to Dupuy, 22 May 1896, in [Spain], *Diplomatic Correspondence*, 9–13. This is an American government translation of three Spanish Red Books published in 1898 and 1899. Readers must use the Spanish documents with caution. Madrid often deleted passages without indicating editorial changes. I cite these documents only where I have verified the original in the Spanish archives and because the English translation is readily available in U.S. libraries.

30. O'Donnell y Abreu, *Apuntes del ex-ministro de estado duque de Tetuán* 1:87–94; Fernández Almagro, *Historia política de la España* 2:290–95; Comellas García-Llera, *Cánovas*, 341–44.

31. Tetuán, Circular Memorandum to the European Powers, 28 July 1896, Política, legajo 2416, AMAE.

32. Ibid.; Pilapil, "Spain in the European State System," 15–17; Jules Patenôtre (Madrid) to Hanotaux, 24 July 1896, Espagne, 16, FAMAE.

33. Tetuán to Cánovas, 11 August 1896, Política, legajo 2416, AMAE; McWilliams, *Hannis Taylor*, 29–31; Tetuán, Circular Telegram to the European Powers, 14 August 1896, Política, legajo 2416, AMAE.

34. Paul Patenôtre (Washington) to Hanotaux, 19 August 1896, États-Unis 175, FAMAE; Hanotaux to Reverseaux, 22 August 1896, Espagne, 16, FAMAE; Hoyos (Vienna) to Tetuán, 17 August 1896, and Benomar (Rome) to Tetuán, 16 August 1896, Política, legajo 2416, AMAE.

35. Salmeron (Madrid) to Betances, 30 March 1896, and Betances to Estrada Palma, 14 May, 4, 10, 29 September 1896, in Cuba, *Correspondencia diplomática* 3:23–24, 29–30, 65–71.

36. McKee, *National Conventions and Platforms*, 297, 301. McKinley, *The People's Choice*, consists of four volumes of McKinley's campaign speeches, one for each month of the campaign.

37. "Message of the President," *Foreign Relations, 1896*, xxix–xxxvi, lxxx–lxxxvii.

38. Dupuy to Tetuán, 9 December 1896, Política, legajo 2416, AMAE.

39. Quesada to Estrada Palma, 1, 3, 6 December 1896, in Cuba, *Correspondencia diplomática* 5:78–83; *Cong. Rec.*, 54th Cong., 2d sess., 39, 60, 131–33; Atkins, *Sixty Years in Cuba*, 211–13, 244–45.

40. *Cong. Rec.*, 54th Cong., 2d sess., 332; Quesada to Estrada Palma, 1, 3 December 1896, in Cuba, *Correspondencia diplomática* 5:79–82.

41. Eggert, *Richard Olney*, 266.

42. Quesada to Estrada Palma, 10 February 1897, in Cuba, *Correspondencia diplomática* 5:93–98; Garraty, *Henry Cabot Lodge*, 184–85; Coolidge, *Orville H. Platt*, 165–66.

43. Eggert, *Richard Olney*, 267–69; Fernández Almagro, *Cánovas*, 550–52; Fernández Almagro, *Historia política de la España* 2:394–95.

44. Taylor to Olney, 7, 8 January 1897, Despatches from Spain, RG59, M 31, microfilm 122, USNA.

45. Tetuán to Dupuy, 5 February 1897, in [Spain], *Diplomatic Correspondence*, 19–24; Dupuy to Tetuán, 13 February 1897, in ibid., 24; Reverseaux to Hanotaux, 22 January, 11 February 1897, Espagne, 17, FAMAE; Eggert, *Richard Olney*, 267–68; Weigle, "Sugar Interests and American Diplomacy," 222–24.

46. Eggert, *Richard Olney*, 269; Portell Vilá, *Cuba en sus relaciones con los Estados Unidos* 3:231–39.

47. Lee to Olney, 23 February 1897, Consular Despatches from Havana, RG59, T 20, microroll 128, USNA; U.S. Secretary of State, *Report . . . Relative to the . . . Death of Dr. Ricardo Ruiz*, 1–4; *Washington Post*, 22, 23, 24 February 1897.

48. Taylor to Olney, 26 February 1897, Despatches from Spain, RG59, M 31, microroll 122, USNA.

49. Olney to Lee, 24 February 1897, microfilm 60, Olney Papers; Olney to Lee, 21 February 1897, Cleveland Papers; Cleveland to Olney, 28 February 1897, in *Letters of Grover Cleveland*, 469. The fullest discussion of this controversy is in Eggert, *Richard Olney*, 269–72.

50. Lee to Rockhill, 1 March 1897, in *Foreign Relations, 1896*, 845; *Cong. Rec.*, 54th Cong., 2d sess., 2168–69, 2172, 2226–40, 2287, 2311; *Washington Post*, 25, 26 February 1897.

CHAPTER 3

1. Margaret Leech and H. Wayne Morgan have written the best biographies of William McKinley. An excellent study is Gould, *Presidency of William McKinley*. For a good description of McKinley's political style, see Morgan, "William McKinley as a Political Leader." See also Offner, "McKinley and the Origins of the Spanish-American War," 79–81.

2. Offner, "McKinley and the Origins of the Spanish-American War," 66–74; Hilderbrand, *Power and the People*, 8–12; Morgan, *William McKinley*, 323–24; Gould, *Presidency of William McKinley*, 38.

3. Gould, *Presidency of William McKinley*, 13–19; Morgan, *William McKinley*, 249–68. Other cabinet members were Lyman J. Gage, secretary of the treasury; Cornelius N. Bliss, secretary of the interior; James A. Gary, postmaster general; Joseph McKenna, attorney general; and James Wilson, secretary of agriculture.

4. Duncan, "Diplomatic Career of William Rufus Day," 46–54; McLean, *William Rufus Day*, 32–37; Shippee and Way, "William Rufus Day" 9:29–32.

5. DeNovo, "Alvey A. Adee," 69–80; Moore also collected diplomatic documents. His papers in the Library of Congress are a rich source and include many memoirs of people and events. For instance, on Day see Memorandum, 13 September 1897, and Recollections of William R. Day, 20 May 1941, box 214, Moore Papers.

6. Clymer, *John Hay*; Dennett, *John Hay*; Kushner and Sherrill, *John Milton Hay*.

7. Offner, "McKinley and the Origins of the Spanish-American War," 141–42.

8. *Washington Post*, 13, 19 September, 16 October 1897.

9. Lodge to Roosevelt, 2 December 1896, in Lodge, *Theodore Roosevelt and Henry Cabot Lodge* 1:240–41; Reid to McKinley, 5 December 1896, and 2 January 1897, series 1, microfilm 1, McKinley Papers.

10. Quesada to Estrada Palma, 14, 18 January, in Cuba, *Correspondencia diplomática* 5:88–90; Heath, "Work of the President," 282.

11. Parker, *Recollections of Grover Cleveland*, 249–50; Kohlsaat, *From McKinley to Harding*, 64.

12. Richardson, *Messages and Papers of the Presidents* 14:6241–42.

13. Offner, "McKinley and the Origins of the Spanish-American War," 105–12.

14. *Washington Post*, 30 March, 13, 19, 29 April 1897; *Washington Star*, 1, 8, 23, 24, 29 April 1897; Wriston, *Executive Agents in American Foreign Relations*, 754.

15. Robinson, *Thomas B. Reed*, 352–61; Dingley, *Nelson Dingley, Jr.*, 430.

16. Acheson, *Joe Bailey*, 94–96; *Washington Star*, 19 March 1897.

17. Merrill and Merrill, *The Republican Command*, 4–34.

18. "The Week," *Nation* 65 (14 October 1897): 291; Roosevelt, *Autobiography*, 228–31; Roosevelt, *Rough Riders*, 10–11; Coolidge, *Orville H. Platt*, 280–81.

19. *Cong. Rec.*, 55th Cong., 1st sess., 562, 615–21, 642–46, 656–63, 684–94, 847.

20. Ibid., 996, 998, 955.

21. Ibid., 946–49, 951, 996, 998; *New York Tribune*, 13 May 1897.

22. *Cong. Rec.*, 55th Cong., 1st sess., 10 to 20 May 1897, passim.

23. Ibid., 1049, 1081; *Washington Post*, 14, 15, 18 May 1897.

24. *Cong. Rec.*, 55th Cong., 1st sess., 1186.

25. Ibid., 1120, 1187–93; *Washington Star*, 21, 22 May 1897; *New York Tribune*, 22 May 1897; "The Week," *Nation* 64 (27 May 1897): 387.

26. Atkins, *Sixty Years in Cuba*, 261–63; Cortissoz, *Whitelaw Reid* 2:219–20; Duncan, "William Rufus Day," 74–75; *Washington Post*, 24, 26, 29 May 1897.

27. Calhoun, "Report on Ruiz Death," Communications from Special Agents, RG59, M 37, microroll 21, USNA.

28. Calhoun, "Report on Cuban Question," ibid.

29. Ibid.

30. There were many applicants for Lee's job, and Frank Aldrich of Illinois believed in June that he had received it. *Washington Star*, 25 May, 4 June 1897; *Washington Post*, 11 March 1897; *New York Tribune*, 8 October 1897; Eggert, "Our Man in Havana," 477–85.

31. Sherman to Dupuy, 26 June 1897, in *Foreign Relations, 1897*, 507–8.

32. Soldevilla, *El año político, 1896*, 58–59; Soldevilla, *El año político, 1897*, 34–35.

33. Soldevilla, *El año político, 1897*, 86–89, 95, 103–4, 158–68; Fernández Almagro, *Cánovas*, 552–55.

34. Soldevilla, *El año político, 1897*, 149–51, 170–75; Fernández Almagro, *Historia política de la España* 2:366–68, 399; *New York Tribune*, 20 May 1897.

35. Soldevilla, *El año político, 1897*, 178–86, 197.

36. Ibid., 210–14; Baker, "Imperial Finale," 230–33; Taylor to Sherman, 4, 7 June 1897, Despatches from Spain, RG59, M 31, microroll 122, USNA.

37. Taylor to Sherman, 24 June 1897, ibid; Soldevilla, *El año político, 1897*, 230–33.

38. Fernández Almagro, *Historia Política de la España* 2:407; Baker, "Imperial Finale," 223–24.

39. Dupuy to Sherman, 30 June 1897, Notes from the Spanish Legation, RG59, M 59, microroll 28, USNA; Tetuán to Dupuy, 4 Aug. 1897, in [Spain], *Diplomatic Correspondence*, 28–35.

40. Tetuán to Dupuy, 4 August 1897, in [Spain] *Diplomatic Correspondence*, 28–35.

41. Varela Ortega, *Los amigos políticos*, 314; Arco, *Montero Ríos*, 109–10.

42. Fernández Almagro, *Cánovas*, 559–61; Comellas, *Cánovas*, 353–57.

CHAPTER 4

1. Foster, *Memoirs* 2:225.

2. Nevins, *Henry White*, 122; Jessup, *Elihu Root*, 196; Dawes, *McKinley Years*, 123; Cortissoz, *Whitelaw Reid* 2:219; *Washington Star*, 27 April 1897.

3. *New York Herald*, 20 June 1897; List of Cuban League Members and Contributors, Cochran Papers; Woodford to McKinley, 21 June 1897, McKinley Papers.

4. Taylor to Sherman, 27 August 1897, Despatches from Spain, RG59, M 31, microroll 123, USNA; Woodford to McKinley, 3, 22 September, 17 October 1897, box 185, Moore Papers; Palmer, *Bliss*, 41–42.

5. Woodford to McKinley, 27 November, 4 December 1897, box 185, Moore Papers. There is no mention in Woodford's letters that he did any additional entertaining.

6. Woodford to Day, 5, 8 April 1898, box 35, Day Papers; Woodford to McKinley, 11 April 1898, box 185, Moore Papers; Palmer, *Bliss*, 39–40; Miscellaneous letters, vol. 4, and newspaper clippings, box 6, Bliss Papers.

7. Day to Woodford, 16 July 1897, Instructions to Spain, RG59, M 77, microroll 150, USNA; *New York Tribune*, 20 June 1897.

8. Sherman to Woodford, 16 July 1897, in *Foreign Relations, 1898*, 558–61.

9. Ibid.

10. Ibid.

11. Ibid.; McKinley's instructions to Woodford were written a few weeks after the Navy Department completed its war plan against Spain. For a copy of the plan, see Grenville, "American Naval Preparations."

12. Quesada to Estrada Palma, 19 July 1897, in Cuba, *Correspondencia diplomática* 5:118–19.

13. Sherman to Woodford, 30 June 1897, Instructions to Spain, RG59, M 77, microroll 150, USNA.

14. Woodford to McKinley, 10, 19 August 1897, box 185, Moore Papers. Woodford's confidential letters are on microfilm as part of the State Department papers, but typed copies are in box 185 of the Moore Papers, and I cite these because they are easier to use. Not all of Woodford's letters appear in *Foreign Relations*; some that are printed are incomplete.

15. Woodford to McKinley, 10 August 1897, box 185, Moore Papers; Hay to McKinley, 6 October 1897, McKinley Papers.

16. Woodford to McKinley, 19 August 1897, box 185, Moore Papers; Porter to Sherman, 19 August 1897, Despatches from France, RG59, M 34, microroll 117, USNA.

17. White, *Autobiography* 2:161–62; Woodford to Sherman, 30 August 1897, Despatches from Spain, RG59, M 31, microroll 123, USNA.

18. Breckinridge to Sherman, 26 August 1897, Despatches from Russia, RG59, M 35, microroll 51, USNA.

19. Woodford to McKinley, 19, 23 August 1897, box 185, Moore Papers.

20. Woodford to McKinley, 3 September 1897, ibid. In Washington, Adee predicted to McKinley that the Spanish were waiting for Woodford's first meet-

ing before determining the makeup of the next ministry. If Woodford proved to be agreeable, Sagasta would assume the leadership; if Woodford's proposals were upsetting, another Conservative government would be formed. Adee to McKinley, 21 August 1897, McKinley Papers.

21. Taylor to Sherman, 24 August 1897, Despatches from Spain, RG59, M 31, microroll 122, USNA; Palmer, *Bliss*, 41–42.

22. Woodford to McKinley, 6 September 1897, box 185, Moore Papers.

23. Woodford to Sherman, 13 September 1897, in *Foreign Relations, 1898*, 562–65.

24. Ibid.; Baker, "Imperial Finale," 239.

25. Woodford to Sherman, 13 September 1897, in *Foreign Relations, 1898*, 562–65; Wolff to Salisbury, 9 September 1897, 72, Spain, 2056, PRO.

26. Portell Vilá, *Cuba en sus relaciones con los Estados Unidos* 3:350–53; True, "Revolutionaries in Exile," 195–96. There is extensive discussion of bond sales in Estrada Palma's letters in Primelles, *Revolución del 95* 3:54–62, 4:199–217, 252–57, 5:11–25.

27. Estrada Palma to Cisneros Betancourt, 22 July 1896, and Gómez to Estrada Palma, 11 August 1896, in Primelles, *Revolución del 95* 5:29–34, 47–49.

28. Portell Vilá, *Cuba en sus relaciones con los Estados Unidos* 3:351–53.

29. McCook to Perier Mercet and Co. (Paris), 17 August 1897, Espagne, 17, FAMAE.

30. McCook to Day, 14, 17 September, 7, 11 October 1897, box 35, Day Papers.

31. Woodford to Sherman, 20, 23 September 1897, in *Foreign Relations, 1898*, 565–73.

32. Ibid; Woodford to McKinley, 24 September 1897, box 185, Moore Papers.

33. Woodford to McKinley, 24 September 1897, box 185, Moore Papers.

34. Ibid.

35. Day to Woodford, 1 October 1897, Diplomatic Instructions, RG 59, M 77, microroll 150, USNA.

36. Woodford to Sherman, 4, 5, 11 October 1897, in *Foreign Relations, 1898*, 573–81.

37. Tetuán to Dupuy, 20 September 1897, Política, legajo 2417, AMAE.

38. Dupuy to Tetuán, 22 September 1897, ibid.

39. Patenôtre to Hanotaux, 29 September 1897, Espagne, 17, FAMAE; Wolff to Salisbury, 26 September 1897, 72, Spain, 2056, PRO.

40. Soldevilla, *El año político, 1897*, 326–27; Baker, "Imperial Finale," 242–44; Varela Ortega, *Los amigos políticos*, 314–15.

41. There is no satisfactory biography of Moret. The best is by González Cavada, *Segismundo Moret*; see also Olmet, *Moret*. For discussions of Moret's di-

plomacy, see Jover Zamora, *Política, diplomacia y humanismo popular,* 130–33, and Morales Lezcano, *León y Castillo,* 11. Baker, "Imperial Finale," 249–53; Reverseaux to Hanotaux, 30 October 1897, Espagne, 43, FAMAE.

42.   There is some biographical information on Pío Gullón in Personal, legajo 128, expediente 6185, AMAE.

43.   Soldevilla, *El año político, 1897,* 339–40; Baker, "Imperial Finale," 303.

44.   Soldevilla, *El año político, 1896,* 475–76; Soldevilla, *El año político, 1897,* 34–35, 103–4, 109, 308.

45.   Woodford to Day, 6 October 1897, Despatches from Spain, RG59, M 31, microroll 123, USNA; Woodford to Sherman, 16 October 1897, in *Foreign Relations, 1898,* 581; Woodford to McKinley, 10, 17 October 1897, box 185, Moore Papers.

CHAPTER 5

1.   Baker, "Imperial Finale," 283–88, 351–53, 365–70; Varela Ortega, *Los amigos políticos,* 317–18.

2.   Reverseaux to Hanotaux, 9 November 1897, Espagne, 18, FAMAE; Baker, "Imperial Finale," 353–70. Baker's analysis of Spanish opinion for and against war is exceptionally thorough.

3.   Soldevilla, *El año político, 1897,* 360, 368–69; Blanco to Dupuy, 1 November 1897, Ultramar, legajo 4923, AHN; Moret to Blanco, 2 December 1897, ibid.; Reverseaux to Hanotaux, 9 November 1897, Espagne, 18, FAMAE. Blanco's reports were usually optimistic despite overwhelming difficulties.

4.   Gullón to Woodford, 23 October 1897, in *Foreign Relations, 1898,* 582–89. Although the note was dated 23 October, Gullón handed it to Woodford on the twenty-fifth.

5.   Ibid.

6.   Woodford to Sherman, 13 November 1897, ibid.; Dupuy to Blanco, 8 November 1897, Ultramar, legajo 4923, AHN; Dupuy to Gullón, 9 November 1897, Política, legajo 2419, AMAE; Gullón to Dupuy, 10 November 1897, ibid.

7.   Dupuy to Gullón, 9 November 1897, Ultramar, legajo 2903, AMAE; Woodford to Sherman, 28 November 1897, in *Foreign Relations, 1898,* 644; Woodford to Sherman, 11, 31 December 1897, in *Foreign Relations, 1897,* 501; Blanco to Moret, 22 January 1898, Ultramar, legajo 4923, AHN.

8.   Woodford to Sherman, 26, 27 November 1897, in *Foreign Relations, 1898,* 616–44.

9.   Baker, "Imperial Finale," 317, 325–26; *El Correo Militar* (Madrid), 11 January 1898; Varela Ortega, "Aftermath of Splendid Disaster," 326.

10.   *El Imparcial* (Madrid), 30 November 1897.

11. Reverseaux to Hanotaux, 10 October, 6 December 1897, Espagne, 18, FAMAE; Wolff to Salisbury, 11, 21 October 1897, 72, Spain, 2056, PRO; Vladimirov, *La diplomacia de los Estados Unidos*, 127–28.

12. Dubsky to Goluchowski, 4 December 1897, Spanien, 59, HHSA.

13. Ibid.; Hanotaux to Reverseaux, 26 October 1897, Espagne, 18, FAMAE; Reverseaux, Memorandum on Meeting with Queen Regent, 20 October 1897, ibid.; Reverseaux to Hanotaux, 6 December 1897, ibid.; Vaurineux (St. Petersburg) to Hanotaux, 11 November 1897, ibid.

14. Wolff to Salisbury, 17 October 1897, 72, Spain, 2056, PRO; Woodford to McKinley, 20 October 1897, box 185, Moore Papers. Another American banker advancing a Cuban financial settlement was Dwight Braman, of Boston and New York. In Washington, he claimed to be a financial correspondent of the Spanish royal family; in Europe, he pointed to conversations with Day and McKinley's cousin William McKinley Osborne. Braman proposed purchasing Cuba from Spain for $250 million and turning the island into a corporation that would issue stocks and bonds, with the United States guaranteeing payments. After Braman toured Europe, he assured Day that his plan had French support. Neither the Cubans nor the Americans encouraged Braman, but his European trip probably fueled the belief that McKinley was searching for a means to purchase the island. Braman to McKinley, 10 October 1897, box 35, Day Papers.

15. Reid to McKinley, 8 March 1898, microfilm 72, Reid Papers.

16. McCook to Perier Mercet and Co. (Paris), 17 August 1897, Espagne, 17, FAMAE; Wolff to Salisbury, 8 November 1897, 72, Spain, 2057, PRO.

17. Reverseaux to Hanotaux, 30 October 1897, Espagne, 43, FAMAE.

18. Dupuy to Gullón, 27 October 1897, Ultramar, legajo 2903, AMAE.

19. Wolff to Salisbury, 10, 22 October, 3, 9 November 1897, 72, Spain, 2056 and 2057, PRO.

20. Wolff to Salisbury, 9 November 1897, 72, Spain, 2057, PRO. Wolff examines the financial proposals in detail, providing a wealth of information.

21. Ibid.

22. Woodford to McKinley, 24 October, 7 November 1897, box 185, Moore Papers.

23. Woodford to Sherman, 13 November 1897, in *Foreign Relations, 1898*, 600–602.

24. Woodford to McKinley, 14 November 1897, box 185, Moore Papers.

25. Woodford to McKinley, 27 November, 4 December 1897, ibid.

26. *Washington Post*, 9 October 1897; Dupuy to Gullón, 19, 20 October 1897, in [Spain], *Diplomatic Correspondence*, 37–38.

27. *Washington Star*, 28 October, 10 November 1897; *New York Tribune*, 29 October, 11 November 1897; *Washington Post*, 28, 30 October 1897; Patenôtre to Hanotaux, 30 October 1897, Espagne, 18, FAMAE.

28. Dupuy to Gullón, 20 October 1897, in [Spain], *Diplomatic Correspon-*

dence, 38; *Washington Star*, 5 November 1897; *New York Tribune*, 4 November 1897; *Washington Post*, 5 November 1897.

29.   *New York Tribune*, 19 November 1897.

30.   Dupuy to Blanco, 19 November 1897, Ultramar, legajo 4923, AHN; Dupuy to Gullón, 19 November 1897, Ultramar, legajo 2903, AMAE; *Washington Post*, 20 November 1897; *Washington Star*, 27 November 1897; Dupuy to Gullón, 29 November, 2 December 1897, in [Spain], *Diplomatic Correspondence*, 42–43.

31.   Taylor, "Review of the Cuban Question"; McWilliams, *Hannis Taylor*, 34–35; Wolff to Salisbury, 2 November 1897, 72, Spain, 2057, PRO.

32.   Wolff to Salisbury, 2, 9 November 1897, 72, Spain, 2057, PRO; Reverseaux to Hanotaux, 9 November 1897, Espagne, 18, FAMAE.

33.   Wolff to Salisbury, 9 November 1897, 72, Spain, 2057, PRO.

34.   Francos Rodríguez, *Canalejas*, 117, 133; Soldevilla, *El año político, 1897*, 239–40, 360–61; Romanones, *Sagasta*, 194–95.

35.   Francos Rodríguez, *Canalejas*, 134; Romanones, *Sagasta*, 191–94.

36.   For Moret and the Austrian ambassador, see text and notes 11 to 13, above.

37.   Francos Rodríguez, *Canalejas*, 134–41, 156–68; Dupuy to Gullón, 14 November 1897, Ultramar, legajo 2903, AMAE.

38.   Betances to Estrada Palma, 22 October 1897, in Cuba, *Correspondencia diplomática* 3:116–17; Estrade, *Colonia cubana de París*, 150; Dupuy to Blanco, 1 November 1897, Ultramar, legajo 4923, AHN; Dupuy to Gullón, 1 November 1897, Ultramar, legajo 2903, AMAE.

39.   Dupuy to Gullón, 12 November 1897, in [Spain], *Diplomatic Correspondence*, 39; Francos Rodríguez, *Canalejas*, 138–39; Romanones, *Sagasta*, 193–94.

40.   Romanones, *Sagasta*, 193–94; Francos Rodríguez, *Canalejas*, 156–58.

41.   Francos Rodríguez, *Canalejas*, 141, 167–68.

42.   Sherman to Dupuy, 6 November 1897, in *Foreign Relations, 1898*, 596–97.

43.   Blanco to Dupuy, 10 November 1897, Ultramar, legajo 4923, AHN; Dupuy to Sherman, 10 November 1897, Notes from the Spanish Legation, RG59, M 59, microroll 29, USNA; Woodford to Sherman, 15 November 1897, in *Foreign Relations, 1898*, 602.

44.   Lee to Day, 17 November 1897, Consular Despatches from Havana, RG59, T 20, microroll 131, USNA.

45.   Day to Lee, 22 November 1897, Instructions to Spain, RG59, M 77, microfilm 150, USNA; Brice (Matanzas) to Day, 17 November, 17 December 1897, in U.S. President, *Condition of Reconcentrados in Cuba*, 29–30; Barker (Sagua la Grande) to Day, 25 November 1897, ibid.; Barker to Day, 20 November 1897, in U.S. Congress, Senate, Committee on Foreign Relations, *Affairs in Cuba*, 561.

46. Lee to Day, 23 November, 7, 14 December 1897, in U.S. Congress, Senate, Committee on Foreign Relations, *Affairs in Cuba*, 552–53.

47. Lee to Day, 23, 26 November 1897, Consular Despatches from Havana, RG59, T 20, microroll 131, USNA.

48. Day to Dupuy, 1 December 1897, in *Foreign Relations, 1897*, 511; Dupuy to Gullón, 2 December 1897, Política, legajo 2419, AMAE; Dupuy to Blanco, 2 December 1897, Ultramar, legajo 4923, AHN.

49. Blanco to Gullón, 3, 5 December 1897, Política, legajo 2419, AMAE; Gullón to Dupuy, 3 December 1897, ibid.

50. Dupuy to Gullón, 5, 6 December 1897, ibid.; Dupuy to Blanco, 4 December 1897, Ultramar, legajo 4923, AHN; Blanco to Gullón, 6 December 1897, Política, legajo 2419, AMAE; Gullón to Dupuy, 6 December 1897, ibid.

51. Sherman to Dupuy, 8 December 1897, in *Foreign Relations, 1897*, 511–12; Lee to Day, 9 December 1897, Consular Despatches from Havana, RG59, T 20, microroll 131, USNA.

52. *El Cubano Libre* (Tampa), 30 October 1897; Estrada Palma, "Work of the Cuban Delegation," 418; Dupuy to Gullón, 2 November 1897, Ultramar, legajo 2903, AMAE; Gómez to Billini, 10 December 1897, in *Cartas de Máximo Gómez*, 36–40.

53. Foner, *Spanish-Cuban-American War* 1:222; Portell Vilá, *Cuba en sus relaciones con los Estados Unidos* 3:355–56; "Agreement of November 18, 1897," Archivo de la delegación del Partido Revolucionario Cubano, Caja 1-W, CNA.

54. "Speech by Andrés Moreno de la Torre, secretary of foreign relations, to the council of the Cuban government, 10 December 1897," Archivo de la delegación del Partido Revolucionario Cubano, Caja 1-W, CNA.

55. Lee to Day, 27 November, 1, 3 December 1897, Consular Despatches from Havana, RG59, T 20, microroll 131, USNA; Day to Lee, 2 December 1897, Instructions to Spain, RG59, M 77, microroll 150, USNA.

CHAPTER 6

1. "Message of the President," 6 December 1897, *Foreign Relations, 1897*, vii–xxxiv.

2. Ibid.

3. "President's Attitude toward Cuba," *Literary Digest* 15 (18 December 1897): 995–96.

4. Dupuy to Gullón, 7 December 1897, Política, legajo 2417, AMAE; Dupuy to Gullón, 8 December 1897, in [Spain], *Diplomatic Correspondence*, 51.

5. Woodford to Sherman, 7 December 1897, in *Foreign Relations, 1898*, 645; Gullón to Dupuy, 8 December 1897, Política, legajo 2417, AMAE; Woodford to McKinley, 1 January 1898, box 185, Moore Papers.

6. *New York Tribune*, 2 December 1897; *Washington Star*, 2, 10, 12 December 1897; *New York Herald*, 6 December 1897; *Washington Post*, 7 December 1897; *New York Journal*, 8 December 1897; Dupuy to Gullón, 3 December 1897, Ultramar, legajo 2903, AMAE.

7. *Washington Star*, 9, 16 December 1897; *Washington Post*, 15 December 1897; *New York Tribune*, 20 December 1897; Dupuy to Gullón, 16 December 1897, in [Spain], *Diplomatic Correspondence*, 52; Dupuy to Gullón, 17 December 1897, Ultramar, legajo 2903, AMAE.

8. Woodford to Sherman, 15, 23 December 1897, in *Foreign Relations, 1898*, 646; Day to Woodford, 17 December 1897, in ibid.

9. Woodford to Sherman, 23 December 1897, in ibid., 646–54.

10. *Washington Post*, 27 December 1897.

11. "L'Espagne et les États-Unis pendant l'insurrection Cubaine, 1895–97," undated, Espagne, 18, FAMAE (this thirty-five-page memorandum was prepared for Hanotaux to use in his talks with León y Castillo); Hanotaux to Patenôtre, 4 January 1898, Espagne, 19, FAMAE; Montebello (St. Petersburg) to Hanotaux, 5 January 1898, ibid.; Patenôtre to Hanotaux, 23 January 1898, in France, *Documents Diplomatiques* 14:46–48.

12. Woodford to McKinley, 26 December 1897, 8 January 1898, box 185, Moore Papers.

13. Woodford to McKinley, 17 January 1898, ibid.

14. Ibid.

15. Ibid.

16. Ibid.

17. Ibid.; Cortés-Cavanillas, *María Cristina de Austria*, 129–30. Cortés-Cavanillas states that in an effort to keep the peace, Woodford passed some of his diplomatic messages from Washington to the queen regent through a trusted third party.

18. Baker, "Imperial Finale," 264–65, 336–38, 371–74. Baker believes the Spanish cabinet's bellicose elements were dominant from 10 January to 10 February 1898.

19. Day to Dupuy, 18 December 1897, Notes to the Spanish Legation, RG59, M 99, microroll 90, USNA; Dupuy to Blanco, 23 December 1897, Ultramar, legajo 4923, AHN; Dupuy to Gullón, 24, 26 December 1897, Política, legajo 2419, AMAE; Gullón to Dupuy, 24 December 1897, ibid.; Congosto to Dupuy, 27 December 1898, Ultramar, legajo 4923, AHN; "Relief of Suffering in Cuba," 8 January 1898, *Foreign Relations, 1898*, 655–56; *Washington Star*, 28 December 1897; Pryor, *Clara Barton*, 302–4.

20. *Washington Star*, 3, 4, 8, 12 January 1898; Lee to Day, 8 January 1898, Despatches from Havana, RG59, T 20, microroll 131, USNA. A file on Spanish relief efforts, including correspondence between Moret and Blanco, is located in Ultramar, legajo 4970, AHN.

21. "Birthright for a Mess of Potage," Cuba, *Correspondencia diplomática* 5:202–4.

22. *New York Tribune*, 19, 20 December 1897; Blanco to Dupuy, 22 January 1898, Ultramar, legajo 4923, AHN; Foner, *Spanish-Cuban-American War* 1: 134–35.

23. Congosto to Dupuy, 25 December 1897, Ultramar, legajo 4923, AHN; Soldevilla, *El año político, 1897*, 437; Lee to Day, 31 December 1897, Despatches from Havana, RG59, T 20, microroll 131, USNA.

24. Congosto to Dupuy, 12 January 1898, Ultramar, legajo 4923, AHN; Lee to Day, 12, 13, 14, 15 January 1897, in *Foreign Relations, 1898*, 1024–25; *Washington Post*, 13 January 1898. *El Correo Militar* (Madrid), 14 January 1898, boasted that there were one hundred thousand Spaniards in Cuba who opposed autonomy. A complete file of Blanco's and Moret's correspondence on the riot is in Ultramar, legajo 4970, AHN.

25. Blanco to Moret, 15, 16 January 1898, Ultramar, legajo 4959, AHN; Moret to Blanco, 13, 15, 18 January 1898, Ultramar, legajo 4970, AHN; Baker, "Imperial Finale," 310–12.

26. Lee to Day, 18 January 1898, Despatches from Havana, RG59, T 20, microroll 131, USNA; Moret to Blanco, 18 January 1898, Ultramar, legajo 4959, AHN.

27. Dupuy to Gullón, 14 January 1898, in [Spain], *Diplomatic Correspondence*, 60.

28. Dupuy to Gullón, 16 January 1898, Ultramar, legajo 2904, AMAE; Lee to Day, 15 January 1898, Despatches from Havana, RG59, T 20, microroll 131, USNA.

29. Dupuy to Gullón, 16 January 1898, in [Spain], *Diplomatic Correspondence*, 64–65; Gullón to Dupuy, 17, 19 January 1898, in ibid., 64, 66.

30. Sigsbee, *Maine*, 9–10; Dupuy to Gullón, 16 December 1897, Ultramar, legajo 2903, AMAE; U.S. Secretary of the Navy, *Annual Report*, 325.

31. Foner, *Spanish-American-Cuban War* 1:229; U.S. Secretary of the Navy, *Annual Report*, 3.

32. *Washington Star*, 14 January 1898; Journal, 14 January 1898, Long Papers; *New York Tribune*, 15 January 1898.

33. *Washington Star*, 17, 18 January 1898.

34. Lee to Day, 25 January 1898, box 35, Day Papers.

35. Dupuy to Gullón, 5 January 1898, Política, legajo 2419, AMAE; *Cong. Rec.*, 55th Cong., 2d sess., 582.

36. *Cong. Rec.*, 55th Cong., 2d sess., 730–39, 760–64, 769.

37. Ibid., 739, 767–69, 772–74. The consular reports, which McKinley regularly read, portrayed the devastating effects of reconcentration. Submitting these reports to Congress was certain to create an emotional outburst against

Spain. Dupuy considered the American consuls in Matanzas, Sagua la Grande, and Santiago de Cuba to be active agents of the insurgents. Dupuy to Gullón, 22 October 1897, Ultramar, legajo 2903, AMAE.

38. *Washington Star*, 19, 21 January 1898; *New York Tribune*, 19, 21 January 1898; Dupuy to Gullón, 20 January 1898, in [Spain], *Diplomatic Correspondence*, 67; Rubens to Quesada, 23 January 1898, Fondo Donativo y Remisiones, Fuera de caja, 62–64, CNA; Quesada to Estrada Palma, 21 January 1898, in Cuba, *Correspondencia diplomática* 5:122–23.

39. Memorandum of Conversation with Dupuy, undated (from context, it was held on 20 January 1898), box 35, Day Papers.

40. Lee to Day, 21 January 1898, Despatches from Havana, RG59, T 20, microroll 131, USNA. From the first, Lee often asked for a naval ship. During December and January he repeatedly requested one.

41. Lee to Day, 12 January 1898, box 35, Day Papers; McKinley to Day, undated, ibid.; Day to Lee, 22 January 1898, and Lee to Day, 22 January 1898, in *Foreign Relations, 1898*, 1025; Memorandum of Conversation with Dupuy, 24 January 1898, box 35, Day Papers; Dupuy to Gullón, 24 January 1898, in [Spain], *Diplomatic Correspondence*, 68; Journal, 24 January 1898, Long Papers; *Washington Star*, 24 January 1898.

42. Lee to Day, 24, 25 January 1898, and Day to Lee, 24 January 1898, in *Foreign Relations, 1898*, 1026; Sigsbee, *Maine*, 24–25.

43. *Washington Post*, 25 January 1898; *New York Tribune*, 25 January 1898.

44. Dupuy to Blanco, 25 January 1898, Ultramar, legajo 4923, AHN; Dupuy to Gullón, 24 January 1898, in [Spain], *Diplomatic Correspondence*, 68; Gullón to Woodford, 26 January 1898, in ibid., 70.

45. *Washington Post*, 26 January 1898; Sigsbee, *Maine*, 25–50.

46. Dupuy to Gullón, 28 January 1898, in [Spain], *Diplomatic Correspondence*, 71. This appears to be the only time McKinley and Dupuy spoke to one another about Cuba.

CHAPTER 7

1. Foner, *Spanish-Cuban-American War* 1:134–36; *New York Tribune* 3, 4, 7 February 1898.

2. Soldevilla, *El año político, 1898*, 43–44; Romanones, *Sagasta*, 191–92. This is the third of three documents Romanones found in Sagasta's file on Cuba.

3. Converse (Matanzas) to Navy Department, 6 February 1898, Miscellaneous letters, RG59, M 179, microroll 990, USNA.

4. Atkins, *Sixty Years in Cuba*, 270–72; U.S. Congress, Senate, Committee on Foreign Relations, *Affairs in Cuba*, 485–89. Information on the deplorable

conditions in Cuba was abundant. Since it was often sensational, I have included Atkins's observations because he was pro-Spanish and anti-interventionist.

5. Sigsbee to Long, 1 February 1898, Miscellaneous Letters, RG59, M 179, microroll 990, USNA; Lee to Day, 2 February 1898, box 35, Day Papers; Day to Lee, 4, 5 February 1898, in *Foreign Relations, 1898*, 1027; Lee to Day, 4 February 1898, in ibid., 1027–28.

6. Dupuy to Gullón, 7 February 1898, in [Spain], *Diplomatic Correspondence*, 79–80.

7. Dupuy to Blanco, 3 February 1898, Ultramar, legajo 4923, AHN; Moret to Blanco, 14, 15 February 1898, Ultramar, legajo 4959, AHN; Baker, "Imperial Finale," 371; Varela Ortega, "Aftermath of Splendid Disaster," 320–22.

8. Gullón to Woodford, 1 February 1898, in *Foreign Relations, 1898*, 658–64; Dubsky to Goluchowski, 30 January, 3 February 1898, Spanien, 59, HHSA. According to Gullón, Sagasta delayed the response until 1 February because he did not want Spain to appear to be replying angrily to the arrival of the *Maine* in Havana.

9. Woodford to McKinley, 4, 7 February 1898, box 185, Moore Papers; Woodford to Sherman, 14 February 1898, Despatches from Spain, RG59, M 31, microroll 123, USNA.

10. Moret to Blanco, 2 December 1897, 23 January 1898, Ultramar, legajo 4923, AHN; Moret to Blanco, 20 January 1898, Ultramar, legajo 4970, AHN; Blanco to Moret, 22 January 1898, Ultramar, legajo 4923, AHN; Blanco to Moret, 23 January 1898, Ultramar, legajo 4970, AHN; Dubsky to Goluchowski, 3 February 1898, Spanien, 59, HHSA.

11. Woodford to Sherman, 24, 25 January 1898, Despatches from Spain, RG59, M 31, microroll 123, USNA; Woodford to McKinley, 28, 31 January, 4 February 1898, box 185, Moore Papers.

12. Baker, "Imperial Finale," 373–74; Cervera y Topete, *Spanish-American War*, 12–13, 16, 22–25, 27–29, 31–36; Moret to Blanco, 7 February 1898, Gobierno Autonómico, caja 6, CNA; Rodríguez González, *Política naval de la Restauración*, 475–86; Bliss to Corbin, 5 February 1898, Bliss Papers.

13. Gullón to conde de Rascón, 30 January 1898, Estado, legajo 8664, AHN; Gullón, Circular telegram to Paris, London, Berlin, Vienna, Rome, St. Petersburg, 8 February 1898, in [Spain], *Diplomatic Correspondence*, 80.

14. Pabón y Suárez de Urbina, *El 98*, 75–76; Tabouis, *Jules Cambon*, 91; Patenôtre to Hanotaux, 6 February 1898, in France, *Documents Diplomatiques* 14:74–76; Hanotaux, Memorandum, 10 February 1898, in ibid., 85–87; Hanotaux to Patenôtre, 18 February 1898, Espagne, 19, FAMAE; Shippee, "Germany and the Spanish-American War," 756.

15. Woodford to McKinley, 7 February 1898, box 185, Moore Papers.

16. Dupuy to Canalejas, undated, in *Foreign Relations, 1898*, 1007–8. See the

Appendix for the State Department's translation of the letter. Popular and scholarly treatments of this event always use the term *de Lôme letter*. The name "de Lôme" is inaccurate. The Spanish minister's complete surname was "Dupuy de Lôme," and he signed his telegrams "Dupuy."

17. Rubens, *Liberty*, 287; Foner, *Spanish-Cuban-American War* 1:232–34; Sworn statement of Gustavo Escoto y Castello, 10 February 1898, Fondo Donativo y Remisiones, folio 366, CNA; Rubens to Quesada, 9 February 1898, Fondo Donativo y Remisiones, fuera de caja, epistolaria, 62–64, CNA.

18. Rubens, *Liberty*, 288.

19. "De Lôme Incident," *Literary Digest* 16 (19 February 1898): 212–13. There are more than a dozen studies of newspaper opinion and the coming of the war. During the 1930s, Wilkerson, *Public Opinion and the Spanish-American War*, and Wisan, *The Cuban Crisis as Reflected in the New York Press*, concluded that the sensational press was a primary cause of the war, and these works spawned many additional studies. See Gould and Roell, *William McKinley: A Bibliography*, 78–90.

20. Rubens, *Liberty*, 289; Duncan, "William Rufus Day," 104; Sherman to Woodford, 23 February 1898, in *Foreign Relations, 1898*, 1018–20.

21. Memorandum of Conversation with Dupuy de Lôme, 9 February 1898, Papiers D'Agents, Jules Cambon, 8, FAMAE; Cambon to Hanotaux, 10, 11 February 1898, Espagne, 19, FAMAE. Dupuy never explained why he wrote to Canalejas, but perhaps the Spanish diplomat, a member of the Conservative Party, wanted to sustain a close association with Canalejas, who might someday succeed Sagasta as head of the Liberal Party. Perhaps Dupuy was trying to impress Canalejas with his wit and intelligence in order to lay a basis for future assignments; if so, the disclosure mocked his efforts by ending his career.

22. Rubens, *Liberty*, 291; McKinley, Handwritten Memorandum, and Day, Memorandum, undated, box 9, Day Papers; Day to Woodford, 9 February 1898, in *Foreign Relations, 1898*, 1008; *Washington Star*, 11, 12 February 1898.

23. Dupuy to Gullón, 8, 9 February 1898, in [Spain], *Diplomatic Correspondence*, 80–81.

24. Soldevilla, *El año político, 1898*, 40–43.

25. Gullón to Dupuy, 10 February 1898, in [Spain], *Diplomatic Correspondence*, 81–82; Gullón to conde de Rascón, 13 February 1898, Estado, legajo 8664, AHN. From his study of Dupuy, García Barrón concluded that the Spanish minister regularly erred on the optimistic side and thereby misled Madrid about Washington.

26. Blanco to Moret, 12 February 1898, Ultramar, legajo 4959, AHN; Moret to Blanco, 12 February 1898, Ultramar, legajo 4970, AHN; Moret to Congosto, 12, 20 February 1898, Ultramar, legajo 4923, AHN.

27. Dubsky to Goluchowski, 16 February 1898, Spanien, 59, HHSA.

28. Woodford to Sherman, 11 February 1898, in *Foreign Relations, 1898*, 1009; Woodford to Gullón, 14 February 1898, and Gullón to Woodford, 15 February 1898, in ibid., 1009, 1012–13.

29. Day to Woodford, 12 February 1898, in ibid., 1012–13; Woodford to McKinley, 15, 19, 23, 26 February 1898, box 185, Moore Papers.

30. Gullón to Woodford, 15 February 1898, in [Spain], *Diplomatic Correspondence*, 84–85; Woodford to Sherman, 17 February 1898, in *Foreign Relations, 1898*, 1014.

31. Woodford to McKinley, 15, 19, 23, 26 February 1898, box 185, Moore Papers.

32. Soldevilla, *El año político, 1898*, 46–47.

33. *Cong. Rec.*, 55th Cong., 2d sess., 1534–35, 1574–85, 1605, 1681–82, 1703, 1876, 2088; *New York Tribune*, 15 February 1898.

34. Lee to Day, 16 February 1898, in *Foreign Relations, 1898*, 1029; Lee to Day, 15 February 1898, Despatches from Havana, RG59, T 20, microroll 132, USNA; *Washington Post*, 16 February 1898.

35. Rickover, *How the Battleship* Maine *Was Destroyed*, 45.

36. Ibid., 20–21, 45–47; *Washington Star*, 16 February 1898; Mayo, *America of Yesterday*, 162–66.

37. "Disaster to the 'Maine,'" *Literary Digest* 16 (26 February 1898): 241–44. See also note 19 above.

38. *Washington Star*, 16 February 1898; *Washington Post*, 17 February 1898; *New York Tribune*, 17 February 1898.

39. *Washington Star*, 16 February 1898; *Washington Post*, 17, 19 February 1898; *New York Tribune*, 17, 19 February 1898.

40. Olcott, *William McKinley* 2:12–13. Long and Dawes recorded similar statements. Dawes, *McKinley Years*, 143–45; Journal, 17 February 1898, Long Papers.

41. Rickover, *How the Battleship* Maine *Was Destroyed*, 48–50; *Cong. Rec.*, 55th Cong., 2d sess., 1873–79.

42. Rickover, *How the Battleship* Maine *Was Destroyed*, 57.

43. Du Bosc to Gullón, 16, 18 February 1898, and Gullón to Du Bosc, 16, 17 February 1898, in [Spain], *Diplomatic Correspondence*, 86–87.

44. Rickover, *How the Battleship* Maine *Was Destroyed*, 50–53.

45. Roosevelt to Long, 19 February 1898, in *Letters of Theodore Roosevelt* 1:779–81; Foster, *Diplomatic Memoirs* 2:25–26; Morgan, "The DeLôme Letter."

CHAPTER 8

1. Lee to Day, 22 February 1898, Despatches from Havana, RG59, T 20, microroll 132, USNA; *Washington Star*, 23 February 1898; *Washington Post*, 24 February 24, 1898.

2. *Washington Star*, 28 February 1898; *New York Tribune*, 1 March 1898.

3. Lee to Day, 1 March 1898, Despatches from Havana, RG59, T 20, microroll 132, USNA; Mayo, *America of Yesterday*, 171–72; *New York Tribune*, 3 March 1898.

4. Lee to Day, 8 March 1898, Despatches from Havana, RG59, T 20, microroll 132, USNA; *Washington Star*, 26 February 1898; *Washington Post*, 12 March 1898.

5. *Washington Post*, 25, 26 February 1898; *Washington Star*, 26 February 1898; *Journal of John D. Long*, 216; Cambon to Hanotaux, 25 February 1898, Espagne, 19, FAMAE.

6. *Washington Star*, 1, 2, 3 March 1898; *Washington Post*, 2, 3 March 1898.

7. *Papers of John Davis Long*, 41–42, 53–55; Mayo, *America of Yesterday*, 167–69; Journal, 24 February 1898, Long Papers. Long considered all modern battleships to be experimental and potentially self-destructive.

8. *New York Tribune*, 5, 6 March 1898; Memorandum, 6 March 1898, 800, Private Papers, 179, PRO; Roosevelt to Colwell (London), and Colwell to Roosevelt, 5 March 1898, and Roosevelt to Dyer (Madrid), 5 March 1898, Department of the Navy, Cable Correspondence, RG38, USNA. Dyer (Madrid) never made an estimate of the fighting quality of the Spanish navy. Colwell (London) was much more energetic but had a breakdown in early April. As a result, Sims (Paris) moved to London while Colwell took a rest in Paris. When the war started, the two men reversed posts again. Both Colwell and Sims established extensive espionage networks during the war. Before leaving Madrid, Dyer hired an agent who consistently provided unreliable information. The importance of these clandestine intelligence reports to decision makers is unknown. Presumably, the members of the Naval War Board read the reports. There is no indication that the secretary of state or president read them or that the reports influenced diplomatic policy. The best account of naval intelligence activities is in Trask, *War with Spain*, 87–88. For the most interesting espionage reports, see Department of the Navy, Reports submitted by Lieutenant William S. Sims relative to affairs in France and Spain, Department of the Navy, International Relations and Politics, RG45, USNA.

9. *Washington Post*, 5 March 1898.

10. Busbey, *Uncle Joe Cannon*, 186–90; Dingley, *Nelson Dingley, Jr.*, 45–55; *Washington Post*, 8 March 1898; *Cong. Rec.*, 55th Cong., 2d sess., 2569, 2602–20, 2631–32.

11. Diary, 9 March 1898, Hinds Papers.

12. Mayo, *America of Yesterday*, 172–73; "Measures of National Defense," *Literary Digest* 16 (19 March 1898): 331–33; "The Week," *Nation* 66 (10 March 1898): 175; White (London) to Porter (White House), 12 March 1898, box 56, Cortelyou Papers.

13. Woodford to Day, 14 March 1898, Despatches from Spain, RG59, M 31, microroll 123, USNA; Roosevelt to Evans, 16 March 1898, in *Letters of Theodore Roosevelt*, 795; *Papers of John Davis Long*, 71–73.

14. Cambon to Hanotaux, 11 March 1898, Espagne, 20, FAMAE. Ireland, who had been educated in France, was a good friend of Cambon's.

15. For an especially good study of Proctor's speech, see Linderman, *Mirror of War*, 37–59.

16. Roosevelt to Foraker, 5 November 1897, Foraker Papers; Cullom, *Fifty Years of Public Service*, 283; *Washington Post*, 26 February 1898; Proctor to Day, 1 March 1898, box 9, Day Papers.

17. Proctor to Day, 1, 4 March 1898, box 9, Day Papers.

18. *Washington Star*, 11, 14 March 1898; *Washington Post*, 18 March 1898; Rubens to Quesada, Fondo Donativo y Remisiones, fuera de caja, 62–64, CNA.

19. *Cong. Rec.*, 55th Cong., 2d sess., 2916–19.

20. Ibid., 2916.

21. Ibid.

22. Ibid., 2917.

23. Ibid.

24. Ibid., 2918.

25. Ibid.

26. Ibid.

27. Ibid., 2919.

28. Alger, *Spanish-American War*, 4–5; Pratt, *Expansionists of 1898*, 246–47; Tarbell, "President McKinley in War Times," 218–19; "Senator Proctor on Cuba's Desolation," *Literary Digest* 16 (26 March 1898): 361; "Right of Intervention," *Literary Digest* 16 (2 April 1898): 391–94; *Wall Street Journal* (New York), 19 March 1898, as quoted in Pratt, *Expansionists of 1898*, 246.

29. "Religious Press on the Prospects of War," *Literary Digest* 16 (16 April 1898): 471–72; Pratt, *Expansionists of 1898*, 284–86.

30. *Washington Star*, 21 March 1898; Hastings to McKinley, 27 March 1898, microfilm 3, McKinley Papers.

31. *Washington Post*, 19 March 1898; Dawes, *McKinley Years*, 147.

32. *Washington Post*, 16 March 1898; Acheson, *Joe Bailey*, 97; *New York Press*, 18 March 1898; Dawes, *McKinley Years*, 146–47.

33. *New York Tribune*, 20, 21 March 1898; *Washington Star*, 21 March 1898; Day to Woodford, 20 March 1898, in *Foreign Relations, 1898*, 692–93; Polo to Gullón, 24 March 1898, Política, legajo 2424, AMAE.

34. *Washington Post*, 22, 23, 24, 27 March 1898; *Washington Star*, 23, 24 March 1898; *New York Tribune*, 24, 25 March 1898; Dawes, *McKinley Years*, 148–49. Journalists noted the following congressional visitors to McKinley: Senators Arthur P. Gorman, Gray, Morgan, Francis M. Cockrell, Turpie, Foraker, Allison, Elkins, Shelby M. Cullom, Spooner, Fairbanks, Davis, Charles J. Faulkner, James K. Jones, and Aldrich; Representatives Reed, Hitt, Grosvenor, and Bailey. Reed told Cambon that McKinley had decided to submit to Congress both the *Maine* report and the consular reports. Cambon to Hanotaux, 23 March 1898, Espagne, 20, FAMAE.

35. *Washington Star*, 26 March 1898; *Washington Post*, 27 March 1898; *Cong. Rec.*, 55th Cong., 2d sess., 3278–79.

36. The U.S. Navy has investigated the *Maine* explosion three times, once in 1898, a second time in 1911, and a third in 1975. The first court of inquiry determined that an external explosion had caused the disaster. In 1911 the navy built a coffer dam around the wrecked ship and pumped out the water to expose the damaged parts. With more complete information, the second inquiry concluded that the first was incorrect. Nevertheless, the second held that an external explosion at a different part of the hull had caused the ship's magazines to blow up. The navy then towed the remains of the *Maine* to sea and sank them in deep water. In 1975, Admiral Hyman Rickover directed a third investigation of the explosion. Using the evidence developed in 1911, his engineering staff determined that there had been no external explosion and that all the facts of the wreckage were consistent with an internal explosion. Rickover was especially critical of the first investigation because it lacked expert advice on munitions and ship architecture. Rickover, *How the Battleship* Maine *Was Destroyed*, 75–106.

37. May, *Imperial Democracy*, 133–47, describes the "hysteria" in American public opinion; see also *Washington Star*, 28, 29 March 1898; *Washington Post*, 28, 29 March 1898; "Report on the *Maine* Disaster," *Literary Digest* 16 (9 April 1898): 422–24.

38. Soldevila, *El año político, 1898*, 63–64; Woodford to Sherman, 28 February 1898, in *Foreign Relations, 1898*, 665–66.

39. Moret and Blanco exchanged many telegrams concerning the election. For example, see Moret to Blanco, 23 March 1898, Ultramar, legajo 4959, AHN. A large number of election telegrams are also located in Ultramar, legajo 4970, AHN. These files suggest that the Spanish regime was more interested in controlling the election than in fighting the war. The careful selection of candidates conformed to the *cacique* system of control used widely in Spain.

40. Baker, "Imperial Finale," 253–58; McCook to Day, 9 March 1898, box 9, Day Papers; Porter to Sherman, 14 March 1898, Despatches from France, RG59, M 34, microroll 118, USNA.

41. Dubsky to Goluchowski, 26 January 1898, Spanien, 59, HHSA; Cervera

y Topete, *Spanish-American War*, 26–27, 30, 38–39; *El Correo Militar* (Madrid), 23 February, 2 March 1898; *Correo de Madrid*, 13 March 1898; Varela Ortega, "Aftermath of Splendid Disaster," 319–21.

42. Du Bosc to Gullón, 25 February 1898, in [Spain], *Diplomatic Correspondence*, 88; Gullón to Du Bosc, 26 February 1898, in ibid.; Gullón to Paris, Berlin, Vienna, London, St. Petersburg, Rome, and the Holy See, 16 March 1898, in ibid.; Blanco to Polo, 12 March 1898, Ultramar, legajo 4923, AHN; Gullón to Polo, 13 March 1898, and Polo to Gullón, 16 March 1898, Ultramar, legajo 2904, AMAE; Moret to Blanco, 12 March 1898, Ultramar, legajo 4959, AHN.

43. Polo to Gullón, 18 March 1898, in [Spain], *Diplomatic Correspondence*, 90; Soldevilla, *El año político, 1898*, 75; Woodford to McKinley, 9 March 1898, in *Foreign Relations, 1898*, 681–85; Moret to Blanco, 8 March 1898, Ultramar, ASHM; Moret to Blanco, 10 March 1898, Ultramar, legajo 4959, AHN.

44. Gullón to Rascón, 11 March 1898, Estado, legajo 8664, AHN.

45. Du Bosc to Gullón, 9 March 1898, Ultramar, legajo 2904, AMAE.

46. Polo to Gullón, 11, 12, 16 March 1898, in [Spain], *Diplomatic Correspondence*, 91–92; Gullón to Polo, 17 March 1898, in ibid., 93; Polo to Gullón, 12, 17 March 1898, Ultramar, legajo 2904, AMAE; Gullón to Polo, 14, 22 March 1898, ibid.

47. Polo to Blanco, 12, 19 March 1898, Ultramar, legajo 2904, AMAE; Blanco to Polo, 11 March 1898, ibid.; Polo to Gullón, 19 March 1898, in [Spain], *Diplomatic Correspondence*, 93; Polo to Blanco, 26 March 1898, Política, legajo 2424, AMAE; Lee to Day, 1, 24 March 1898, Despatches from Havana, RG59, T 20, microroll 132, USNA; *New York Tribune*, 28 March 1898; Long to Sherman, 28 February 1898, in *Foreign Relations, 1898*, 679–80; Polo to Day, 26, 28 March 1898, Notes from the Spanish Legation, RG59, M 59, microroll 29, USNA.

48. Polo to Blanco, 19 March 1898, Ultramar, legajo 2904, AMAE; Polo to Gullón, 21, 22 March 1898, ibid.

49. Polo to Gullón, 22 March 1898, Ultramar, legajo 2904, AMAE; Polo to Gullón, 24 March 1898, Política, legajo 2424, ibid.

50. *El Correo Militar* (Madrid), 24 March 1898.

51. Gullón to Polo, 27 March 1898, in [Spain], *Diplomatic Correspondence*, 102; Moret to Blanco, 23 March 1898, Ultramar, legajo 4959, AHN.

CHAPTER 9

1. Woodford to McKinley, 2 March 1898, in *Foreign Relations, 1898*, 673–75.

2. *Washington Post*, 20 February, 27 March 1898; Cambon to Hanotaux, 11 March 1898, Espagne, 20, FAMAE; McCook to Day, 1 March 1898, box 9, Day Papers; Reid to McKinley, 8 March 1898, microfilm 72, Reid Papers; Foner,

Spanish-Cuban-American War 1:247–48. Foner believes that Gómez offered to buy independence in order to prevent American military intervention.

3.   Sherman to Woodford, 1 March 1898, in *Foreign Relations, 1898*, 666–69.

4.   Patenôtre to Hanotaux, 11 March 1898, Espagne, 20, FAMAE; Woodford to McKinley, 9, 17, 19 March 1898, in *Foreign Relations, 1898*, 681–88, 693; Gullón to Polo, 21 March 1898, Ultramar, legajo 2904, AMAE; Gullón to Rascón, 21 March 1898, Estado, legajo 8664, AHN; Maura y Gamazo, *Historia crítica del reinado de don Alfonso XIII durante su menoridad* 1:359–60.

5.   Woodford to McKinley, 17, 18 March 1898, in *Foreign Relations, 1898*, 685–92.

6.   Straus to McKinley, 12, 23, 24 March 1898, and Straus to McCook, 12 March 1898, and Straus to Angell, 22 March 1898, box 2, Straus Papers; Straus diary, date of entry unclear, box 22, ibid.

7.   Cortissoz, *Whitelaw Reid* 2:220–22.

8.   Unsigned memorandum, 24 March 1898, box 35, Day Papers. Day to Moore, 25 March 1898, box 6, Moore Papers. During the emergency, Day asked Moore to come at once to Washington.

9.   Woodford to McKinley, 2 March 1898, in *Foreign Relations, 1898*, 673–76; Day to Woodford, 3 March 1898, in ibid., 680–81.

10.   *Washington Post*, 6 March 1898; *Washington Star*, 7 March 1898; Moret to Blanco, 4 March 1898, Ultramar, legajo 4959, AHN.

11.   Woodford to McKinley, 9 March 1898, in *Foreign Relations, 1898*, 681–85.

12.   Woodford to McKinley, 19 March 1898, box 185, Moore Papers.

13.   Day to Woodford, 20 March 1898, in *Foreign Relations, 1898*, 692–93.

14.   Woodford to McKinley, 22, 23, 25 March 1898, in ibid., 696–701. In Política, legajo 2420, AMAE, is a collection of twelve documents that appear to make up Gullón's working file on the coming of the war. The first document is Woodford's 22 March submission of the *Maine* report.

15.   Soldevilla, *El año político, 1898*, 85–88; *El Heraldo de Madrid*, 23 March 1898; Gullón, circular telegram to all Spanish diplomats, 24 March 1898, in [Spain], *Diplomatic Correspondence*, 95–96.

16.   Soldevilla, *El año político, 1898*, 88–90.

17.   Polo to Gullón, 25 March 1898, in [Spain], *Diplomatic Correspondence*, 97–98; Gullón to Polo, 26 March 1898, and Polo to Gullón, 28 March 1898, Política, legajo 2424, AMAE.

18.   Woodford to McKinley, 24 March 1898, in *Foreign Relations, 1898*, 697; Woodford to McKinley, 25 March 1898, box 185, Moore Papers.

19.   Woodford to McKinley, 25 March 1898, box 185, Moore Papers.

20.   Woodford to Sherman, 25, 26 March 1898, in *Foreign Relations, 1898*, 698–703.

21.   Woodford to McKinley, 26 March 1898, in ibid., 703–4.

22. *Washington Post*, 29 March 1898; Unsigned memorandum, 11 April 1898, box 121, Chandler Papers. The senators were Platt (Conn.), Fairbanks, Spooner, Hanna, Allison, Hale, and Aldrich.

23. *Cong. Rec.*, 55th Cong., 2d sess., 3293–94, 3341, 3401.

24. *Washington Star*, 29 March 1898; *Washington Post*, 30 March 1898; *New York Tribune*, 30 March 1898.

25. *Cong. Rec.*, 55th Cong., 2d sess., 3379–82, 3390–92, 3670; *Washington Post*, 31 March 1898; Diary, 31 March 1898, Hinds Papers.

26. Tarbell, "McKinley in War Times," 219–23; *Washington Star*, 30 March 1898; *Washington Post*, 30, 31 March 1898; Chandler to Dana, 31 March 1898, box 120, Chandler Papers. Apparently Day agreed that public opinion would support an armistice only if the Cubans did. See Hansborough to Day, undated (probably sent 30 March 1898), box 8, Day Papers.

27. *Washington Star*, 31 March 1898; *New York Tribune*, 31 March 1898.

28. *Cong. Rec.*, 55th Cong., 2d sess., 3433–45.

29. Nelson to Hill, 31 March 1898, Hill Papers; Lodge to Higginson, 4 April 1898, Higginson Papers; Roosevelt to Root, 5 April 1898, in *Letters of Theodore Roosevelt* 2:812–14; Rhodes, *McKinley and Roosevelt Administrations*, 59; Jessup, *Elihu Root* 1:96–97; *New York Times*, 1 April 1898; Merrill and Merrill, *Republican Command*, 48–53.

30. Day to Woodford, 28, 29, 30 March 1898, in *Foreign Relations, 1898*, 713, 718, 721. McKinley wrote the draft of the 30 March warning, box 9, Day Papers.

31. Polo to Gullón, 29 March 1898, Política, legajo 2424, AMAE.

32. Polo to Gullón, 30 March 1898, ibid.

33. Sherman to Woodford, 26 March 1898, in *Foreign Relations, 1898*, 1036–37.

34. Day to Woodford, 26, 27, 28 March 1898, and Woodford to Day, 27 March 1898, in ibid., 704, 711–13.

35. *El Heraldo de Madrid*, 25 March 1898; *El Correo de Madrid*, 27, 28 March 1898; *El Imparcial* (Madrid), 29 March 1898; Barclay to Salisbury, 29 March 1898, 72, Spain, 2062, PRO; Dubsky to Goluchowski, 29 March 1898, Spanien, 68, HHSA; Polo to Blanco, 28 March 1898, Política, legajo 2424, AMAE.

36. Woodford to Gullón, 28 March 1898, and Woodford to McKinley, 29 March 1898, in *Foreign Relations, 1898*, 718–21, 1043–44; Barclay to Salisbury, 29, 30 March 1898, 72, Spain, 2068, PRO; Soldevilla, *El año político, 1898*, 100–103.

37. Barclay to Salisbury, 30 March 1898, 72, Spain, 2062, PRO; Dubsky to Goluchowski, 30 March, 1898, Spanien, 68, HHSA; Soldevilla, *El año político, 1898*, 106–10; *El Correo de Madrid*, 1 April 1898; Moret to Blanco, 27 March 1898, and Blanco to Moret, 29 March 1898, Ultramar, legajo 4959, AHN.

38. Reply of Council of Ministers to Woodford, 31 March 1898, in [Spain], *Diplomatic Correspondence*, 107–8.

39. Gullón to Polo, 31 March 1898, and Polo to Gullón, 31 March 1898, Política, legajo 2424, AMAE.

40. *El Correo de Madrid*, 2 April 1898; *El Heraldo de Madrid*, 31 March 1898; *El Imparcial* (Madrid), 31 March 1898.

41. Woodford to McKinley, 1 April 1898, in *Foreign Relations, 1898*, 727–28; Woodford to McKinley, 31 March 1898, box 185, Moore Papers. Contemporary observers and later historians disagreed over the importance of public opinion in pressuring the Sagasta ministry to take a nationalistic stand against the United States. Nearly all agree, however, that the army was extremely important in limiting Sagasta's ability to negotiate a withdrawal from Cuba. See Romanones, *Sagasta*, 194–95; Rivas Santiago, *Sagasta*, 123; Lema, *Mis recuerdos*, 210–12; Fernández Almagro, *Política naval de la España*, 197; Varela Ortega, *Los amigos políticos*, 314–18. The French ambassador wrote an incisive analysis of Sagasta's choices; see Patenôtre to Hanotaux, 30 March 1898, in France, *Documents Diplomatiques* 14:174; Baker, "Imperial Finale," 326–31, 353–57, 364–65. Varela Ortega states that the queen regent, fearful of losing her throne, sent personal effects to a castle in Austria.

42. *Washington Star*, 1, 2 April 1898; *Washington Post*, 1, 2 April 1898; *New York Tribune*, 2 April 1898; *New York Times*, 2 April 1898; Polo to Gullón, 1 April 1898, Política, legajo 2424, AMAE. The French and German diplomats were critical of McKinley's giving in to Congress. Ambassador Theodor Ludwig von Holleben believed that if Cleveland had been president, he would have resisted Congress, despite the resulting domestic conflict. Cambon thought that McKinley failed because he associated his policy with Congress. Sooner or later, he had to follow the lead of Congress. Vagts, *Deutschland und die Vereinigten Staaten* 2:1297–98; Cambon to Hanotaux, 1 April 1898, Espagne, 21, FAMAE.

CHAPTER 10

1. A good description of European diplomacy in response to the developing Spanish-American crisis is in May, *Imperial Democracy*, chapters 12 through 15.

2. Offner, "Washington Mission."

3. Soldevilla, *El año político, 1898*, 68–69.

4. Dubsky to Goluchowski, 11, 14 March 1898, Spanien, 68, HHSA; Reverseaux to Hanotaux, 13 March 1898, Espagne, 20, FAMAE; Hanotaux, Memorandum of Conversation with León y Castillo, 15 March 1898, in France, *Documents Diplomatiques* 14:142–44; Dubsky to Goluchowski, 16 March 1898, Spanien, 68, HHSA.

5. Dubsky to Goluchowski, 12 March 1898, Spanien, 68, HHSA; Cambon to Hanotaux, 15 March 1898, Espagne, 20, FAMAE. The queen regent also appealed to the tsar.

6. Dubsky to Goluchowski, 24, 25 March 1898, Spanien, 68, HHSA; Gullón, Circular telegram, 25 March 1898, in [Spain], *Diplomatic Correspondence*, 98–99.

7. Mendez de Vigo (Berlin) to Gullón, 28 March 1898; Mazo (Rome) to Gullón, 27 March 1898; and Villagonzalo (St. Petersburg) to Gullón, 30 March 1898, in [Spain], *Diplomatic Correspondence*, 101–9; Reverseaux to Hanotaux, 27 March 1898, and Hanotaux to Patenôtre, 31 March 1898, in France, *Documents Diplomatiques* 14:165–66; Francisca Nava to Rampolla, 27 March 1898, Rubrica 249, 43229, ASV; León y Castillo to Gullón, 30 March 1898, Política, legajo 2417, AMAE; Balfour to Barclay, 31 March 1898, 72, Spain, 2067, PRO.

8. Merry to Gullón, 25 March 1898, in [Spain], *Diplomatic Correspondence*, 99–100; Dubsky to Goluchowski, 26 March 1898, Spanien, 68, HHSA.

9. Francisca Nava to Rampolla, 27 March 1898, and Rampolla to Francisca Nava, 28 March 1898, Rubrica 249, 43205, 43229, ASV. Some authors hold that Germany prompted papal mediation. The German chancellor did suggest papal mediation and the possible arbitration of the *Maine*. Bülow thought that Spain would willingly take Leo XIII as a mediator but that McKinley would likely reject arbitration. Therefore, to prevent war, he suggested a trade-off: Spain would leave Cuba immediately if the United States would agree to allow the pope to arbitrate the *Maine* dispute. This proposal was no more attractive to Madrid than to Washington. Gottschall, "Germany and the Spanish-American War," 36; Francisca Nava to Rampolla, 8 April 1898, Rubrica 249, 43494, ASV; Barclay to Salisbury, 31 March 1898, 72, Spain, 2068, PRO.

10. Unsigned note to Keane, 27 March 1898, Rubrica 249, 43158, ASV; Keane to Rampolla, Rubrica 249, 43164, ASV; Offner, "Washington Mission," 563.

11. Offner, "Washington Mission," 563–64.

12. Ireland to Rampolla, 1, 2 April 1898, Ireland Papers; Cambon to Hanotaux, 12 April 1898, Espagne, 22, FAMAE.

13. Dubsky to Goluchowski, 2, 3 April 1898, Spanien, 68, HHSA; Merry to Gullón, 2 April 1898, and Gullón to Merry, 3 April 1898, in [Spain], *Diplomatic Correspondence*, 109–10. Dubsky stated that Woodford organized the diplomats to seek a papal appeal to Spain.

14. Woodford to McKinley, 3 April 1898, in *Foreign Relations, 1898*, 732; Soldevilla, *El año político, 1898*, 114–15.

15. Day to Woodford, 3 April 1898, in *Foreign Relations, 1898*, 732–33.

16. Storer (Brussels) to Ireland, 11 May 1898, Ireland Papers.

17. Polo to Gullón, 4 April 1898, Política, legajo 2424, AMAE; Gullón to

Merry, 5 April 1898, and Merry to Gullón, 3, 6 April 1898, Política, legajo 2417, AMAE; Francisca Nava to Rampolla, 8 April 1898, Rubrica 249, 43494, ASV.

18. Moret to Blanco, 31 March and 2 April 1898, Ultramar, legajo 4959, AHN; *El Imparcial* (Madrid), 5 April 1898; Soldevilla, *El año político, 1898*, 114–15.

19. Ireland to Rampolla, 3 April 1898, Ireland Papers; Elkins Journal, 3 April 1898, ibid. The original journal is in the Ireland Papers, which suggests that Elkins wrote it for Ireland. Ireland probably wanted Elkins's testimony for his defense against Vatican charges that he failed in his Washington assignment. The journal is quite detailed, and Elkins probably wrote it with Ireland's telegrams to Rampolla at hand. Polo to Gullón, 4 April 1898, Política, legajo 2417, AMAE; Cambon to Hanotaux, 4 April 1898, Espagne, 21, FAMAE.

20. Elkins Journal, 3, 4 April 1898, Ireland Papers; Polo to Gullón, 4, 5 April 1898, Política, legajos 2424, 2417, AMAE.

21. Elkins Journal, 5 April 1898, Ireland Papers; Rampolla to Ireland, 4, 5 April 1898, ibid.; Gullón to Polo, 5 April 1898, and Merry to Gullón, 5 April 1898, Política, legajo 2417, AMAE; Woodford to McKinley, 5 April 1898, in *Foreign Relations, 1898*, 734–35.

22. Ireland to Rampolla, 5 April 1898, Ireland Papers; Elkins Journal, 5 April 1898, ibid.

23. Offner, "McKinley's Final Attempt to Avoid War."

24. Balfour to Pauncefote, 2, 4 April 1898, and Pauncefote to Salisbury, 5, 8 April 1898, 5, America, 2515, 2365, PRO.

25. Joint Note of the Powers and the President's Reply, 6 April 1898, in *Foreign Relations, 1898*, 740–41.

26. Polo to Blanco, 7 April 1898, Política, legajo 2424, AMAE; Polo to Gullón, 7 April 1898, Política, legajo 2417, ibid.

27. *Washington Post*, 3, 4 April 1898; Davis to Day, 5 April 1898, box 8, Day Papers; Day to Spooner, 5 April 1898, Spooner Papers; *New York Times*, 6 April 1898; Mayo, *America of Yesterday*, 177.

28. Lee to Day, 6 April 1898, Despatches from Havana, RG59, T 20, microroll 132, USNA; Diary, 6 April 1898, box 52, Cortelyou Papers; *New York Tribune*, 7 April 1898.

29. *Washington Star*, 7 April 1898.

30. *Cong. Rec.*, 55th Cong., 2d sess., 3669–73, 3681–87.

31. *New York Times*, 5, 7 April 1898; Foner, *Spanish-Cuban-American War* 1:258–61.

32. Foner, *Spanish-Cuban-American War* 1:261; Elkins Journal, 6, 7, 8, 9 April 1898, Ireland Papers; *New York Times*, 8 April 1898; *Washington Post*, 8 April 1898.

33. Polo to Blanco, 11 April 1898, and Blanco to Polo, 13 April 1898, Ultra-

mar, legajo 4923, AHN. Pérez provides a good account of the poor communication and coordination of the Cubans in *Cuba between Empires*, 189.

34. Polo to Day, 5 April 1898, in *Foreign Relations, 1898*, 737–39.

35. Soldevilla, *El año político, 1898*, 119–20; *El Imparcial* (Madrid), 6, 7 April 1898.

36. Francisca Nava to Rampolla, 8 April 1898, Rubrica 249, 43494, ASV.

37. *El Imparcial* (Madrid), 7 April 1898; Woodford to Gullón, 6 April 1898, in *Foreign Relations, 1898*, 743; Gullón to Woodford, 6 April 1898, in [Spain], *Diplomatic Correspondence*, 112. Woodford may have blundered because of extreme fatigue and nervous strain. See his letter to Day, 5 April 1898, Despatches from Spain, RG59, M 31, microroll 123, USNA.

38. Francisca Nava to Rampolla, 8 April 1898, Rubrica 249, 43494, ASV.

39. Dubsky to Goluchowski, 6 April 1898, Spanien, 68, HHSA; Rampolla to Ireland, 8 April 1898, Ireland Papers; Cambon to Hanotaux, 9 April 1898, Espagne, 21, FAMAE.

40. Woodford to Gullón, 7 April 1898, in *Foreign Relations, 1898*, 744; Polo to Gullón, 7 April 1898, Política, legajo 2417, AMAE; Ireland to Rampolla, 7, 9 April 1898, Ireland Papers; Merry to Gullón, 8 April 1898, Política, legajo 2417, AMAE.

41. Francisca Nava to Rampolla, 9 April 1898, Rubrica 249, 43520, ASV; Gullón to Merry, 8 April 1898, Política, legajo 2417, AMAE.

42. *El Imparcial* (Madrid), 8, 9 April 1898.

43. Francisca Nava to Rampolla, 9 April 1898, Rubrica 249, 43520, ASV.

44. Ibid. By early April, Silvela favored autonomy for Cuba, arbitration of the *Maine*, opposition to U.S. intervention in Cuba, and a political truce of all political parties in Spain to strengthen Sagasta's hand. *Heraldo de Madrid*, 3, 5 April 1898.

45. Patenôtre to Hanotaux, 9 April 1898, Espagne, 21, FAMAE; Barclay to Salisbury, 9, 10 April 1898, 72, Spain, 2068, PRO; Dubsky to Goluchowski, 9 April 1898, Spanien, 68, HHSA; Francisca Nava to Rampolla, 9 April 1898, Rubrica 249, 43520, AVS.

46. Francisca Nava to Rampolla, 9 April 1898, Rubrica 249, 43520, AVS; *El Imparcial* (Madrid), 10 April 1898.

47. Bride, *Guerre Hispano-Américaine*, 74–75; Soldevilla, *El año político, 1898*, 124–30; *El Imparcial* (Madrid), 10 April 1898.

48. Gullón to Dubsky, 9 April 1898, Gullón to Merry, 9 April 1898, and Gullón, Circular telegram, 9 April 1898, in [Spain], *Diplomatic Correspondence*, 114–15; Moret to Blanco, 11 April 1898, Ultramar, legajo 4959, AHN.

49. Gullón, Circular telegram, 9 April 1898, in [Spain], *Diplomatic Correspondence*, 115; Merry to Gullón, 9 April 1898, Política legajo 2417, AMAE; Rampolla to Ireland, 10 April 1898, Ireland Papers; Baker, "Imperial Finale,"

391–97. Baker calls Madrid's belief in European support a "diplomacy of illusions."

50. Soldevilla, *El año político, 1898*, 144; Baker, "Imperial Finale," 331–33, 398–99; *El Imparcial* (Madrid), 9, 10 April 1898; *El Correo Militar* (Madrid), 9 April 1898; Moret to Blanco, 11 April 1898, Ultramar, legajo 4959, AHN; Baker, "Imperial Finale," 360–63; Francisca Nava to Rampolla, 13 April 1898, Rubrica 249, 43551, AVS.

CHAPTER 11

1. Woodford to McKinley, 10 April 1898, in *Foreign Relations, 1898*, 747; Ireland to O'Connell, 8 April 1898, O'Connell Papers; Cambon to Hanotaux, 10 April 1898, Espagne, 21, FAMAE.

2. Elkins Journal, 9 April 1898, and Ireland to Rampolla, 11 April 1898, Ireland Papers; Polo to Gullón, 10 April 1898, Política, legajo 2417, AMAE.

3. *New York Times*, 11 April 1898.

4. Ibid., 10, 11 April 1898; Rubens, *Liberty*, 334–38; Elkins Journal, 11 April 1898, Ireland Papers; Matías Romero (Washington) to Ignacio Mariscal (Mexico City), 11 April 1898, SREM.

5. Blanco to Polo, 10 April 1898, and Polo to Blanco, 10 April 1898, Política, legajo 2424, AMAE; *El Imparcial* (Madrid), 12 April 1898.

6. Polo to Gullón, 10 April 1898, Política, legajo 2417, AMAE; Day, Memorandum of Interview with Polo, 10 April 1898, and Adee to Day, 10 April 1898, box 35, Day Papers; Elkins Journal, 10 April 1898, Ireland Papers.

7. Polo to Blanco, 10 April 1898, Política, legajo 2424, AMAE.

8. Polo to Sherman, 10 April 1898, and Polo to Gullón, 12 April 1898, in [Spain], *Diplomatic Correspondence*, 120–22.

9. Gullón to Polo, 11, 12 April 1898, Política, legajo 2417, AMAE; *El Imparcial* (Madrid), 12 April 1898.

10. *New York Times*, 11 April 1898. Sherman did not attend the cabinet meetings; Day represented the State Department.

11. Ibid.; Cambon to Hanotaux, 11, 12 April 1898, Espagne, 22, FAMAE; Cousins, *Memorial Address*; Garraty, *Henry Cabot Lodge*, 189.

12. McKinley, Message to Congress, 11 April 1898, in *Foreign Relations, 1898*, 760.

13. Duncan, "William Rufus Day," 120; Long to Robbins, 12 April 1898, Long Papers; Atkins, *Sixty Years in Cuba*, 281; Coolidge, *Orville H. Platt*, 277–78; *Washington Star*, 12 April 1898.

14. Allen to Day, 2 April 1898, two scholarly memoranda on intervention,

undated and unsigned, quoting Lawrence and Hall on international law, and Adee to Day, 7 April 1898, box 35, Day Papers; Vahle, "Congress, the President, and Overseas Expansion," 39–44; *Washington Post*, 5 April 1898; *Washington Star*, 4 April 1898; *New York Times*, 5 April 1898.

15. Polo to Gullón, 11 April 1898, Política, legajo 2417, AMAE; Pauncefote to Salisbury, 12 April 1898, 5, America, 2517, PRO; Foner, *Spanish-Cuban-American War* 1:261–65.

16. *Washington Star*, 11 April 1898; *Washington Post*, 12 April 1898; Journal, 11 April 1898, Long Papers.

17. McKinley, Message to Congress, in *Foreign Relations, 1898*, 750–60.

18. Ibid.

19. U.S. President, *Condition of Reconcentrados in Cuba*. Newspapers carried extensive coverage of the consular reports; see, for example, *New York Tribune*, 12 April 1898. Polo to Gullón, 13 April 1898, Política, legajo 2424, AMAE.

20. Duncan, "William Rufus Day," 120; Dawes, *McKinley Years*, 151–54; Alger to McKinley, 5 April 1898, McKinley Papers; Journal, 4 April 1898, Long Papers.

21. *Washington Star*, 11 April 1898; *New York Tribune*, 12 April 1898; *Washington Post*, 12 April 1898.

22. Polo to Gullón, 11 April 1898, Política, legajo 2417, AMAE; Pauncefote to Salisbury, 12 April 1898, 5, America, 2517, PRO.

23. Ireland to Rampolla, 12 April 1898, Ireland Papers.

24. Neale, "British-American Relations." This is the best study of the Anglo-German controversy over the origins and development of the second Great Power demarche; Neale did not use French and Austrian archival documents. See also Einstein, "British Diplomacy in the Spanish-American War." My account and those cited are all drawn from 5, America, 2517, PRO.

25. Polo to Gullón, 14 April 1898, Política, legajo 2424, AMAE; Pauncefote to Salisbury, 14 April 1898, 5, America, 2517, PRO; Cambon to Hanotaux, 14, 15 April 1898, Espagne, 22, FAMAE; Paul Cambon (London) to Delcassé, 26 February 1902, Cuba, 1, ibid. Paul Cambon recalled that the Austrian, Russian, and Italian diplomats made no contribution to the proposal.

26. Balfour to Pauncefote, 17 April 1898, 5, America, 2517, PRO; León y Castillo to Gullón, 18 April 1898, Política, legajo 2417, AMAE; Noailles (Berlin) to Hanotaux, 19 April 1898, Espagne, 22, FAMAE; Pauncefote to Salisbury, 16 April 1898, 5, America, 2517, PRO.

27. *Heraldo de Madrid*, 13 April 1898; *El Correo de Madrid*, 13 April 1898; Soldevilla, *El año político, 1898*, 144–45.

28. *El Imparcial* (Madrid), 13 April 1898; *El Correo Militar* (Madrid), 12 April 1898.

29. *El Correo de Madrid*, 13 April 1898; Soldevilla, *El año político 1898*, 147; *El Correo Español* (Madrid), as quoted in Baker, "Imperial Finale," 334.

30. Beránger interview, *Heraldo de Madrid*, 6 April 1898; *El Correo Militar* (Madrid), 2, 16 April 1898; *El Imparcial* (Madrid), 18 April 1898; Pabón y Suárez de Urbina, *El 98*, 18–19; Fernández Almagro, *Historia política de la España* 3:75–78; Sims (Paris) to Roosevelt, 25 March 1898, Cable Correspondence, RG38, USNA.

31. *Cong. Rec.*, 55th Cong., 2d sess., 3847; Chandler to Dana, 13 April 1898, Chandler Papers.

32. *New York Tribune*, 13 April 1898; Diary, 13 April 1898, Hinds Papers.

33. *Cong. Rec.*, 55th Cong., 2d sess., 3815–16.

34. Ibid., 3817–21.

35. Ibid., 3773, 3776.

36. Ibid., 3791, 3954.

37. Ibid., 3773–90, 3827–49, 3876–3906, 3943–87, Appendix 286–300, 652–55.

38. Dawes, *McKinley Years*, 154; *Washington Star*, 14 April 1898.

39. Portell Vilá, *Cuba en sus relaciones con los Estados Unidos* 3:357–65; Foner, *Spanish-Cuban-American War* 1:270–74; Holbo, "Cuban-Bond 'Conspiracy' of 1898"; Ellis, *Henry Moore Teller*, 307–12; *New York Tribune*, 1 April 1901.

40. *Cong. Rec.*, 55th Cong., 2d sess., 3988–93.

41. Ibid., 4017–18, 4027–43, 4062; Diary, 19, 21 April 1898, Hinds Papers; *New York Tribune*, 18, 19 April 1898. See Elkins's journal of 20 April 1898 for an interesting account of back-room Senate deliberations.

42. Spooner to Bryant, 23 April 1898, Spooner Papers; Chandler to Dana, 19 April 1898, Chandler Papers (italics added by Chandler).

43. Patenôtre to Hanotaux, 17 April 1898, Espagne, 22, FAMAE; Polo to Gullón, 18 April 1898, Política, legajo 2424, AMAE; Storer to Ireland, 14 April 1898, Ireland Papers; Diary, 16 April 1898, box 52, Cortelyou Papers.

44. *Journal of John D. Long*, 223; Woodford, "McKinley and the Spanish War"; Pritchett, "Recollections of President McKinley," 401; Elkins Journal, 20 April 1898, Ireland Papers; Diary, 20 April 1898, box 52, Cortelyou Papers; Polo to Sherman, 20 April 1898, in *Foreign Relations, 1898*, 765; Blockade of Cuban Ports, 22 April 1898, in ibid., 769–70; *Cong. Rec.*, 55th Cong., 2d sess., 4228–29, 4244, 4252.

45. *El Imparcial* (Madrid), 15, 16 April 1898; *El Correo de Madrid*, 14, 20 April 1898; *El Correo Militar* (Madrid), 15 April 1898.

46. Soldevilla, *El año político, 1898*, 152–53; *El Imparcial* (Madrid), 19 April 1898; Woodford to Sherman, 20 April 1898, in *Foreign Relations, 1898*, 1080–84.

47. Soldevilla, *El año político, 1898*, 156–57, 164; Dubsky to Goluchowski, 20 April 1898, Spanien, 69, HHSA.

48. Soldevilla, *El año político, 1898*, 165–73.

49. *La Independencia* (Manzanilla), 15 April 1898; *El Cubano Libre* (Camagüey), 10 May 1898; Foner, *Spanish-Cuban-American War* 1:261.

1. Quesada to Estrada Palma, 19 May and 8 July 1898, in Cuba, *Correspondencia diplomática* 5:127–29, 145. The impact of American rejection on the Cubans is well covered in Pérez, *Cuba between Empires*, 188–97.

2. The best military history of the war is Trask, *War with Spain*.

3. Polo to Gullón, 21, 22, 23, 24, 25, 26 April 1898, Política, legajo 2424, AMAE. Política, legajo 2420, contains seventy messages from Montreal to Madrid, 23 May to 21 September 1898, largely devoted to military intelligence. They reveal that Spain had Washington contacts during the war; at the Paris peace conference, Sarah Atkinson, a stenographer attached to the American delegation, provided information to the Spanish.

4. Trask, *War with Spain*, 87–88. In retrospect, Colwell's and Sims's reports were often reliable and timely. Long sent the first counterintelligence request to Sims (Paris) on 31 May 1898, Department of the Navy, Cable Correspondence, RG38, USNA. See also Allen to Sims (Paris), 1 June 1898, ibid.; *New York Times*, 12, 13 June 1898; Torre del Río, *Inglaterra y España*, 133–38; Jover Zamora, *Teoría y práctica de la redistribución colonial*, 47–53.

5. *New York Times*, 18, 25, 28 June, 8, 16, 22 July 1898; *El Imparcial* (Madrid), 1, 9, 12, 16 July 1898. Apparently the navy did consider sending a fleet to raid Spanish commerce. See Long to Sims (Paris), 18 June 1898, Department of the Navy, Cable Correspondence, RG38, USNA. In a retrospective report on the effect of Watson's fleet on Spanish thinking, Sims's agent in Madrid believed that Sagasta was convinced the American navy would attack the Spanish coasts and acted to defend the peninsula rather than forward ships and arms to the Philippines. Sims, Report number 13, 9 September 1898, Department of the Navy, International Relations and Politics, Spain, RG45, USNA. For a description of Spanish panic, see Wolff to Salisbury, 18 July 1898, 72, Spain, 2069, PRO.

6. Hay to McKinley, 13 June 1898, box 56, Cortelyou Papers; Wolff to Salisbury, 5, 7 May 1898, 72, Spain, 2068, 2063, PRO; Cambon to Delcassé, 23 June 1898, États-Unis, 7, FAMAE; Vladimirov, *La diplomacia de los Estados Unidos*, 203–7; Montebello (St. Petersburg) to Hanotaux, 11 May 1898, and Hanotaux, Circular telegram, 29 May 1898, in France, *Documents Diplomatiques* 14:279–81, 312–13.

7. Soldevilla, *El año político, 1898*, 196–98, 205, 208; Francisca Nava to Rampolla, 3, 12 May 1898, Rubrica 249, 43937, 44079, ASV; Baker, "Imperial Finale," 407–8.

8. *El Imparcial* (Madrid), 17, 18, 27 May 1898; Dubsky to Goluchowski, 20 June 1898, Spanien, 69, HHSA; Baker, "Imperial Finale," 408–9.

9. León y Castillo, *Mis tiempos* 2:99, 109–11; Gullón to Rascón, 20 May 1898, Estado, legajo 8664, AHN.

10. Wolff to Salisbury, 25 May 1898, 29 December 1898, 72, Spain, 2068,

PRO; Francisca Nava to Rampolla, 22 May 1898, Rubrica 249, 44259, ASV; Dubsky to Goluchowski, 25 May 1898, Spanien, 59, HHSA.

11. Francisca Nava to Rampolla, 22 May 1898, Rubrica 249, 44259, ASV.

12. Porter to Day, 24 May, 3 June 1898, Despatches from France, RG59, M 34, microroll 119, USNA; Vladimirov, *La diplomacia de los Estados Unidos*, 229–30; Foner, *Spanish-Cuban-American War* 1:254.

13. Patenôtre to Hanotaux, 10, 13 May 1898, Espagne, 24, FAMAE.

14. Trask, *War with Spain*, 110; Patenôtre to Hanotaux, 14, 15, 26 May 1898, Espagne, 24 and 25, FAMAE; Wolff to Salisbury, 21 May 1898, 72, Spain, 2068, PRO.

15. Hay to Day, 8 May 1898, box 185, Memorandum on terms of settlement, 9 May 1898, box 186, and Memorandum, untitled and undated, box 193, Moore Papers.

16. Memorandum, untitled and undated, box 193, Moore Papers.

17. Salisbury to Pauncefote, 10 May 1898, 5, America, 2364, PRO; Pauncefote to Salisbury, 16 May 1898, 2365, ibid.

18. Garvin, *Joseph Chamberlain* 3:301–5; Torre del Río, *Inglaterra y España*, 204–10, 253–77; Wolff to Salisbury, 15 May 1898, 72, Spain, 2068, PRO; Wolff to Salisbury, 19 May 1898, 2064, ibid.; Almodóvar to Rascón, 19 June 1898, Estado, legajo 8663, AHN.

19. Torre del Río, *Inglaterra y España*, 211; Heindel, *American Impact on Great Britain*, 58–59, 64–65.

20. Hay to McKinley, 27 May 1898, box 56, Cortelyou Papers; Day to Hay, 3 June 1898, box 192, Moore Papers.

21. Pauncefote to Salisbury, 4, 11 June 1898, 5, America, 2365, PRO; Hay to Day, 6 June 1898, box 193, Moore Papers.

22. Memorandum, 6 June 1898, box 186, and Hay to Day, 8 June 1898, box 185, Moore Papers. For other Hay telegrams, see box 193, Moore Papers.

23. Cambon to Hanotaux, 6, 7, 11 June 1898, and Patenôtre to Hanotaux, 11 June 1898, Espagne, 26, FAMAE; *New York Times*, 6, 11 June 1898.

24. Hay to Day, 15 June 1898, box 193, Moore Papers; Courcel (London) to Hanotaux, 15 June 1898, Espagne, 26, FAMAE; Monson (Paris) to Salisbury, 14 June 1898, 27, France, 3400, PRO; Hay to Day, 15 June 1898, box 193, Moore Papers. An explanation of why Spain turned to Britain for help is given in Torre del Río, *Inglaterra y España*, 222–24.

25. Hanotaux, Memorandum of conversation with Porter, 4 May 1898, and Hanotaux to Patenôtre, 12 May 1898, in France, *Documents Diplomatiques* 14:260–61, 281–82. Porter asserted on 18 May that Spain could obtain peace promptly if it would cede Cuba. If the war continued much longer, Porter expected McKinley to recall him to Washington to become secretary of war. Hanssen, Memorandum of conversation with Porter, 18 May 1898, in ibid., 293.

26. Hanotaux, Memorandum of conversation with Porter, 2 June 1898, in ibid., 316–17.

27. Hanotaux, Memorandum of conversation with Porter, 6 June 1898, in ibid., 322; Hanotaux to Cambon, 9 June 1898, Paris, Espagne, 26, FAMAE; Porter to Day, 7, 10, 13 June 1898, Despatches from France, RG59, M 34, microroll 119, USNA. Sims's secret agent said that León y Castillo was authorized to negotiate an armistice after the Spanish won a victory at Santiago. The Spanish expected the American public to become weary of war. Sims (Paris) to Bureau of Navigation, 15 June 1898, Department of the Navy, Cable Correspondence, RG38, USNA.

28. Day to Porter, 18 June, 6 July 1898, Diplomatic Instructions, RG59, M 77, microroll 64, USNA; Porter to Day, 8 July 1898, Despatches from France, RG59, M 34, microroll 119, USNA.

29. Porter to Day, 21 June 1898, Despatches from France, RG59, M 34, microroll 119, USNA; Hanotaux, Memorandum of conversation with León y Castillo, 9 June 1898, and Memorandum of conversation with Porter, 14 June 1898, Espagne, 26, FAMAE. In all probability, León y Castillo had no special negotiating instructions, and he and Hanotaux were fishing for an opening with Porter. See Dubsky to Goluchowski, 23, 26 May 1898, Spanien, 59, HHSA.

30. Soldevilla, *El Año político, 1898*, 277–78, 283–84; Porter to Day, 1 July 1898, Despatches from France, RG59, M 34, microroll 119, USNA; *La Estafeta*, 30 June 1898, quoted in Fernández Almagro, *Historia política de la España* 3: 151–52.

31. Trask, *War with Spain*, 257–65; Varela Ortega, "Aftermath of Splendid Disaster," 322–24; *Washington Post*, 7 July 1898.

32. Soldevilla, *El año político, 1898*, 304–5, 311–13; *El Imparcial* (Madrid), 6 July 1898; Dubsky to Goluchowski, 6 July 1898, Spanien, 69, HHSA.

33. Francisca Nava to Rampolla, 8 July 1898, Rubrica 249, 45010, ASV; Patenôtre to Delcassé, 7, 9 July 1898, Espagne, 27, FAMAE; Quesada (Madrid) to Alcorta (Buenos Aires) 9 July 1898, Caja 651, 89, MREA; Varela Ortega, "Aftermath of Splendid Disaster," 321–22.

34. Correa to Blanco, 6 July 1898, and Blanco to Correa, 9 July 1898, Política, legajo 2424, AMAE.

35. Wolff to Salisbury, 11 July 1898, 72, Spain, 2069, PRO; Patenôtre to Delcassé, 9 July 1898, Espagne, 27, FAMAE; Dubsky to Goluchowski, 9, 12 July 1898, Spanien, 69, HHSA; Varela Ortega, "Aftermath of Splendid Disaster," 325–26.

36. Toral to Blanco, 12 July 1898, Política, legajo 2424, AMAE. McKinley was tougher than Shafter toward Toral and was impatient with army and navy delays in taking Santiago de Cuba by force. See Trask, *War with Spain*, 299–306.

37. Dubsky to Goluchowski, 14 July 1898, Spanien, 69, HHSA; Sagasta to

Blanco, 12 July 1898, quoted in Rodríguez Martínez, *Los desastres*, 81; Correa to Blanco, 12 July 1898, Política legajo 2424, AMAE.

38. Blanco to Correa, 13, 14, 15 July 1898, Política, legajo 2424, AMAE; Blanco to Sagasta, 14 July 1898, quoted in Rodríguez Martínez, *Los desastres*, 81; Soldevilla, *El año político, 1898*, 320.

39. Wolff to Salisbury, 15 July 1898, 72, Spain, 2064, PRO; Dubsky to Go-luchowski, 16 July 1898, Spanien, 69, HHSA; *El Imparcial* (Madrid), 16 July 1898; Soldevilla, *El año político, 1898*, 317–18.

40. Blanco to Correa, 15 July 1898, and Correa to Blanco, 16 July 1898, Política, legajo 2424, AMAE; Blanco to Correa, 17 July 1898, quoted in Rodrí-guez Martínez, *Los desastres*, 81–82.

41. *El Correo Militar* (Madrid), 13 July 1898; *La Correspondencia Militar*, 13 July 1898, quoted in Soldevilla, *El año político, 1898*, 316.

42. Romanones, *Sagasta*, 200; Arco, *Montero Ríos*, 112. Sagasta consulted Montero Ríos and Vega de Armijo (presidents respectively of the upper and lower houses of the Cortes), Martínez de Campos, Tetuán, Romero Robledo, Silvela, Azcárraga, Canalejas, and Generals Fernando Primo de Rivera, López Domínguez, and Emilio Calleja.

CHAPTER 13

1. Long to Samson, 15 July 1898, and Mahan, Memorandum, 18 July 1898, Department of the Navy, Naval War Board Records, RG80, USNA.

2. Almodóvar to León y Castillo, 20 July 1898, in [Spain], *Diplomatic Corre-spondence*, 201; *New York Times*, 16 July 1898; *El Imparcial* (Madrid), 16 July 1898.

3. Patenôtre to Delcassé, 17 July 1898, Espagne, 27, FAMAE; Patenôtre to Delcassé, 23 July 1898, in France, *Documents Diplomatiques* 14:399.

4. Almodóvar to León y Castillo, 18 July 1898, in [Spain], *Diplomatic Corre-spondence*, 200; Bécker, *Relaciones exteriores de España* 3:903–5.

5. Delcassé to Cambon, 19 July 1898, Espagne, 27, FAMAE; Delcassé, Memoranda, 20, 21, 22 July 1898, Papiers D'Agents, T. Delcassé, 2, FAMAE; León y Castillo to Almodóvar, 20, 21 July 1898, in [Spain], *Diplomatic Correspon-dence*, 201–2. For the French view of the negotiations, see Offner, "United States and France."

6. León y Castillo to Almodóvar, 24 July 1898, in [Spain], *Diplomatic Corre-spondence*, 204; Trask, *War with Spain*, 357.

7. Cambon to Delcassé, 21 July 1898, Espagne, 27, FAMAE.

8. Almodóvar to McKinley, 22 July 1898, in *Foreign Relations, 1898*, 819–20.

9. Patenôtre to Delcassé, 22 July 1898, and Cambon to Delcassé, 24 July

1898, Espagne, 27, FAMAE; Francisca Nava to Rampolla, 23 July 1898, Rubrica 249, 45148, ASV; Dubsky to Goluchowski, 23 July 1898, Spanien, 69, HHSA.

10. Memorandum of interviews with the French Ambassador, undated, box 185, Moore Papers. Day wrote this thirteen-page memorandum after the final meeting with Cambon to provide a detailed account of the McKinley-Cambon meetings. He noted that McKinley read and corrected the manuscript before it was typed. Cambon to Delcassé, 27, 28 July 1898, Espagne, 27, FAMAE.

11. *Washington Post*, 27 July 1898; *New York Times*, 27 July 1898; Diary, 31 July 1898, box 52, Cortelyou Papers.

12. *Washington Post*, 27, 28 July 1898; *New York Times*, 28 July 1898.

13. *New York Times*, 29, 30 July 1898; *Washington Post*, 30 July 1898; Wilson to Allison, 3 August 1898, Allison Papers; Hay to Day, 28 July 1898, McKinley Papers; Leech, *In the Days of McKinley*, 285–86.

14. *Washington Post*, 28, 30 July 1898; *New York Times*, 29 July 1898.

15. Draft note and attached changes, 30 July 1898, box 185, Moore Papers.

16. Ibid.

17. Ibid.; Leech, *In the Days of McKinley*, 284–85.

18. Wilson to Allison, 3 August 1898, Allison Papers.

19. Day to Almodóvar, 30 July 1898, in *Foreign Relations, 1898*, 820–21.

20. León y Castillo to Almodóvar, 28 July 1898, and Almodóvar to León y Castillo, 28 July 1898, in [Spain], *Diplomatic Correspondence*, 208–10.

21. Almodóvar to León y Castillo, 28 July 1898, in ibid.

22. *New York Times*, 31 July 1898; Memorandum of interviews with the French Ambassador, undated, box 185, Moore Papers; Cambon to Almodóvar, 31 July 1898, in [Spain], *Diplomatic Correspondence*, 213–14; Cambon to Delcassé, 1 August 1898, in France, *Documents Diplomatiques* 14:418–20; *Washington Post*, 1 August 1898.

23. Memorandum of interviews with the French Ambassador, undated, box 185, Moore Papers; Cambon to Delcassé, 1 August 1898, in France, *Documents Diplomatiques* 14:418–20; Cambon to Almodóvar, 31 July 1898, in [Spain], *Diplomatic Correspondence*, 213–14.

24. Memorandum of interviews with the French Ambassador, undated, box 185, Moore Papers; Cambon to Delcassé, 1 August 1898, in France, *Documents Diplomatiques* 14:418–20; Cambon to Almodóvar, 31 July 1898, in [Spain], *Diplomatic Correspondence*, 213–14; *Washington Post*, 3 August 1898.

25. Dubsky to Goluchowski, 2 August 1898, Spanien, 71, HHSA; Patenôtre to Delcassé, 31 July 1898, Espagne, 27, FAMAE; Patenôtre to Delcassé, 4 August 1898, Espagne, 28, FAMAE.

26. *New York Times*, 3 August 1898; Picó, *1898*, 64–79; Almodóvar to Cambon, 1 August 1898, in [Spain], *Diplomatic Correspondence*, 214–15; Patenôtre to Delcassé, 2 August 1898, Espagne, 27, FAMAE; Wolff to Salisbury, 4 August 1898, 72, Spain, 2069, PRO.

27. Cambon to Almodóvar, 4 August 1898, in [Spain], *Diplomatic Correspondence*, 216–17; Cambon to Delcassé, 4, 5 August 1898, in France, *Documents Diplomatiques* 14:427–28, 430–32; Memorandum of interviews with the French Ambassador, undated, box 185, Moore Papers; Memorandum on French mediation, undated, box 214, ibid.

28. Cambon to Delcassé, 5 August 1898, in France, *Documents Diplomatiques* 14:430–32; Cambon to Delcassé, 5 August 1898, Papiers D'Agents, T. Delcassé, 2, FAMAE.

29. Cambon to Delcassé, 5 August 1898, Papiers D'Agents, T. Delcassé, 2, FAMAE.

30. *Washington Post*, 4 August 1898; *New York Times*, 4, 5 August 1898; Long to Sampson, 4 August 1898, Department of the Navy, Naval War Board Records, RG80, USNA.

31. León y Castillo to Almodóvar, 5 August 1898, and Almodóvar to Cambon, 7 August 1898, in [Spain], *Diplomatic Correspondence*, 217–19; *El Imparcial* (Madrid), 5, 6, 7 August 1898; Patenôtre to Delcassé, 7 August 1898, Espagne, 28, FAMAE; Dubsky to Goluchowski, 6, 12 August 1898, Spanien, 71, HHSA. During three days of conferences, Sagasta consulted Montero Ríos, Canalejas, and Vega de Armijo of the Liberal Party, Silvela, Martínez de Campos, Tetuán, and Romero Robledo of the Conservative Party, Nicolás Salmerón of the Republican Party, Generals Polavieja, Azcárraga, José Chinchilla, Fernando Primo de Rivera, López Domínguez, Weyler, Emilio Calleja, and Gonzalo Chacón, and José Mier, a Carlist.

32. Almodóvar to Day, 7 August 1898, in *Foreign Relations, 1898*, 822–23.

33. *Washington Post*, 10 August 1898; Memorandum of interviews with the French Ambassador, undated, box 185, Moore Papers; Cambon to Almodóvar, 11 August 1898, in [Spain], *Diplomatic Correspondence*, 219–20; Cambon to Delcassé, 19 August 1898, Espagne, 28, FAMAE; Protocol, *Foreign Relations, 1898*, 824–25. Underlining by Cambon. See the Appendix for the protocol.

34. Cambon to Almodóvar, 11 August 1898, in [Spain], *Diplomatic Correspondence*, 221–22.

35. Almodóvar to León y Castillo, 12 August 1898, in ibid., 222–23.

36. *Washington Post*, 13 August 1898; Cambon to Almodóvar, 12 August 1898, in [Spain], *Diplomatic Correspondence*, 223–24; Dubsky to Goluchowski, 14 August 1898, Spanien, 71, HHSA; Memorandum of interviews with the French Ambassador, box 185, Moore Papers.

37. Pérez, *Cuba between Empires*, 199–227; Estrada Palma to Rodríguez, 17 August 1898, Archivo de la delegación del Partido Revolucionario Cubano, legajo 1, CNA.

BIBLIOGRAPHY

· · · · · · · · · · · · · · · · · ·

In attempting to research a balanced account of the Spanish-American War, one discovers an uneven collection of documents. There are many more sources available for the United States than for Spain and Cuba. The United States possesses a rich record, which is open to public research. Besides the diplomatic archives, there are the papers of McKinley, his private secretary, the secretary of state, the secretary of the navy, and several unofficial advisers. The debates of Congress are illuminated by many collections of senatorial papers. Newspapers, published memoirs, and letters of participants are also valuable.

By contrast, Spanish private papers are almost nonexistent, and those fragmentary records that do remain are often in private collections, which are difficult for foreign scholars to use. There are no Sagasta papers, none for his foreign ministers, and only a few scattered letters of cabinet officers. Spain published diplomatic documents in three Red Books in 1898 and 1899, but it produced these to win European sympathy. The Red Books are unreliable; the foreign ministry edited many documents and gave no indication where the cuts were made. Unfortunately, many scholars have gone no farther than these documents, which are available in English translation ([Spain], *Spanish Diplomatic Correspondence*). Since the English text is more useful to my readers, I have cited Red Book documents where possible, but only after comparing them with the original Spanish messages and making certain that the Red Book translations are correct. Spain's diplomatic archives are complete and well ordered, but its colonial records are scattered and in disarray, particularly toward the end of Cuban rule, when colonial organization was breaking down. Most military records are beyond the reach of foreign scholars, and the diplomatic initiatives of the queen regent are not available. Fortunately, Spain had a liberal press law, and Madrid's newspapers carried a great deal of information about political and diplomatic events. In addition, foreign diplomats in Madrid were knowledgeable and wrote regular reports about Spanish politics.

The Cuban record is also incomplete. Having no foreign ministry or centralized bureaucracy, the Junta did not have well-organized records. The Cuban government began in the 1920s to collect, organize, and preserve the historical record, but many documents had already been lost or mutilated. The Cuban government published two useful collections of 1895–98 documents, and the archives in Havana contain some additional valuable material. Important Cuban leaders left few memoirs; Rubens produced a book long after the events of 1898, and his recollections must be handled cautiously. Cuban newspapers were issued sporadically, and those remaining are often propagandistic rather than newsworthy.

Many American historians begin with the premise that the United States caused the war. Without foreign research, often drawing on limited and single-purpose materials, and picturing Spain as having surrendered nearly all diplomatic points and ready to give even more, these authors have attempted to find the causes of the war in the political, economic, intellectual, and psychological flaws of American society. Among the more widely accepted causes are newspaper sensationalism and economic interests. Marcus W. Wilkerson and Joseph Wisan elaborated the sensational press theory; the outstanding advocate of economic interests is Walter LaFeber. After World War I, historians of the 1920s and 1930s depicted McKinley as weak and manipulated by outside forces, a situation that resulted in a needless war of imperialism. The weaker McKinley appeared to historians, the more significant became the forces that pressured him. The "chocolate eclair backbone" became a standard description of the president; Walter Millis, who exemplified this view, ridiculed America's passion for war and the president's compliance. Other historians have stressed the influence of naval developments and strategy, imperialism, the depression of the 1890s, populism, progressivism, Cuban propaganda, mass hysteria, a "psychic crisis," manifest destiny, evangelistic missionary views, Social Darwinism, and the scheming of a few political insiders to create a "large policy." Some eclectic historians have added all the ingredients together, whether logical or not. James A. Field, Jr., has protested the resulting irrationality.

One facet of the American historical confusion is the role of William McKinley. Joseph A. Fry has ably traced the changing historical interpretation of McKinley. Several corrective studies of the president have appeared since the late 1950s. Margaret Leech contributed the best biography, and H. Wayne Morgan provided a fine study of the politician. Lewis L. Gould's study of McKinley's presidency eliminated many of the stereotypes of a weak and manipulated person; he portrayed McKinley as an innovative modern president. David F. Trask has written the best history of the Spanish-American War, and he also gave McKinley high marks as an able politician and military strategist. In addition, Trask broke new ground through his expanded treatment of the Spanish side of the war. Ernest R. May stands alone in the quality of his multi-archival study of the diplomacy of the war. Unfortunately, he did not have the valuable insights of Gould and Trask when he wrote his book, using instead the standard view of

McKinley as a weak president. May also focused on European attitudes rather than the Cuban-Spanish-American conflict.

Spanish historiography of the diplomacy of the war is poor. Historians have done little multi-archival work, and there are no good biographies of their statesmen and diplomats, such as Sagasta, Moret, Gullón, and Almodóvar. Melchor Fernández Almagro wrote an excellent biography of Cánovas, but no one has provided a good treatment of Cánovas's American diplomacy. There are a few autobiographies, such as Fernando de León y Castillo's, but they are disappointing. Spanish historians have been more interested in domestic political history, and there are several good accounts, such as José Varela Ortega's, of the 1890s. These studies criticize the weaknesses of Spanish government and society, such as newspaper excesses and military influence, which contributed to the war spirit. An imaginative approach is that of José María Jover Zamora, who placed Spain's misfortunes in the larger setting of a general redistribution of colonies at the turn of the century based on changes in national power and wealth. Carlos Serrano's more recent study embodies many current Spanish viewpoints. Thomas Hart Baker, Jr., produced an excellent study of Spanish politics and the war in his well-researched dissertation.

Cuban historians have done more research on the diplomacy of the Spanish-American War than have their Spanish colleagues. Duvon C. Corbitt provides insight into Cuban historians and their changing historiography. In the 1920s, Emilio Roig de Leuchsenring started a school of historical interpretation that criticized the United States for unnecessarily entering the Cuban war. In his view, the United States acted to deny Cuba its independence and social justice. Roig's interpretation is still current in Cuban historiography and bolsters the legitimacy of the Castro regime. In the 1930s, Herminio Portell Vilá produced a massive study of Cuban-American diplomatic relations, a study that still has value. But his four volumes are more than fifty years old, and the author did not have access to the wealth of U.S. presidential and private papers now available to modern researchers. As a result, many of his arguments are flawed. The Cuban perspective has been carried on in the United States by Philip S. Foner and Louis A. Pérez, Jr.

ARCHIVAL SOURCES

AHN. Archivo Histórico Nacional, Madrid, Spain.
  Sección
    Estado,
      legajos 8663–64, correspondence of the conde de Rascón, ambassador
        to Great Britain

Ultramar,
 legajo 4923, Cuba
 legajo 4959, Telegramas [between Moret and Blanco, 1898]
 legajo 4970, Cuba
AMAE. Archivo Ministerio de Asuntos Exteriores, Madrid, Spain.
 Archivo Histórico
 Política,
  legajos 2415–26, Estados Unidos
 Ultramar,
  legajos 2901–4, Cuba
 Personal,
  legajo 128, Pío Gullón y Iglesias
  legajo 269, Luis Polo de Bernabé
ASHM. Archivo Servicio Histórico Militar, Madrid, Spain.
ASV. Archivo Segreto Vaticano, the Vatican City.
 Segreteria di Stato
  Rubrica 249 (1901)
   Protocol number 43034 (22 March 1898) to 45148 (23 July 1898)
CNA. Archivo Nacional de la República de Cuba, Havana, Cuba.
 Sección
  Archivo de la delegación del Partido Revolucionario Cubano en Nueva
   York (1892–98)
  Archivo Máximo Gómez
  Fondo Donativo y Remisiones
  Gobierno Autonómico (January–August 1898)
  Revolución del 1895
FAMAE. Archives, Ministère des Affaires Étrangères, Paris, France.
 Correspondence Politique, Nouvelle Série
  Cuba,
   1, Établissement de l'Indépendance
  Espagne,
   16–28, Possessions d'Outre-Mer, Cuba et Porto Rico
   43, Finances Publiques (1898–1902)
  États-Unis,
   175, Correspondence Politique (July–December 1896)
   7, Politique Étrangère (1897–1914)
  Papiers D'Agents,
   Jules Cambon, vol. 8
   T. Delcassé,
    vol. 16, Médiation entre l'Espagne et les États-Unis
    vol. 2, Lettres de diplomates, Jules Cambon

HHSA. Haus-, Hof-, und Staatsarchiv, Vienna, Austria.
  Politisches Archiv,
    Spanien, XX, 68–71
MREA. Archivo Ministerio de Relaciones Exteriores, Buenos Aires, Argentina.
  Caja 651, Legación en España
PRO. Public Record Office, London, England.
  Foreign Office
    5, America, Diplomatic
    27, France, Diplomatic
    72, Spain, Diplomatic, Insurrection in Cuba, War between the United
      States and Spain
    800, Private Papers of Sir Francis Bertie
SREM. Archivo Secretaria de Relaciones Exteriores, Mexico City, Mexico.
  Independencia de Cuba (1895–98), Tomo III, L-E–1335
USNA. United States, National Archives, Washington, D.C.
  RG38. Entry 100. Department of the Navy. Cable Correspondence, U.S.
    Naval Attachés, Spanish-American War. 2 vols. London, Paris, St.
    Petersburg, Berlin, Rome, Tokyo, Madrid, Miscellaneous.
  RG45. Entry 464. Department of the Navy. International Relations and
    Politics, 1790–1910. Spain.
  RG59. Department of State. Communications from Special Agents, 1794–
    1906. M 37.
  RG59. Department of State. Despatches from U.S. Consuls in Havana,
    Cuba, 1783–1906. T 20.
  RG59. Department of State. Despatches from U.S. Ministers to France,
    1789–1906. M 34.
  RG59. Department of State. Despatches from U.S. Ministers to Russia,
    1808–1906. M 35.
  RG59. Department of State. Despatches from U.S. Ministers to Spain,
    1792–1906. M 31.
  RG59. Department of State. Diplomatic Instructions of the Department of
    State, 1801–1906. M 77.
  RG59. Department of State. Miscellaneous Letters of the Department of
    State, 1789–1907. M 179.
  RG59. Department of State. Notes from the Spanish Legation to the
    Department of State, 1790–1906. M 59.
  RG59. Department of State. Notes to Foreign Legations in the United States
    from the Department of State, 1834–1906. M 99.
  RG80. Entry 194. Department of the Navy. Naval War Board Records, April
    6, 1898–August 13, 1898.

MANUSCRIPT COLLECTIONS

Boston, Massachusetts
    Massachusetts Historical Society
        John Davis Long Papers
Cambridge, Massachusetts
    Baker Library
        Henry L. Higginson Papers
Carlisle, Pennsylvania
    U.S. Military History Research Collection
        Tasker Howard Bliss Papers
Cincinnati, Ohio
    Cincinnati Historical Society
        Joseph Benson Foraker Papers
Des Moines, Iowa
    Iowa State Archives
        William B. Allison Papers
London, England
    British Museum Library
        Arthur James Balfour Papers
New York City, New York
    New York Public Library
        Wm. Bourke Cochran Papers
Richmond, Virginia
    Richmond Diocese Archives
        Dennis J. O'Connell Papers
St. Paul, Minnesota
    James Jerome Hill Reference Library
        James J. Hill Papers
    Minnesota Historical Society
        John Ireland Papers
Washington, D.C.
    Library of Congress
        William Eaton Chandler Papers
        Grover Cleveland Papers
        George B. Cortelyou Papers
        William Rufus Day Papers
        Asher C. Hinds Papers
        William McKinley Papers
        John Bassett Moore Papers
        Richard Olney Papers
        Whitelaw Reid Papers

John Coit Spooner Papers
Oscar S. Straus Papers

DOCUMENT COLLECTIONS

Cervera y Topete, Pascual. *The Spanish-American War: A Collection of Documents Relative to the Squadron Operations in the West Indies.* Arranged by Rear Admiral Pascual Cervera y Topete. Translated by the Office of Naval Intelligence. Washington, D.C.: Government Printing Office, 1900.

Cuba. Partido revolucionario cubano. *Correspondencia diplomática de la legación cubana en Nueva York durante la guerra de independencia de 1895–1898.* 5 vols. Havana: Los Talleres del Archivo Nacional, 1943–46.

France. Commission de publication des documents relatifs aux origines de la guerre de 1914. *Documents Diplomatiques Françaises, 1871–1914.* 41 vols. Paris: Imprimerie Nacionale, 1929–59.

McKinley, William. *McKinley, The People's Choice: Full Text of Each Speech or Address Made by Him from June 18 to August 1, 1896.* Compiled by Joseph P. Smith. Canton: Repository Press, 1896.

———. *McKinley's Speeches in August.* Compiled by Joseph P. Smith. Canton: Repository Press, 1896.

———. *McKinley's Speeches in September.* Compiled by Joseph P. Smith. Canton: Repository Press, 1896.

———. *McKinley's Speeches in October.* Compiled by Joseph P. Smith. Canton: Repository Press, 1896.

Primelles, León, ed. *La revolución del 95 según la correspondencia de la Delegación cubana en Nueva York.* 5 vols. Havana: Editorial Habanera, 1932–37.

Richardson, James D., comp. *A Compilation of the Messages and Papers of the Presidents.* 14 vols. New York: Bureau of National Literature, 1912.

[Spain. Minister of State.] *Spanish Diplomatic Correspondence and Documents, 1896–1900: Presented to the Cortes by the Minister of State.* (Translated by the United States.) Washington, D.C.: Government Printing Office, 1905.

U.S. Congress. *Congressional Record.* 54th Cong., lst sess., 2d sess., 55th Cong., lst sess., 2d sess.

———. Senate. Committee on Foreign Relations. *Report Relative to Affairs in Cuba.* 55th Cong., 2d sess. S. Rept. 885. Serial 3624. Washington, D.C.: Government Printing Office, 1898.

U.S. Department of State. *Papers Relating to the Foreign Relations of the United States.* Washington, D.C.: Government Printing Office, 1897–1901.

U.S. Department of War. *Report of the Census of Cuba, 1899.* Washington, D.C.: Government Printing Office, 1900.

U.S. President. *Message in Response to the Resolution of the Senate, Dated February 14, 1898, Calling for Information in Respect to the Condition of Reconcentrados in Cuba, the State of the War and the Country, and the Prospects of Projected Autonomy in that Island.* 55th Cong., 2d sess. S. Doc. 230. Serial 3610. Washington, D.C.: Government Printing Office, 1898.

U.S. Secretary of the Navy. *Annual Report of the Navy Department of the Year 1898.* Washington, D.C.: Government Printing Office, 1898.

U.S. Secretary of State. *Report in Response to Senate Resolution, February 23, 1897, Relative to the Arrest, Imprisonment, and Death of Dr. Ricardo Ruiz in the Jail of Guanabacoa, on the Island of Cuba.* 54th Cong., 2d sess., 4 March 1897. S. Doc. 179. Serial 3471. Washington, D.C.: Government Printing Office, 1897.

MEMOIRS, DIARIES, LETTERS, AUTOBIOGRAPHIES

Alger, Russell A. *The Spanish-American War.* New York: Harper and Brothers, 1901.

Atkins, Edwin F. *Sixty Years in Cuba: Reminiscences.* Cambridge: Riverside Press, 1926.

Cleveland, Grover. *The Letters of Grover Cleveland, 1850–1908.* Edited by Allan Nevins. Boston and New York: Houghton Mifflin, 1933.

Cullom, Shelby M. *Fifty Years of Public Service.* Chicago: A. C. McClurg, 1911.

Dawes, Charles G. *A Journal of the McKinley Years.* Edited by Bascom N. Timmons. Chicago: Lakeside Press, 1950.

Estrada Palma, Tomás. "The Work of the Cuban Delegation." In *The American-Spanish War.* Norwich, Conn.: Charles C. Haskell and Son, 1899.

Foster, John W. *Diplomatic Memoirs.* 2 vols. Boston: Houghton Mifflin, 1909.

Gómez, Máximo. *Cartas de Máximo Gómez.* Edited by Emilio Rodríguez Demorizi. Ciudad Trujillo: J. R. Vda. García, 1936.

Heath, Perry S. "The Work of the President." In *The American-Spanish War.* Norwich, Conn.: Charles C. Haskell and Son, 1899.

Kohlsaat, Herman H. *From McKinley to Harding: Personal Recollections of Our Presidents.* New York: Charles Scribner's Sons, 1923.

Lema, Salvador Bermúdez de Castro y O'Lawlor, marqués de. *Mis recuerdos (1880–1901).* Madrid: Ibero-Americana, 1930.

León y Castillo, Fernando de, marqués del Muni. *Mis tiempos.* 2 vols. Madrid: Librería de los successores de Hernando, 1921.

Lodge, Henry C., ed. *Selections from the Correspondence of Theodore Roosevelt and Henry Cabot Lodge, 1884–1918.* 2 vols. New York: Charles Scribner's Sons, 1925.

Long, John Davis. *The Journal of John D. Long*. Edited by Margaret Long. Ridge, N.H.: Richard R. Smith, 1956.

———. *Papers of John Davis Long, 1897–1904*. Edited by Gardner Weld Allen. Boston: Massachusetts Historical Society, 1959.

Mayo, Lawrence Shaw, ed. *America of Yesterday, as Reflected in the Journal of John Davis Long*. Boston: Atlantic Monthly Press, 1923.

O'Donnell y Abreu, Carlos Manuel, duque de Tetuán. *Apuntes del ex-ministro de estado duque de Tetuán para la defensa de la política internacional y gestión de diplomática del gobierno liberal-conservador desde el 28 de marzo de 1895 a 29 de septiembre de 1897*. 2 vols. Madrid: Raoul Péant, 1902.

Parker, George F. *Recollections of Grover Cleveland*. New York: Century, 1909.

Pritchett, Henry S. "Some Recollections of President McKinley and the Cuban Intervention." *North American Review* 189 (1909): 397–403.

Roosevelt, Theodore. *An Autobiography*. New York: Macmillan, 1919.

———. *The Letters of Theodore Roosevelt: The Years of Preparations, 1868–1900*. Edited by Elting E. Morison et al. 2 vols. Cambridge: Harvard University Press, 1951.

———. *The Rough Riders*. New York: Charles Scribner's Sons, 1899.

Rubens, Horatio S. *Liberty: The Story of Cuba*. New York: Brewer, Warren, and Putnam, 1932.

Sigsbee, Charles D. *The Maine, an Account of Her Destruction in Havana Harbor: Personal Narrative*. New York: Century, 1899.

Soldevilla, Fernando. *El año político, 1896*. Madrid: Enrique Fernández-de-Rojas, 1897.

———. *El año político, 1897*. Madrid: Ricardo Rojas, 1898.

———. *El año político, 1898*. Madrid: Enrique Rojas, 1899.

Taylor, Hannis. "A Review of the Cuban Question in Its Economic, Political, and Diplomatic Aspects." *North American Review* 165 (November 1897): 610–35.

White, Andrew D. *Autobiography of Andrew Dickson White*. New York: Century, 1905.

Wilson, William L. *The Cabinet Diary of William L. Wilson, 1896–1897*. Edited by Festus P. Summers. Chapel Hill: University of North Carolina Press, 1957.

Woodford, Stewart Lyndon. "McKinley and the Spanish War." *Yearbook of the Oneida Historical Society* 10 (1905): 140–44.

NEWSPAPERS

El Correo Militar (Madrid). 1 January 1897–15 August 1898.
El Cubano Libre (Tampa).

El Heraldo de Madrid. 1 January 1896–15 August 1898.
El Imparcial (Madrid). 1 January 1896–15 August 1898.
La Independencia (Manzanilla). 1897–1898.
Literary Digest (New York). 1 January 1896–15 August 1898.
Nation (New York). 1 January 1897–15 August 1898.
New York Herald.
New York Times. 1 January 1897–15 August 1898.
New York Tribune. 1 January 1897–15 August 1898.
Washington Post. 1 January 1895–15 August 1898.
Washington Star. 1 January 1895–15 August 1898.

BOOKS

Abel, Christopher, and Nissa Torrents, eds. *José Martí: Revolutionary Democrat.* Durham: Duke University Press, 1986.

Abrahamson, James L. *America Arms for a New Century: The Making of a Great Military Power.* New York: Free Press, 1981.

Acheson, Sam H. *Joe Bailey: The Last Democrat.* New York: Macmillan, 1932.

Arco, Juan del. *Montero Ríos.* Madrid: Purcalla, 1947.

Bécker, Jerónimo. *Historia de la relaciones exteriores de España, durante el siglo XIX.* 3 vols. Madrid: Editorial Voluntad, 1926.

Beisner, Robert L. *From the Old Diplomacy to the New, 1865–1900.* 2d ed. The American History Series. Arlington Heights, Ill.: Harlan Davidson, 1986.

Benton, Elbert J. *International Law and Diplomacy of the Spanish-American War.* Baltimore: Johns Hopkins Press, 1908.

Bride, Charles. *La Guerre Hispano-Américaine de 1898.* Paris: R. Chapelot, 1899.

Busbey, L. White. *Uncle Joe Cannon: The Story of a Pioneer American.* New York: Henry Holt, 1927.

Camacho, Pánfilo Daniel. *Estrada Palma, el gobernante honrado.* Havana: Editorial Trópico, 1938.

Carr, Raymond. *Modern Spain, 1875–1980.* Oxford and New York: Oxford University Press, 1980.

Carreras, Julio Angel. *Cuba: Contradicciones de classes en el siglo XIX.* Havana: Editorial de Ciencias Sociales, 1985.

Chadwick, French E. *The Relations of the United States and Spain: The Spanish-American War.* New York: Charles Scribner's Sons, 1911.

Clymer, Kenton J. *John Hay: The Gentleman as Diplomat.* Ann Arbor: University of Michigan Press, 1975.

Comellas García-Llera, José Luis. *Cánovas.* Madrid: Cid, 1965.

Coolidge, Louis A. *Orville H. Platt: An Old Fashioned Senator of Connecticut*. New York: G. P. Putnam's Sons, 1910.

Cortés-Cavanillas, Julián. *María Cristina de Austria: Reina regente de España de 1885 a 1902*. 2d ed. Barcelona: Juventud, 1980.

Cortissoz, Royal. *The Life of Whitelaw Reid*. 2 vols. New York: Charles Scribner's Sons, 1921.

Corzo Pi, Daniel. *Historia de don Tomás Estrada Palma*. Havana: Imprente de Diaz y Castro, n.d.

Cousins, Robert G. *Memorial Address on the Life and Services of the Late Senator Jonathan P. Doliver*. N.p. 1911.

Dennett, Tyler. *John Hay: From Poetry to Politics*. New York: Dodd, Mead, 1934.

Dingley, Edward N. *The Life and Times of Nelson Dingley, Jr.* Kalamazoo: Ihling Brothers and Everand, 1902.

Eggert, Gerald G. *Richard Olney: Evolution of a Statesman*. University Park: Pennsylvania State University Press, 1974.

Ellis, Elmer. *Henry Moore Teller, Defender of the West*. Caldwell, Idaho: Caxton Printers, 1941.

Estrade, Paul. *La colonia cubana de París, 1895–1898: El combate patriótico de Betances y la solidaridad de los revolucionarios franceses*. Havana: Editorial de Ciencias Sociales, 1984.

Fernández Almagro, Melchor. *Cánovas: Su vida y su política*. 2d ed. Madrid: Tebas, 1972.

———. *Historia política de la España contemporánea*. Vol. 2, *1885–1897*; vol. 3, *1897–1902*. 2d ed. Madrid: Alianza, 1974.

———. *Política naval de la España moderna y contemporánea*. Madrid: Instituto de Estudios Políticos, 1946.

Foner, Philip S. *The Spanish-Cuban-American War and the Birth of American Imperialism, 1895–1902*. 2 vols. New York and London: Monthly Review Press, 1972.

Francos Rodríguez, José. *La vida de Canalejas*. Madrid: Revista de Arch., 1918.

Garraty, John A. *Henry Cabot Lodge: A Biography*. New York: Alfred A. Knopf, 1953.

Garvin, James L. *The Life of Joseph Chamberlain*. 6 vols. London: Macmillan, 1932–69.

González Cavada, Antonio. *Segismundo Moret*. Madrid: Purcalla, 1947.

Gould, Lewis L. *The Presidency of William McKinley*. Lawrence: Regents Press of Kansas, 1980.

Gould, Lewis L., and Craig H. Roell. *William McKinley: A Bibliography*. Westport, Conn.: Meckler, 1988.

Healy, David. *Drive to Hegemony: The United States in the Caribbean, 1898–1917*. Madison: University of Wisconsin Press, 1988.

Heindel, Richard H. *The American Impact on Great Britain, 1898–1914: A Study of the United States in World History*. Reprint. New York: Octagon Books, 1968.

Hilderbrand, Robert. *Power and the People: Executive Management of Public Opinion, 1897–1921*. Chapel Hill: University of North Carolina Press, 1981.

Jessup, Philip C. *Elihu Root*. 2 vols. New York: Dodd, Mead, 1938.

Jones, Stanley L. *The Presidential Election of 1896*. Madison: University of Wisconsin Press, 1964.

Jover Zamora, José María. *Política, diplomacia y humanismo popular: Estudios sobre la vida Española en el siglo XIX*. Madrid: Turner, 1976.

———. *1898: Teoría y práctica de la redistribución colonial*. Madrid: Fundación Universitaria Española, 1979.

Kern, Robert W. *Liberals, Reformers, and Caciques in Restoration Spain, 1875–1909*. Albuquerque: University of New Mexico Press, 1974.

Kushner, Howard I., and Anne Hummel Sherrill. *John Milton Hay: The Union of Poetry and Politics*. New York: Twayne, 1977.

LaFeber, Walter. *The New Empire: An Interpretation of American Expansion, 1860–1898*. Ithaca: Cornell University Press, 1963.

Leech, Margaret. *In the Days of McKinley*. New York: Harper Brothers, 1959.

Le Riverend, Julio. *Historia económica de Cuba*. 2d ed. Havana: Editorial de Ciencias Sociales, 1985.

Lewis, Cleona. *America's Stake in International Investments*. Washington, D.C.: Brookings Institution, 1938.

Linderman, Gerald F. *The Mirror of War: American Society and the Spanish-American War*. Ann Arbor: University of Michigan Press, 1974.

McKee, Thomas H. *The National Conventions and Platforms of All Political Parties, 1789–1900*. Baltimore: Friedenwald, 1900.

McLean, Joseph E. *William Rufus Day: Supreme Court Justice from Ohio*. Baltimore: Johns Hopkins University Press, 1946.

McWilliams, Tennant S. *Hannis Taylor: The New Southerner as an American*. University: University of Alabama Press, 1978.

Maura y Gamazo, Gabriel, duque de Maura. *Historia crítica del reinado de don Alfonso XIII durante su menoridad bajo la regencia de su madre doña María Cristina de Austria*. 2 vols. Barcelona: Montaner y Simón, 1919–25.

May, Ernest R. *Imperial Democracy: The Emergence of America as a Great Power*. New York: Harcourt, Brace and World, 1961.

Meléndez Meléndez, Leonor. *Cánovas y la política exterior española*. Madrid: Instituto de estudios políticos, 1944.

Merrill, Horace Samuel, and Marion Galbraith Merrill. *The Republican Command, 1897–1913*. Lexington: University of Kentucky Press, 1971.

Millis, Walter. *The Martial Spirit: A Study of Our War with Spain*. Boston: Houghton Mifflin, 1931.

Morales Lezcano, Víctor. *León y Castillo, embajador (1887–1918): Un estudio sobre la política exterior de España*. Las Palmas: Cabildo insular de Gran Canaria, 1975.

Morgan, H. Wayne. *From Hayes to McKinley: National Party Politics, 1877–1896*. Syracuse: Syracuse University Press, 1969.

———. *William McKinley and His America*. Syracuse: Syracuse University Press, 1963.

Nevins, Allan. *Henry White: Thirty Years of American Diplomacy*. New York: Harper and Brothers, 1930.

Nido y Segalerva, Juan del. *Historia política y parlamentaria del Excmo. Sr. Práxedes Mateo Sagasta*. Madrid: Congresso de los Diputados, 1915.

Olcott, Charles S. *The Life of William McKinley*. 2 vols. Boston: Houghton Mifflin, 1916.

Olmet, Luis Antón del, and Arturo García Carraffa. *Moret*. Vol. 5 of *Los grandes españoles*. Madrid: Juan Pueyo, 1913.

Pabón y Suárez de Urbina, Jesús. *El 98, acontecimiento internacional*. Madrid: Ministerio del Asuntos Exteriores, 1952.

Palmer, Frederick. *Bliss, Peacemaker: The Life and Letters of General Tasker Howard Bliss*. New York: Dodd, Mead, 1934.

Payne, Stanley G. *A History of Spain and Portugal*. 2 vols. Madison: University of Wisconsin Press, 1973.

———. *Politics and the Military in Modern Spain*. Stanford: Stanford University Press, 1967.

Pérez, Louis A., Jr. *Cuba and the United States: Ties of Singular Intimacy*. Athens and London: University of Georgia Press, 1990.

———. *Cuba between Empires, 1878–1902*. Pittsburgh: University of Pittsburgh Press, 1983.

Picó, Fernando. *1898: La guerra después de la guerra*. Río Piedras, Puerto Rico: Ediciones Huracán, 1987.

Portell Vilá, Herminio. *Historia de Cuba en sus relaciones con los Estados Unidos y España*. 4 vols. Havana: Jesús Montero, 1938–41.

Poyo, Gerald E. *"With All, and for the Good of All": The Emergence of Popular Nationalism in the Cuban Communities of the United States, 1848–1898*. Durham: Duke University Press, 1989.

Pratt, Julius W. *Expansionists of 1898: The Acquisition of Hawaii and the Spanish Islands*. Baltimore: Johns Hopkins Press, 1936. Reprint. Baltimore: Peter Smith, 1949.

Pryor, Elizabeth B. *Clara Barton: Professional Angel*. Philadelphia: University of Pennsylvania Press, 1987.

Ramos Oliveira, Antonio. *Politics, Economics and Men of Modern Spain, 1808–1946*. Translated by Teener Hall. London: Victor Gollancz, 1946.

Rhodes, James F. *The McKinley and Roosevelt Administrations, 1897–1909*. New York: Macmillan, 1922.

Rickover, Hyman G. *How the Battleship* Maine *Was Destroyed*. Washington, D.C.: Department of the Navy, Naval History Division, 1976.

Rivas Santiago, Natalio. *Sagasta: Conspirador-tribuno-gobernante*. Madrid: Editorial Purcalla, 1946.

Robinson, William A. *Thomas B. Reed: Parliamentarian*. New York: Dodd, Mead, 1930.

Rodríguez González, Agustín Ramón. *Política naval de la Restauración (1875–1898)*. Madrid: Editorial San Martin, 1988.

Rodríguez Martínez, José. *Los desastres y la regeneración de España*. N.p.: Coruña, 1899.

Roig de Leuchsenring, Emilio. *Cuba no debe su independencia a los Estados Unidos*. Habana: Sociedad Cubana de Estudios Históricos a Internacionales, 1950.

Romanones, Alvaro Figueroa y Torres, conde de. *Sagasta o el político*. Bilbao: Espasa-Calpe, 1930.

Scott, Rebecca J. *Slave Emancipation in Cuba: The Transition to Free Labor, 1860–1899*. Princeton: Princeton University Press, 1985.

Serrano, Carlos. *Final del imperio: España, 1895–1898*. Madrid: Siglo veintiuno, 1984.

Tabouis, Geneviève. *The Life of Jules Cambon*. Translated by C. F. Atkinson. London: Jonathan Cape, 1938.

Torre del Río, Rosario de la. *Inglaterra y España en 1898*. Madrid: Peñalara, 1988.

Trask, David F. *The War with Spain in 1898*. The Macmillan Wars of the United States, edited by Louis Morton. New York and London: Macmillan, 1981.

Vagts, Alfred. *Deutschland und die Vereinigten Staaten in der Weltpolitik*. 2 vols. London: Lovat, Dickson, and Tomson, 1935.

Varela Ortega, José. *Los amigos políticos: Partidos, elecciones y caciquismo en la Restauración, 1875–1900*. Madrid: Alianza, 1977.

Vladimirov, Leonid Sergeevich. *La diplomacia de los Estados Unidos durante la guerra hispano-americana de 1898*. Moscow: Ediciones en lenguas extranjeres, 1958.

Wilkerson, Marcus W. *Public Opinion and the Spanish-American War*. Baton Rouge: Louisiana State University Press, 1932.

Wisan, Joseph. *The Cuban Crisis as Reflected in the New York Press*. New York: Columbia University Press, 1934.

Wriston, Henry M. *Executive Agents in American Foreign Relations*. Baltimore: Johns Hopkins Press, 1929.

Artola, Miguel. "El sistema político de la Restauración." In *La España de la Restauración: Política, economía, legislación y cultura*, edited by José Luis García Delgado. Madrid: Siglo veintiuno, 1985.

Auxier, George W. "The Propaganda Activities of the Cuban *Junta* in Precipitating the Spanish-American War, 1895–1898." *Hispanic American Historical Review* 19, no. 3 (August 1939): 286–305.

Corbitt, Duvon C. "Cuban Revisionist Interpretations of Cuba's Struggle for Independence." *Hispanic American Historical Review* 43, no. 3 (August 1963): 395–404.

DeNovo, John A. "The Enigmatic Alvey A. Adee and American Foreign Relations, 1870–1924." *Prologue* 7, no. 2 (1975): 69–80.

Eggert, Gerald G. "Our Man in Havana: Fitzhugh Lee." *Hispanic American Historical Review* 47, no. 4 (November 1967): 463–85.

Einstein, Lewis. "British Diplomacy in the Spanish-American War." *Proceedings of the Massachusetts Historical Society* 76 (1964): 30–54.

Field, James A., Jr. "American Imperialism: The 'Worst Chapter' in Almost Any Book." *American Historical Review* 83, no. 3 (June 1978): 644–68.

Fry, Joseph A. "William McKinley and the Coming of the Spanish-American War: A Study in the Besmirching and Redemption of an Historical Image." *Diplomatic History* 3, no. 1 (Winter 1979): 77–98.

García Barrón, Carlos. "Enrique Dupuy de Lôme and the Spanish American War." *Americas* 36, no. 1 (July 1979): 39–58.

Grenville, John A. S. "American Naval Preparations for War with Spain, 1896–1898." *Journal of American Studies* 2, no. 1 (April 1968): 33–47.

Holbo, Paul S. "The Convergence of Moods and the Cuban-Bond 'Conspiracy' of 1898." *Journal of American History* 55, no. 1 (June 1968): 54–72.

———. "Economics, Emotion, and Expansion: An Emerging Foreign Policy." In *The Gilded Age*, edited by H. Wayne Morgan. Rev. ed. Syracuse: Syracuse University Press, 1970.

Morgan, H. Wayne. "The De Lôme Letter: A New Appraisal." *Historian* 26 (November 1963): 36–49.

———. "William McKinley as a Political Leader." *Review of Politics* 28, no. 4 (October 1966): 417–32.

Neale, Robert G. "British-American Relations during the Spanish-American War: Some Problems." *Historical Studies: Australia and New Zealand* 6, no. 21 (November 1953): 72–89.

Offner, John. "President McKinley's Final Attempt to Avoid War with Spain." *Ohio History* 94 (Summer–Autumn 1985): 125–38.

———. "The United States and France: Ending the Spanish-American War." *Diplomatic History* 7, no. 1 (Winter 1983): 1–21.

————. "Washington Mission: Archbishop Ireland on the Eve of the Spanish-American War." *Catholic Historical Review* 73, no. 4 (October 1987): 562–75.

Pérez, Louis A., Jr. "Insurrection, Intervention, and the Transformation of Land Tenure Systems in Cuba, 1895–1902." *Hispanic American Historical Review* 65, no. 2 (May 1985): 229–54.

————. "Toward Dependency and Revolution: The Political Economy of Cuba between Wars, 1878–1895." *Latin American Research Review* 28, no. 1 (1983): 127–42.

————. "Vagrants, Beggars, and Bandits: Social Origins of Cuban Separatism, 1878–1895." *American Historical Review* 90, no. 5 (December 1985): 1092–1121.

Pletcher, David M., "Caribbean 'Empire,' Planned and Improvised." *Diplomatic History* 14, no. 3 (Summer 1990): 447–59.

————. "Rhetoric and Results: A Pragmatic View of American Economic Expansion, 1865–1898." *Diplomatic History* 5, no. 2 (Spring 1981): 93–106.

Poyo, Gerald E. "Evolution of Cuban Separatist Thought in the Emigré Communities of the United States, 1848–1895." *Hispanic American Historical Review* 66, no. 3 (August 1986): 485–507.

Pritchett, Henry S. "Some Recollections of President McKinley and the Cuban Intervention." *North American Review* 189 (March 1909): 397–403.

Shippee, Lester B. "Germany and the Spanish-American War." *American Historical Review* 30, no. 4 (1925): 754–77.

Shippee, Lester B., and Royal B. Way. "William Rufus Day." In *American Secretaries of State and Their Diplomacy*, edited by Samuel F. Bemis. 10 vols. New York: Alfred A. Knopf, 1928.

Tarbell, Ida. "President McKinley in War Times." *McClure's Magazine* 11, no. 3 (July 1898): 208–24.

Varela Ortega, José. "Aftermath of Splendid Disaster: Spanish Politics before and after the Spanish American War of 1898." *Journal of Contemporary History* 15 (1980): 317–44.

DISSERTATIONS

Baker, Thomas Hart, Jr. "Imperial Finale: Crisis, Decolonization, and War in Spain, 1890–1898." Ph.D. diss., Princeton University, 1976.

Duncan, George William. "The Diplomatic Career of William Rufus Day, 1897–1898." Ph.D. diss., Case Western Reserve University, 1976.

Gottschall, Terrell D. "Germany and the Spanish-American War: A Case Study of Navalism and Imperialism, 1898." Ph.D. diss., Washington State University, 1981.

Offner, John Layser. "President McKinley and the Origins of the Spanish-American War." Ph.D. diss., Pennsylvania State University, 1957.

Pilapil, Vincente R. "Spain in the European State System, 1898–1913." Ph.D. diss., Catholic University of America, 1964.

Readnour, Harry Warren. "General Fitzhugh Lee, 1835–1905: A Biographical Study." Ph.D. diss., University of Virginia, 1971.

True, Marshall MacDonald. "Revolutionaries in Exile: The Cuban Revolutionary Party, 1891–1898." Ph.D. diss., University of Virginia, 1965.

Vahle, Cornelius Wendell, Jr. "Congress, the President, and Overseas Expansion, 1897–1901." Ph.D. diss., Georgetown University, 1967.

Weigle, Richard D. "The Sugar Interests and American Diplomacy in Hawaii and Cuba, 1893–1903." Ph.D. diss., Yale University, 1939.

INDEX

• • • • • • • • • • • • • • • • •

Adams, Representative Robert, Jr., 20–21, 97–98, 151–52, 187–88

Adee, Assistant Secretary of State Alvey A., 40, 96, 117, 157, 194–95

Aguinaldo, Emilio, 214

Aldrich, Senator Nelson W., 43

Alfonso XII, king of Spain, 7–9

Alfonso XIII, king of Spain, 8

Alger, Secretary of War Russell A., 39, 128, 131, 153, 184, 195, 213

Allison, Senator William B., 43

Almodóvar del Río, duque de, Minister of State Juan Manuel Sánchez Gutiérrez de Castro, 197, 216; and peace negotiations, 211, 218, 220–22

Argulo, Manuel Rafael, 114

Armistice, 149–51, 154–58. *See also* Blanco y Erenas, marqués de Piña Plata, Gen. Ramón: armistice and suspension of hostilities; Correa y García, Gen. Miguel; Ireland, Archbishop John; Junta, Cuban; McKinley, President William; Moret y Prendergast, Minister of Colonies Segismundo; Polo de Bernabé, Minister Luis; Spain, government of; Woodford, Minister Stewart L.

Atkins, Edwin F., 2, 25, 46, 112, 170

Auñón y Villalón, Capt. Ramón, 198

Austria-Hungary, 30, 72–73, 116, 160, 162–63, 200–201

Azcárraga, Gen. Marcelo, 51–52, 60–66

Bailey, Representative Joe, 43, 45, 88, 135, 151–53

Balfour, Arthur J., 185

Barton, Clara, 82, 93, 131. *See also* Red Cross

Barton, Stephen E., 93

Belmont, August, 137

Beránger, Adm. José María, 186

Bermejo, Segismundo, 115, 196–97

Betances, Ramón, 5, 13, 30–31, 79

Bishop of Havana, 81–82

Bismarck, Prince Otto von, 161

Blanco y Erenas, marqués de Piña Plata, Gen. Ramón, 48, 50, 66, 71, 75, 78, 84, 87, 91, 99, 132, 138, 140, 207; doubts about reforms, 70, 112; and relief for *reconcentrados*, 71, 80–82, 92–93, 140, 170–71, 225; and Canalejas visit, 79–80; implementation of autonomy, 93–94, 111–12, 137; and January riot, 94–95; and tariff negotiations, 114–15; and de Lôme letter, 116, 119; and *Maine* disaster, 122, 125, 128, 138, 184; critical of Lee, 146–47; and armistice and suspension of

Merry del Val, Ambassador Rafael, 165

Mexico, 178–79

Montero Ríos, Senator Eugenio, 196–97

Montgomery, USS, 112, 115

Montojo, Adm. Patricio, 196

Moore, Assistant Secretary of State John Bassett, 40, 199–200, 214–15, 221, 229

Moreno de la Torre, Andrés, 83–84

Moret y Prendergast, Minister of Colonies Segismundo, 76, 79, 87–88, 112, 142; Cuban reforms and autonomy, 50, 65–66, 69–71, 137, 225; cultivates Woodford, 56, 74–76; influence in government, 65–66; seeks European support, 72–73, 115–16; financial schemes, 73–74; appeal to end Junta, 90–92, 100, 114; and January riot, 94–95; tariff negotiations, 114–15, 119–20; war warnings, 115, 137–38; and de Lôme letter, 119–21; and *Maine* disaster, 138, 155; sale of Cuba, 145, 147; complaint about Lee, 146–47; and McKinley's Cuban plan, 147–48, 155; proposes Cuban armistice, 149–50, 155–56; and suspension of hostilities, 165, 226; and papal appeal, 172; military support, 175; leaves cabinet, 192, 196–98

Morgan, Senator John T., 18, 22, 43–45, 49

Nelson, Senator Knute, 153

New York Herald, 55, 117

New York Journal, 19, 21, 39, 95; and de Lôme letter, 117, 122, 227, 229

New York Times, 201, 213

New York Tribune, 77

New York World, 39

Nicaraguan canal, 38

Olney, Secretary of State Richard, 15, 17, 22, 24–25, 30, 36, 39, 42, 64, 72; warns Spain, 25–26, 28, 70–71; and Lee mission, 26–27, 35; and Cameron resolution, 33; and Spanish reforms, 33–34; and Cuban policy, 35; and Ruiz death, 35

Pando y Sánchez, Gen. Luis Manuel de, 112

Paris. *See* France

Partido revolucionario cubano. See Junta, Cuban

Patenôtre, Ambassador Jules, 115–16, 173, 218

Pauncefote, Ambassador Sir Julian, 167–68, 180, 184–85, 200–201

Peralta y Pérez de Salcedo, Gen. Joaquín, 207

Philippine Islands, 48, 213–14, 222; role in peace settlement, 196, 199, 200–202, 209–18, 220–21

Platt, Senator Orville H., 43

Platt, Senator Thomas C., 55

Polavieja, Gen. Camilo García de, 10, 48–49, 52, 65–66, 79, 205

Polo de Bernabé, Minister Luis, 121, 135, 139–40, 148–49, 170, 189, 191, 195; and *Maine* disaster, 138, 141; and Proctor, 140–41; and congressional revolt, 153–54, 156; and Ireland, 166; and suspension of hostilities, 178; fails to gain U.S. cooperation, 179–80; and Spanish peace efforts, 180, 185

Porter, Ambassador Horace, 40, 59–60, 198, 210; tentative peace discussions with Hanotaux, 201–3

Sanguily, Julio, 23, 35

Santiago de Cuba, battle of, 195, 203–7

Sensational press, 39, 146–47, 229–30. *See also* Hearst, William Randolph; *New York Journal*

Shafter, Gen. William R., 205

Sherman, Secretary of State John, 19, 21, 39, 44, 58, 76, 79

Sicard, Rear Adm. Montgomery, 131

Sigsbee, Capt. Charles D., 96, 99, 113, 122

Silvela, Francisco, 10, 50, 52, 196, 220

Sims, Lt. William S., 195

Smith, Postmaster General Charles Emory, 213

Smith, R. A. C., 46

Spain, business interest in: and Cuba, 10–11, 68, 71, 75

Spain, government of: and autonomy for Cuba, 11, 50, 69–71, 75; and military costs of war, 13–14, 72, 112, 203; and Cuban Junta, 27–28; and Ruiz, 34–35; sale of Cuba, 46; finances of, 68, 137, 198; possibility of surrendering Cuba to U.S. armed forces, 69, 228; U.S. notes to, 70–71, 89; and U.S. prisoners, 71, 77; and Taylor's article, 78; and *reconcentrados*, 82; and war preparations, 115, 129–30; and de Lôme letter, 118–22; and *Maine* investigation, 125, 141–42; and possibility of war, 137–38; and papal mediation, 164–65; and suspension of hostilities, 166, 172–76, 180, 192; U.S. naval dispositions toward, 166–67; and demarche of Great Powers in Washington, 168; Woodford's ultimatum to, 171–72; and

papal appeal, 172–73; and McKinley's message to Congress, 185–86; and Chamberlain's speech, 200; and Philippine Islands, 201; and battle of Santiago de Cuba, 203–4; and U.S. control of the seas, 204; preparations for peace, 204–5, 207, 209–11; and peace terms for Cuba, 211, 216–18, 220–21; and peace terms for Puerto Rico, 217–18, 220; and peace terms for Philippine Islands, 217–18, 220–21; and Cortes approval, 220–21; and peace protocol, 221–22; overview of Cuban policy, 225; Cuban war stalemated, 227–28

Spain, public opinion in: newspapers' role in shaping, 11; on *Maine* disaster, 99; and jingoism, 137–38, 186; and suspension of hostilities, 156–57, 175; on McKinley's Cuban message, 186; on congressional resolutions, 191–92; and military defeats, 195, 204, 207

Spooner, Senator John C., 43, 168, 190

Stillman, Oscar B., 34

Storer, Minister Bellamy, 190

Straus, Oscar, 145–46

Sulzer, Representative William, 169

Taylor, Minister Hannis, 22, 30, 33, 55, 77–78, 87

Teller, Senator Henry M., 188

Teller amendment, 188–89, 199, 214, 219, 227

Tetuán, duque de, Minister of State Carlos Manuel O'Donnell y Abreu, 29–31, 33, 49–50, 70, 220; and Woodford's mission, 60–61, 63–65